6/10
HU

THE ENCYCLOPEDIA OF

OF

ALIEN

ENCOUNTERS

ALAN BAKER

Facts On File, Inc.

The Encyclopedia of Alien Encounters

First Published in Great Britain in 1999 by
Virgin Publishing Ltd.
Thames Wharf Studios
Rainville Road
London W6 9HT

Checkmark Books
An imprint of Facts On File, Inc.
11 Penn Plaza
New York, NY 10001

Library of Congress Cataloging-in-Publication Data
Baker, Alan, 1964–
The encyclopedia of alien encounters / Alan Baker:
p. cm.
Includes bibliographical references.
ISBN 0-8160-4226-8 (alk. paper)—ISBN 0-8160-4227-6 (pbk.:alk. paper)
1. Human-alien encounters—Encyclopedias.   I. Title.
BF2050.B35   2000
001.942′03—dc21   99-086105

Text design by Roger Kohn Designs
Cover design by Max Media
Phototypeset by Intype London Ltd.

Printed in the United States of America

MP Hermitage 10 9 8 7 6 5 4 3 2 1
PBK 10 9 8 7 6 5 4 3 2 1
This book is printed on acid-free paper.

CONTENTS

INTRODUCTION **5**

Entries A–Z **9**

BIBLIOGRAPHY AND

SUGGESTED FURTHER

READING **269**

INDEX **273**

To Piero, Renza and Dalia, for love, hospitality and many inspiring conversations

INTRODUCTION

I t is generally accepted that the "modern" age of the UFO began with Kenneth Arnold's sighting of nine strange objects on June 24, 1947, while he was aiding in the search for a missing military transport plane in the Cascade Mountains, Washington State. Arnold described the movement of the crescent-shaped objects as similar to a "saucer" skipping over water. One of the journalists to whom he spoke after the encounter, perhaps through misunderstanding, coined the term "flying saucers" to describe the objects themselves, rather than their mode of flight. Thus began an obsession that has come to occupy a central position in the mythology of our times.

And yet, can we truthfully say that sightings of unidentified objects in the skies—and associated encounters with apparently nonhuman beings—constitute an exclusively *modern* phenomenon? From our vantage point in the late 20th century, the appearance of metallic disks in the skies strongly implies the presence of travelers from some distant planet, who have come to our world as a result of the same curiosity that drives our own efforts to explore space. This is the so-called extraterrestrial hypothesis, which many UFO researchers have come to accept as the only viable explanation for the thousands of reports made over the five decades since that fateful day in 1947. It is certainly a seductive notion, but it is far from being the only possible answer.

From the moment our remote ancestors developed the intellect to register the immensity and grandeur of the skies, humanity has been haunted by the question of what lies out there,

beyond the comforting orb of the Moon, in the depths of the fathomless void through which our tiny world floats. From the very beginning, our species has striven to fill the void of our ignorance by looking to that other void, and the countless godlike beings we believed it to contain. In this way, an imaginary celestial history was created and modified over the millennia, in which civilizer-gods descended to Earth, guiding the progress of the human race through the development of agriculture, to the creation of cities and the formulation of architecture, mathematics and astronomy. The many rich and diverse mythological systems developed by human cultures across the globe would seem to agree that we have always shared our planet and our lives with supernatural beings whose appearance, behavior and origins constitute a truly vast panoply. However, the rise of Christianity resulted in a strongly marked demarcation between good and evil, with the vast majority of supernatural beings placed firmly in the latter category. This is exemplified in the word *demon*, meaning an evil or unclean spirit, which is descended from the Greek word *daimon*, meaning a divine power or god.

In the West, the elementals and nature spirits of the pre-Christian era were banished by the God of the New Testament to the realm of mythological memory, there to work their magic on the subconscious mind and to emerge from time to time in the guise of fairies, sylphs, kobolds, goblins and many other beings who seemed anxious that we should not forget them.

Although it would not seem so at first glance, there is evidence that these beings are not simply the denizens of a remote and pagan past. Some UFO researchers, such as Jacques Vallée, dissatisfied with the simplism of the extraterrestrial hypothesis, have studied the folklore and legends of many cultures, and have discovered striking correlations between them and the numerous modern reports of "alien" encounters. For instance, there is a strong implication that the diminutive gray beings who abduct travelers on lonely roads at night share a common origin with the "Gentry" of Celtic legend, who likewise waylaid those journeying through isolated places, and frequently carried them away into another world. From the victim's point of view, only a few minutes might pass in this realm, but when they returned to the normal world, they would discover that many hours or even days had passed. One merely has to look at the modern reports of "missing time" to see the link between the two encounters.

There are numerous other correlations, which will be explored in the appropriate entries in this book. However, the one cited above is sufficient to give an idea of the striking implication that human interaction with the denizens of a mysterious "other world" is as ubiquitous in history as it is in locality. When this idea is combined with the evidence in support of the modern phenomenon (in the form of UFO sightings, encounters with nonhuman creatures and the physical traces that are sometimes left behind), it can be seen that a genuine mystery exists, even if we are still a long way from explaining it to everyone's satisfaction.

This, surely, is the reason for our continuing fascination with the paranormal in general, and UFO/alien encounters in particular. And yet we must also take into account our own advances in science and technology, which have placed our species on the threshold of space. If, as some researchers suggest, the intelligence behind nonhuman encounters has been continuously modifying their surface details to conform with humanity's world view at each moment in history, then it would seem entirely logical that their latest guise is that of explorers from elsewhere in the Universe. The *reason* for this activity is, of course, the greatest mystery. It has been suggested that it may actually originate in the collective unconscious of humanity, constituting a system of intellectual evolution by which an intelligent species pulls itself toward an as yet unknown cosmic destiny.

It is for the reasons mentioned above that reports of apparent alien encounters form one of the most significant puzzles currently facing us, and as such they demand a far more considered response than that usually offered by sceptics: that we are wasting our time in considering what is, essentially, an invented mystery. While there have, of course, been countless UFO-related books, of varying quality, published over the five decades since Kenneth Arnold, I believe there remains a place for a book such as the one you now hold. For one thing, many previous books on ufology are no longer in print, making the information they contain difficult to obtain. In addition, information pertaining to the wide-ranging and important subject of "alien contact" (as opposed to UFO sightings) is scattered throughout the vast literature of the paranormal, which is an additional obstacle to those requiring information on the subject in general, or on one or more of its particular aspects.

The Encyclopedia of Alien Encounters is intended for the widest possible readership, and will hopefully provide a reliable reference work for those approaching the subject for the first time, as well as those who have read more widely in this and related fields. It differs from other paranormal encyclopedias in its concentration on the field of alien or nonhuman encounters, allowing the subject to be treated comprehensively in a way that has not been possible in past books, due to the unavoidable constraints of space incurred in dealing with other facets of general ufology.

Although some paranormal encyclopedias present their information in chapter form, *The Encyclopedia of Alien Encounters* contains alphabetical entries, thus making it easier to use from a reference point of view. The entries themselves cover various aspects of the alien contact phenomenon, in addition to entries on the fiction that has been inspired by reports of such contacts. There is, for example, an entry on *The X-Files*, together with information on how such fictional treatments relate to the reported phenomena that have inspired them. The fictional aspects of the alien contact phenomenon have been included because they illustrate the reactions in the media and wider population to encounter reports, and provide important clues as to how these phenomena have influenced the popular mythology of the late 20th century.

Since we are dealing with a rather emotive subject, which has elicited strong views both favorable and critical over the years, I have attempted to follow a policy of impartiality. However, it is worth mentioning now that I will refrain for the most part from using words such as *allegedly, apparently, supposed* and so on in the text. The reason for this is that, were I to include them as often as warranted, the text would quickly become very tedious indeed. I trust that the reader will appreciate that, in the absence of the long-awaited irrefutable evidence for the existence of aliens or other nonhumans, all sightings and contacts with such entities are "alleged."

In bringing together information from diverse times, locations and sources, the intention of *The Encyclopedia of Alien Encounters* is to provide a comprehensive historical reference work, detailing the events, encounters, personalities and theories that have created this fascinating field of human experience and enquiry.

ABDUCTION

An event in which human beings are taken from their normal surroundings against their will, and are forced to interact in various ways with nonhuman entities. For the last 40 years or so, this has been by far the most commonly reported type of alien contact. In more recent years, the most common type of entity reported has been the **Gray.** Although abductions can occur at any time and in any place, the standard scenario involves the victim being alone, whether in bed, or in an isolated location, such as a lonely stretch of road in a rural area. There may be an initial intimation that something is not quite right, such as the sighting of a light in the sky, or, in the case of bedroom encounters, the presence of a (usually) blue light in the room. At this point the victim frequently experiences a sudden dislocation in time, and realizes that he or she has instantaneously traversed several miles of road, or awakens the following morning in

bed. In each case, there is no memory of what has transpired in the intervening hours.

The American historian and UFO researcher David M. **Jacobs** has identified five distinct phases in an abduction. Although all five may not be present in every abduction event, the vast majority of abductions do seem to contain one or more of these phases.

Phase one involves the arrival of the entities in the victim's environment. They frequently display a total mastery over normal matter, and are as likely to enter a room through the walls as through a door. The victim is immediately immobilized through unknown means, and is "floated" out of his or her surroundings and into a waiting UFO, which may be parked on the ground, or hovering overhead.

Phase two begins inside the object, where the victim is usually undressed, and is physically examined by the entities, who manipulate the limbs and joints, often paying close attention to the spine. In some cases, one entity will stare with great intensity into the victim's eyes, prompting some researchers to suggest that this constitutes a kind of "bonding" between entity and human, resulting in a sense of familiarity, and thus a lessening of fear in subsequent abductions. During this phase, tiny devices are frequently either implanted in or retrieved from the abductees' bodies, usually, but not exclusively, the sinus cavity. The exact nature and function of these **implants** is not known. Reproductive procedures then take place: egg harvesting from females and sperm extraction from males, followed by either the implantation of embryos or extraction of fetuses. Much speculation has arisen from these events, most prominent among which is the notion that the entities are engaged in producing a race of human/alien **hybrids.**

Phase three includes various examinations with complex machines, which seem to scan the abductee's physiological systems. These machines are variously described as floating above the abductee or hanging from the ceiling. Occasionally, they are likened to huge, artificial "eyes." During this phase, the abductee will also be shown various images on a monitor screen. These may include images of mass destruction or more pleasant scenes of romantic encounters. The purpose of such "visualizations" is unclear, but may imply an interest on the part of the entities in human emotions. Female abductees are then taken into an "incubatorium" and a "nursery" and are shown infant hybrids, which they are encouraged to hold and nurture. Many abductees comment on the sickliness of these infants, and it may be that they desperately require at least some form of human contact in order to survive.

Phase four is perhaps the most distressing part of what is generally a distressing experience, although not all abductees report it. This phase includes what David Jacobs calls "ancillary experiences," which include immersion in a tank of liquid (for reasons unknown), cures for various illnesses (more for maintenance of the "specimen" than for any altruistic reasons), the examination of pain thresholds (perhaps to investigate the structure of neural pathways), and sexual activity (in which abductees are forced to copulate with each other, and which seems to be a variation on the entities' "breeding program").

Phase five concludes the abduction experience, with the abductee being returned to his or her normal environment. Interestingly, they are not always returned to precisely the place from which they were taken: sometimes, they may be left some way away from their homes, and are obliged to find their own way back, obviously in some confusion. In other cases, they may be left upside down in bed, with their nightclothes on inside out. In the majority of cases, they have no conscious memory of what has happened to them. It is unclear whether this memory block is imposed by the entities or is a natural response to the enormity of what has just transpired.

It should be emphasised that by no means all abduction experiences are unpleasant: some abductees report feelings of great love and companionship between themselves and the entities. Others, notably Whitley **Strieber**, believe that the terror of an abduction is a necessary obstacle, beyond which lies a more profound understanding of human existence and destiny.

ACCOUNT OF A MEETING WITH DENIZENS OF ANOTHER WORLD, AN (DAVID LANGFORD)

Fictional UFO encounter, written by the British physicist and science-fiction author David Langford. The book has an interesting and amusing provenance in the literature of UFOs and alien encounters, since it has been taken by many to be absolutely true, whereas in fact it is a spoof created by Langford in 1979. The book tells the story of an undertaker and carpenter named William Robert Loosley (1838–93), who was out walking in the woods near his home in High Wycombe on the evening of October 4, 1871, when he saw what he took to be a shooting star. Returning to the scene the following day, he was set upon by strange machines, which ripped his clothes, took samples of his skin and attempted to communicate with him by means of holographic projections.

Loosley wrote an account of this astonishing experience, which he placed in a secret drawer of a desk he had made. The account was discovered in the 1970s by his great-great-granddaughter, Hazel (Langford's wife), and was published under the title *An Account of a Meeting with Denizens of Another World, 1871, by William Robert Loosley.* The book was edited by David Langford himself, who also provided a commentary.

Many ufologists pointed to the book as being a fascinating example of an early alien encounter, while others took a more skeptical stance, having paid attention to various clues provided by Langford, not least of which was the inclusion of a short biography, which made it perfectly clear (several times) that Langford was a successful science-fiction writer. In one of his many subsequent attempts to point out that the book was a spoof, Langford told *UFO Brigantia* magazine in 1990 that it had originally been the idea of Paul Barnett, his editor at the publishers David & Charles. The intention had been to write an account of alien contact, and then to examine it with a physicist's eye, while also testing the credulity of ufologists.

Unfortunately, many failed the test, and Loosley's encounter has been reprinted as genuine in numerous UFO-related books, in spite of Langford's protestations, notably in the May 26, 1988, issue of *New Scientist.* The only genuine element in the case is William Loosley himself, who really did live in High Wycombe toward the end of the 19th century.

This fact was confirmed by UFO researchers, some of whom mistakenly took it as supportive evidence for the veracity of his encounter. Loosley's encounter is an interesting example of **disinformation** (albeit of a good-natured kind), by virtue of its skilful mixing of fact and fantasy. There are many such **hoaxes** on record.

ADAMSKI, GEORGE

The most famous of the **contactees**, who encountered a **humanoid** UFO pilot in the Californian desert on November 20, 1952. Born in Poland on April 17, 1891, Adamski emigrated to the United States with his family when he was a year old. Throughout his 20s and 30s, he had a variety of jobs, including maintenance man in Yellowstone National Park, flour mill worker in Portland, Oregon, and concrete contractor in Los Angeles. In the 1930s, he turned his hand to philosophy, and styled himself "Professor" George Adamski, founding a monastery in Laguna Beach, California. He managed to secure a license to produce wine for the monastery during Prohibition, and it seems that the wine found its way outside those religious confines, to the extent that Adamski claimed to two of his followers that he was "making a fortune." Indeed, Adamski was somewhat disappointed by the repeal of Prohibition, and would later comment that were it not for the legalization of alcohol, he would not have had to "get into this saucer crap." This, of course, hardly bodes well for the veracity of the story he would subsequently tell to the world.

At the time of his famous encounter with a man from another world, Adamski was running a hamburger stand a few miles from the Mount Palomar Observatory. Having heard of flying saucer activity in the region, Adamski made several trips into the desert, hoping to make contact, and finally succeeded on November 20, 1952. He and several associates were having lunch near Desert Center, when they saw a gigantic, silvery, cigar-shaped object hovering in the sky. Assuming that the ship was looking for him, Adamski went off into the desert by himself, and watched as a "scout ship" left the parent object and landed close by. Adamski then became aware of a man standing in a ravine about a quarter of a mile away. As he approached, Adamski saw that the man was wearing a brown single-piece suit. Communication then took place through a combination of hand signals and telepathy. The visitor claimed that he was from Venus, and that his race were deeply concerned at humanity's misuse of nuclear power, which threatened both life on Earth and in the rest of space, a claim that was to be frequently echoed by other so-called **Space Brothers**.

The Venusian also stated that Earth was being visited by races from other planets in the Solar System, including Jupiter and Saturn. When, after an hour, the meeting drew to a close, the visitor asked if he might borrow one of the film holders from Adamski's camera, promising to return it at a later date. Adamski agreed, and also decided to take plaster casts of the Venusian's footprints. (Just why he happened to have some plaster in the trunk of his car at that time is unclear.) The scout ship returned on December 13, 1952, and Adamski watched as one of the portholes opened and a hand tossed out the film holder.

Adamski wrote an account of these events and sent it to the British writer Desmond Leslie, who was sufficiently impressed to include it in a book he had just completed. *Flying Saucers Have Landed* was published in September 1953 and sold more than 100,000 copies.

Adamski's claims of alien contact have been virtually totally discredited, not least because of the fact that Venus cannot possibly harbor intelligent life of any kind, let alone humanoid (its surface temperature is high enough to melt lead). The same

goes for the other planets in the Solar System said by him to harbor humanlike aliens. In addition, the Venusian scout ship, as revealed in the photographs he took, looks decidedly "50s-retro," with its big, circular portholes and spherical undercarriage. Adamski himself played a rather cynical game with the **FBI**, at first claiming that his "material had been cleared" with them, and then, after they had contacted him and told him not to make false claims about government organizations, claiming that they had "warned [him] to keep quiet." The final blow to Adamski's claims came in January 1955, when four of the people who had been with him on November 20 admitted that they had seen nothing of what Adamski had claimed.

AERIAL PHENOMENA ENQUIRY NETWORK (APEN)

Mysterious and rather sinister organization, which first came to the attention of ufologists in 1974 when researcher Jenny Randles received a one-hour tape cassette, with no return address, containing various TV and radio broadcasts on UFOs. Occasionally, voices would interrupt, making statements on the hostility of UFOs and uttering various threats. More bizarrely, snippets from German wartime propaganda broadcasts and a Nazi marching tune were also included on the tape.

The following year, Randles and other researchers began to receive strange letters (also without any return address) describing various UFO events, including an alleged crash landing in North Wales. Randles notes that this case, which occurred in Llandrillo, has recently come to be regarded as comparable in importance to the **Roswell** incident, but at the time was not taken particularly seriously by UFO investigators. APEN thus seemed privy to some significant information.

Randles relates the experience of a man named Peter Bottomley who in 1975 had just joined the

British UFO Research Association (BUFORA), whereupon he was visited one night by two smartly dressed men claiming to be APEN operatives. After describing the organization's research activities, the two men told Bottomley that he had been chosen to be APEN's "mediator," a position that carried some payment for "expenses." The men then left, saying that they would telephone Bottomley for an answer to their offer.

Bottomley contacted Jenny Randles, who described the apparent nature of APEN and advised him to have nothing to do with them. When an APEN representative subsequently telephoned him, Bottomley declined their invitation to join the organization. Although APEN did not press the matter with him, Jenny Randles had an unnerving experience when she moved some weeks later. Waiting for her at her new address was a "Welcome to Your New Home" card, with an additional message: "Never call anyone bigger than yourself stupid."

It seems that APEN was not above a little breaking and entering. An East Midlands UFO group discovered that the house containing their files had been broken into, and although nothing was taken, the files themselves had been disturbed. APEN later wrote to the group, apologizing for the activities of their agents.

Randles was further victimized by APEN. Wondering why some of her correspondents had ceased contact, she learned that APEN had been writing letters to them in her name (her signature had been badly forged), offering them jobs in a secret government UFO study group. According to Randles, "All they had to do in return was withdraw from normal UFO research and tell nobody what they were doing." The recipients of the letters had apparently drawn the conclusion that Randles was really a government agent, and had thus lost their trust in her.

Although it is less active now, APEN is still apparently on the scene, or perhaps more accurately, is still skulking *behind* the scenes, occasionally making life difficult for UFO researchers. Their true agenda remains as mysterious as ever, but they are clearly intent on disrupting UFO research and propagating distrust among ufologists as much as possible.

AETHERIUS SOCIETY

Organization founded in 1954 by George **King**, who was contacted by an alien intelligence representing the **Interplanetary Parliament**. King, who was working as a taxi driver in London at the time, was in his apartment in Maida Vale, when the alien voice suddenly announced itself. Eight days later, an Indian swami teleported into the apartment and instructed him on how to open a line of communication with a Venusian named Aetherius. King later formed the Aetherius Society to aid in spreading the aliens' message to the people of Earth.

The society has branches throughout the world, and its teachings (one of which has it that Jesus Christ now lives on Venus) have prompted many ufologists to regard it as little more than a flying saucer **cult**. One of their quasi-technological devices is the so-called "prayer battery," which can store up to 700 hours of psychic energy, keeping it fresh and ready to use for 10,000 years. At times of great crisis, this beneficent energy can be directed anywhere in the world, dispersing violence and strife and promoting love and harmony (a process which, in view of the last 40 years of human history, perhaps works better in theory than in practice). For their part, however, the Aetherians claim that their prayer energy has actually averted numerous disasters.

In the 1950s, King published a book entitled *You Are Responsible*, in which he told of numerous interplanetary adventures, including a trip to Mars in which he helped the Martians to destroy an "intelligent meteorite," which was threatening their civilization. Like George Adamski and other

contactees, the Aetherius Society ran into problems when probes from Earth established beyond any doubt that planets such as Mars and Venus do not harbor humanoid life. The society's solution was both ingenious and in keeping with the quasi-religious nature of their teachings. According to them, Aetherius and the other alien entities contacted by King are not physical beings at all, but are spiritual entities, capable of manipulating matter and energy (although this would seem to render their spacecraft superfluous).

On one occasion, the society was challenged to prove the veracity of its claims; in response, it asked the Interplanetary Parliament to send a large spaceship to hover over Los Angeles. The Interplanetary Parliament complied, but in order to avoid panic, rendered the ship invisible to all but Aetherius Society members.

A FOR ANDROMEDA (TV SHOW)

Seven-part serial first aired in 1961, written by Fred **Hoyle** and John Elliot and starring Peter Halliday, Esmond Knight, Mary Morris and Julie Christie. Signals from an intelligence in outer space are picked up by a radio telescope. Part of the message is a set of instructions for building a highly sophisticated computer, which, once operational, goes on to electrocute one of the scientists, who is reborn possessing the alien computer's consciousness. The central element in the story, that of an extraterrestrial intelligence achieving a presence on Earth through the initial transmission of information, was repeated in the 1995 film *Species*.

ALIEN (FILM)

Made in 1979, directed by Ridley Scott and starring Tom Skerrit, Sigourney Weaver, John Hurt, Ian Holm, Yaphet Kotto, Harry Dean Stanton and Veronica Cartwright. Diverted from their journey back to Earth, the crew of a commercial starship investigate an alien-generated distress signal coming from an uncharted planet. Their ship is subsequently infected by an apparently invincible and extremely violent being, which dispatches the astronauts one by one, leaving a single survivor who eventually succeeds in destroying the monster.

All four films in the series (which includes *Aliens* [1986], *Alien³* [1992] and *Alien: Resurrection* [1997]) are notable not only for their superb special effects, but also for their treatment of extraterrestrial life as being truly incomprehensible. The alien creatures, while exhibiting signs of intelligence, cannot be communicated or reasoned with, and seem utterly inimical to all other forms of life. This is actually rather refreshing, and the incomprehensibility—the complete *otherness*—of the aliens is, ironically, more in keeping with what we might reasonably expect in a genuine encounter with an extraterrestrial being.

The behavior and physiology of the aliens (known as "xenomorphs" in the films) have subtle and intriguing parallels with nonhuman entities reported in the literature on UFOs. For instance, the fictional aliens behave much like insect drones, building large nests for an egg-laying "queen." People who have encountered the **Grays** frequently report an insectlike appearance and behavior, as if the abductors belong to a hive society and lack the individuality experienced by humans. In addition, the xenomorphs have a rather imaginative way of reproducing, which relies on the combination of alien DNA with that of the host creature. Thus, in the first two films, the xenomorphs are humanoid, while in the third film, the alien seed is implanted in a dog, and the resulting creature displays canine characteristics.

The process of hybridization has been referred to on numerous occasions with regard to the possible motives for an extraterrestrial presence on Earth, with the combination of human and alien DNA playing a major part. It may not be stretching the point too far to suggest that these particular parallels may constitute a minor element in a process of cultural feedback, which in turn is an important concept in the **psychosocial hypothesis** of nonhuman encounters.

ALIEN AUTOPSY: FACT OR FICTION? (FILM DOCUMENTARY)

(See **Roswell Autopsy Footage**)

ALIEN BIG CATS (ABCs)

Generic name given to various feline animals that are encountered far from their natural habitats (the word *alien* in these cases meaning "out of place" rather than "extraterrestrial"). These animals, which include leopards, panthers, pumas, servals, lynxes and lions, have been sighted in more than 30 counties in England, as well as in Northern Ireland, Wales and Scotland. Numerous photographs of the cats have been taken, although the vast majority are rather fuzzy and indistinct, leading some skeptics to suggest that large house or farm cats are being mistaken for ABCs.

However, there is much additional evidence in the grisly form of sheep and calf carcasses, which have been discovered in farmers' fields stripped of their flesh, and with claw marks on the neck and belly. In September 1993 the remains of a sheep were discovered in Whorlton, County Durham. Nearby were some droppings, which were analyzed by Dutch zoologist Dr. Hans Kruuk of the Institute of Terrestrial Ecology at Aberdeen. After his analysis, he was quoted as saying: "My examinations all point to a puma or leopard, but since no sightings exist in Durham of a spotted creature my conclusions would favor a puma."

According to Paul Sieveking, writing in *Fortean Times* Number 80, at least four Asian leopard cats (*Felis bengalensis*) have been shot or found dead in Britain in the last 10 years or so. Alien Big Cats have been seen from time to time on the Isle of Wight for the last hundred years, and there have been more than 300 in the last 10 years alone.

For the most part, the cats confine their predations to farm animals, but there have been several documented attacks on humans. For instance, in December 1993, Nick and Sally Dyke, of Stourbridge in the West Midlands, were searching for the so-called Beast of Inkberrow in the county of Hereford and Worcester, when they encountered a large, black and very wild feline in St. Peter's churchyard, Inkberrow. Nick Dyke literally stumbled over the cat, which turned, knocked him to the ground and ran toward Sally, knocking her down with a single swipe. Its claws penetrated the several layers of her clothing and left three five-inch-long wounds in her side.

Perhaps the most famous of all Alien Big Cats is the legendary "Beast of Bodmin," which haunts the moorlands around Bodmin, Cornwall. This creature has also been seen on numerous occasions, and was videotaped in December 1993 and 1994 by Rosemary Rhodes of Ninestones Farm. She stopped keeping sheep after four of her ewes were ripped to pieces by an unknown animal. Her videotape shows what appears to be a black leopard.

It has been suggested by some commentators that Alien Big Cats are the descendants of escapees from zoos and private collections of exotic animals, while others have put forward the intriguing but perhaps unprovable theory that the animals have stumbled into space warps and have been teleported from one location (their natural habitat) to another (the British countryside).

ALIENS

By far the most widely accepted explanation for the numerous reports of encounters with nonhuman entities is that they are aliens, who have arrived on Earth from some other planet in the Universe. This view is most strongly adhered to in the United States, and is known as the **extraterrestrial hypothesis**. Over the 50 or so years since the "modern era" of ufology began, an astonishing variety of aliens has been encountered. Contrary to popular assumptions, the **Grays**, while they have come to be regarded as the quintessential alien being, are merely one species out of many that have been seen, met and communicated with by puzzled or terrified humans.

The sheer variety of alien physical types is enormous, so much so that it has been cited in opposition to the extraterrestrial hypothesis for nonhuman encounters. Even the Grays themselves can be split into several different subgroups, based on height, skin color and texture, the number of fingers on their hands and their eyes. Other aliens are described as being indistinguishable from humans, and yet some of these seem to require breathing apparatus in our atmosphere, while others do not. There are yet more entities that bear absolutely no similarity to the humanoid form whatsoever.

This diversity of form has led many researchers to speculate that Earth is the object of exploration of numerous space-faring races from diverse planets, and this point of view has resulted in several attempts to classify aliens into groups. The most comprehensive of these classification systems was formulated in the late 1960s by the Brazilian researcher Jader U. Pereira, who chose as his principal characteristic the ability, or otherwise, to breathe our atmosphere. As the American researcher Patrick Huyghe states, this is logical enough, since entities able to breathe oxygen would be profoundly different, biologically, from those who could not. However, this criterion results in a large number (the majority, in fact) of physically diverse entities who are able to breathe our atmosphere being placed in the same group, and it is unsatisfactory for this reason.

Pereira himself accepted this fault in his system, and so added other criteria, such as the presence and length of hair, types of clothing worn, language and the use of tools. Once again, however, Patrick Huyghe points out the inadequacy of this system, since these characteristics are "cultural rather than somatic."

The American folklorist Thomas Bullard of the University of Indiana has also attempted to formulate an alien classification system, based on **abduction** reports. His results reveal three basic types of entity: the entirely human, the **humanoid** (similar to humans, but with noticeable differences) and the nonhumanoid. Here, however, we encounter the same problem that beset Pereira's system: each group of entities (especially the nonhumanoid) contains numerous subgroups, which are not adequately addressed, and which may constitute entirely different species. Indeed, as Huyghe notes, most researchers have come to the conclusion that the formulation of any completely comprehensive alien classification system is all but impossible, such is the astonishing diversity of aliens encountered. Huyghe himself has made a brave attempt at classification, dividing reported aliens into Classes, Types and Variants. The Humanoid Class contains five Types: Humans, Short Grays, Short Non-Grays, Giants and Nonclassics; the Animalian Class contains another five Types: Hairy Mammalian, Reptilian, Amphibian, Insectoid and Avian; the Robotic Class contains two Types: Metallic and Fleshy; and the Exotic Class also contains two Types: Physical and Apparitional. Each of the Types are further divided into Variants. The result is perhaps the most comprehensive and inclusive system to date.

This amazing variety of alien forms is perhaps no more than we should expect: given the size of our own galaxy (not to mention that of the whole Universe) and the likelihood that there are many millions of inhabited planets out there, it seems logical enough that the denizens of those worlds should differ widely in their physical form. However, we are left with a serious problem with regard to the majority of reported aliens: their humanoid appearance. Many evolutionary biologists maintain that humanoid life on other planets is incredibly unlikely. The reason for this is to be found in the physical attributes of our own world, which has had a direct bearing on the form into which human beings have evolved over the past 3 billion years or so. We are the result of a great many factors, including the period of Earth's revolution around the Sun, its mean distance from its parent star, its axial rotation period, its average radius and its mass. Then there is the composition of the atmosphere and the resulting amount of solar radiation (the engine of evolution) that is allowed through to the surface. There is also the presence of a large moon to consider, without the steadying influence of which Earth would have oscillated wildly in its axial rotation, and the seasons would have been so diverse as to make life itself impossible. When these and many other factors are taken into account, it does indeed seem extremely unlikely that a being from a world differing even slightly from our own would look anything like us—the more so when we consider the many thousands of random genetic mutations that have given rise to the human form, mutations that could not be repeated identically on another world, no matter how similar to Earth it was.

And yet, we are nevertheless faced with many different alien races, which, while sharing the basic humanoid form (two arms, two legs, torso, head, etc.), display sufficient differences to imply origins on many different planets. However, other evolutionary biologists suggest that "parallel evolution" may occur throughout the Universe, with life-forms arising as a result of essentially the same chemical and genetic processes. According to Huyghe, "The chemistry of the compounds making up the genetic code seems to demand that all life be similar." Thus a successful oceanic predator would look pretty much like a shark, no matter which planet it happened to inhabit; and a successful intelligent being on an Earth-like planet would possess two legs for rapid locomotion (any more would use up valuable processing capacity in the brain, and would have been selected out through evolution), a head placed at the highest point on the body in order to see as much of the environment as possible, and so on. It therefore seems at least feasible that some alien life-forms visiting Earth would possess basically humanoid forms, while still retaining variations on that genetic theme.

ALLAGASH ABDUCTIONS

One of the most impressive and extensively investigated accounts of abduction by aliens involved four art students, who encountered a UFO while on a camping trip on the Allagash River in Maine. The students, brothers Jack and Jim Weiner, Charlie Foltz and Chuck Rak, left Boston, Massachusetts, on Friday, August 20, 1976. They had been camping and canoeing for four days when they and several other campers noticed a bright object hanging in the night sky. After some moments, the light "extinguished from the outside edge . . . to the center."

Two days later, on the night of Thursday, August 26, they set up camp on the shore of East Lake, lit a large fire and set out on to the lake to fish for trout. Chuck Rak became uneasy, feeling as if he were being watched. He turned around to see a large, spherical light hovering to the southeast at an altitude of 200 to 300 feet. Charlie Foltz took a flashlight and signaled to the light, which immediately began to approach the group, projecting a beam of light onto the surface of the lake as it did so. Suddenly terrified, the four young men began to row toward the shore, but the object outpaced them, and they were quickly engulfed in the beam of light.

The next thing they knew, they were standing on the shore, watching the object as it shot up into the sky and disappeared. They noted in surprise that their campfire had burned down to a few glowing embers. It seemed that the men had experienced a period of **missing time**: the state of their campfire implied that they had been away for several hours, even though they only remembered being on the water for about 20 minutes.

Several years later, Jim Weiner sustained a head injury and went to the Beth Israel Hospital. During his treatment, the doctors expressed concern that he was not getting enough sleep. Jim knew the reason, but felt unable to confide in them that he was being visited at night by nonhuman entities. Eventually, Jim described his **bedroom visitors** to his own doctor, who was familiar with the literature on UFOs and abductions, and who suggested that he attend a lecture in Waltham, Massachusetts, given by the famous and respected researcher Raymond E. Fowler.

Jim described his experiences to Fowler, who put together a **Mutual UFO Network (MUFON)** investigation team in January 1989. According to Fowler, the team "consisted of MUFON investigator and [abduction] specialist David Webb (solar physicist), MUFON hypnosis consultant Anthony (Tony) Constantino (professional hypnotist) and myself (MUFON National Director of Investigations)."

After satisfying themselves, through various background inquiries, that the four witnesses were trustworthy individuals, the MUFON team began a series of **hypnotic regression** sessions to recover their lost memories. The four men promised that they would not discuss the sessions (conducted individually) with one another until the program had been completed.

Under hypnosis, each of the men recalled being taken up into the UFO through the beam of light. Once inside, they encountered several humanoid entities, and were forced (through some form of mind control) to undress and sit in a mist-filled room. They were then given a detailed physical examination by the beings, who probed their bodies with various instruments and then took samples of their saliva, blood, skin, feces, urine and sperm.

When their ordeal was finally over, the men were taken into another room containing a circular portal, through which they were forced to walk. They found themselves outside the UFO once again, floating down through the light beam and into their waiting canoe. During the hypnosis sessions, it also emerged that Jack and Jim Weiner had been abductees since childhood. In addition, Jack recalled an abduction experienced with his wife, Mary, while at their mountain home in Townshend, Vermont, on the night of May 20, 1988.

One of the most intriguing elements of this case involved an "anomalous lump," which Jack had had removed several years previously. After the operation, the lump had been sent by the mystified local pathologist to the Centers for Disease Control in Atlanta, Georgia, for analysis. Fowler asked for copies of Jack's medical records, but when the latter asked the records clerk for them, he discovered that the lump had been sent for analysis to military pathologists in Washington, D.C. When he asked why the lump had been sent to the Armed Forces Institute of Pathology (AFIP) instead of the Centers for Disease Control, he was told that it was "less costly," an explanation that didn't make much sense, since Jack was covered by medical insurance.

The four witnesses were invited to appear on *The Joan Rivers Show*, which was broadcast in May 1993. The show's producers offered to pay for a lie-detector test. However, while the witnesses were treated respectfully by Joan Rivers, the polygraph examiner arrived several hours late, and said that he had only time to test two of the men. Jack Weiner and Chuck Rak volunteered, but were treated very badly by the examiner, who was "very aggressive, bordering on hostile." He later claimed that Chuck Rak had failed the test and Jack Weiner was borderline, but refused to allow Fowler to see the test results. Fowler was rightly furious, pointing out that the examiner's hostile attitude caused a great deal of anxiety in Jack and Chuck, which may well have accounted for the results.

The producers of the TV show *Unsolved Mysteries* then offered to pay for another polygraph test, to be conducted by Ernest C. Reid, a Certified Stress Analyst based in Massachusetts. All four witnesses were tested, and all passed. Fowler's comprehensive report on the case was later condensed into the book *The Allagash Abductions* (1993).

ALLINGHAM, CEDRIC

On February 18, 1954, Cedric Allingham was walking along the Scottish coast between Lossiemouth and Buckie, when he became aware of a strange "swishing" sound. Looking up to the sky, he saw a dark, saucer-shaped object. The saucer moved out over the sea, but later returned and landed nearby, while Allingham took several photographs of it. A door in the object opened and a figure, indistinguishable from an ordinary human being, climbed out and approached the witness.

According to Allingham, the visitor was six feet tall, about 32 years old and was wearing some kind of breathing apparatus. Like **Adamski**'s Venusian, he was wearing a shimmering, one-piece suit. The saucer occupant then began to communicate with Allingham, using a combination of sign language and sketches drawn in the sand. In an attempt to discover which planet the visitor came from, Allingham drew a circle and then pointed to the Sun. He then drew a series of concentric circles, representing the orbits of the planets. The visitor pointed to the fourth circle, indicating that he came from Mars.

Presently, the spaceman climbed back into his craft and departed, leaving Allingham to bemoan the fact that there had been no other witnesses to corroborate his astonishing adventure. However, as luck would have it, he encountered a fisherman on his walk back to Lossiemouth, who said that he had seen Allingham and the Martian from a nearby hilltop. The fisherman, named James Duncan, signed a statement confirming that he had witnessed the historic meeting.

Allingham wrote and published a book entitled *Flying Saucer from Mars*, which appeared in 1954 and became a best-seller. Not surprisingly, however, there were numerous skeptics, notably the British journalist Robert Chapman, who wrote about the case in his well-balanced and acclaimed 1969 book, *UFO: Flying Saucers over Britain.* Chapman was unhappy about every aspect of Allingham's encounter, not least the unaccountably fuzzy photographs of the Martian spacecraft, which bore an uncanny resemblance to Adamski's Venusian "scout ship." Chapman approached the publishers of *Flying Saucer from Mars*, Frederick Muller, requesting an interview with Allingham. The latter replied that an interview was out of the question, since Allingham had gone to America to meet George Adamski. Later they claimed that Allingham was in Switzerland, recovering from an undisclosed illness. Not long after this, Allingham apparently died.

According to researchers Jenny Randles and Peter Hough, the fisherman, James Duncan, was eventually traced. He said that he had seen something from the hilltop, "but it was rather different and less spectacular than Allingham's book alleges." Randles and Hough go on to relate how two skeptical researchers, Christopher Allan and Steuart Campbell, conducted their own investigation of the affair, which led them to suspect that "Cedric Allingham" was actually the British astronomer and TV personality Patrick Moore.

Frederick Muller then gave Allan and Campbell the name of an old friend of Moore's, a journalist named Peter Davies, who claimed that *Flying Saucer from Mars* was indeed a hoax, written by a person he refused to name and then revised by Davies to disguise the original writer's style. The royalties from the book were split between Davies and the other author. For his part, Patrick Moore has steadfastly denied writing the Allingham book, and it seems that the identity of Peter Davies's mysterious coauthor will remain unknown.

ALMAS

A Mongolian word (meaning "wildman") describing a race of half-human, half-ape creatures, which are said to live in the Altai Mountains of western Mongolia and the Tien Shan Mountains of China. In the early 15th century, a Bavarian nobleman named Hans Schiltberger encountered the Almases when he was taken prisoner by Mongols and forced to travel through the Tien Shan Mountains. He described them as being covered with fur, except for the face and hands, and as having "nothing in common with other human beings."

The American anomalist Jerome Clark cites a late-18th-century Mongolian manuscript containing a drawing of an Almas, noting that all of the other illustrations are of real animals, implying that the Almases were not considered to be supernatural beings, but were seen as "flesh and blood" creatures.

A scientific study of the Almases was conducted by Professor Tsyben Zhamtsarano early in the 20th century. However, the results of his extensive research were lost following his death in one of Stalin's prison camps. One of Zhamtsarano's colleagues later reported that Almas sightings declined in the last years of the 19th century, possibly because the creatures were migrating westward in an effort to avoid the growing human population.

According to the Russian anatomist Dr. Marie-Jeanne Kofman, a female Almas was captured in the forests of Mount Zaadan in the Caucasus Mountains in the late 19th century. It seems that while captive in the village of Tkhina, she became pregnant by one of the villagers and gave birth to several children. In 1964, the famous Russian scientist Dr. Boris Porshnev spoke to two people who claimed to be the grandchildren of the Almas. They said that, unlike the Almas, their parents had been capable of human speech. The American cryptozoologist Dr. Karl Shuker notes that, not only do the areas frequented by the Almases contain fossil Neanderthal remains, but "some anthropologists believe that the Neanderthals vanished not through actual extinction but by interbreeding with modern humans until their separate identity was lost." (*Homo sapiens neanderthalensis* lived in many parts of Eurasia but seems to have disappeared around 30,000 years ago.)

The connection with Neanderthals is not accepted by all anthropologists, however. Chris Stringer, for instance, while willing to accept that Almases might well exist, states that their descriptions ("long arms . . . small flat noses, 'Mongolian' cheekbones, and a lack of . . . culture, meat-eating and fire") do not match what we know about Neanderthals.

AMNESIA

A partial or total loss of memory, especially through shock or some other psychological disturbance, brain damage or illness, and one of the defining elements in an alien **abduction** experience. In this context, the amnesia said to result from an encounter with nonhuman entities is also known as **missing time**. Skeptics claim that such periods of amnesia (in which, for instance, a car journey might pass much faster than the driver realizes, leaving him or her unable to account for the intervening time) are completely natural, are the result of the nervous system switching to a kind of "autopilot" while performing a mundane task, and are experienced by virtually everybody in the course of normal daily activities.

ANCIENT ASTRONAUTS

A theory propounded in the mid-20th century, first by Jacques Bergier and then (much more famously) by Erich von **Däniken**, which states that at some point in the remote past, Earth was visited by creatures from other planets, and that they helped in the construction of many of the most impressive monuments of the ancient world, in addition to instructing humanity in the basics of civilization. While the theory itself describes an intriguing possibility, its principal "evidence," as cited in most of the literature on the subject, is based on the patronizing assertion that ancient architects were simply not clever enough to have built their own monuments. In addition, other artifacts from the remote past are claimed to contain imagery that could only have been inspired by the presence of alien space travelers.

Two of the most famous examples of the latter are the Nazca Lines in Peru and the tomb lid of the Mayan king Pacal at Palenque. Von Däniken and his colleagues have always maintained that the Nazca Lines, a series of vast representations of animals and straight tracks etched into the desert floor, can only be seen properly from the air, and thus must have been created as a form of communication with extraterrestrials in their spacecraft. The straight lines themselves, so the theory goes, were constructed to serve as runways for alien ships. The German mathematician and archaeologist Maria Reiche, who spent much of her life investigating the artifacts of the Nazca Plain, responded to the ancient astronaut theory by pointing out that the terrain is composed of soft, pebble-strewn sand—totally useless as a landing field. "I'm afraid the spacemen would have got stuck," she commented wryly. Apart from this, it is difficult to imagine why a spacecraft capable of interstellar travel would require a runway to land.

With regard to the pictures, which include a monkey, a hummingbird and a spider, anthro-pologists have suggested a much more feasible explanation. Agreeing that the gigantic images were indeed designed to be seen from high in the air, they suggest that they form part of an elaborate representation of the cosmos, to be viewed by the souls of shamans during their out-of-body journeys, while the lines, which reach to the horizon when viewed from the ground, are likely to be pointers leading to sources of water.

The tomb lid of King Pacal is a beautiful and fascinating object, although not for the reason suggested by von Däniken et. al. It contains the carving of a man in profile who, according to the ancient astronaut theorists, is sitting in the cockpit of a spacecraft and is manipulating a set of complex controls. There is, they claim, even an exhaust plume issuing from the rear of the vehicle.

In fact, the tomb lid of Pacal (who died in A.D. 683) contains images common throughout Mayan art, and whose meaning is well understood by archaeologists. The "rocket ship" in which the figure sits is actually a maize tree, which the Mayans revered as a giver of life; the figure is not manipulating "controls," but plucking a fruit. Neither is Pacal sitting in a "cockpit"; rather, he is suspended between life and death, above an elaborate representation of the entrance to the underworld—*not* the engine of a spaceship.

While the *exact* methods of construction of the colossal monuments of the ancient world, such as the pyramids at Giza and the ruined cities of Central and South America, remain puzzling, we nevertheless have a pretty good idea of how they were built, and this certainly does not include the use of antigravity beams or spacecraft with crane attachments. All of the archaeological evidence points to the Egyptians, the Mayans, the Incas and so on as being the true architects of these and other wonders, requiring no help from "out there."

There is, however, one element in the ancient astronaut theory that carries considerably more weight: the so-called Sirius Mystery. According to the American scholar Robert K. G. Temple, there is considerable evidence to suggest that Earth was indeed visited in the distant past by a race of amphibious beings called Nommos, which played an important role in the development of the first human civilization on the shores of the Persian Gulf, and memories of which survived in the legends of Babylonia, Egypt and Greece.

ANDREASSON, BETTY

Alien abductee, whose case was investigated with characteristic diligence by Raymond E. Fowler. Betty first encountered the entities on January 25, 1967, at her home in Ashburnham, Massachusetts. She was able to recall consciously how a light appeared outside the house, and how her father, who was visiting with her mother, saw a number of strange beings approaching the house. These beings then entered through the walls, at which point Betty's memories of the incident ceased.

It wasn't until several years later, in 1974, that Betty contacted first the *National Enquirer* and then the Mutual UFO Network (MUFON), at which point Fowler became involved in the case. Three years later, in 1977, Betty began to undergo regressive hypnosis to recover her memories of what had happened in 1967.

According to her recollections, Betty was taken aboard a UFO, where she met an entity of the Gray type, who introduced himself as **Quazgaa**. (This in itself is interesting, since **Grays** almost never reveal their names, although the **Space Brothers** of the **contactee** era had no qualms about doing so.) Betty was subjected to the standard medical examination, in which an **implant** was inserted into her nose.

Betty's experiences with Quazgaa and the other entities have developed into an incredibly complex scenario, which Fowler has chronicled in a whole series of books: *The Andreasson Affair* (1979), *The Andreasson Affair—Phase Two* (1982), *The Watchers* (1991), *Watchers II* (1995) and *The Andreasson Legacy* (1997).

One of the central elements of this ongoing series of encounters is a vitally important message given to Betty by the entities, but which she was not allowed to remember during the early phases of her experience, since the time was not yet right. When she was finally able to remember and relate the message, it proved to be that the "Watchers," as they came to be called, are the caretakers of life on Earth, and that abductions are carried out in order to monitor environmental effects upon the human body. In addition, the Watchers have always coexisted with humanity, and the two species are genetically linked.

Their genetic manipulation of humanity through the production of hybrid offspring is due to the fact that the human race will shortly become sterile as a result of our relentless pollution of the planet, and the Watchers are here to "collect and preserve Earth's life-forms for existence elsewhere." However, the future is not as depressing as might be supposed, for Fowler reports that the Watchers possess a "paraphysical" aspect that implies a continuing existence after death. Indeed, the Watchers told Betty on several occasions that human beings are "more than flesh and blood," that life on Earth is only a preparation for what is to come afterward. This intriguing concept is also to be found in the work of Whitley **Strieber**, who has speculated that the "visitors" (to use his term for them) may be intimately involved with what happens to us after we die. He has also suggested that our living form may only be a kind of "larva," from which the mature human emerges upon the physical death of the body.

These paraphysical elements mark Betty Andreasson's experiences as among the most bizarre of abduction accounts; indeed, Fowler himself comments on their **high strangeness**, but maintains his belief that Betty has actually had the experiences, that they are objective rather than subjective. As far as the entities' message is concerned, it is basically a reiteration of the numerous warnings about the state of our planet that have been given over the years by aliens of every description, from the **Space Brothers** to the Grays.

ANGELUCCI, ORFEO

Contactee who encountered a UFO on May 24, 1952, while driving home from the night shift at the Lockheed Aircraft factory in Burbank, California. The UFO first appeared as an indistinct red light, which Angelucci followed until it disgorged two globes of green light before shooting up into the sky. The globes hovered in front of his parked car, and a voice asked him to get out of the vehicle. When he had done so, the globes moved together, and between them there appeared a kind of monitor screen, displaying the head and shoulders of a man and woman. Angelucci later described the beings as radiantly beautiful, perfect and noble.

After transmitting various abstract concepts through telepathy, the man and woman vanished from the screen, and the voice proceeded to give a brief lecture on the now familiar concerns of the aliens for the future of our world. The voice promised a further contact, and with that the green globes departed.

Two months later, in July 1952, Angelucci was walking home after a visit to a snack bar when he discovered a UFO in a vacant lot underneath an elevated freeway. His curiosity understandably piqued, he climbed aboard to discover that the craft was remote controlled. Immediately it took off and headed into outer space, from which he looked back on the blue orb of Earth. (Inside the craft, hidden loudspeakers played the song "Fools Rush In"!) There then followed another lecture delivered by a voice,

which evinced such compassion that Angelucci was reduced to tears at his miserable human state. A beam of white light was projected upon him from the ceiling, causing a kind of awakening of cosmic consciousness, in which he realized that human beings were "trapped in eternity."

Angelucci had a number of subsequent adventures with the space people, who apparently didn't need spacecraft, only displaying them for the benefit of humans. On one occasion, while out walking at night, he was met by a spaceman who introduced himself as Neptune, and informed Angelucci that where he came from Earth was known as the "home of sorrows." He added that unless humanity sorted itself out a disaster called "The Great Accident" would destroy Earth in 1986.

In January 1953, Angelucci was spiritually transported to another planet, where he met a beautiful alien woman named Lyra and another man called Orion. Angelucci was told that in a previous life he, too, had been an alien, also called Neptune.

When he tried to inform others of the presence of the aliens, Angelucci was confronted with derision and even outright hostility. In spite of this, he produced a book in 1955 entitled *Secret of the Saucers*, and a small newspaper, *The Twentieth Century Times*, reporting on the activities and philosophy of the space people. Eventually, public hostility began to be replaced by curiosity and, by many, acceptance.

APPLETON, CYNTHIA

British **contactee** who encountered an alien being in her house in Birmingham, England, on November 18, 1957. A housewife, Cynthia was at home with her children when a figure materialized by the fireplace in the living room. The being was tall, with long blond hair, and was dressed in a tight-fitting silvery suit. Like many of the **Space Brothers**, the being communicated through telepathy, telling Cynthia that he was from another world. Although he did not say which one, he said that "like yours, it is governed by the Sun," implying that it lay within our Solar System. The visitor explained that his race was visiting Earth because the planet's oceans contained some element they needed. He also advised her that human beings used the wrong kind of power, and that his people had mastered gravity.

The being returned to the Appleton house on January 8, 1958, accompanied by another spaceman. This time, they said (verbally) that they came from Venus, and that they were actually projections. Cynthia was advised not to touch them. (This sounds rather like an application of the science of holographic projection—see **holographic theory**.)

On a subsequent visit in September 1958, Cynthia was told that she would have a baby boy, a prophecy that turned out to be accurate. During one visit, one of the beings burned his finger, and left behind a small piece of skin in a bowl of water. When this physical evidence was analyzed, it was found to be more like animal than human tissue.

AREA 51

Ultrasecret military test facility located in Groom Lake, a dry lake bed 120 miles northwest of Las Vegas, Nevada. Geographically remote and shrouded in secrecy since its construction in 1954, Area 51 was the home of the U-2 spy plane and its replacement, the Lockheed SR-71 Blackbird. In the late 1970s and early 1980s, it was also the construction and test site for the B-2 Stealth Bomber and F-117A Nighthawk fighter. The intense secrecy surrounding both Area 51 and its neighboring site, S-4, has aroused the suspicions of UFO researchers, who believe that captured extraterrestrial technology is being tested and experiments in **reverse engineering** conducted there.

An unnamed congressman, who visited the base and, due to his high security clearance, was shown some of the work being done there, claimed that a "mysterious technology" was being developed, one that was "not part of the official program of the U.S. government." In 1984 the Pentagon made an application to appropriate 89,000 acres of public land in Nevada. The main reason for this was that too many aviation enthusiasts (not to mention UFO enthusiasts) were frequenting the area. It was later discovered that there remained three vantage points from which to observe the facility, so the Pentagon promptly made a further application to seize the land containing the vantage points, 4,000 acres in all.

However, these precautions have been unable to prevent some very impressive sightings of highly maneuverable aircraft in the region, and even aviation commentators, not known for their acceptance of UFOs, concede that some extremely advanced technology is indeed being developed and tested at Area 51 and S-4.

In 1989, Robert **Lazar** claimed in a Las Vegas TV interview that he had worked at the S-4 site between 1987 and 1989. His task was to reverse engineer the propulsion system of an alien spacecraft in the possession of the U.S. government. Lazar also claimed that as many as nine flying disks were kept at S-4, one of which had a large hole in its rim, implying that it had been shot down. According to Lazar, the alien ships are powered by a substance known as **Element 115**.

ARNOLD, KENNETH
(See **Introduction**)

ARTIFACTS (ALIEN)
Throughout the modern era of ufology, the "Holy Grail" for investigators has been the discovery of actual artifacts left behind by alien beings on their departure from Earth. Unfortunately, for most of that time the final proof of alien presence has been unforthcoming, despite numerous claims to the contrary. On the occasions when a piece of material

has been retrieved and sent for analysis, it is invariably discovered to consist of materials commonly found on Earth. However, this may be an unfair criticism of such objects, in view of the fact that the various elements found on our planet are common throughout the known Universe, and so, should a genuine alien artifact ever be retrieved, it could reasonably be expected to consist of materials familiar to us. The true test of an alleged alien artifact would center on the methods by which known materials were combined: if it were found to be constructed through the use of unfamiliar processes, it would be much more compelling as evidence of extraterrestrial intelligence.

Impressive claims have recently been made by Derrel **Sims** for certain objects removed from several abductees. Whitley **Strieber** has also commented on such implants, citing the results of professional analysis, which has concluded that some of them are made of boron, an element that is not easy to stumble across in the course of everyday life.

The concept of alien artifacts is not confined to anything that might be found on Earth, however. In 1959, the U.S. **National Aeronautics and Space Administration** (NASA) commissioned the highly respected Brookings Institute in Washington, D.C., to conduct a study into the implications of space exploration. The resulting document was entitled *Proposed Studies on the Implications of Peaceful Space Activities for Human Affairs.* The most intriguing part of the report, in the context of alien artifacts, was entitled "Implications of a Discovery of Extraterrestrial Life," and dealt with "the need to investigate the possible social consequences of an extraterrestrial discovery and to consider whether such a discovery should be kept from the public in order to avoid political change and a possible 'devastating' effect on scientists themselves—due to the discovery that many of their own most cherished theories could be at risk." The report went on to state

that "artifacts left at some point in time by these life-forms might possibly be discovered through our space activities on the Moon, Mars or Venus."

As it turns out, the Brookings Institute report seems to have been somewhat prophetic, since apparent artifacts have indeed been discovered on both the Moon and Mars, although their exact nature is still extremely controversial. By far the best known of these strange objects is the so-called Face on Mars, or the Martian Sphinx, which was photographed during the *Viking* missions to Mars in 1976. Located in the region of Cydonia, the "Sphinx" is a mile-long mesa, which appears to have been carved to represent a humanoid face. When the photographs were first released, NASA assured intrigued journalists that it was merely the result of a trick of light and shadow upon an object that, in reality, bore no resemblance to a face. However, a second frame containing the mesa was later discovered. Taken with the Sun at a different angle, the second frame revealed identical features, proving that the face was what it appeared to be. Subsequent computer enhancement undertaken by Richard Hoagland, Vincent Di Pietro and Gregory Molenaar among others has revealed that the face possesses eyeballs, teeth and an apparent "headdress" containing horizontal striations.

In addition to the Sphinx, there are a number of other anomalous objects nearby on the Cydonia Plain, including a five-sided pyramid, one of whose walls seems to have collapsed, and a circular mound, known as the "Tholus," which seems to contain a spiral ramp.

The researchers mentioned above have also suggested that a geometric pattern links the various features, expressing two mathematical constants: *pi* (the ratio of the circumference of a circle to its radius) and *e* (the base of natural logarithms). Hoagland has also suggested that the geographical location of the Cydonia objects, at 19.5 degrees North latitude, is extremely significant, since it echoes the location of various "geophysical disturbances" on other planets in the Solar System, including Earth. "From the latitude of the largest volcanic 'upwelling' on Earth (the Hawaiian shield volcano), to the siting of the two major suspected active volcanic complexes on Venus, Alpha and Beta Regio, to the location of the Great Red Spot on Jupiter and its recently discovered counterpart on Neptune—the Great Dark Spot—ALL occur (within a degree or so) *at either 19.5 North or South—or both!*" [Original emphasis.]

Earth's own Moon also holds some fascinating mysteries. For instance, at the center of the lunar disk as seen from Earth, in a region known as *Sinus Medii* (Central Bay), there is a crater called Ukert. At the center of this 16-mile-wide crater lies a perfect equilateral triangle. In 1967, NASA's *Lunar Orbiter III* probe photographed more anomalous objects. Southwest of *Sinus Medii* stands a one-and-a-half-mile-high object, which Hoagland has christened the "Shard," on account of its apparent glasslike composition. Not far from the Shard is another towering object—this one approximately seven miles high—which is topped by an enormous cubical structure.

In 1994 the military probe *Clementine* mapped the entire lunar surface, and captured images of geometric objects hanging up to nine miles above the surface, apparently supported by some kind of framework. Richard Hoagland suggests that these may be the remnants of vast domes designed to cover and protect alien cities, long fallen into disrepair. Hoagland also claims that the Apollo astronauts explored these ruined cities, and that this was actually the real reason for the Apollo program.

This, of course, begs the question: why hasn't the public been informed of these monumental discoveries? The Brookings Institute report, and in particular the section dealing with the implications of the discovery of alien artifacts on other planets, may hold the answer.

ASHTAR (AKA ASHTAR COMMAND)

Space being, a member of an interstellar organization called the Council of Seven Lights, which is said to be monitoring and protecting Earth, notably from harmful cosmic radiation, which is being deflected away from the planet by their orbiting spacecraft. Ashtar is the commander of a space station from the planet Shanchea; his first **contactee** was George **van Tassel**, the designer of the **Integratron**, although in the years since contact was made in 1951, many people claimed to have received messages from Ashtar and the council through the practice of **channeling**. These messages are the familiar ones of cosmic philosophy: advice on conduct and warnings about various disasters—such as a predicted shift in Earth's axis, threatening human survival—together with information on plans for the future evacuation of the planet. Much of this material is naïve in the extreme, referring, for instance, to "wondrous stars which are really suns!" It also smacks of bad science fiction, mentioning such beings as Elcar, of the 6th projection, 42nd wave, 4th sector patrol.

ASKET

Alien being encountered by the Swiss **contactee** Eduard "Billy" **Meier**. Asket belongs to a race known as the Timars, which originated in a parallel universe called the DERN universe, but which migrated to another universe called the DAL 50,000 years ago. The Timars are related to both the **Pleiadians/Plejarans** and the human race. The two alien races engage in an ongoing exchange of wisdom and technology: the Timars offer their highly advanced technical knowledge in exchange for the enormous spiritual wisdom of the Pleiadians/Plejarans. As a result, both races are approximately 8,000 years ahead of humanity in these fields.

Asket was Billy Meier's guide for 12 years, during which she helped him to learn about the cultures and belief systems of Earth. She also took Billy on many journeys through time, in order to observe firsthand the key events of human history. Asket and the Timars help the Pleiadians/Plejarans to monitor the activities of humanity, since we are at a particularly dangerous point in our evolution. In common with many other space people, Asket informed Billy that our destructive tendencies will soon present a threat to the inhabitants of other planets.

According to Meier, Asket is no longer active on Earth, and as a farewell gesture, she took him on board her spacecraft and allowed him to photograph her. The resulting, slightly blurred, picture shows a young, strikingly attractive woman with long blond hair and curiously elongated earlobes—apparently the only anatomical difference between the Timars and humans. Unfortunately, this photograph was later discovered to be of a Swedish fashion model.

AVELEY, ESSEX, U.K.

Location of an alien abduction on October 27, 1974. John and Elaine Avis were driving home with their three children, when they saw an oval blue light in the sky, which puzzled them. They discussed it briefly as they continued their journey, but presently they encountered a curious green mist on the road, into which they drove.

Upon arriving home, John Avis switched on the TV to discover that the stations had closed down for the evening (this was before the days of 24-hour schedules), and that they had arrived two and a half hours later than they should have done. Unable to remember what had occurred during the missing time, John and Elaine decided to undergo hypnotic regression.

During the sessions, it emerged that, once inside the green mist, the family were taken from their car and into a waiting UFO, and were subjected to the medical examination described by numerous other abductees. Their captors were four feet tall and dressed in white gowns. Most curiously, they had the faces of animals, with large eyes and pointed ears, and they seemed to be covered with fur. These creatures were apparently under the command of another group of entities on board the craft. These were much taller (about six and a half feet) and were virtually indistinguishable from humans, the only difference being that their eyes were pink. These beings then showed John and Elaine Avis around the craft, which had three decks. Its propulsion system was described, and the abductees were then shown a holographic depiction of the destruction of the aliens' home planet through pollution.

Their alien captors then returned the family to their car. As is often the case with alien abductees, the attitudes of the family subtly changed after their experience, becoming gradually more spiritually orientated. John Avis began to develop artistic skills, and the family reported various psychic phenomena, including apparitions, in their home.

AVIARY

Group of 12 so-called whistle-blowers within the U.S. intelligence community, who were the "Deep Throat" sources of researcher William **Moore**. The group includes "Falcon" and "Condor," two intelligence agents who claim that the U.S. government is in ongoing contact with **Gray** aliens. Falcon, who was actually a counterintelligence agent with the Air Force Office of Special Investigations named Richard C. Doty (this may not be his real name) originally contacted researcher Linda Moulton **Howe**, offering to contribute some film of UFOs for a documentary she was planning. The film was never supplied, due, according to Doty, to "political reasons." During a meeting with Howe, Doty showed her a "Briefing for the President of the

United States of America," which contained information on **extraterrestrial biological entities (EBEs)**, which had crashed in their spacecraft near **Roswell**, New Mexico in 1947, prompting President Harry Truman to create the **MJ-12** group (also known as **Majestic 12** and Majority 12).

According to researcher Robert Hastings, Condor is the code name of Robert M. Collins, a former U.S. Air Force captain who worked in the Plasma Physics group at the top secret Sandia National Laboratories, Kirtland Air Force Base until 1988, when he retired. Condor claims that the USAF Project **Blue Book** was actually nothing more than a public relations exercise, and that the most interesting UFO reports were diverted to higher authorities for investigation. Condor and Falcon maintained that the **Area 51** facility in Nevada is partly operated by aliens, who have forged a "secret treaty" with the U.S. government, whereby they are allowed to operate unchallenged on Earth, in return for items of their highly advanced technology.

AZTEC, NEW MEXICO

Site of a hoax UFO **crash-retrieval**, which was written up by entertainment columnist Frank Scully in his 1950 book *Behind the Flying Saucers*. According to the story, a craft 99.99 feet in diameter crashed near Aztec, killing its 16 crew. The ship was taken to **Wright-Patterson Air Force Base** for study. Inside the UFO the investigators discovered books containing strange hieroglyphics and small wafers—apparently food.

This information was originally given by one Silas M. Newton in a public lecture at the University of Denver on March 8, 1950. Newton, who claimed to be a Texas oil millionaire, repeatedly referred to a friend of his, named "Dr. Gee," who participated in the study of the craft and its occupants. However, both Newton and "Dr. Gee" (whose real name was Leo G. GeBauer) were actually con men, who defrauded investors out of thousands of dollars with an instrument they claimed could detect oil, and which was based on recovered alien technology.

BADAJOZ, SPAIN

Location of an early-morning encounter with an apparition-like alien. On November 12, 1976, two Spanish soldiers were on sentry duty in the guardhouse on the Talavera la Real air force base near the border with Portugal. Alerted by a sudden, extremely high-pitched noise, they rushed outside to see a bright light hanging in the sky. At this point, they were joined by a third soldier, and together they decided to search the fuel stockpiles for possible sabotage.

They were unable to find any evidence of an intrusion, until they were suddenly caught in a powerful wind from an unknown source. There was a sound of breaking twigs in a nearby clump of bushes, and the soldiers sent their German shepherd dog to challenge whoever or whatever was hiding there. Moments later, the dog staggered back to them in a disorientated state.

At that point, a ghostly figure appeared in front of them. It was humanoid and extremely large—about nine feet tall. Surrounded by a greenish glow, it seemed to be dressed in a kind of a space suit and was wearing a helmet through which its humanlike face could be seen. Most bizarrely, its lower arms and hands were missing, as were its calves and feet.

One of the soldiers raised his rifle, but instantly fell to the ground, paralyzed and temporarily blinded. His companions, however, succeeded in firing a number of rounds into the creature, which promptly vanished in a flash of light.

When the soldiers reported what had just happened, more men were dispatched to search the area, while the paralyzed man was hospitalized, where he later recovered. Even though other personnel had heard the shots, no spent cartridge cases were found at the scene, and there were no bullet holes in the wall in front of which the entity had appeared.

A similarly incomplete entity was encountered by a British soldier at **Dakelia Barracks** on Cyprus in 1968.

BADEN-WÜRTTEMBERG, GERMANY

At 2:00 A.M. on February 24, 1977, Lothar Schaefler, a 25-year-old railway worker from Langenargen, Baden-Württemberg, dropped off his friend, an innkeeper, after an evening at a local bar. The two men watched as a pair of blue lights approached through the early-morning sky; the lights came to a halt, moved together and then disappeared.

Once inside his house, Schaefler's friend went upstairs and saw through a window that the lights had returned. He was about to move to the window for a better view when he became paralyzed. Schaefler, still outside, became terrified when two entities appeared. Although he wanted to run, he, too, found he could not move. The beings were humanoid, about four feet tall, with long arms reaching to their knees. Their heads were hairless and perfectly spherical, with slanted eyes and a circular mouth but no nose or ears. Around their necks were greenish frills.

Suddenly, Schaefler was able to move again, and he ran around a neighboring house, frantically searching for a way in. In utter desperation, he smashed a windowpane on the front door and let himself into the hall, where he collapsed in a petrified heap on the floor. Awoken by this commotion, the occupants of the house called the police, who found Schaefler in the hall, with his hand covered with blood. The beings had departed.

Suspecting that Schaefler's bizarre story was the result of drunkenness, the police took him to a hospital, where his blood alcohol level was checked and found not to be particularly high. Schaefler suffered from insomnia for some time after his encounter, and subsequently developed a stomach ulcer, probably caused by the stress of his experience.

BAHÍA BLANCA, ARGENTINA

Not all alien encounters are outrageous and terrifying; nor are they obviously otherworldly at their outset. One such case occurred in Bahía Blanca, Buenos Aires, Argentina, at 3:00 A.M. on August 8, 1972, and subsequently became known as the "Hitchhiker From Space."

A car mechanic named Eduardo Fernando Dedeu was driving home when his car radio developed a problem. He stopped and got out to check the aerial. As he was doing so, he noticed a hitchhiker standing at the side of the road. He asked the man if he wanted a lift, and the man responded by getting into the car. As they started off, Dedeu attempted to start a conversation with his passenger, but could not understand a thing he said.

The passenger was about six and a half feet tall and heavily built. He wore a nondescript coat with the collar turned up. On his head was an odd hat that looked a little like a shallow helmet. The only truly unusual thing about him was his chin, which was extremely long, reaching to his upper chest.

Dedeu and his curious passenger drove in silence for the next 15 miles, until the car's engine malfunctioned and they coasted to a halt. Dedeu then saw a large, brightly lit object drifting over a neighboring field. He left the car to get a better look at the UFO, and when he turned back, he saw that his passenger was nowhere to be seen. The passenger door was open, and the door handle lay in the road, having been pulled off.

Dedeu watched the UFO depart and then returned to his car, which now started with no problem. Although he drove around for a while looking for the hitchhiker, he could not find him.

For the following seven months, other entities matching the description of Dedeu's mysterious passenger were seen in Argentina, and were seen in the United States in September 1994.

BASES (ALIEN)

Although the best-known base said to be operated (at least partly) by aliens is Area 51/S-4, there are many others reputed to be scattered throughout the United States. One is said to lie beneath the small New Mexico town of Dulce, and is home to an enormous number of **Grays**—18,000, according to some estimates. Some of the literature on the Dulce Base (notably that produced by Commander **X**) claims that the Grays are actually native to Earth and are agents employed by a hostile race of reptilian creatures called the DRACO, who are at this moment approaching Earth inside a colossal planetoid star ship. The Dulce Base is being used as a genetics laboratory, in which the Grays conduct hideous experiments on their hapless human victims, crossbreeding them with a variety of animals, although the reason for this is not clear. Other experiments involve the transplantation of souls between bodies.

In 1971, while vacationing in Arizona, a man named Brian Scott was teleported into a UFO in a base beneath the Superstition Mountains. He was undressed and examined by several seven-foot-tall creatures with leathery skin and appallingly bad breath. Scott suffered terrible head pains, "like 10,000 migraine headaches," during the examination, which resulted in his intelligence being enhanced.

The beings occupying the base beneath Mount Shasta in northern California are unusually benevolent toward humans, and are said to be the descendants of the fabled Lemurians. In 1977, UFO researcher William F. Hamilton III was contacted by a beautiful woman calling herself "Bonnie" and claiming to have come from a city called Telos, a mile beneath the mountain. She described to Hamilton how both the Atlanteans and Lemurians had fled underground after the catastrophes that had destroyed their civilizations. According to Bonnie, the Lemurians originally came from the planet Aurora, but their colonization of Earth's surface was short-lived, due to harmful radiation from the Sun. They migrated to the interior of the planet, building vast cities inside natural cavern systems. Many, however, remained on the surface and degenerated into modern humans.

There are a number of alien bases in Canada (perhaps due to the country's sparse population in relation to its area). According to some researchers, there is an aeons-old city beneath Toronto, the center of which lies beneath the junction of Gerrard Street and Church Street. Apparently, the magnetic machinery, much of which is still in working order, accounts for the above-average rate of traffic accidents there.

Rumors of underground alien bases seem to be a contemporary adaptation of the claims of Richard S. **Shaver**, regarding a race of monstrous creatures known as **Deros**, while the concept of underground civilizations itself can be traced back through mythological history. Some Native Americans believe that humanity was born underground, later finding its way to the surface. The notion of the "underworld" also played an important role in the myth-systems of the Central and South American civilizations, as well as classical Greece and Rome.

BEBEDOURO, BRAZIL

UFO researchers who subscribe to the **extraterrestrial hypothesis** are not particularly keen on the idea that some (if not all) nonhuman entities might be modern variations on the creatures of **folklore** that have been encountered throughout history. Some cases, however, would seem to admit to few other reasonable interpretations.

One such case occurred in Bebedouro, Minas Gerais, Brazil, on May 4, 1969. A military policeman named José Antônio da Silva was fishing by himself on the shores of a lagoon, when he heard voices behind him, and turned to see two, four-foot-tall beings in silver suits and helmets. One of the beings fired a beam of light at him, and da Silva fell to the ground, whereupon the beings dragged him to a waiting cylindrical object.

Once inside, the beings placed another helmet on their captive, who felt the craft rise into the air. After some considerable time, during which the beings conversed in an unknown language, da Silva felt another jolt, which seemed to indicate that the craft had landed. He was then blindfolded and led into a large room. Once they had removed his blindfold, the beings took off their helmets, and da Silva was able to see their faces for the first time.

The beings had waist-long, reddish hair, thick eyebrows, large eyes, ears and wide mouths, and large, crooked noses. They also sported extremely long beards. These strange, dwarflike creatures took an immediate interest in da Silva's fishing equipment. While they were examining it, the military policeman looked around the room and saw a large shelf containing four human bodies. He became extremely frightened, but his captors managed to calm him down, and gave him a dark green liquid to drink. (This is an interesting and often reported element in abductions, and Whitley **Strieber** has suggested that the liquid may have amnesia-causing qualities.)

The "leader" of the creatures, who was slightly taller than the others, began a conversation of sorts with da Silva, conducted in sign language and diagrams, and regarding various types of weaponry. Da Silva suspected that the beings wanted him to help them deal with humans in some way, and he then made it clear to them that he wanted to leave.

The leader then noticed da Silva's crucifix and rosary, and took it away from him, which caused the man to begin praying. At this point, astonishingly, his prayers were apparently answered, for a figure resembling Christ appeared before him. The dwarfs then decided it was time for their captive to be returned home. They took him back into the craft, and as it landed, da Silva lost consciousness, waking up about 250 miles from where he had been abducted. He later discovered that he had been gone for four and a half days, and had suffered three wounds on his neck where the helmet had chaffed against his skin.

This case is extremely puzzling, due not only to the resemblance of the "aliens" to creatures of folklore, but also to its religious element. In the light of his obvious religious faith, it is possible that the Christ-like figure was a projection from da Silva's unconscious, in response to his fear and desperation.

BEDROOM VISITORS

Generic name given to entities that are seen by percipients while in bed at night. Many (although by no means all) alien abductions begin in the victim's bedroom, although an outright abduction need not necessarily take place, and numerous people have reported no more than a vague sense of a strange and unexplainable presence somewhere in the room.

Typically, the percipient will either be on the point of falling asleep, or will have just woken up when he or she suddenly has the feeling that there is "someone" in the room who should not be there. Frequently, this feeling is accompanied by an utter inability to move, a discovery that invariably makes the percipient afraid. On looking around the room, he may see a group of ill-defined shapes or apparent entities around the bed. Appalling as this may sound, it only lasts for a few seconds before movement returns and the shapes disappear.

This is known as sleep paralysis, and is regarded as perfectly natural, in spite of the fear it causes. The paralysis occurs because the sleeping brain is "disconnected" from the muscles of the limbs, to prevent us from physically acting out our dreams. Upon awakening, there can sometimes be a short delay before movement is re-enabled. The strange and frightening shapes are hallucinations experienced on the edge of sleep. The boundary between waking and sleeping is called the hypnagogic state, and the corresponding boundary between sleeping and waking is called the hypnopompic state. In these states, the percipient has awareness of his surroundings, but is still so close to sleep that material from the unconscious may be "seen" within his immediate environment.

It is possible that some supposed alien abductions may actually be hypnagogic or hypnopompic hallucinations. After such an experience, percipients may assume, especially upon fully awakening, that something terrible has happened to them during the night, and that they are witnessing the departure of alien creatures from their bedroom. This, of course, cannot explain *all* abductions, especially those experienced in full wakefulness during the course of the day.

BELGRAVE, AUSTRALIA

Site of an encounter with demonic entities on August 8, 1993. The percipients, 27-year-old Kelly Cahill and her husband, were driving home from a friend's house in the Dandenong Hills when they saw a large UFO with lights and windows hovering above the road ahead. The object was close enough for Kelly to discern figures moving in the windows. It departed quickly, and the couple continued their journey.

A few minutes later the car was bathed in an intense light, which unnerved Kelly and her husband. Suddenly, she felt calm again, and said that she felt as if she had had a blackout. She also smelled strongly of vomit, and when they arrived home, the couple realized that they had lost an hour of time. Later, when she was undressing for bed, Kelly discovered a triangular mark on her abdomen. She later suffered from severe stomach pains and a uterine infection, both of which forced her to go to the hospital.

Kelly spontaneously recalled part of their UFO encounter, in which the 150-foot-diameter craft landed in a field not far from the road. Her husband stopped the car, and they both got out for a better look at the craft. Kelly noticed that another car had stopped not far away, and the three passengers were also staring at the object in the field. Presently, they were able to discern a black figure standing in the field. It was about seven feet tall, very thin and with large eyes that glowed red. Suddenly, the field seemed to be full of the beings, some of which glided toward the frightened witnesses, while others approached the people from the other car.

The beings then took hold of them and, as she struggled against their grip, Kelly felt the urge to be sick. At that point, her memories of the experience ended. Interestingly, Kelly later said that she had the feeling the creatures were evil, that they had no souls. She subsequently had several dreams about them, during one of which an entity leaned over her abdomen. The creatures were superficially similar in appearance to the **Grays**, in that their heads were extremely large and hairless, their eyes were huge and they had spindly limbs. The main difference was their color: Kelly described them as being not the *color* black, but more like *holes in space* than material beings.

The people in the other car later confirmed Kelly's story, making this a rare and important multiple witness case.

BENDER, ALBERT K.

Legendary UFO investigator and victim of the **Men in Black (MIBs)**. In 1953, Bender founded the International Flying Saucer Bureau (IFSB), based in Bridgeport, Connecticut, and began to publish a journal called *Space Review*. Soon afterward, Bender claimed to have stumbled upon the solution to the flying saucer mystery, but wrote in *Space Review* that he had been prevented from disclosing any information by a "higher source." He then ceased publication of his journal and closed down the IFSB.

According to the American researcher Gray Barker in his book *They Knew Too Much About Flying Saucers* (1956), Bender was in his apartment when he was overcome by a fit of dizziness and had to lie down. Presently, he became aware of three men, dressed in black suits and Homburg hats, standing in his bedroom. Their faces were hidden in shadow, and as Bender watched, their eyes suddenly lit up "like flashlight bulbs," causing a stabbing pain in his head. Bender later said: "It was then I sensed that they were conveying a message to me by telepathy."

The MIBs' message was a confirmation that Bender had indeed discovered the true nature of UFOs, and they supplied additional information that so terrified him that he gladly complied with their order to shut down both *Space Review* and the IFSB, and to cease UFO investigations immediately. They also swore him to silence, on his honor as an American citizen.

Although he refused to be drawn by his former colleagues on what the Men in Black had told him, in 1962 Bender finally published a book entitled *Flying Saucers and the Three Men*, the contents of which were so outrageous that Gray Barker advised his friends not to believe it. The book describes how the Men in Black were disguised aliens, whose true appearance was monstrous. They abducted him, he claimed, and took him to their flying saucer base in Antarctica, where they told him that they came from the planet Kazik and were on Earth to extract a certain element from the sea (see the **Cynthia Appleton** case). The reason Bender was able finally to tell his story was that the creatures' mission was scheduled to end in 1960, after which they told him he would be free to release the information.

Although Gray Barker believed that Bender may have been suffering from delusions, he nevertheless believed that his friend had indeed stumbled upon some important piece of information that had brought him to the attention of the **CIA** or some other organization, which had warned him off. In Barker's opinion, the Men in Black were human, not alien.

Shortly after publication of *Flying Saucers and the Three Men*, Bender moved to the other side of the country and made his telephone number unlisted, having shown little interest in promoting his book.

BENNEWITZ, DR. PAUL

Physicist, manager of a small electronics company and resident of Albuquerque, New Mexico, who in 1980 recorded unusual electromagnetic activity and photographed a number of UFOs in the vicinity of his home. The objects appeared to come from the direction of the nearby top secret Sandia Military Reservation. At the time, there were several intrusions by UFOs into restricted military airspace, especially the Manzano Nuclear Weapons Storage Area.

Bennewitz contacted the U.S. Air Force about these "intrusions," and spoke with a Major (now Lieutenant Colonel) Ernest Edwards, who in turn contacted Special Agent Richard **Doty**.

Bennewitz attempted to decipher the electromagnetic signals he was receiving and recording, with the intention of establishing electronic communication with the UFOs. At this point, according to William **Moore**, Bennewitz became the target of a coordinated program of **disinformation**, designed to unbalance him mentally and thus undermine his credibility. His own investigation of Myrna **Hanssen**'s terrifying close encounter led Bennewitz to believe that there was an alien **base** beneath the town of Dulce, New Mexico, and this belief was heavily reinforced by the government's disinformation.

At the Las Vegas **Mutual UFO Network (MUFON)** meeting of July 1989, William Moore claimed that he had been employed by the Air Force Office of Special Investigations (AFOSI) to supply Bennewitz with information on UFOs and the presence of evil aliens that was calculated to drive him to a nervous breakdown. According to Moore, the hapless Bennewitz had detected an experimental air force signal that actually had nothing to do with UFOs. Security officers approached him and asked him to cease his efforts to intercept the signals, but he refused, in the mistaken belief that the air force was trying to hide genuine UFO activity.

BETHURUM, TRUMAN

Contactee who published a book in 1954, entitled *Aboard a Flying Saucer,* which chronicled his experiences with the people of the planet Clarion. Clarion, it seems, is within our Solar System, but is never seen from Earth, since it is on the other side of the Moon (a typically stupid assertion). A highway maintenance worker, Bethurum was on the night shift on July 27, 1952, and took a break by driving into the desert around Mormon Mesa, Nevada. Awakening from a short nap, he saw that his truck was surrounded by 10 short (between four and five feet) olive-skinned men. Nearby hovered a gigantic metallic disk 300 feet in diameter.

The men invited Bethurum into their "scow" to meet their captain, who turned out to be a beautiful woman named Aura Rhanes. Bethurum noted her unusual mode of dress: a black velvet bodice, red pleated skirt and a red and black beret. She informed her guest that all the planets of the Solar System had breathable atmospheres, and many were inhabited. Over the next three months, Bethurum would meet Aura Rhanes eleven times. They told each other about life on their home planets (although highly advanced, the people of Clarion followed a simple and harmonious way of life), and Aura hinted that

one day Truman might be allowed to visit Clarion. However, this never came to pass, and after her 11th visit, Aura Rhanes never returned.

BIGFOOT

Large, hairy, extremely elusive anthropoid creature said to inhabit the forests of the American Pacific Northwest (although sightings have been made throughout the North American continent), which is occasionally seen in conjunction with apparent UFO activity. According to cryptozoologist Dr. Karl Shuker, the typical Bigfoot's face is "apelike with a sloping brow, prominent eyebrow ridges, light-reflecting eyes (usually a nocturnal adaptation), broad flattened nose and lipless slitted mouth. It has a powerful, muscular chest, very long arms whose pawlike hands have thick fingers and hairless palms, sturdy muscular legs, and no tail."

It has been suggested that Bigfoot (known as Sasquatch in Canada) might be a surviving population of *Gigantopithecus,* which may have crossed the land bridge now occupied by the Bering Strait, although no archaeological evidence has yet been found to support this theory.

The UFO connection is one of the most bizarre and intriguing aspects of the Bigfoot mystery, with some researchers suggesting that the giant hairy creature might be under alien control for some unknown reason, or might even itself be an alien.

BLACK HELICOPTERS

Unmarked helicopters that have frequently been seen in connection with UFO/alien activity, and which often fly low over the properties of witnesses. There is little doubt that black helicopters *do* exist, even if their origin and purpose remain shrouded in mystery. On May 7, 1994 in Harahan, Louisiana, a black helicopter chased a teenager for 45 minutes, while the occupants pointed some kind of instrument at the boy. Although the incident was reported to the local police, the chief said that the aircraft was owned by the federal government, and that he was unable to take the matter any further.

The following year, a black helicopter sprayed an unidentified substance on the rural property of a couple in Fallon, Nevada. The livestock were also sprayed, and 13 of them died the following day, while all the plants that had been sprayed died within six months. Again, the helicopter's activities were reported to the authorities, but all knowledge of the machine was denied.

According to conspiracy researcher Jim Keith, between 1971 and 1985, black helicopters, carrying no insignia or registration markings of any kind, were seen in the vicinity of **cattle mutilations**. Keith also states that some civilians who have managed to photograph the helicopters have been harassed by men in black uniforms without insignia.

A hunter in the Red Mountain region near Norris, Montana, had a rather unnerving encounter with a black helicopter and its crew in the autumn of 1976. The aircraft, which was displaying no registration markings (a legal requirement), flew behind a nearby hill and apparently landed. The hunter climbed the hill and saw what appeared to be a Bell Jet Ranger on the ground. Seven men in civilian clothing disembarked and climbed up the hill toward the witness, who waved and shouted a greeting. As the men drew closer, he realized that they were Asian. The men then turned and walked back toward the helicopter, breaking into a run when they saw that the hunter was following them. They then climbed into their aircraft and took off.

Conspiracy researchers like Keith wonder whether the reason black helicopters are hardly ever reported in the media (despite their sightings being comparable to UFOs in number) is that they are "too sensitive a subject" to be given any attention. In short, "does it mean that major media sources have been told to keep quiet about the black helicopters?"

At least two official agencies are definitely known to operate such machines: the Drug Enforcement Agency (DEA) and the Federal Emergency Management Agency (FEMA), an organization designed to ensure the continuance of national administration in the event of a major catastrophe.

The fact that black helicopters are so often seen in the vicinity of cattle mutilations has led to the speculation that the U.S. government is secretly conducting biological weapons experiments in isolated rural areas, and is excising the internal organs of farm animals to monitor the effects of these weapons. Jim Keith reminds us that the FBI admitted to releasing flu germs in urban areas in the 1950s and 1960s, "to determine how susceptible the U.S. was to germ warfare attack," adding that 12 people died as a result of these experiments. The CIA has also exposed citizens to harmful chemicals, notably LSD, which was sprayed on San Francisco residents to test its mind control capabilities.

BLOB, THE (FILM)

Made in 1958, directed by Irwin S. Yeaworth and starring Steve McQueen and Anita Corseaut. In this unintentionally hilarious film, a meteorite lands in a small American town, disgorging a small lump of protoplasm, which feeds on living flesh and gradually grows into a colossal, bloodred lump that goes on the rampage, eating anyone it encounters. It is left to Steve (Steve McQueen) to figure out that the thing is sensitive to temperature, and that extreme cold incapacitates it. Eventually, the Blob is captured and dumped in the Arctic (perhaps in preparation for a nonexistent sequel).

Interestingly (and perhaps suspiciously), this film was made the same year that Hans Gustafsson and Stig Rydberg had their terrifying encounter with similar **blob**like creatures in Sweden.

BLOBS (ALIENS)

In 1958, an event occurred that made headlines across Europe, although today it is largely forgotten, and rarely turns up in the recent UFO literature. Early on the morning of December 20, 1958, two young Swedish men, Hans Gustafsson and Stig Rydberg, were driving from Hoganas to Helsingborg. At about 3:00 A.M., a thick mist descended over the road, forcing them to slow down. The road was surrounded by a dense forest, but nearby there was a clearing, in which they saw a bright light.

Curiosity got the better of them, and they left the car to investigate. As they approached the clearing, they saw that the light was coming from a disk-shaped object, standing on legs about two feet long. According to Gustafsson, the disk "seemed to be made of a peculiar, shimmering light that changed color."

Suddenly the men saw a group of "blobs, like protozoa, just a bit darker." They were bluish in color and were jumping around the disk "like globs of animated jelly." The blobs then attacked Gustafsson and Rydberg and began pulling them toward the object. The creatures displayed great strength, not to mention a dreadful odor like "ether and burnt sausage." Rydberg later said that it was almost impossible to resist the blobs. "It almost seemed as if the creatures could read my mind. They parried every move before I made it. Their strength was not so great as the technique with which they wielded it."

Eventually, Rydberg managed to wrestle himself away from the blobs, made a dash for the car and began to honk the horn in a frantic attempt to get someone's attention. Perhaps surprised or frightened by the sudden, blaring noise, the blobs instantly broke off their attack and retreated to the object, which then rose into the air and quickly flew away.

Exhausted and terrified, Gustafsson and Rydberg continued on their journey home. They would not have told anyone of their dreadful experience, had it not been for the awful stench that clung to them for days and made them sick. They consulted a physician, who could find no physical injuries. Haunted by their memories of the blobs, they decided to report their encounter officially, and were subsequently questioned for 12 hours by members of the Swedish defense staff, doctors and psychologists. The investigators could find no inconsistencies in the testimonies.

Gustafsson and Rydberg took the defense officials and members of the press to the scene of their encounter, where they discovered three indentations in the ground where the disk had stood. They were later hypnotized by psychologists who concluded that they genuinely believed what they were saying. Whatever the true nature of the encounter, it appeared not to be a hoax.

BLUE BOOK (PROJECT)

U.S. Air Force UFO investigation project, established by the Pentagon in March 1952 out of the remnants of Project **Grudge**, and based at **Wright-Patterson Air Force Base** in Dayton, Ohio. Although it ran for a considerable time compared to the other three official air force UFO projects (**Twinkle, Sign** and Grudge), finally being disbanded in 1969, it was actually little more than a face-saving public relations exercise, staffed by a small number of low-ranking officers who were required to divide their time between Blue Book and other, unrelated duties, and who were in no position to make any demands for information concerning the UFO problem from those higher up in the military hierarchy.

The project was originally headed by Captain Edward J. Ruppelt, whose positive conclusions regarding the extraterrestrial nature of some UFOs were included in his 1956 book *The Report on Unidentified Flying Objects* (only to be reversed in a later edition). According to the astronomer Professor

J. Allen **Hynek,** who served as a consultant to Blue Book, the project was something of a shambles from the outset. "Blue Book was a 'cover-up' to the extent that the assigned problem was glossed over for one reason or another. In my many years association with Blue Book, I do not recall even one serious discussion of methodology, of improving the process of data gathering or of techniques of comprehensive interrogation of witnesses."

The leadership of Blue Book changed several times during the 1950s and 1960s, until the dismissive conclusions of the University of Colorado Condon Committee, which conducted an investigation into UFOs in 1968, prompted the air force to announce that "the continuation of Project Blue Book cannot be justified either on the ground of national security or in the interest of science." When the project was finally disbanded in 1969, it brought to an end 22 years of official government interest in UFOs.

BLUE ROOM

Legendary repository of various alien artifacts said to be located somewhere on **Wright-Patterson Air Force Base**. Also known as "Hangar 18" and "Building 18-F, 3rd Floor," the Blue Room, whether or not it really exists, has entered the mythology of UFO research, becoming a kind of shrine, a place where the truth about the Universe and our place in it is known by the select few with clearances high enough to allow them into the "inner circle."

In the early 1960s, Senator Barry Goldwater, former chairman of the Senate Intelligence Committee, requested entry to the Blue Room in order to view whatever it contained, but was refused permission by General Curtis LeMay. Goldwater later informed various researchers that the subject of UFOs was "still classified above Top Secret."

The Blue Room served as the inspiration for the film *Hangar 18.*

BOAS, ANTONIO VILLAS

One of the most unsettling elements in alien abductions is the sexual or reproductive procedures that are carried out on humans by alien beings. The first reported "cosmic seduction" happened in Brazil in 1957. At 1:00 A.M. on October 16, a young farmer named Antonio Villas Boas was out on his tractor plowing fields near São Francisco de Sales when he noticed a red "star" approaching. The object quickly grew in size until it became a roughly circular craft, with a bright red light at the front and a rotating cupola on top. When the object lowered a set of landing gear, the young farmer decided to get out of the field and drove away on his tractor. However, he had not gone very far when the engine and lights of the vehicle died. Antonio jumped down from the tractor and was about to make a run for it when he was grabbed by a five-foot-tall humanoid being. Antonio struggled free but was seized by three taller beings, who proceeded to drag him toward the craft. They were dressed in gray coveralls and wore helmets.

Once inside the craft, which they had entered via a retractable metal ladder, the beings took Antonio first to a small, brightly lit room, and then to a larger semicircular chamber containing some chairs and a low table. After undressing him, taking some samples of his blood and spreading a clear liquid over his body, the beings led him to another room where he was left alone for about half an hour, whereupon some kind of gas was pumped through the walls, which made him violently sick.

After another long wait, Antonio was shocked to see a beautiful woman enter the room. She was about five feet tall and was completely naked. Her face was entirely human, except for her large catlike eyes and rather pointed chin. She had long white hair, although her pubic hair was bright red. In spite of this outrageous situation, Antonio became sexually aroused (he later surmised that the curious liquid smeared on his body might have been an aphrodisiac), and he and the woman had sex. Her technique was rather unusual: she nipped him on the chin and barked.

When it was over, she smiled at him, rubbed her stomach and pointed upward, apparently meaning that she would have his baby somewhere in space. With that, the woman left the room; the other beings returned, gave Antonio his clothes and then gave him a short tour of the craft. Antonio attempted to steal a small, clocklike device as proof of his encounter, but the beings spotted the ploy and took the device away from him.

Antonio was then allowed to leave the ship, the beings indicating that he should stand well away from the ladder when he reached the ground. The cupola on top of the craft then began to spin faster and faster, and it took off, glowing brightly, and disappeared into the early-morning sky. When he arrived home, Antonio discovered that about four hours had passed during his experience.

In the weeks that followed, Antonio suffered from nausea and weakness, and eventually wrote to a well-known journalist named Joao Martins, author of several UFO-related articles. Martins in turn contacted Dr. Olavo Fontes in Rio de Janeiro, and together they interviewed and examined Antonio. Dr. Fontes concluded that the farmer's symptoms suggested mild radiation sickness.

After a delay of several years, the encounter was reported in *Flying Saucer Review*, although Antonio himself refused to speak publicly about his experience until 1980, when he added that the woman had also taken a sample of his sperm after intercourse.

BRITISH UFO RESEARCH ASSOCIATION (BUFORA)

Private UFO investigative organization founded in 1964 through the merger of the London UFO Research Association (founded in 1959) and the British UFO Association (founded in 1962). Based in London, England, BUFORA maintains contact with researchers throughout the world via the International Committee for UFO Research. According to the Chairman, John Spencer, BUFORA's aims are:

1. To encourage, promote and conduct unbiased scientific research of unidentified flying object (UFO) phenomena throughout the United Kingdom
2. To collect and disseminate evidence and data relating to unidentified flying objects (UFOs)
3. To coordinate UFO research throughout the United Kingdom and to cooperate with others engaged in such research throughout the world

BUKIT MERTAJAM, MALAYSIA

Nonhuman entities vary as much in size as appearance. While some are reported to be 20 feet tall, others, such as those in this case from Malaysia, seem to be ridiculously small. On August 19, 1970, six young boys (Mohamad Zulkifli, Abdul Rahim, David Tan, Sulaiman, K. Wigneswaran and Mohamed Ali—no relation) were in the playground of the Stowell English Primary School in Bukit Mertajam, Penang, when a flying disk the size of a dinner plate landed nearby and disgorged five ugly, three-inch-tall humanoid creatures. Four of them wore blue uniforms, while the fifth, which the boys took to be the leader, on account of his two horns, wore a yellow tunic covered with stars.

The tiny creatures proceeded to install some kind of aerial-like device in a tree. Wigneswaran tried to capture the leader, whereupon the ufonauts whipped out their laser pistols and began firing on the boys. All of them except Wigneswaran ran away. He was later found by a schoolteacher, lying in some bushes, sporting a red mark on his leg where he had been hit by a miniature laser gun.

Some of the boys reported encounters with the tiny spacemen on the following day. School officials questioned the boys, suspecting (not unreasonably) that they had invented the whole thing. They remained adamant, however, that their story was true. Interestingly, their description of the entities is reminiscent of some demonic supernatural creatures in Far Eastern mythology.

CARACAS, VENEZUELA

The following case illustrates the inadvisability of attempting to apprehend any alien beings one might encounter: failure is virtually guaranteed, and physical injury is always a possibility. At 2:00 A.M. on November 28, 1954, Gustavo Gonzales and José Ponce were on their way to an all-night market in nearby Petare, when a 10-foot-diameter luminous sphere descended onto the road ahead, blocking their way.

Gonzales, who was driving, brought the truck to a halt and both men got out to examine the sphere, which was now hovering about six feet above the road. At that moment, a strange, hairy, apelike little creature emerged from the bushes at the side of the road and approached them. Acting on impulse, Gonzales grabbed the entity, which weighed only about 35 pounds and whose body was extremely hard. As Gonzales discovered to his cost, the creature was also immensely strong: with one shove, it sent the man flying through the air. Looking around frantically, Ponce saw two more creatures coming out of the bushes. He decided to make a dash for it and ran to a nearby police station, while the first creature set upon Gonzales with its sharp claws.

Apparently handy in a fight, Gonzales whipped out a knife and stabbed the ape-creature, but the blade could not penetrate its incredibly tough skin. One of the other creatures, which had been collecting rocks from the roadside, then pointed a small tube at Gonzales and fired a beam of light at him. Gonzales clutched at his face, temporarily blinded, while the three creatures climbed aboard the sphere, which then took off and flew away.

After recovering his sight, Gonzales made his way to the police station, where he and Ponce were questioned by police, who assumed that they must be drunk. They were not so sure, however, when

Gonzales revealed the long, deep scratch that the creature had given him.

CASPAR MUMMY

The Caspar, Wyoming, mummy was discovered by two gold prospectors in October 1932. Cecil Main and Frank Carr were exploring a gulch in the Pedro Mountains, 60 miles west of the town of Caspar, when they found traces of gold in one of the walls. Setting dynamite charges, they blew away part of the wall, revealing a cave, four feet by four feet, and about 15 feet deep. All thoughts of gold left them when they saw what the cave contained. Sitting cross-legged on a ledge was the tiny figure of a "man." His body was a dark bronze in color, and he was only 14 inches tall.

The prospectors took the man back to Caspar, where word of the discovery quickly spread, and eventually reached the anthropologists at the Wyoming State Historical Society, who arranged for the body to be X-rayed. The X rays revealed a complete internal structure, including skull, spine, bones and even a complete set of teeth. The anthropologists found that the little man weighed 12 ounces and was probably about 65 years old when he died.

The mummified body was also examined by anthropologists from Harvard, the American Museum of Natural History and the Boston Museum Egyptian Department, who concluded that the mummy was an adult rather than a child, and that the embalming methods were comparable to those of the Egyptian pharaohs. The manner of the man's death was also established: he had been hit over the head with some blunt object, which had smashed open the skull and exposed the brain, which remained as a dark, gelatinous substance covering the top of the head.

The mummy was sold to a car dealer in Caspar named Ivan Goodman, who allowed all the tests to be carried out on it. He died in 1950, and the mummy became the property of one Leonard Wadler, although its current location is not known.

There have been a number of theories put forward to explain the strange little man, who came to be known as "Pedro," after the mountains in which he was discovered. In 1979, Professor George Gill, an anthropologist at the University of Wyoming examined Pedro's X rays and concluded that the remains were those of an infant who had suffered from a condition known as anencephaly, in which development of the brain and cranium is incomplete, resulting in brain matter being exposed. As Karl Shuker notes, while this "could account for Pedro's flattened head and its covering of congealed blood and brain tissues . . . anencephaly cannot explain Pedro's adult features and dentition."

An alternative theory is that Pedro was a member of a prehistoric Native American culture that has eluded discovery by archaeologists. Interestingly, Native Americans themselves claim that there is a race of small, aggressive and extremely elusive people still living on the continent.

CATTLE MUTILATIONS

Since the late 1960s, the phenomenon of cattle mutilations has puzzled and disturbed both farmers and UFO researchers. Although to date more than 10,000 animals have been killed by unknown predators, no perpetrator has been apprehended, and no definitive explanation has been settled upon. The first widely publicized case occurred in 1967, when an Appaloosa mare called "Lady" was found with her head completely stripped of flesh in the Sand Dune Valley near Alamosa, Colorado.

Throughout the 1970s, the attacks spread across the United States. In the summer of 1975, police officers in Colorado were investigating up to three mutilations per day. The carcasses were found to be missing various parts of their anatomies, usually skin, eyeballs, ears, tongues, rectums and genitals. In many cases, the animal was completely drained of blood, and there was no sign of any tracks that might have given a clue as to the nature of the predator, even when the ground was muddy or covered with snow. In some cases, the animal decomposed with unnatural speed, while in others decomposition took much longer than it should have done. Many farmers reported that scavengers, which would normally pick at a carcass, kept well away from the mutilated animals.

UFOs have often been reported in areas suffering from strange animal deaths. One of the most interesting cases involves a witness named Larry Gardea, who was bear hunting near Luhan Canyon in New Mexico on September 13, 1994. Making his way through a pasture at 4:00 P.M., he discovered a cow lying on her side with her vagina and rectum missing. Less than 10 feet away, Gardea saw another cow on its knees, apparently dead also.

At that point, he heard a strange sound, which he likened to an arc welder's torch, coming from the nearby forest. The other cows in the pasture immediately moved away from the sound, except for one, which according to Gardea *floated* over the fence enclosing the pasture and toward the edge of the forest. At the same time, another cow floated down out of the air and landed in the pasture.

As the cow disappeared into the forest, Gardea aimed his rifle in the direction of the noise and fired twice. The sound abruptly ceased. According to Gardea, "That's when I felt afraid for the first time. I figured I had just attracted attention to myself and if the sound could move that cow, it could move me. So I turned around and ran back to the ranch house to call the sheriff."

Gardea returned to the pasture about 40 minutes later, along with the Mora County sheriff's deputy and a number of local residents. They were unable to find either the cow that had been pulled away by the sound or the one sitting apparently dead on its knees.

Another very puzzling feature of the cattle mutilation phenomenon, and which has led to the theory that the mutilators are aliens, is the nature of the wounds themselves, which, it is claimed by researchers, show signs of having been cut with an instrument operating at extremely high temperatures, which cauterizes the wounds. It is not feasible that human beings could have wielded such instruments, since our own lasers (at least those powerful enough to cut an animal apart) are large and cumbersome, and there would be little point in hefting such an instrument through countless fields when sharp knives would serve just as well.

The total blood loss observed in many cases is another puzzle. In order for this to be achieved, the animal's throat would have to be cut, and it would then have to be hung upside down while the heart pumped out the three to four gallons of blood. There have never been any indications at mutilation sites that this was done.

In addition, many animals are apparently dropped from the air and found in inaccessible places, such as mountaintops, sometimes with their legs broken. As mentioned above, there is a lack of tracks around the carcass, again implying the use of aircraft of some kind.

Some researchers, such as Jim Keith, have suggested that the aircraft used are the **black helicopters** reported countless times by people throughout the United States, who claim to have been harassed by the unmarked aircraft. Keith notes that many mutilated animals are found to have been sprayed with fluorescent paint, perhaps to mark them as targets for mutilation at night. There are a number of **conspiracy theories** associated with cattle mutilation, one of which suggests that the U.S. government is using the hapless farmers' cattle and other animals in biological warfare experiments.

The best known and respected of researchers in the cattle mutilation phenomenon is Linda Moulton **Howe**, who has produced books and videos, such as *A Strange Harvest,* which detail numerous cases and investigations. Howe was recently the subject of a highly critical article by a **debunker** named Jack Hitt, which was published in the February 1997 issue of the magazine *Gentleman's Quarterly*. In his article, entitled "Operation Moo," Hitt makes reference to the investigations of a former FBI agent, Ken Rommel, who concluded that the wounds on the animals were the result of scavenging action by birds pecking at the soft tissue (which is, admittedly, the first target of scavengers). Rommel has also suggested that the smooth and regular incisions are the result of postmortem gases expanding in the animals' bodies and stretching the skin. This theory seems quite sensible, but it fails to account for the evidence of cauterization at high temperatures. Nor does it explain the total absence of blood in many cases.

In a critique of Hitt's article in *GQ,* Mark Williams points out that cows' udders are frequently removed with apparently surgical precision, while the underlying tissue is left completely untouched, which would seem to rule out normal scavenging activity. Indeed, the farmers whose animals are mutilated maintain that they know very well what wounds left by scavengers look like, and that victims of anomalous mutilations do not exhibit such wounds.

Williams also notes Hitt's implication that Linda Howe is getting rich through her books and videos (his suggestion is that she has made approximately $600,000 so far). However, Williams then points out that Howe's self-published books, which sell for $39.95, cost her $40.00 to print.

Cattle mutilations continue to be reported, in the United States as well as in the United Kingdom and Europe. It seems that, until a perpetrator is actually caught in the act, they will remain a disturbing and, for the farmers involved, expensive mystery.

CENTER FOR UFO STUDIES (CUFOS)

The Chicago-based Center for UFO Studies (CUFOS) was founded in 1973 by Dr. J. Allen **Hynek**, professor of astronomy at Ohio State University, and later chairman of the Astronomy Department at Northwestern University. The main activities of CUFOS are:

1. To maintain its library of UFO material, including books, articles, various documents and encounter reports

2. To publish its quarterly magazine, the *International UFO Reporter (IUR)*, its annual *Journal of UFO Studies,* a variety of books on UFO-related subjects and various scientific monographs

3. To conduct investigations into UFO sightings and encounters

The information gathered from its activities is summarized and stored in a computer database called UFOCAT.

In honor of Hynek's contribution to ufology, the center's name was changed on his death in 1986 to the J. Allen Hynek Center for UFO Studies.

CENTRAL INTELLIGENCE AGENCY (CIA)

The Central Intelligence Agency (CIA) was established by the National Security Act of 1947, and is led by the Director of Central Intelligence (DCI). The CIA is an independent agency, and is responsible to the president of the United States through the DCI. It is also accountable to the American people through the intelligence oversight committee of the U.S. Congress. The agency's mission is to provide accurate foreign intelligence to the president and the National Security Council, while conducting various counterintelligence activities related to foreign intelligence and national security.

In 1997 the CIA published an article in its journal *Studies in Intelligence*. The article, entitled "CIA's Role in the Study of UFOs, 1947–90," was prepared by a National Reconnaissance Office (NRO) historian named Gerald Haines, and documents the CIA's interest in the UFO phenomenon, in spite of frequent denials by the agency that any such interest existed. Indeed, some officials in the CIA believed that there was a possibility that some UFOs were interplanetary spacecraft, and therefore considered it necessary to investigate all sightings.

In 1953 the CIA commissioned the **Robertson Panel** to report on the national security implications of UFOs, fearing that, should a major wave of sightings occur, the Soviet Union would be able to take advantage of the clogging of communications channels by people making reports of what they had seen.

According to researcher Jon Elliston, "From the time of their earliest forays into UFO territory, 'Air Force and CIA officials agreed that outside knowledge of Agency interest in UFOs would make the problem more serious' [Haines]—the 'problem' being public concerns about strange lights in the skies." In his article, Haines adds: "Agency officials purposefully kept files on UFOs to a minimum to avoid creating records that might mislead the public if released." He concludes that this was ultimately damaging to the CIA, since it led to public concerns about an official cover-up of UFO-related information, and a concomitant erosion of trust in government.

That the CIA indeed covered up its interest in UFO reports can no longer be doubted, since, on its own admission, it did precisely this in relation to test flights of the then brand-new U-2 spy plane, which was first tested in 1955, and resulted in a large number of UFO reports (over half of reports from the late 1950s and 1960s, according to Haines).

Elliston states that in the 1970s and 1980s the Office of Scientific Intelligence (OSI) suggested that the Soviet Union might be able to infiltrate and use civilian UFO groups to obtain information on sensitive U.S. weapons programs. When asked if the CIA investigated such civilian groups, Haines replied that the CIA does not conduct "domestic operations," adding that the agency did suggest that the FBI should "look into" the activities of these groups.

CHANNELING

Although better known as a method of establishing contact with spiritual entities, channeling has also been claimed to allow communication with extraterrestrial entities. According to some practitioners and commentators, the channeler is able to relay information that originates outside the human consciousness, whether from God, angels, spirits, demons or aliens.

The practice of channeling is extremely ancient, and is shared by all of Earth's cultures, from the **shamanic** peoples of Asia and North America, to the ancient Greeks with their oracles, to the Spiritualists of the mid-19th and 20th centuries, to the modern channelers who claim to be in contact with extraterrestrial civilizations. Indeed, the Spiritualist movement marked an important democratizing development in the field of nonhuman contact: hitherto, such contact had been the privilege and responsibility of a select few (priests, shamans, oracles and so on); but with Spiritualism came the realization that anyone could make the attempt to speak directly with discarnate entities, and perhaps even succeed.

Channeling can either be spontaneous or induced; in either case, the subject falls into a trance (in the former, involuntarily; in the latter, various induction methods are used, including meditation, self-hypnosis, fasting, chanting and so on). With regard to the field of alien contact, the most significant channelers were the so-called **Martian mediums** of the late 19th century; there has also been much material published concerning communications received via channeling from an extraterrestrial organization known as the **Council of Nine**.

Psychologists are divided on the true nature of channeled information. The Freudian interpretation has it that such information represents material that has been suppressed by the conscious mind, while followers of C. G. **Jung** suggest that it represents archetypes from the **collective unconscious**. Some channelers are sympathetic to the Jungian view, although they are more inclined to see the collective unconscious as representative of a Higher Self or "oversoul," an aspect of humanity that is intimately connected with the Universe, which is seen as a conscious entity.

CHILDREN'S CIRCLES

An element in alien abductions first reported and examined by Whitley **Strieber**, notably in his book *The Secret School* (1997). According to Strieber, the Children's Circles are profoundly important in the relationship between what he calls the "Visitors" and abductees in their early lives. The circle, which he attended in his youth, was (and perhaps still is) located in the Olmos Basin in his home town of San Antonio, Texas. It was here that he and many other children from the area had their first encounters with the Visitors, one of whom he came to call the "Sister of Mercy," apparently because the female being appeared as a nun.

The children who are involved in a circle usually feel a powerful urge to leave their homes in the dead of night and make their way to the site where the encounters take place. During these times, the seeds of a lifelong relationship with the Visitors are sown, and many lessons are given, which seem to be designed to introduce the children

to the idea that humanity is capable of reaching beyond the physical, into profound cosmic and spiritual realms. Partly due to his memories of the children's circle, Strieber has come to the conclusion that the Visitors are intimately connected with the afterlife and are anxious to ensure the progress of human souls. Indeed, they have referred to Earth as a "school."

CHUPACABRAS (GOATSUCKER)

An extremely violent and dangerous anomalous animal, which made its first appearance in the years following an unexplained subterranean explosion in the Cabo Rojo area of Puerto Rico in 1987. Since the early 1970s, the Caribbean island has been host to various kinds of bizarre activity, from UFOs to **Men in Black**. The Chupacabras derives its name from its appetite for the blood of various animals (not just goats), which it drains through small holes made in the animal's body. Frequently, the principal incision is made in the back of the animal's head, killing it instantly.

Witnesses describe the Chupacabras as being about four feet tall, with powerful hind legs and extremely thin, bony forearms armed with razor-sharp claws. Its face is pointed, and it has large fangs and huge, red eyes. In fact, a drawing of the animal by the Puerto Rican investigator Jorge Martin is rather reminiscent, facially at least, of a **Gray** alien.

The creature's unpleasant activities began in earnest early in 1995 in the town of Orocovis, deep in the hinterland, but quickly spread to the coastal town of Canovanas. Residents of the town commented that the presence of the Chupacabras seemed to be connected with the brightly lit unidentified objects frequently seen entering and leaving El Yunque (the Puerto Rican rain forest). With regard to this connection, one witness, Lucy Batista, told Jorge Martin that the "creature being seen everywhere in

Canovanas must be an extraterrestrial. The drawings that are going around show a combination of extraterrestrial and terrestrial animal."

According to the American anomalist Scott Corrales, there have been countless sightings of this bizarre creature. He cites "the industrial complex that couldn't find any security guards to work the graveyard shift, because three Goatsucker-like creatures had been seen at the same time; the people waiting for the bus in broad daylight who saw the Chupacabras walking down the street; the driver waiting at a stoplight who thought a dog was crossing the street in front of him, only to realize that it was a creature he had never seen before; the woman who looked out the window in the midst of Hurricane Luis only to see the Chupacabras standing at a distance, impervious to the rain, wind and lightning . . ."

The Chupacabras was apparently not content to remain an exclusively Puerto Rican curiosity, for reports of mysterious attacks on domestic animals spread from the island to Brazil, then to Mexico, and then into the United States, mainly to the Latin American communities in Florida and Texas.

Like the **cattle mutilations** that have been plaguing farmers throughout rural America since the late 1960s, attacks by the Chupacabras have been dismissed by skeptics as the work of dogs or other mundane animals. While this is certainly true in some cases, the assertion conveniently ignores the countless sightings that have been made of an unknown beast.

As might be expected, the UFO community has lost no time in formulating theories to account for the existence of the Chupacabras. These include biological weapons experiments that have gone disastrously wrong, as well as a hideously successful attempt to cross alien DNA with that of terrestrial animals.

CIA

(See **Central Intelligence Agency**)

CIMARRON, NEW MEXICO

Location of a particularly terrifying alien abduction, which came to the attention of Dr. Paul **Bennewitz**, and served partly as the inspiration for the **disinformation** supplied to him by William **Moore**, and which subsequently drove him to a nervous breakdown. The victim of the abduction, Myrna Hanssen, was hypnotized by abduction researcher Dr. Leo Sprinkle in several sessions between May 11 and June 3, 1980.

Myrna's experience began when she was driving with her six-year-old son near the town of Cimarron. They witnessed the arrival of five UFOs, which landed in a nearby pasture and captured a cow. Myrna and her son were then abducted and were forced to witness the mutilation of the animal. She was then informed by the **Gray** beings that it had to be done.

There followed the standard physical examination on Myrna and her son, after which a tall, "jaundiced-looking" man appeared, and, astonishingly, apologized to her, saying that her abduction should not have occurred, that it had been a mistake, and that those responsible would be punished. The creatures' mode of dress was equally bizarre, and included a "Franciscan monk's collar" and a collar (worn by a square-headed female entity) "gathered at the neck like a pilgrim with ruffles."

Myrna and her son were then taken, via a hidden elevator in the New Mexican desert, to what she described as an underground "base city of operation" by another group of beings whom she described as entirely human. Inside this vast complex, she saw a large number of human beings working alongside Gray-type entities.

When her son was taken away from her, Myrna lost control and ran, screaming, away from her captors, eventually finding herself in a dimly lit room full of large vats. Looking into one of the vats, she was horrified to see human body parts suspended in bubbling liquid. As she collapsed in a sobbing heap, the beings found her and took her to another room, where she was implanted with several devices. These devices were later detected with CAT scans.

Finally, Myrna and her son were taken to an area where they were subjected to intense flashes of light, which apparently had the effect of erasing their memories of their encounter. They were then taken to another UFO and flown back to the point of their abduction.

Whether or not Myrna Hanssen's experience was grounded in objective reality, it remains fascinating as a possible example of a modern variation on the concept of Hell. The central elements—encountering evil creatures, being taken into some kind of underworld, seeing humans being "boiled" in vats—are reminiscent of religious retribution, perhaps more so than the activities of extraterrestrial beings.

CLARION (PLANET)

(See **Bethurum, Truman**)

CLOSE ENCOUNTERS

Generic term denoting experiences in which human beings witness or directly interact with phenomena that cannot adequately be explained within current scientific paradigms, and which may have an intelligent but nonhuman origin. J. Allen **Hynek** divided close encounters into three types: Close Encounters of the First Kind, in which "observers report a close-at-hand experience without tangible physical effects"; Close Encounters of the Second Kind, in which "measurable physical effects on the land and on animate and inanimate objects are reported"; and Close Encounters of the Third Kind, in which "animated entities (often called 'humanoids,'

'occupants,' or sometimes 'ufonauts') have been reported." Subsequent additions to this classification system are Close Encounters of the Fourth Kind, in which human beings are taken from their normal surroundings against their will, and are forced to interact in various ways with nonhuman entities; and Close Encounters of the Fifth Kind, in which human beings report ongoing (and usually benign) contacts with aliens, much in the manner of the **contactees** of the 1950s and 1960s.

Although the concept of close encounters is assumed by many to refer exclusively to extra-terrestrial entities and their technology, the range of experiences that can be so labeled is much wider, and includes interaction with all nonhuman beings. The envelope of close encounters is thus widened to include the entities of **folklore**, mythology and parapsychology. The American paranormal researcher Rosemary Ellen Guiley has identified 10 aspects of the encounter phenomenon that can be found in reports of a wide variety of such events:

Despite a great variety in the types of encounters . . . records through the ages show a marked similarity in characteristics: (1) feelings of friendliness, love, wonder, awe, fearlessness; (2) being anointed as a messenger to humanity; (3) instruction, initiation, rite of passage, or enlightenment; (4) psychokinetic feats such as levitation, flying, passing through material objects; (5) the appearance of unusual or overpowering light, or beings of light; (6) trans-portation to a nonordinary realm; (7) passage across a threshold or border; (8) an inkling of the ineffable; (9) revelations; and (10) extrasensory perception (ESP). (Guiley [1991], p. 181)

There are a number of theories to explain close encounters, which will be addressed under the appropriate headings in this encyclopedia.

CLOSE ENCOUNTERS OF THE THIRD KIND (FILM)

Made in 1977, directed by Steven Spielberg and starring Richard Dreyfuss, Melinda Dillon, Teri Garr and François Truffaut. A power company employee has a **close encounter** with UFOs and is driven to the edge of a nervous breakdown by the recurring mental image of a peculiarly shaped mountain. When he discovers that the mountain (Devil's Tower, Wyoming) actually exists, he sets out in the company of a woman whose small son has been abducted by aliens. Meanwhile, a research team led by a French ufologist manages to decode an electronic communication from the aliens, giving the coordinates of their intended landing site—Devil's Tower.

A flawed masterpiece, *Close Encounters* was the first major film to attempt a serious treatment of the subject of UFOs and alien contact. J. Allen **Hynek** served as a technical consultant, while the François Truffaut character, "Claude Lacombe," was inspired by the ufologist Jacques **Vallée**. The film's vast success has also led some skeptical commentators on the UFO phenomenon to suggest that the physical appearance of the aliens (which are dead ringers for the now ubiquitous **Grays**) has resulted in widespread cultural feedback in subsequent reports of alien encounters and abductions.

COLD, INDRID

(See **Derenberger, Woodrow**)

COLLECTIVE UNCONSCIOUS

Concept formulated by the Swiss psychologist Carl G. Jung in the early years of the 20th century. The unconscious is a region of the mind that is not directly known by the conscious human being, and consists of the personal unconscious (which contains "lost memories, painful ideas that are repressed [and] subliminal perceptions") and the collective unconscious, a much more ancient and impersonal area of the mind containing mental patterns and images, which are shared by all human beings. Jung suggested the existence of the collective unconscious partly in response to the observed fact that certain mythological motifs recur in cultures throughout the world.

These recurring, universal motifs were termed "archetypes" by Jung, who identified the four principal ones as: the persona, or "outward face" a person presents to his or her society; the shadow, a primitive aspect of the personal unconscious, which is the antithesis of the civilized persona; the anima and animus, which are the female and male aspects of the psyche, respectively, and which are incorporated into both sexes; and the self, which functions as principal organizer of the personality, bridging the gap between the conscious and unconscious.

There are many other archetypes, perhaps the most important of which with regard to UFO encounters is the "mandala," or circle, which represents universal unity, and to which Jung refers in his book *Flying Saucers: A Modern Myth of Things Seen in the Sky* (1959). Jung's suggestion that the shape of the "classical flying saucer" (a circle or disk) is of great significance, and constitutes an externalization of humanity's own yearning for unity, is not palatable to many ufologists who subscribe to the **extraterrestrial hypothesis**. Some, however, who are more sympathetic to alternatives (such as the **psychosocial hypothesis**), consider it a useful starting point from which to explore possible explanations for UFO and alien encounters that are grounded more in the (still largely unknown) nature of the human mind.

COMING RACE, THE (NOVEL)

Written by Edward Bulwer-Lytton, first baron Lytton, and published in 1871, *The Coming Race* was an immediate popular success, and has been enormously influential, both in Western occultism and in the **conspiracy theories** of modern ufology. Although in terms of its principal concerns it belongs with British utopian science fantasy novels of the late 19th century (such as Samuel Butler's *Erewhon* [1872] and Anthony Trollope's *The Fixed Period* [1880]), Lytton's novel takes its initial inspiration from Jules Verne's *Journey to the Center of the Earth* (1864), taking place inside Earth, as opposed to some undiscovered Pacific island, as in the other works mentioned.

The novel recounts the adventures of an American mining engineer, who discovers an unknown and highly advanced subterranean civilization. These tall and extremely beautiful people, the Vril-ya, utilize a mysterious and immensely powerful force known as Vril. Since it requires years of training to master the Vril force without the user destroying himself, it has been seen by some as a fairly accurate prediction of nuclear energy on Lytton's part. Although principally concerned with the major themes of the late 19th century, such as Darwinian evolution, democracy and the emancipation of women, *The Coming Race* is perhaps of greater importance for its treatment of the idea that there are powerful races sharing the planet with humanity, of which the normal person knows nothing. It has, for instance, been instrumental in shaping the legends of the **Hollow Earth**, much loved by ufologists in the 1950s and 1960s (notably Raymond **Palmer** and Richard **Shaver**), and which have recently undergone a significant revival in the form of rumors concerning vast underground alien **bases**.

The similarity between Lytton's novel and the legends of underground realms such as Agharti and Shamballah has, over the years, prompted many to suggest that he might have based his story of the Vril-ya on a genuine body of esoteric knowledge—in short,

that *The Coming Race* is actually fact disguised as fiction. Without doubt, the most infamous figure to have taken the idea of a mythical superrace seriously was Adolf Hitler. However, the significance of the so-called Vril Society in Nazi ideology may well have been overstated, based as it is on the testimony of a German rocket engineer named Willy Ley, who went to the United States in 1933. In an article entitled "Pseudoscience in Naziland," Ley claimed (while admitting that his knowledge on the subject was limited) that the Vril Society (or *Wahrheitsgesellschaft*—Society for Truth) was based on an acceptance of the reality of the Vril force.

COMMITTEE FOR THE SCIENTIFIC INVESTIGATION OF CLAIMS OF THE PARANORMAL (CSICOP)

Highly skeptical organization, founded in 1976 and based in Buffalo, New York. Originally an offshoot of the American Humanist Association, CSICOP's aims are to encourage the "critical investigation of paranormal and fringe-science claims from a responsible, scientific point of view and [to disseminate] factual information about the results of such inquiries to the scientific community and the public."

According to the information presented on its Internet website, the committee:

1. Maintains a network of people interested in critically examining paranormal, fringe science, and other claims, and in contributing to consumer education
2. Prepares bibliographies of published materials that carefully examine such claims
3. Encourages research by objective and impartial inquiry in areas where it is needed
4. Convenes conferences and meetings
5. Publishes articles that examine claims of the paranormal

6. Does not reject claims on a priori grounds, antecedent to inquiry, but examines them objectively and carefully

While CSICOP has undoubtedly performed a valuable service in exposing numerous paranormal frauds and hoaxes, it has nevertheless come under attack from researchers and skeptics alike for its hostile attitude to the paranormal, with some going so far as to complain that the organization has a hidden religious agenda.

COMMUNICATIONS WITH ALIENS

Given the vast number of close encounters of various kinds that have occurred over the years (particularly in the five decades since Kenneth Arnold), it might be expected that communication between aliens and their human percipients has frequently taken place. Indeed, an enormous amount of such material, received in a variety of ways, has been recorded in the literature on UFOs and alien contact. To anyone unfamiliar with the subject, the idea that aliens are capable of communicating with humans (and that humans are themselves capable of understanding such communications) might offer, potentially at least, unequivocal proof of the presence of intelligent nonhuman life on Earth. Unfortunately, this is far from the case.

With the benefit of hindsight, we can see that from the early days of the modern era of ufology, those intelligences had no intention of providing humanity with information that would prove their existence. This is one of the central pillars of the skeptical argument against the existence of an alien intelligence capable of interacting with human beings: never have "they" volunteered any information, such as a previously unknown and revolutionary scientific principle, that could be tested in the laboratory and successfully implemented. (Of course, those who accept the extraterrestrial nature of the **Roswell** incident, not to mention the claims of Colonel Philip J. **Corso**, would contest this.)

In terms of content, the main thrust of alien communications concerns the future of Earth. This is just as true today as it was in the 1950s and 1960s, when **contactees** such as George **Adamski** and Orfeo **Angelucci** met people from outer space. The main difference is in the nature of the threat to our planet: in the early days of ufology, the aliens' fears reflected our own cold war concerns, and centered on the threat of nuclear annihilation. Today, the great threat is to the environment. Some ecologists have suggested a worst-case scenario in which global warming may result in the proliferation of super-resistant diseases, which could cause the extinction of humanity. Other scientists point to the steady decline in human fertility, which could have similarly catastrophic results. It seems that the aliens share these concerns, and frequently warn their percipients of the dangers of ecological collapse (the so-called "Watchers" encountered by Betty **Andreasson** have stated unequivocally that the human race will become sterile in the near future).

Aliens are very fond of prophesying various disasters, such as earthquakes, plane crashes and assassinations, and, while these do occur, they usually happen months or even years after the dates given, and thus can be accounted for by the frequently unpleasant nature of life on Earth, rather than any special wisdom on the part of the aliens. This does not prove that nonhuman intelligences do not exist, merely that they are far more parsimonious with genuinely useful information than they would have us believe. By far the most striking example of nonhuman prophecy is related by the American anomalist John A. **Keel** in his book *The **Mothman** Prophecies*. The **ultraterrestrials**, as Keel calls them, made three key predictions during the visitations in Point Pleasant, West Virginia, in 1967–8: that the pope would be fatally stabbed in the Near East in 1968; that

Robert Kennedy would come to harm in a hotel kitchen; and that the United States would suffer a nationwide power failure on December 24, 1968. As it turned out, the pope was stabbed (but recovered) in Manila in 1969; Robert Kennedy was assassinated in a hotel kitchen; and in December 1968, the Silver Bridge over the Ohio River collapsed, killing 46 people.

Researchers who approach the field from different perspectives to that of the extraterrestrial hypothesis, such as Keel and Jacques **Vallée**, have commented extensively on the apparently symbolic nature of alien communications. Indeed, Vallée has suggested that the absurdity of alien behavior itself constitutes a form of symbolic language. He offers the example of a UFO percipient who was asked the time by an alien entity. When he replied (somewhat bemused) that it was 2:30 P.M., the entity cried: "You lie! It is four o'clock." Whereupon, he climbed back into his UFO and departed. However, the percipient maintained that it *had* been 2:30 P.M. It is possible that this apparently nonsensical exchange was actually an attempt by the entity to impart some information concerning the relative nature of time.

The concept of communications with alien civilizations is, of course, also of great interest to orthodox science, in particular those in the field of astronomy who support the **Search for Extraterrestrial Intelligence (SETI)** program. (See also **Sagan, Carl**)

COMMUNION (CONCEPT)

With the publication in 1987 of abductee Whitley **Strieber**'s book *Communion: A True Story,* the general public became aware as never before, not only of alien abductions, but also of the immense complexity inherent in the phenomenon. In fact, Strieber, perhaps more than any other commentator on the subject of alien encounters, has emphasized the unlikelihood that humanity has even begun truly to understand the nature and intentions of the beings he has come to call the Visitors. (This itself is an indication of Strieber's unwillingness to assume that the final answer is to be found in the extraterrestrial hypothesis: on the contrary, he seems to believe—quite reasonably—that to call them "aliens" is at once to limit the potential of our understanding of them.)

The concept of communion, as expressed by Strieber, refers to the powerful, at times traumatic, but utterly essential interaction that is taking place between humanity and the Visitors. This interaction is not confined to the present century, but has been taking place, in various forms, throughout human history. The ultimate goal of communion is far from clear, but may be concerned with human evolution: Strieber himself has suggested that nonhuman encounters may be what the process of evolution looks like when applied to a conscious species. This evolutionary process in which the Visitors seem so interested may well also extend to what awaits us after death, and it is conceivable that life on Earth is itself no more than a preparation for our future activities in the spiritual realm. This is, of course, a familiar idea; but, according to Strieber, it has received confirmation of a kind from the Visitors themselves. He reports how, one night when he fell into a trance, his wife, Anne, began to ask questions, which Strieber would answer, apparently through a form of **channeling**. One of the questions she asked was: "What is the Earth?" The reply came immediately: "It's a school."

Skeptics and believers alike have frequently asked: "Why don't they just land on the White House lawn?" The nature and purposes of communion seem to demand that human beings are contacted on an individual basis, bypassing all forms of authority and officialdom, perhaps because the Visitors consider them ephemeral and irrelevant.
(See also **children's circles**)

COMMUNION (FILM)

Made in 1989, directed by Philippe Mora, written and produced by Whitley **Strieber** and starring Christopher Walken, Lindsay Crouse, Frances Sternhagen and Andreas Katsulas. Adaptation of the best-selling book by Whitley Strieber, which recounts his experiences at the hands of alien beings.

Although the film is a brave attempt to treat the abduction phenomenon in a serious way on the big screen, it is deeply flawed, and the responsibility for this must rest with Strieber, who was inexperienced in the art of screenwriting. Although Strieber was (quite laudably) prepared to include images of **high strangeness** in the film, he misjudged the public's willingness to accept such material. One notorious scene in particular, in which Christopher Walken dances with the aliens to some funky space music, had audiences rolling in the aisles with laughter, which was hardly the desired effect. In addition, the film could not hope to capture the existential ponderings that made the book so engaging.

Nevertheless, *Communion* is both touching and entertaining, not least for its portrayal of Strieber's eccentric sense of humor.

CONDOR

(See **aviary**)

CONSPIRACY THEORIES

The incredible richness, diversity and complexity of the UFO and alien encounter phenomena has led some commentators to suggest that, regardless of whether such events actually take place in the objective world, they have nevertheless attained the status of modern mythology. Regardless of whether one subscribes to this view, it is clear that what began as a very simple concept (the sighting of metallic, disk-shaped objects in the sky) has developed into a vast body of reports, commentaries, theories, arguments and counterarguments, each of which can

be subdivided into numerous categories. Indeed, the ufologist who decides to undertake a *fully comprehensive* history of the subject will be worthy of admiration and pity in equal measure.

One of the most complex and controversial areas of ufology is conspiracy theory. Just as alien encounters themselves frequently shade into other areas of the paranormal, UFO conspiracy theories merge with conspiracies of other kinds, such as the suspicion among certain U.S. militia groups that the United Nations is preparing to invade their country and turn it into a totalitarian nightmare under the control of the New World Order.

With regard to the alien presence on Earth, the central conspiracy theory can be summarized as follows. Some time in the late 1940s or early 1950s, the United States government (and possibly other world governments also) entered into a secret treaty with hostile **Grays**, whereby the aliens were allowed to abduct and experiment upon certain human beings in return for selected items of alien technology. A number of underground **bases** were constructed for the aliens' use, and a worldwide network of subterranean tunnels was established for secret transportation.

However, the aliens quickly reneged on their part of the agreement and began unauthorized abductions of large numbers of people without informing their human hosts. Realizing the gravity of their situation (not to mention that of the planet), the government decided to begin work on a number of sophisticated weapons projects, in the hope that they would be able to defeat the alien aggressors. These projects include "Excalibur," a missile capable of penetrating more than a kilometer into the ground to destroy the alien bases, and other projects based on electromagnetic and laser technology to shoot down alien spacecraft.

This basic scenario has spawned a number of other theories, none of which bodes particularly well for the future of humanity. Perhaps the most outrageous of these is the infamous **Montauk Project**. Another theory, which had its genesis in a spoof television documentary, is known as "Alternative 3," and involves the ultrasecret migration of Earth's power elites to a new home on Mars. The reason for this jumping ship is that our world will shortly become uninhabitable due to humanity's irresponsible pollution of the biosphere. According to the scenario, three alternatives were examined, by which global catastrophe might be averted: Alternative 1 involved detonating nuclear bombs at high altitudes, blowing holes in the upper atmosphere, through which the harmful greenhouse gases might escape into space; Alternative 2 involved the construction of gigantic subterranean cities, to which a small percentage of the population would be evacuated, leaving the rest to take their chances on the devastated planet's surface. These two alternatives were abandoned as unworkable, leaving Alternative 3.

Some of the people who disappear without trace each year throughout the world (upward of 100,000, according to some estimates) are abducted aboard alien-designed craft, turned into mindless slave laborers through surgical and chemical means, and are doomed to spend the rest of their lives in the Martian colonies.

While it is possible that such nightmarish scenarios are really occurring, we can nevertheless see how they came to develop as a subcategory within the wider mythological context of UFO and alien encounters. That there has been a cover-up of government interest in UFOs can no longer be gainsaid (see **Central Intelligence Agency**). That in itself would have been enough to raise suspicions among the more paranoid members of the UFO fraternity. It should be remembered, however, that governments have shown themselves to be utterly untrustworthy on many occasions completely unrelated to UFOs. This lack of trust in official institutions has shown itself not only in the writings of UFO conspiracy theorists, but also of the most impeccable of political commentators. For instance, the great American linguistic philosopher and dissident Noam Chomsky has pointed to the ongoing attempts by corporate elites throughout the world to "destroy human rights, eliminate the curse of democracy, except in a purely formal way, move power into the hands of absolutist, unaccountable institutions which will run the world in their own interests, without looking at anyone else, enhance private power, and eliminate workers' rights, political rights, the right to food, destroy it all." This has resulted in a situation in which confidence in politicians throughout the world has virtually evaporated. When public perceptions regarding UFO activity and alien encounters are combined with those regarding the general untrustworthiness of our political leaders, it is not difficult to see how the most extreme conspiracy rumors can develop, unencumbered by the unlikelihood of there being much (if any) truth to them. (See also **Illuminati** and **Jason Society**)

CONTACT (NOVEL, FILM)
(See **Sagan, Carl**)

CONTACTEES
People who claim an ongoing relationship with alien beings are known as contactees. In an effort not only to add relative respectability to such claims, but also to recognize that many contactees claim peaceful interaction with beings normally associated with the frightening and intrusive **abductions**, ufologists have in recent years abandoned the word in favor of "Close Encounters of the Fifth Kind." The first contactees came to prominence in the 1950s, when the idea that there might be someone, or something, inside UFOs was only just beginning to be seriously considered. Even then, many serious ufologists dismissed the

claims of people such as George **Adamski**, Orfeo **Angelucci** and Truman **Bethurum** as either delusion or outright lies. Throughout the modern (post-1947) era of ufology, the contactees have relayed messages from the **Space Brothers** promoting peace, harmony and the abandonment of nuclear weapons, which apparently—and rather implausibly—are threatening the "balance of the cosmos" and the well-being of civilizations throughout the Universe. Precisely why a nuclear explosion on Earth would be a threat to beings on the other side of the Universe has never been adequately explained.

Indeed, the contactees had the air of barely competent Hollywood sci-fi scriptwriters, with their tales of bikini-clad female aliens, glittering Venusian cities and galactic federations. In addition, when the United States and the Soviet Union began to send unmanned probes to Mars, Venus and the more distant planets of our Solar System, it became apparent that Earth was the only planet within the system capable of supporting humanoid life. When this information became available to the general public, many contactees claimed to have met aliens from farther out in the galaxy, sometimes from planets orbiting real stars, sometimes from unknown star systems.

While a significant proportion of contactee reports were (and are) crude hoaxes, betrayed by a paucity of imagination, the phenomenon itself does present a problem. Firstly, many contactees are adamant that they do not receive any publicity or financial remuneration whatsoever for their stories, making the charge of cynical, money-motivated hoax a little difficult to sustain. (We must not, however, discount the possibility of delusion or **fantasy-prone personalities** being responsible for many such reports.) Secondly, it has been suggested by some researchers, such as Jacques **Vallée**, that some governments may be involved in the testing of psychological warfare techniques, in which alien encounters are staged, with the use of sophisticated props, hypnosis and hallucinogenic drugs. Perhaps the most interesting and detailed example of this is the **UMMO** controversy. Alternatively, there is the possibility that contactee reports may indeed have an intelligent nonhuman origin, and that the intelligence is itself staging apparently absurd events according to some unknown agenda.

COOPER, MILTON WILLIAM

Born in 1943, conspiracy theorist Milton William "Bill" Cooper is one of the most controversial and vocal figures in the fields of ufology and alien contact. He is perhaps the chief proponent of the idea that evil aliens have forged a secret treaty with the U.S. government (see **conspiracy theories**), an idea that he later modified to include the Alternative 3 conspiracy. His interest in UFOs began when he was serving aboard the United States naval submarine USS *Tiru* in 1966. While on duty as port lookout, he witnessed a UFO, which was also seen by other members of the crew, including the captain, who immediately classified the incident.

Since then, Cooper has released numerous documents purporting to support his claims. Some of his assertions regarding the true agendas of other UFO researchers (including William **Moore**, Robert **Lazar** and Stanton **Friedman**, whom he alleges are secret government agents) have resulted in charges of paranoia and even mental imbalance being leveled against him.

CORSO, COLONEL PHILIP J.

Formerly a member of President Eisenhower's National Security Council and former chief of the U.S. Army's Foreign Technology Desk at the Pentagon's Research and Development Department under the command of General Arthur Trudeau, Philip Corso burst on to the UFO scene with the publication in 1997 of his book *The Day After Roswell*. Corso claims to have been instrumental in the analysis of a large number of artifacts retrieved from the Roswell, New Mexico, **crash-retrieval** of 1947, and to have guided the subtle inclusion of alien technology into various military and industrial research and development projects, which eventually brought about the end of the cold war. These **reverse engineering** projects were carried out by various companies, including IBM, Hughes Aircraft and Bell Labs, which, however, were told that the items under study had been captured from foreign terrestrial powers, rather than a crashed alien spacecraft. This research resulted in many of the advances in technology that we now take for granted, including fiber optics and integrated circuit chips.

As might be expected, Corso's book (written in collaboration with writer William J. Birnes) has elicited strong reactions both favorable and critical in the ufology field and beyond. Stanton T. **Friedman**, who has perhaps spent more time investigating the allegations surrounding Roswell than any other ufologist, looked into Corso's background and confirmed that his claims regarding his military background are indeed truthful. However, Friedman, in common with many others who have studied *The Day After Roswell,* finds it "most unsatisfactory," pointing to the somewhat incoherent opening in which the background to Roswell is described. It seems that Corso, who admits he was not present at the UFO retrieval, has drawn on virtually every published account of the events around July 4, 1947, and the result is somewhat garbled (and unreferenced).

Friedman also criticizes the book for not offering any documentation to substantiate its claims regarding the seeding of alien technology into human research and development programs. In fact, the only substantial official document included in the book refers to the U.S. Army's Project Horizon, an abandoned plan to build a military outpost on the Moon, which has long been available from the army archives. Curiously, the book also contains several factual inaccuracies concerning military hardware (for instance, that the B-2 Stealth bomber is built by Lockheed, when in fact it is produced by Northrop, and that the Soviet Backfire bomber was operational in the 1950s, when actually it was not deployed until the 1980s). These are mistakes that should not have been made by a man with Corso's background, and this raises the possibility that *The Day After Roswell* could conceivably be an exercise in **disinformation**.

CORTILE, LINDA

American abductee, whose case has come to be regarded by many ufologists as perhaps the most significant in the history of the phenomenon and by skeptics as one of the most elaborate hoaxes. Linda Cortile's experiences were extensively investigated by Budd **Hopkins**, and written up in his book *Witnessed: The True Story of the Brooklyn Bridge Abduction* (1996). Cortile, then 45, first contacted Hopkins in April 1989, after reading his book *Intruders: The Incredible Visitations at Copley Woods,* telling him of her belief that she might have been abducted by aliens. On November 30 of the same year, she telephoned him, saying that she had just been abducted again. She had been up late doing some laundry, and had gone to bed at 3:00 A.M. A paralysis then came over her, and she saw a small **Gray** alien standing in the bedroom. After managing to throw a pillow at the creature, Cortile blacked out briefly (her husband slept beside her, unaware of what was happening).

Cortile was then taken out through the closed window of their 12th-story apartment in Manhattan's Lower East Side by three of the creatures, and together they floated up into a hovering UFO. She later recalled under **hypnotic regression** a typical physical examination, before being returned to her bedroom and her still-sleeping husband. He and their two sons seemed to have been placed into an abnormally deep sleep while the abduction was in progress.

Nearly two and a half years later, Hopkins received the first in a series of letters and tape recordings from two men who initially claimed to be New York policemen. Using the pseudonyms "Richard" and "Dan," they claimed that they had witnessed the abduction from their patrol car beneath the underpass of FDR Drive. They had watched as a group of figures, one of which was wearing a white nightgown, floated up from a high-rise apartment block and into a large, brightly lit object, which had then plunged into the East River, near Pier 17, behind the Brooklyn Bridge.

According to Cortile, she was visited by Richard and Dan several weeks later, and they both became very emotional when they recognized her as the woman they had seen. Meanwhile, Hopkins had made inquiries with the New York Police Department and had been unable to trace these two "officers." He subsequently received a letter from Richard, who admitted that they were not policemen, but security agents who had been driving a political VIP to a heliport in lower Manhattan at the time of the abduction. When the engine of their limousine had died, they had pushed the car into the FDR Drive underpass.

In April 1991, Cortile was abducted by Richard and Dan while out walking in Manhattan. They interrogated her in their car, and told her they suspected she was an alien. In October of that year, she was abducted again, this time by Dan, who took her to a "safe house" on a beach on Long Island and forced her to put on a white nightgown similar to the one she had been wearing on the night of her UFO abduction. While there, she caught a glimpse of some stationery bearing the seal of the **Central Intelligence Agency**. She managed to escape from the house, but Dan caught her on the beach and

repeatedly ducked her head into the sea. Richard then arrived and managed to sedate Dan before taking Cortile back to Manhattan.

About a month later, she was again contacted by Richard, who told her that Dan had become dangerously obsessed with her since witnessing her alien abduction, and had been committed to a mental hospital.

Meanwhile, Hopkins had received a letter from a retired telephone operator from Putnam County, New York, who said that her car had stalled on the Brooklyn Bridge on the night of November 30, 1989, and that she too had witnessed the abduction. Hopkins would subsequently locate five more independent witnesses to the event.

The VIP who had been in the limousine with Richard and Dan turned out to be none other than the then United Nations secretary-general, Javier Perez de Cuellar, who wrote to Hopkins about his experience, but said that if it were ever made public, he would deny everything. In fact, Perez de Cuellar had also been abducted that night, along with Richard, Dan and several other dignitaries, including the Canadian prime minister, Brian Mulroney!

While many abduction researchers had high hopes that the Brooklyn Bridge case would be the final proof of the reality of alien abductions, other researchers were beginning to have doubts about the whole thing. Among them were an abductee named Rich Butler and his friend Joe Stefula, a former army military detective and New Jersey state director of the **Mutual UFO Network (MUFON)**. Butler and Stefula began to uncover troubling discrepancies in the case; for instance, Cortile told them that the 1989 abduction had begun while she was sitting on the couch in her living room, not while she was in bed. In addition, Butler and Stefula drove down to the underpass beneath FDR Drive to check the view of Cortile's apartment building, and found that it was too far away to have allowed a witness to see the details described by Richard, Dan and the woman from Putnam County. They also noted that the building was only yards away from the loading dock of the *New York Post,* and stated that the abduction should therefore have been seen by many workers there (although Hopkins would later counter that the loading dock was enclosed, and faced away from the apartment block).

Rich Butler then contacted the UN Security Investigation Unit and asked whether there had been any unusual incidents reported on the night of November 30, 1989. He received the reply that there had been none. Joe Stefula discussed the case with a friend of his who was a security consultant, and who had served as personal security officer to U.S. defense secretary Dick Cheney. He suggested that the story about Pérez de Cuéllar's car stalling and being pushed beneath the underpass did not ring true. Whenever a UN secretary-general went anywhere, there was a huge amount of logistical planning, which included numerous checkpoints that had to be passed on time. Any delay would have brought an instant response from the UN security service.

There also seemed to be another problem with the Downtown Heliport at Pier Six on the East River, toward which Perez de Cuellar's limousine had been traveling. The normal hours for helicopter flights were between 7:00 A.M. and 7:00 P.M., and no record could be found in the logs for a departure in the early hours of November 30, 1989.

For these reasons, the Brooklyn Bridge abduction has become one of the most controversial in ufology and, since the investigation is ongoing, it will doubtless continue to elicit strong reactions both for and against.

COUNCIL OF NINE

Interstellar organization, composed of disembodied beings of light, also known as "The Nine," which originally contacted the Israeli psychic Uri Geller when he was three years old; a representative informed him of the council's concerns about the future of humanity. Geller later began to channel more information about The Nine (see **channeling**), and these events were written up in the book *Uri* (1974) by the neurologist Andrija Puharich. Geller would later disavow the claims in the book.

In the years following 1974, the Council of Nine concentrated on a trance medium named Phyllis Schlemmer, who published the results of many channeled question-and-answer sessions in her 1994 book *The Only Planet of Choice.* Much of this information takes the form of detailed expositions of the council's cosmic philosophy, which, not unexpectedly, is characterized by spiritual harmony, respect for other forms of life, and so on, although the council has assured us that a massed landing of spacecraft will occur in the near future, after which new technologies will be introduced to humanity.

The Council of Nine has stated that the barbarity of life on Earth is holding back the spiritual development of the galaxy and indeed the entire Universe, a familiar idea that is reassuringly (and somewhat suspiciously) anthropocentric in nature.

CRASH-RETRIEVALS

Term coined by the respected American researcher Leonard H. Stringfield to describe the discovery and retrieval for analysis of alien spacecraft that have crashed on the surface of the Earth. Crash-retrievals first came to public attention with show business columnist Frank Scully's best-selling 1950 book *Behind the Flying Saucers*, which told of three UFO crashes in the southwestern United States, including one which came down near Aztec, New Mexico, in 1948. Several small humanoid beings were discovered inside the wreckage.

In spite of the fact that the information on which Scully's book was based was later discovered to have been totally fabricated by two con men, the seductive notion of crashed flying saucers (the most famous being the **Roswell** incident) took root in the public imagination, and remains one of the most compelling and controversial aspects of ufology. Indeed, like UFO sightings themselves, crashes of alien spacecraft seem to have a provenance stretching much farther back in history than 1947, when the modern era of ufology is deemed to have begun. As British researcher Jenny Randles notes, "There are over a century of documented claims for us to investigate." Unfortunately, it seems that the vast majority of these UFO crashes are either hoaxes or contain insufficient information to support a reliable conclusion.

Although many crash-retrieval reports come from the United States, the phenomenon is not confined to that country. For instance, Jenny Randles has done much research on an apparent UFO crash on a mountain near the small village of Llandrillo in Clwyd, North Wales. There is some evidence to suggest that the RAF was involved in the retrieval of an unknown, glowing object from the side of the mountain.

While Roswell remains the most convincing and extensively investigated crash-retrieval, there are serious doubts about the veracity of many (if not most) other such events. Indeed, without wishing to be cynical, given the large number of alleged UFO crashes over the years, there is a case for the aliens benefiting more from our space technology than we from theirs. In spite of the serious problems surrounding crash-retrievals, they have nevertheless come to occupy a central position in the **conspiracy theories** that have been spawned by the UFO phenomenon.

CROP CIRCLES

A worldwide unexplained phenomenon in which often elaborate designs, usually based around a circle, are discovered in cultivated fields. They usually occur during the spring and summer seasons, and are reported in every country in the world, except for China and South Africa (the reason for this is unknown). Crop circles first came to the attention of the British public in the early 1980s, although the phenomenon seems to have a history of several hundred years. The first report of a crop circle is to be found in Robert Plott's *The Natural History of Stafford-Shire* (1686); the circle seems to have been discovered after a Nicolaea Lang-Berhand saw a group of fairy-like beings dancing in a circle.

The modern era of crop circles began in Australia in the late 1960s, where they were known as "saucer nests," the assumption being that they were landing traces left behind by UFOs. Since then there have been thousands of reports, with the most complex designs being found mainly in the United Kingdom.

As might be expected, this phenomenon is extremely controversial, with a number of competing theories having been put forward to account for it. The most obvious theory is that crop circles are the work of hoaxers. In 1991, two 60-year-old men, Doug Bower and David Chorley, came forward and admitted that they were responsible for the curious designs. Although they undoubtedly faked some of the circles, the frequency and geographical distribution of the designs precluded their having faked *all* of them. In addition, the circles that "Doug and Dave" created for the media fell far short of the quality of the most elaborate designs. Other theories to account for crop circles include weather-based hypotheses such as small, localized whirlwinds; the activities of UFOs; messages of warning from the Earth Mother **Gaia** herself; and laser beam experiments conducted in secret by the military. There is absolutely no doubt that the complex and beautiful crop circles are the work of an intelligence of some kind. Whether that intelligence ultimately proves to be alien or all too human is still very much open to debate.

CSICOP
(See **Committee for the Scientific Investigation of Claims of the Paranormal**)

CUFOS
(See **Center for UFO Studies**)

CULTS
UFO cults are groups of people who believe not only that benevolent extraterrestrial beings are visiting the Earth but also that they are worthy of worship. Virtually every serious ufologist frowns on such groups, which are seen as dangerously naïve and as dragging ufology into the nebulous realm of superstition, when it should be viewed as a scientific mystery.

Although UFO cultism began in the 1950s, inspired by the claims of the **contactees**, a number are still active (see the **Aetherius Society**), the most notorious being the Heaven's Gate sect, headed by the late Marshall Applewhite. On March 22, 1997, 39 members of the cult, including Applewhite, committed suicide through poisoning and suffocation. Apparently, their intention was to leave Earth behind and rendezvous with a gigantic UFO flying alongside the comet Hale-Bopp. The cult maintained that the crew of this spacecraft existed at the "Evolutionary Level" above humanity.

CULTURAL SOURCE HYPOTHESIS
(See **psychosocial hypothesis**)

CYCLOPS (ALIEN)
An extremely tall, humanoid entity that was encountered by three boys on the evening of August 28, 1963, in Belo Horizonte, Minas Gerais, Brazil. The boys, 12-year-old Fernando Eustáquio Gualberto, his seven-year-old brother, Ronaldo, and their friend, seven-year-old José Marcos Gomes Vidal, were in the brothers' back garden when they witnessed the arrival of a 10-foot-wide spherical object, which hovered over the house. The object was transparent, and the boys could see several beings inside, wearing space suits and transparent bubblelike helmets.

The object then projected two beams of light on the ground, and one of the beings floated down between them. As the being reached the ground, the boys saw that it had a single eye, beneath a pronounced eyebrow ridge, and was completely hairless. The being, which was about 10 feet tall, walked toward the three boys, gesturing with its hands and speaking loudly in an unintelligible language.

Fernando picked up a piece of rock and was about to throw it at the entity, when the creature turned toward him. A beam of light shot out from a small rectangular object on the front of its space suit, striking the boy's hand and making him drop the rock. The being then continued its attempts at communication, before floating back up to the UFO, which then departed.

The three terrified boys told Fernando and Ronaldo's parents what had happened. Their father later examined the garden and discovered several small triangular indentations in the ground where the being had walked.

CYDONIA COMPLEX
(See **artifacts** (alien))

DAKELIA BARRACKS, CYPRUS

Scene of a particularly terrifying and bizarre encounter, which occurred at three o'clock on a September morning in 1968. The percipient, who told his story to British ufologist Jenny Randles, was a British Army NCO, who was alerted to a possible intruder by his dog, a fierce Turkish wolfhound. Thinking that the growling of the dog might signal a terrorist attack on the barracks, the soldier moved carefully and silently to the door of his room, while the wolfhound uncharacteristically scampered under the bed and began to whimper.

The NCO then heard a curious, high-pitched humming sound that seemed to be coming from somewhere outside his room. He slowly opened the door and stepped out on to the landing, from which a flight of wooden stairs led down to the ground floor. What he saw floating up the stairs appalled and terrified him beyond imagining. The soldier later

described an incomplete humanoid being—only the head and shoulders were visible—dressed in a light blue suit with a collarless neck. The scowling face, inclined forward, was bright orange in color; the hair was red, and the eyes were large and unblinking. As it approached the top of the stairs and the petrified soldier, the being turned its head fully 180 degrees.

In panic, the soldier ran back to his room, slammed the door and sat on the edge of his bed, while the humming noise continued to rise in pitch until it reached a deafening level. Added to it was a sliding sound, which the soldier took to be that of the being moving toward his room. Rather than face the unimaginable, he grabbed an underwater speargun and fired it through the door.

Instantly, the humming and sliding noises stopped, leaving the NCO alone in his room, where he was found an hour later by a relief guard. He later suffered briefly from muscular paralysis, but made a complete recovery, unlike his unfortunate wolf-hound, which remained fearful of the slightest noise for the rest of its life.

DÄNIKEN, ERICH VON

Born on April 14, 1935, in Zofingen, Switzerland, Erich Anton Paul von Däniken rose to worldwide fame (not to mention notoriety) with the publication in 1968 of his book *Chariots of the Gods?* In this best-selling work and the many others that followed, von Däniken developed the theory that Earth was visited in prehistory by extraterrestrial beings, which manipulated human DNA in combination with their own to produce modern *Homo sapiens*, citing various literary, historical and archaeological references in support of his claims.

His later books include *Gods from Outer Space* (1969), *The Gold of the Gods* (1972), *In Search of Ancient Gods* (1973), *Miracles of the Gods* (1974) and *Von Däniken's Proof* (1977). These books have been translated into 32 languages, and have sold approximately 54 million copies worldwide. These sales figures alone demonstrate how popular these **ancient astronaut** concepts put forward by von Däniken and others have become. However, the Swiss writer has been heavily criticized for shoddy research and falsification of much of his evidence, a charge he categorically denies.

DAY THE EARTH STOOD STILL, THE (FILM)

Made in 1951, directed by Robert Wise and starring Michael Rennie, Patricia Neal and Lock Martin, this is one of the finest science-fiction films of the 1950s, and contains many of the themes that would be promulgated by the **contactees** throughout this and the next decade. The film was made the year before George **Adamski** had his famous encounter with a Venusian in the Californian desert, which is perhaps significant, given the basic premise of the plot: that a kind of interstellar federation has noticed humanity's use of atomic weapons, and dispatches a representative (named Klaatu) in a "classic" flying saucer to warn the people of Earth that they are upsetting the balance of the cosmos, and must follow the path of peace or be destroyed. Indeed, one glance at Michael Rennie's peaceful but powerful, entirely human-looking alien reminds us of Adamski's Venusian (admittedly, Rennie's hairstyle is in keeping with 50s fashion), right down to his iridescent space suit.

DEBUNKERS

Commentators on UFO and other paranormal phenomena, whose intention is to explain every reported incident in mundane, scientifically accept-able terms, and who maintain the stance that the possible reality of such phenomena is not worth serious consideration. While the former intention is in itself laudable enough, and has resulted in many hoaxes being exposed (which serious ufologists applaud as much as anyone else), the debunkers' utterly dismissive stance results in an unfortunate tendency to pronounce themselves satisfied with explanations that are patently absurd, in spite of overwhelming evidence that a genuine mystery exists, which perhaps cannot be explained within the context of current scientific paradigms.

A classic example of an exercise in debunking is to be found in the notorious Condon Committee report on UFOs, which was financed by the U.S. Air Force and conducted at the University of Colorado under the direction of Dr. Edward U. Condon, a highly respected nuclear physicist. The committee was established in 1966, and presented its report three years later. Although proclaiming itself totally impartial (which was far from the truth and resulted in some resignations by disgruntled members), the committee placed its (negative) conclusions at the beginning of the report, rather than at the end. In addition, although approximately one third of the cases studied were labeled as "unexplained," the report concluded that UFOs were of no scientific significance.

(See also **Klass, Philip Julian**)

DEFENSE INTELLIGENCE AGENCY (DIA)

In its own words, the Defense Intelligence Agency, which was established in 1961, is "a designated Combat Support Agency and the senior military intelligence component of the Intelligence Community." Its primary function is to provide "all-source" intelligence to the United States armed forces. "Additionally, DIA plays a key role in providing information on foreign weapons systems to U.S. weapons planners and the weapons acquisition community."

Although the DIA has denied any interest in or investigation of UFOs and related phenomena, the same denials made by the CIA have proved demonstrably false. While it does not of necessity follow that the DIA is also being "economical with the truth," its stated function of providing information on foreign weapons systems would make it ideally placed to assess the defense implications of UFO activity.

DEMONS

The word *demon* derives from the Greek *daimon*, meaning "divine power," "fate" or "god." Originally, the word was used to denote spiritual entities intermediate between humans and gods, and as such could be either good or evil. Although rarely alluded to in the literature on UFOs and alien encounters, demonic attributes play a significant part in many reports of human/alien interactions. Those nefarious riders in the night skies, the **Grays,** are frequently described as demonic, or hideously evil (the American abductee Whitley **Strieber** originally suspected them of wishing to devour his soul). Indeed, it is interesting to note how the gradual transformation of alien intentions, from the frequently altruistic in the 1950s and 1960s, to the frequently malevolent in the 1980s and 1990s, curiously echoes the transformation of attitudes toward demons, from the "divine powers" of the Greeks to the exclusively evil entities of the Christian era.

There is an additional parallel to be found in the preoccupation with human sexuality evinced by both demons and aliens. The former were very fond of tormenting their human victims sexually (men being seduced by succubi, women by incubi); the latter are obsessed with impregnating human females and extracting the sperm of human males, some of whom have related appalling tales of being physically seduced by female Grays. The often reported scars and "scoop marks" (indentations in the skin, where tissue has apparently been removed) on the bodies of abductees likewise seem comparable to the skin blemishes by which medieval witches could be detected.

Although ufologists and abduction researchers who subscribe to the **extraterrestrial hypothesis** would balk at such comparisons, they are nevertheless worth bearing in mind, since they strongly imply a profound connection between the various forms of human/nonhuman contact that have occurred through the centuries.

DERENBERGER, WOODROW

Contactee who claimed to have met alien beings from the planet Lanulos. Derenberger's experiences seem to be integral to the **Mothman** visitations, which occurred in West Virginia between 1966 and 1968. These events, among the most bizarre in the field of alien encounters, were extensively investigated by journalist John A. **Keel** and described in his 1975 book *The Mothman Prophecies*.

At 7:00 P.M. on November 2, 1966, Derenberger, an appliance salesman, was on his way home after work, and was in the Parkersburg area of West Virginia, when he witnessed the landing of a UFO, about the size of a car and shaped like "an old-fashioned kerosene lamp chimney, flaring at both ends, narrowing down to a small neck and then enlarging in a great bulge in the center." The UFO landed in the road in front of Derenberger's panel truck, and a man climbed out.

As the man, grinning broadly, approached Derenberger's vehicle, with his arms tucked tightly under his armpits, Derenberger saw that he was about five feet 10 inches tall, heavily tanned and wearing a dark coat beneath which glistened a green metallic suit. Apparently through the use of telepathy, the man told Derenberger not to be afraid, saying: "We mean you no harm. I come from a country much less powerful than yours . . . My name is Cold. I sleep, breathe, and bleed even as you do."

Looking at the lights of nearby Parkersburg, Cold asked what kind of place it was. When Derenberger replied that it was called a "city," the visitor replied that on his world, they called cities "gatherings." While this conversation was taking place, Cold's ship lifted off and hovered high in the air to avoid the attention of passing motorists. Cold suggested that Derenberger should report the meeting to the authorities, and he would come forward at a later date to confirm the story.

Presently, Cold said that he would contact Derenberger again soon. His craft descended once more, he climbed aboard and departed.

Two days later, on November 4, Derenberger was driving past Parkersburg with a coworker when he received a telepathic communication from Cold, who explained that he was from the planet Lanulos, "located close to the galaxy of Ganymede." (This is one of the many pieces of nonsense spoken by aliens: Ganymede is not a galaxy, but one of Jupiter's satellites.) After passing on various bits of information about life on Lanulos, Cold withdrew from Derenberger's mind.

The following year, Derenberger had several meetings with Cold, whose first name he discovered was Indrid, and who took him on a guided tour of the Lanulosan mothership, which was orbiting the Moon. Eventually, Cold agreed to take Derenberger on a trip to Lanulos itself (which took about half an hour). There he was introduced to Cold's wife, Kimi, and their three children. Derenberger was surprised (and rather embarrassed) to learn that the Lanulosans were nudists (a trait they apparently shared with the Venusians, whose world was a constant 104°F).

Woodrow Derenberger quickly achieved celebrity status, which turned out to be extremely damaging and disruptive to his family life. He was plagued with crank calls, warning him to shut up about his contacts with the Lanulosans, in addition to several curious phone calls, which consisted of electronic noises (a familiar experience of UFO witnesses). In March 1968, during one of his radio talk-show appearances, a 21-year-old psychology student called in to say that he, too, had met the Lanulosans, although his contact was named Vadig. However, the young man, whose name was Thomas Monteleone, turned out to be a hoaxer (Monteleone later became a well-known science-fiction writer).

Although several members of his family also claimed to have met the Lanulosans, Derenberger is dismissed as a hoaxer by many ufologists, and not without reason. In a 1996 interview with conspiracy researcher Jim Keith, John Keel stated that Derenberger was a very complicated character, and that there was no doubt that he did fabricate many of his experiences. According to Keel: "Derenberger came up with some interesting MIB [**Men in Black**]-type experiences, when he didn't know anything about any of this [the Mothman visitations]. Derenberger had some strange experiences with men who came into where he was working, and so on."

When Jim Keith asked Keel if he thought that Derenberger's claims were partly the result of genuine paranormal experiences and partly tall tales, Keel replied that that was true of all contactees. "Once they got a little attention, they started making up stories. The same thing happens in spiritualism, where people have unusual spiritualistic experiences, and start making up stories, and this is a well-known thing, it's been discussed in many books."

DEROS

An extremely violent and unpleasant race of subterranean beings, originally brought to the public's attention by Richard S. **Shaver** in the early 1940s. The word *Dero* is a contraction of "Detrimental Robot," although they are living beings rather than robots in the conventional sense. The Deros are descendants of a highly advanced extraterrestrial race which migrated to Earth (which they called "Lemuria") many thousands of years ago, and which founded the legendary civilization of Atlantis. These aliens colonized both the surface and interior of Earth, but were all but destroyed in the geological cataclysm that brought about the end of Atlantis. In addition, the Sun began to send out harmful radioactive elements, which forced many of the remaining Lemurians to leave Earth in search of new homes on other planets, while others decided to take their chances in the Earth's interior, and moved their homes far underground.

As the millennia passed, those in the vast subterranean cities gradually deteriorated both mentally and physically, due to the harmful emanations from the Sun, into a race of hideous, moronic, unthinkably evil monsters. Although they have long since forgotten how to operate most of the miraculous machinery left behind by their ancestors, the Deros still use deleterious ray machines, which transmit harmful influences to the surface. These machines are the cause of the world's ills. The Deros also possess teleportation technology, which they use to abduct people from Earth's surface. The hapless souls are used as sexual slaves, and for food.
(See also **Teros**)

DESVERGERS, D. S.

UFO and alien witness, whose encounter took place on the evening of August 19, 1952, in woods near West Palm Beach, Florida. At about 9:00 P.M., scoutmaster D. S. "Sonny" Desvergers was traveling back from a meeting, when he and the three boys who were with him noticed some strange lights in the woods. Desvergers stopped his car and went to investigate, leaving the boys in the vehicle.

A few minutes later, the boys saw a red ball of fire at treetop height, which then moved down toward the spot where they had last seen the scoutmaster. They continued to wait for Desvergers, and when he failed to return, one of them ran to a nearby house and telephoned the local sheriff.

The sheriff arrived in time to see Desvergers stumble out of the forest, exhausted and clearly very frightened. He told the sheriff that he had reached a clearing, when he saw a metallic, disk-shaped object hovering above him. Shining his flashlight upward, he saw that there was a kind of "turret" on top of the 25-foot-diameter saucer. A panel in the turret then opened, revealing a creature so terrifying that Desvergers steadfastly refused to describe it, saying it was simply too dreadful for words. At that point, a fiery spray of gas shot out from the turret, burning his arms and knocking him to the ground. When he recovered his senses a few moments later, the UFO had departed.

The sheriff saw that Desvergers's arms were indeed badly reddened, and when he examined the clearing, he found a scorched patch on the ground.

The suspicions of some UFO researchers were raised when it was revealed that Desvergers refused to talk to reporters about the incident, holding his story for sale to a magazine. While this does weigh against the veracity of Desvergers's claims, it should be remembered that there were three other witnesses (the scouts) to the initial appearance of the UFO. This story is rather interesting, since it contains one of the first descriptions of a truly alien being associated with a UFO (as opposed to the entirely benevolent and human-looking **Space Brothers** so beloved of the **contactees** of the period).

DIA

(See **Defense Intelligence Agency**)

DISINFORMATION

A technique favored by many governments and intelligence organizations, by which false information is placed in the public domain, in order either to lead unauthorized people away from sensitive information or to discredit them in the eyes of their peers and the wider public. In the latter case (and especially with regard to UFO research), the disinformation is usually of an extreme or sensational nature. The more gullible ufologists will take its apparent origin in the realms of officialdom as conclusive proof of its veracity, which is far from being invariably the case. When such ufologists subsequently publish this material, they are derided by the majority of people (including the more prudent members of their fraternity—a fact not always acknowledged by skeptics).

DOGON

The Dogon tribe of Mali, West Africa, have certain religious traditions, which strongly imply an ancient contact with extraterrestrial intelligence. Between 1946 and 1950, two French anthropologists, Marcel Griaule and Germaine Dieterlen, lived with and studied the Dogon, and were astonished to discover that the head priests of the tribe possessed amazingly accurate astronomical information.

The Dogon priests knew that the star Sirius is actually a binary system, Sirius A having a much smaller and fainter companion, Sirius B, which is a white dwarf, and is completely invisible to the naked eye. (Sirius B was not even photographed until 1970.) The priests told Griaule and Dieterlen that Sirius's companion is made of a substance that is "heavier than all the iron on Earth." The white dwarf Sirius B is incredibly dense, and thus immensely heavy. The Dogon also knew that Sirius B takes 50 years to orbit Sirius A, that the orbit is elliptical rather than circular, and the position of Sirius A in relation to the orbit.

According to the historian Robert K. G. Temple, the Dogon inherited this information from the civilizations of Babylonia, Egypt and Greece, its ultimate source being a group of amphibious extraterrestrial beings who came to Earth from Sirius, and landed near the Persian Gulf at the dawn of human civilization. The Dogon legends tell how these alien explorers (whom they call Nommos) descended to Earth in a great "ark." Temple points to the strong parallels between the Nommos and Oannes, a civilizing sea god who, along with others of his kind, taught the ancient Babylonians the principles of agriculture, astronomy and written language. According to the *Babylonian History* of the priest Berossus: "The whole body of [Oannes] was like that of a fish; and it had under a fish's head another head, and also feet below, similar to those of a man, subjoined to the fish's tail. His voice, too, and language, were articulate and human; and a representation of him is preserved even to this day."

The suggestion that the Dogon received their astronomical knowledge indirectly from an extraterrestrial source has been challenged by some researchers, who maintain that, although Sirius B's existence was not established until 1862 (by the American astronomer Alvan Clark), it is possible that some missionaries may have passed through Mali at some point in the century before the arrival of the

French anthropologists, and passed on the knowledge of the white dwarf to the Dogon, who then incorporated it into their mythology. However, there is a way in which the extraterrestrial intervention theory might one day be vindicated. The Dogon also speak of *another* star in the Sirius system . . . one that was only confirmed by astronomers in 1995.

DOLPHINOIDS (ALIENS)

A rare type of aquatic alien being that communicates telepathically. While on Earth, dolphinoids confine themselves to large bubbles filled with liquid. Little is known about these creatures, other than that they are enemies of the **Reptoids** and thus of some types of **Gray** also. Like many other aliens, the dolphinoids have stated that they intend to make their presence known to the public in the near future (needless to say, such assurances by aliens have never been adhered to), by means of a telepathically transmitted high-pitched tone. According to rumor, the bright object that was apparently accompanying the comet Hale-Bopp is one of their spacecraft. However, since this object was not actually a genuine UFO, but a misperceived distant star, this rumor should be taken with a large pinch of salt.

DOTY, RICHARD

(See **Aviary**)

DOVER DEMON

A nonhuman entity, which was seen by three independent witnesses in the vicinity of Dover, a suburb of Boston, Massachusetts in 1977. The first sighting occurred at 10:30 P.M. on April 21. Seventeen-year-old Bill Bartlett was driving with two friends when he saw something moving along a low wall on the left side of the road. The car's headlights illuminated a strange humanoid figure, which turned and stared at the car as it passed. Bartlett later described it as being between three and four feet tall, with a spindly, hairless body and a very large, melon-shaped head. He could discern no nose, mouth or ears, but the eyes were large and glowed a bright orange. The creature's skin was peach-colored, and seemed to have a rough texture. Its fingers and toes were long and flexible and were curled tightly around the stones of the wall. Bartlett's friends, who were looking in other directions at the time, did not see the entity, but later confirmed that Bill had been quite disturbed by what he had seen.

The next sighting occurred about two hours later, at 12:30 A.M., as 15-year-old John Baxter was making his way home from his girlfriend's house, and was roughly a mile from the scene of the first encounter, when he saw a diminutive figure approaching him. Baxter momentarily mistook it for one of his friends and called out to it. Both he and the figure came to a standstill, but when Baxter took another step forward, the figure fled into a nearby gully. Giving in to curiosity, the teenager chased after the little creature, which he found standing on the other side of the gully about 30 feet away, clinging tightly to a tree. For the first time, he saw the thing clearly. Realizing that this was no human being, Baxter left the creature to its own devices and quickly resumed his journey home. He would later describe exactly the same entity that Bartlett had seen. Both boys drew pictures of the entity, which resembled each other to a remarkable degree.

The third and final sighting of what the press would christen the "Dover Demon" occurred on the following day, April 22. Fifteen-year-old Abby Brabham was being driven home by Will Taintor, 18, a good friend of Bill Bartlett (who had told him about the strange creature), when she saw a small, monkeylike figure in the car's headlights. Taintor only caught a very brief glimpse, and could offer no clear description, but Abby described exactly the same entity as had been seen by the first two witnesses—with one interesting discrepancy: Abby said that the creatures eyes were bright green, not orange.

The Dover Demon was never seen again. The anomalist Loren Coleman investigated the case, and found all three principal witnesses to be perfectly credible, an opinion shared by all the people who knew them, including teachers and police officers.

The nature and identity of the Dover Demon are a complete mystery; however, cryptozoologist Dr. Karl Shuker speculates intriguingly that it may have been connected somehow with one of the legends of the Cree nation of eastern Canada. The Cree "speak of a mysterious race of pygmy entities called the Mannegishi, who delight in playing tricks upon travelers. According to the Cree, the Mannegishi have round heads, long thin legs, arms with six fingers on each hand, and they live between rocks in the rapids."

DRACO

(See **bases (alien)**)

DRAKE EQUATION

A formula developed by the American astronomer and founder of the **Search for Extraterrestrial Intelligence (SETI)**, Frank Drake, which has the potential to determine "the number of advanced, communicative civilizations that [exist] in space." The Drake Equation is written thus:

$$N = R\, f_p\, n_e\, f_l\, f_i\, f_c\, L$$

Drake's explanation of the factors in the equation is as follows:

The number (N) of detectable civilizations in space equals the rate (R) of star formation, times the fraction (f_p) of stars that form planets, times the number (n_e) of planets hospitable to life, times the fraction (f_l) of those planets where life actually emerges, times the fraction (f_i) of planets where life evolves into intelligent beings, times the fraction (f_c) of planets with intelligent creatures capable of interstellar communication, times the length of time (L) that such a civilization remains detectable. (Drake and Sobel [1993], p. 52)

Although Drake admits that he has no real values for most of the factors in his equation, he points out that it is not as speculative as some critics have suggested, since "each phenomenon it assumes to take place in the universe is an event that has already taken place at least once." After working through the equation with a number of colleagues, Drake reached the conclusion that there are between 1,000 and 1 million advanced civilizations in our galaxy.

DREAMLAND

(See **Area 51**)

DREAMS

The extremely bizarre nature of some UFO sightings and many alien encounters (which is sometimes described as **high strangeness** or the **Oz Factor**) has prompted many researchers to examine a possible connection with dreams. Skeptics maintain that dreams (or, more accurately, waking dreams) are a cause of a significant proportion of reported alien encounters. In such circumstances, the percipient may inadvertently slip into a dream state, for instance while driving along a monotonous stretch of road, in which an unusual event is observed.

However, those who accept that such encounters constitute a genuine mystery with a likely nonhuman origin, have suggested that they may bring about an altered state of consciousness, in which dreamlike imagery may combine with the original stimulus to produce an essentially adulterated experience. These cases are especially problematic, in that it is extremely difficult to differentiate between the stimulus and the psychological reactions to it, which may have little bearing on what actually happened to the percipient.

DULCE, NEW MEXICO
(See **bases (alien)**)

EARTHLIGHTS

Theory developed in the mid-1970s by Paul Devereux to account for UFO sightings (such as those reported at Marfa in Texas, and Hessdalen in Norway) and alien encounters. According to the Earthlights hypothesis, what are reported as UFOs (especially in the form of lights in the sky) are actually balls of electrical energy generated by tectonic processes within Earth's crust. When rock masses in geological fault lines move against each other, they can produce a luminous discharge of electromagnetic energy, which may then escape into the atmosphere. In view of the fact that UFOs are often reported to emerge from and plunge into the ground, this hypothesis would seem to promise a solution to some otherwise unexplained sightings.

The phenomena described by Devereux and other researchers, such as Michael Persinger and Ghislaine Lafrenière, have been duplicated to a certain extent in the laboratory. Dr. Brian Brady of the U.S. Bureau of Mines subjected samples of quartz rock to a pressure of 32,000 lbs. per square inch, resulting in a discharge of small lights as the rock was crushed. These discharges, however, only lasted for a few moments, whereas genuine light phenomena have been observed for several minutes.

There is also some evidence to suggest that such electromagnetic discharges may have a "scrambling" effect on the electrical activity of the brain, resulting in vivid hallucinations. These hallucinations might be influenced by the cultural background of the percipient, who might place a technological interpretation on an unexplained light seen in the sky. If this light is assumed to be an exotic machine of some kind (perhaps a craft from outer space), the accompanying hallucination might well be heavily influenced by this assumption, and alien beings could then be expected to figure strongly in the following, subjective experience.

Michael Persinger has conducted some research along these lines, applying electromagnetic fields to the temporal lobes of volunteers. One such volunteer, the skeptical parapsychologist Dr. Susan Blackmore, experienced feelings of fear, accompanied by the sensation of being touched by something that she could not see. The parallels between this and the classic alien abduction experience are sufficiently strong to suggest that further research along these lines should be conducted.

ELEMENT 115

A transuranic heavy element, which, according to Robert **Lazar**, is used by extraterrestrials to power their spacecraft. Element 115 does not exist on Earth, and thus, if a sample could ever be secured and subjected to independent analysis, it would constitute unequivocal proof of an alien presence on our planet. Interestingly, when Lazar was interviewed by ufologist Dr. Jacques **Vallée**, the latter mentioned that he didn't think super-heavy elements were stable, to which Lazar replied that there is a "zone of stability for higher numbers, above 110." This proves, if nothing else, that Lazar is rather knowledgeable about physics, since current theories predict that elements with higher atomic weights are relatively stable.

ELEMENTALS

Elementals are spirits of nature, which form an integral part of mythological systems throughout the world. They also bear some striking resemblances to the various kinds of entities associated with UFO encounters. Possessed of a wide variety of dispositions, from playful and helpful to extremely malevolent and dangerous, they appear in many different forms, some being indistinguishable from humans, while others resemble animals or human-animal hybrids.

Some elementals are viewed as being essential to the continued harmony of nature, a function which is reminiscent of the concerns expressed by the **Space Brothers**. Malevolent elementals are fond of causing accidents and suffering to humans, and are not above the occasional murder; there are numerous tales in folklore of people who have encountered such beings and are never seen again.

The striking parallels between the activities of elementals and those of UFO-related entities have given rise, in part, to the **psychosocial hypothesis**, which attempts to unite the two types of nonhuman encounter, ancient and modern, into a single concept.

ELOHIM
(See **Vorilhon, Claude**)

ENCOUNTER-PRONE PERSONALITIES

Term suggested by the psychologist Dr. Kenneth Ring to describe people who experience various types of nonhuman interaction within the context of another reality (see **Oz Factor**) and who thus seem to possess an innate spiritual sensitivity, which allows them to recognize (unconsciously) the universality of mind, or, as the theoretical physicist Fred Alan Wolf says, that "mind is not confined to individual and separated persons, but is universal, singular, and beyond any conceptual limit we enforce, such as the notion of spacetime confinement." According to Kenneth Ring, people who report alien encounters and **near-death experiences** may represent a human "evolutionary trend," which will ultimately lead to a species-wide perception of the unity between the "self" and the Universe.
(See also **fantasy-prone personalities**)

ENGLISH, WILLIAM
(See **Grudge Report 13**)

"ESTIMATE OF THE SITUATION"

A Top Secret document produced by the U.S. Air Force Air Technical Intelligence Center (ATIC), based at **Wright-Patterson Air Force Base**, Dayton, Ohio. Describing in detail the history of UFO sightings up to 1948 (including the so-called foo fighters, the small, spherical UFOs that plagued both Allied and German pilots during the Second World War), the "Estimate of the Situation" concentrated on reports of the highest quality, from military personnel, pilots and scientists. Its conclusion was that the evidence pointed to the presence of interplanetary spacecraft in our skies.

The document quickly found its way to the office of General Hoyt S. Vandenberg, the air force chief of staff, who disagreed with its astonishing conclusion (he stated that the evidence was not sufficiently impressive), and ordered it to be destroyed.

ET: THE EXTRATERRESTRIAL (FILM)

Made in 1982, directed by Steven Spielberg and starring Drew Barrymore, Peter Coyote, Henry Thomas and Dee Wallace. A departing spacecraft inadvertently leaves behind one of its crew members, who is befriended by a small boy. Although the boy and his brother and sister struggle to keep ET's existence a secret from their mother, the authorities become aware of his presence, and dispatch various sinister scientific types to apprehend the cuddly alien.

ET draws little inspiration from the field of ufology and alien contact (unlike Spielberg's **Close Encounters of the Third Kind**), being primarily a Disneyesque fantasy. However, as the British ufologist John Spencer points out, it is interesting that this film did not result in any similar contact reports from the public, whereas *Close Encounters* (which was influenced to a large extent by the history of ufology—down to the inclusion of J. Allen **Hynek** as technical consultant) did spawn such reports.

Spencer suggests (probably quite rightly) that such apparently culture-driven reports almost certainly constitute a public reaction to "social events at any given time."

EVIL CLOWNS

A rather curious and sinister phenomenon, which may be related in some way to the **Men in Black (MIBs)**. According to the American anomalist Loren Coleman, there was a large number of reports of "phantom clowns" in the early 1980s. The reports began on the East Coast, and quickly spread west as far as Kansas City. They typically describe elusive individuals dressed in garish clown makeup and outfits (occasionally they are reported to be without trousers). The clowns are usually seen driving battered old vans, which, despite detailed descriptions, can never be traced (a trait they share with the large sedans of the MIBs). Most disturbingly, the clowns exclusively target children, attempting to lure them into their vans. However, perhaps the strangest element of these reports is the fact that no Evil Clown has ever managed to abduct a child. In view of the depressing fact that many children are abducted with ease each year, it is most peculiar that the clowns have never succeeded in doing so. This also seems to tie in with the extreme rarity of MIB witnesses coming to harm, despite the frequent threats made against them.

On May 22, 1981, a clown who was driving a yellow van visited no fewer than six elementary schools in Kansas City. He was described as wearing a black shirt with the image of the Devil on the front. The police were unable to apprehend him.

Other waves of Evil Clown activity were reported in Phoenix, Arizona, in 1985, and New Jersey in 1991. The folklorist Jan Harold Brunvand has stated his belief that Evil Clowns are no more than urban legends, perhaps inspired by the myth of the Pied Piper of Hamelin, although he admits to being unable to explain the mechanism by which such legends "keep recurring in the form of scare stories told by American youngsters."

(See also **high strangeness**)

EXTRATERRESTRIAL BIOLOGICAL ENTITIES (EBEs)

Term originally used to describe the alien occupants of a spacecraft, which crashed near **Roswell**, New Mexico, in early July 1947. According to the **Majestic 12** documents, the term *EBE* was suggested by Dr. Detlev Bronk, a member of the ultrasecret MJ-12 group set up to deal with the UFO/alien phenomenon on September 24, 1947.

The EBEs are similar (perhaps identical) to the **Grays**; they are about three to four feet in height, completely hairless, with spindly bodies and large heads. Their eyes are large and almond-shaped and are usually described as black in color, with no differentiated structures such as irises or pupils. According to current **conspiracy theory**, the EBEs have established a powerful presence on Earth, having allied themselves with the U.S. government. As a result, much has been learned of their physiology and the social structure of their civilization.

Not surprisingly, they are an extremely intelligent species, with an average IQ in excess of 200. The brains are larger and more complex than those of humans, containing several additional lobes. Likewise, their internal organs are markedly different from ours: for instance, the EBE's heart and lungs are a single organ, and waste is excreted exclusively through the skin. (According to Preston B. Nichols, who has written extensively on the so-called **Montauk Project**, this makes them smell extremely unpleasant.)

The EBEs' home star system is Zeta Reticuli, a binary system about 37 light-years from Earth. They live on the fourth planet, a barren desert world, which has apparently suffered some sort of catastrophe, whether natural or the result of their activities is uncertain. The EBEs apparently live very simply, in adobe-like huts rather than the vast, glittering cities one might have expected. According to the group known as the **Aviary**, one of the EBEs wrote a book, known as the "Yellow Book," which details their planet, its social structures and their relationships with humans. Unfortunately, little else is known of the contents of this book.

Robert Lazar has stated that the EBEs consider humans to be "containers"—of what he is not entirely sure, but he suspects that we are seen as containers of souls. Lazar also claims that the U.S. government possesses an *"extremely* classified document dealing with religion," and that the great religions of the world were created by the EBEs "so we have some rules and regulations for the sole purpose of not damaging the containers."

EXTRATERRESTRIAL HYPOTHESIS (ETH)

The extraterrestrial hypothesis, which holds that UFOs are the interstellar spacecraft of a scientific expedition from another planet (or planets), is by far the best known and most subscribed-to theory to account for UFO and nonhuman encounters. That this should be so is no surprise, given the current, technology-driven nature of our own civilization here on Earth. When witnesses encounter strange (usually metallic) objects and associated entities, it is understandable that their first reaction should be to assume that the objects are technological artifacts, and the entities alien explorers. Such is our obsession with space travel and the likelihood that we will one day send manned missions to distant planets, that many people are unwilling to consider anything *but* an extraterrestrial interpretation for the thousands of UFO reports that have been made over the years.

However, the extraterrestrial hypothesis is not the only one to have been suggested (other hypotheses will be discussed under the relevant entries in this book), and a number of ufologists are unwilling to accept it as the final answer to the UFO mystery.

The frequency of **close encounters** in the years since the late 1940s is seen by some ufologists as too high for the ETH to be taken seriously. Taking into account such factors as the worldwide nature of the phenomenon, the geographical distribution of encounters, the time of day of encounters and so on, Jacques **Vallée** arrived at a (conservative) figure of 14 million UFO landings in the last 50 years or so. Even for hypothetical civilizations enjoying unlimited resources, it would be utterly nonsensical to land on a planet 14 million times. It should be stressed, however, that this argument need not preclude the suggestion that extraterrestrials have accounted for *some* close encounters. The implication, therefore, is that the phenomenon of UFO and nonhuman encounters, in its entirety, may well have a far more complex origin than that suggested by the ETH alone.

Many UFO entities are described as humanoid in form, which, biologists maintain, would be extremely unlikely. The humanoid configuration (two arms, two legs, torso, head, etc.) is the result of a large number of very important influencing characteristics of our home planet, such as gravity, composition of the atmosphere, distance from the Sun, and many others. Not only is it unlikely that there are many other planets matching Earth's characteristics *exactly*, but even if there were, it is equally unlikely that beings evolving on such planets would follow exactly the same pathways of genetic mutation that humanity has done.

The extraterrestrial hypothesis can thus be seen as only partially acceptable, and then only in isolated cases. While there is very intriguing evidence to suggest that intelligent aliens may have left artifacts on the Moon and Mars (see **artifacts (alien)**), and, ironically, the more outlandish entities described

by witnesses may support an extraterrestrial interpretation for *some* nonhuman encounters, this is not sufficient for us to rely solely on the ETH to explain *all* such experiences.

EXTRATERRESTRIAL TRAVEL AGENTS

A diffuse group of people, mainly active in the 1970s, who claimed to represent extraterrestrial beings, and who tried to persuade people (with some success) to abandon their careers and other pursuits in favor of a new life on another planet. Through lectures and other means, these people, who came to be known as "Extraterrestrial Travel Agents," maintained that Earth was facing imminent destruction, and that benevolent aliens were preparing to evacuate a certain number of humans.

British researchers Peter Hough and Jenny Randles pinpoint the origin of this phenomenon to a man and woman who called themselves "The Two," and who toured the western United States in 1975, proclaiming to anyone who would listen that they had been sent from the "level above human." They assured their followers that they would all return to that level in a spaceship that was due to arrive shortly.

Throughout the rest of the decade, the movement grew, with other Extraterrestrial Travel Agents popping up throughout the United States, persuading people to sell their homes for, quite literally, a few dollars in anticipation of the aliens' arrival. While these doom-laden predictions on the future of Earth, coupled with the assumption that benevolent extraterrestrials would step in to offer help, can be seen as a curious echo of the **contactees'** claims of the 1950s and 1960s, they are also significant because they sowed the seeds of much more dangerous philosophies, most notably that of the Heaven's Gate sect, which also claimed that a spacecraft would arrive to take its members to the "level above human" (see **cults**).

EZEKIEL

A major Hebrew prophet of the sixth century B.C. As a priest in Jerusalem, he was taken captive by King Nebuchadnezzar in 597 B.C., and worked among the exiles in Tel-Abib in Mesopotamia (now Iraq). He prophesied the destruction of Jerusalem, which took place in 586 B.C. Ezekiel is regarded by many ufologists as one of the earliest witnesses to the activities of an extraterrestrial intelligence, which he described in the first chapter of the Book of Ezekiel. He was on the shore of the Chebar River, when the following event took place:

And I looked, and, behold, a whirlwind came out of the north, a great cloud, and a fire infolding itself, and a brightness was about it, and out of the midst thereof as the color of amber, out of the midst of the fire. Also out of the midst thereof came the likeness of four living creatures. And this was their appearance; they had the likeness of a man. And every one had four faces, and every one had four wings. And their feet were straight feet; and the sole of their feet was like the sole of a calf's foot: and they sparkled like the color of burnished brass. And they had the hands of a man under their wings on their four sides; and they four had their faces and their wings. Their wings were joined one to another; they turned not when they went; they went every one straight forward.
(Ezek. 1:4–9)

When viewed from the point of view of the late 20th century, this description sounds remarkably like the arrival of some kind of machine and its nonhuman crew. However, we must remember that in the final verse of the first chapter, Ezekiel says that "This was the appearance of the likeness of the glory of the LORD." He also describes the entire episode as "visions of God," and the creatures he encountered as cherubim. It is still very much a moot point whether Ezekiel witnessed genuine extraterrestrial activity, or was experiencing an altered state of consciousness, resulting in a holy vision. Of course, the possibility remains that he actually interpreted an alien encounter in terms consistent with the world view of the Middle East in the sixth century B.C.

FAIRIES (ALIENS)

Much has been written on the similarities between modern alien encounters and the tales told in **folklore**. The main thrust of this speculation is that there is an ongoing interaction between human beings and a nonhuman intelligence, which is interpreted as extraterrestrial activity according to the late-20th-century world view. In addition, it has been suggested that this mysterious intelligence may be capable of altering its surface appearance, in order to conform to the expectations of each period in history. However, there are reports on record of modern encounters with creatures that seem not to have bothered with these surface alterations, and which still appear as folkloric beings.

One such case occurred on January 4, 1979 in Rowley Regis, west of Birmingham, England. The witness was a Mrs. Jean Hingley, who had just seen her husband off to work and was about to go back into their house, when she noticed an orange sphere, about eight feet in diameter, hovering over the garage. At that moment, her dog was suddenly rendered unconscious, and three small beings flew out of the object and into the house through the open front door.

Mrs. Hingley followed the buzzing noise made by the creatures, and found them in the living room, shaking the Christmas tree. The encounter lasted about an hour, and so Mrs. Hingley was later able to describe her uninvited guests in some detail. They were about three and a half feet tall, and had large, oval wings, similar to a butterfly's. Their heads were hairless, and their eyes, staring at her from inside transparent, bubblelike helmets, were large, black and shiny. The creatures were dressed in long silvery tunics with silver buttons down the front and glittering streamers attached to the shoulders.

Their behavior, like their appearance, was odd and somewhat absurd: after fiddling with the

Christmas tree, they alighted on the sofa and began to jump up and down like unruly children. When Mrs. Hingley asked them who they were and where they were from, the creatures touched the buttons on their tunics and replied unintelligibly in gruff voices. At a loss for anything else to do, Mrs. Hingley offered them some mince pies. When they tried and failed to eat them, the entities apparently grew angry or frustrated, and projected beams of light at their host from the tops of their helmets. These laserlike beams struck Mrs. Hingley on the head, burning the skin and temporarily blinding her. The fairylike beings then proceeded to explore the rest of the room, picking up various objects, such as cassette tapes, and examining them. (They were able to do this despite the fact that their tapering limbs appeared not to have any fingers.)

Eventually, the creatures flew out through the back door and into the glowing spherical object, which had since landed. It then took off, flew away to the north and disappeared.

It took some time for Mrs. Hingley to recover enough to telephone her husband and tell him what had happened. She also called the police, who examined the landing site and discovered two parallel lines in the snow. Mrs. Hingley had trouble with sore eyes for about a week after the encounter, and the burn mark from the light beams took several months to heal. In addition, the television and radio no longer worked properly, and she and her husband later discovered that the cassette tapes the creatures had picked up were also useless.

FALCON

(See **Aviary**)

FALSE MEMORY SYNDROME (FMS)

A psychological condition in which a person's memory is partially distorted, resulting in his or her identity becoming centered around the recollection of one or more traumatic experiences, which are fervently believed to be true, but which are actually objectively false. It is important to distinguish between False Memory Syndrome and false memories *per se*. Inaccurate or incomplete memories are perfectly natural and unavoidable; we all have them, but we are able to get on with our lives with little or no disruption due to them. However, FMS, according to psychologist Dr. John F. Kihlstrom,

may be diagnosed when the memory is so deeply ingrained that it orients the individual's entire personality and lifestyle, in turn disrupting all sorts of other adaptive behaviors . . . False Memory Syndrome is especially destructive because the person assiduously avoids confrontation with any evidence that might challenge the memory . . . The person may become so focused on the memory that he or she may be effectively distracted from coping with the real problems in his or her life. (False Memory Syndrome Foundation Internet website)

False Memory Syndrome has become an extremely controversial subject with regard not only to cases of alleged childhood sexual abuse (often of a "satanic" nature) but also to cases of alleged contact with and abduction by aliens. Opponents of such abduction cases cite FMS as an example of how traumatic memories can be artificially created, and suggest that on many occasions the abduction researchers themselves are to blame, through asking questions, which (intentionally or unintentionally) lead individuals to confabulate spurious stories of traumatic encounters with aliens. The abduction researchers themselves vehemently dispute this, and there is no doubt that some of them are indeed extremely careful not to ask such leading questions during the

hypnotic regression sessions used to retrieve repressed memories. However, not all abductionists are so conscientious, and there is little doubt that some individuals, who suspect that something unusual or unpleasant has happened to them, have been further damaged by the activities of unscrupulous researchers.

FANTASY-PRONE PERSONALITIES

A theory put forward as a possible origin of some reports of alien encounters and abductions. The exact criteria for fantasy proneness have yet to be properly codified; however, such personalities seem to include a high susceptibility to hypnosis, a tendency to report out-of-body experiences (OBEs) and a rich fantasy life, one or more of which may prompt them to generate encounter experiences.

In an attempt to test this hypothesis, the American researcher Joe Nickell has reviewed 13 cases of abduction first presented by the Harvard psychiatrist Professor John E. **Mack** in his 1994 book *Abduction: Human Encounters with Aliens,* paying special attention to a number of possible indicators of fantasy proneness: susceptibility to hypnosis, "paraidentity" (a subject's having had imaginary playmates as a child), psychic experiences (such as telepathy, precognition and so on), out-of-body or "floating" experiences, vivid dreams or visions, **hypnagogic and hypnopompic** hallucinations, and the receipt of inspiration believed to have come from a higher source.

Nickell found that of the 13 cases he reviewed, one exhibited four of the seven indicators, one exhibited five of the indicators, and the rest showed all seven of them. He concludes from this that, while the reports of the abductees may be objectively true, the "burden of proof is on the claimant," and the ability and propensity of a subject to fantasize must be an important consideration in the evaluation of claims of alien abduction.

FATIMA, PORTUGAL

A small town, which was the scene of a number of visions of the Virgin Mary, prophecies and apparent UFO sightings in 1917. The first apparition was seen on May 13, by three children who were watching their sheep. A bright flash of light was followed by the appearance of a woman who asked the children to return to the spot every month.

Word of the children's experience quickly spread, and when they returned the following month, approximately 50 people went with them. Although these people saw nothing, they reported a low buzzing sound as the children knelt and communicated with an unseen person. When this apparent dialogue was over, a small cloud was seen to rise from a nearby tree.

The following month, the number of people who went with the children rose to 4,500. These people again reported the low buzzing sound and the presence of a small white cloud above the same tree, which came to be known as the tree of the apparitions. Several strange lights were also seen in the sky.

Over the following months, word of what was happening at Fatima spread throughout the country, and the number of spectators quickly grew to tens of thousands. On one occasion, a revolving silvery disk was seen, which swooped low over the assembled crowd, terrifying them.

The ufologist Jacques **Vallée** has written extensively on the apparitions at Fatima, and he concludes that

the final "miracle" [the spinning silver disk] had come at the culmination of a precise series of apparitions combined with contacts and messages that place it very clearly, in my opinion, in the perspective of UFO phenomena. Not only was a flying disk or globe consistently involved, but its motion, its falling-leaf trajectory [an often-reported

UFO maneuver], its light effects, the thunderclaps, the buzzing sounds, the strange fragrance, the fall of "angel hair" that dissolves upon reaching the ground, the heat wave associated with the close approach of the disk—*all of these are frequent parameters of UFO sightings everywhere.* [Original emphasis.] (Vallée [1990], p. 200)

The correlations between the events at Fatima (and other so-called BVM—Blessed Virgin Mary—encounters) and the events typically associated with UFO and alien encounters should not be underestimated, since they strongly imply a common source, and thus suggest that the field is far more complex and multifaceted than has been supposed.

FEDERAL BUREAU OF INVESTIGATION (FBI)

The FBI was founded in 1908 (although it did not receive that title until 1935), when Attorney General Charles J. Bonaparte gathered a force of Special Agents to be the investigative arm of the Department of Justice, which is still its principal function today. Its official mission is to uphold the law through the investigation of violations of federal criminal statutes, to protect the United States from hostile intelligence efforts and to provide assistance to other federal, state and local law enforcement agencies.

The FBI is also authorized to conduct background security checks on prospective U.S. Government employees, and to obtain information regarding events and activities that might jeopardize the national security of the United States. In view of this last responsibility, the FBI might be expected to participate in any government involvement in UFO research. Indeed, despite numerous denials of any interest in the phenomenon, the bureau has been proved, through the **Freedom of Information Act**,

to have produced more than 1,000 documents on the subject.

FIRE IN THE SKY (FILM)

Made in 1993, directed by Robert Lieberman, written by Trace Torme and starring D. B. Sweeney, Robert Patrick, Craig Sheffer, Peter Berg, James Garner, Henry Thomas and Kathleen Wilhoite. Adaptation of Travis **Walton**'s book *The Walton Experience* (1978), which describes his abduction by aliens.

Although the film's abduction sequence, presented in the form of a flashback as Walton (Sweeney) cowers under a kitchen table, is genuinely unsettling, it bears little resemblance to what was described in the book. Walton originally described being taken into a pristine, technologically advanced vessel and being given a physical examination; however, in the film, his experience is altogether less pleasant, and includes waking up in a giant tunnel, which seems to be part machine, part biological monstrosity, before being dragged through several filthy corridors by wizened, **Gray**-like creatures, who proceed to fill his mouth with a vile jelly and push a needle into his eye. In response to criticism of the film from some ufologists, the film's makers replied that the alterations had been employed to make the abduction more dramatic and frightening (as if abductions were not already so).

For this reason, *Fire in the Sky* should be seen as pure entertainment, with little of any seriousness to say about the abduction on which it is based.

FLATWOODS, WEST VIRGINIA

The site of an alien encounter, which took place on the night of September 12, 1952. At sunset, a group of boys, Neil Nunley, Ronnie Shaver and Tommy Hyer watched as a meteor-like object descended onto a nearby hill. Intending to investigate, the boys headed off in the direction of the hill, stopping on the way at the home of an acquaintance, Mrs.

Kathleen May. When she heard that a meteor had apparently fallen nearby, she decided to accompany them. With Mrs. May were her two sons, Eddie and Fred, and 17-year-old Gene Lemon, a National Guardsman. The group then left the house and made their way up the hill.

When they reached the hill's crest, the group saw a large sphere "as big as a house," according to one of the boys, which made a strange hissing sound as it hovered in the air. At this point, Gene Lemon saw what he thought were the eyes of an animal in the branches of a nearby tree, and he shone his flashlight in that direction. The flashlight beam illuminated an enormous figure, approximately 15 feet tall, behind the tree. Its circular face was "bloodred", had glowing, greenish orange eyes, and was enclosed in what looked like a pointed hood. Although the lower part of the entity was in shadow, Mrs. May could just make out multiple folds, as of a robe of some kind. As the gigantic apparition began to float towards them, the witnesses fled in terror back down the hill. Mrs. May and the others were violently ill as a result of the acrid stench that had accompanied the apparition, and were treated for shock.

The following day, the editor of the local newspaper explored the crest of the hill where the entity had been seen, and discovered two parallel marks on the ground, together with a circular area of flattened grass. The strange odor could still be detected close to the ground.

The Flatwoods encounter is notable for being one of the first to feature a nonhuman "monster," as opposed to benevolent humanoids.

FLYING HUMANOIDS

Among the most bizarre and disturbing of encounters with nonhuman entities are the numerous reports of flying humanoids, which have been sighted across the world. While there is a clear provenance for such tales in various mythologies (notably those of India and the Far East), the skies of the industrial West have also played host to strange creatures who glide through the air, to the fear and consternation of witnesses. In many cases, the flying humanoids are reported to have wings, but occasionally they are described as wearing some kind of backpack, which they apparently control by manipulating devices on their chests or belts.

One of the early sightings in the 20th century was made by a Mrs. E. E. Loznaya in the Pavlodar region of Kazakhstan in 1936. Loznaya, then 15 years old, was walking along a lane when she looked up to the sky and saw a man, dressed entirely in black, flying past. The man was wearing a helmet whose visor completely obscured his face, and on his back was something Loznaya described as a "rucksack." As he flew through the air, the man held his arms tightly against his body. Not surprisingly, Loznaya grew very frightened, and began to look for a place to hide from the entity; but when she glanced to the sky again, he had vanished.

Twelve years later, on January 6, 1948, a Chehalis, Washington, housewife named Mrs. Zaikowski was outside her barn when she heard a strange buzzing noise. She looked up at the sky to see a man flying past, with a pair of unmoving silver wings strapped to his back. (The wings of flying humanoids, such as **Mothman**, are frequently said not to flap.) The man's altitude was somewhere between 20 and 200 feet, and as Mrs. Zaikowski continued to watch in amazement (presently she was joined by a group of children on their way home from school), he maneuvered through the air, almost as if showing off to them, before touching a device on his chest and shooting straight up into the sky and disappearing.

In the early hours of June 18, 1953, three neighbors in Houston, Texas, Hilda Walker, Howard Phillips and Judy Meyers, were sitting on the porch of their apartment building, seeking respite from a heat wave, when they saw an enormous shadow fall across the lawn. At first they thought it must be the shadow of a moth, distorted by the light from a street lamp, but the shadow then alighted in a nearby tree, and the witnesses were stunned to realize that it was actually the figure of a man with batlike wings. The man was about six feet six inches tall, was dressed in tight-fitting clothes and a cape and seemed to generate a strange grayish light. After about 15 minutes, the figure slowly dematerialized. The witnesses then heard a loud "swoosh" and saw a white rocket-shaped object speed away to the northeast.

A particularly intriguing flying humanoid encounter occurred during the Vietnam conflict. Earl Morrison, serving with the First Marine Division and stationed near Da Nang in August 1969, was on guard duty with two other soldiers. At about 1:00 A.M., they saw something moving through the sky toward them. As the thing drew closer, the men realized that it was a naked woman with batlike wings. Although the woman's skin was jet-black, it nevertheless glowed with an eerie greenish light. The woman flew directly over the men, no more than seven feet above their heads. She made no sound whatsoever. The woman headed off toward the soldiers' encampment, and when she was about 10 feet away, they began to hear the flapping of her wings. It seemed to Morrison, as he watched the bizarre apparition, that the woman's arms had no bones in them.

Flying humanoids, like other anomalous creatures, have occasionally been linked to UFO activity, although the exact nature of the connection is difficult to evaluate. The level of **high strangeness** in such encounters would seem to militate against the **extraterrestrial hypothesis (ETH)**—or at least calls for a radical rethink of the ETH as a possible explanation. Some researchers have suggested that encounters such as these demand, by their very nature, a far subtler and more complex theory to account for them (see **psychosocial hypothesis**).
(See also **Garuda** and **Owlman**.)

FLYING SAUCER REVIEW (FSR) (PUBLICATION)

An international journal, established in 1955 and published quarterly, and regarded by many as the world's leading UFO publication. Produced with the input of more than 70 experts from various countries in Europe, the U.S. and throughout the rest of the world, *FSR* includes reports from the English-speaking world, and numerous reports in translation from many other languages.

As far as the origin of UFOs is concerned, *Flying Saucer Review*'s stance is one of acceptance that some UFOs are structured craft of some kind, although it reserves judgment on whether these craft come from outer space. According to *FSR*'s editor, Gordon Creighton:

There seems to be no evidence yet that any of these craft or beings originate from Outer Space. The whole phenomenon involves a mass of features that conflict with modern science, and many researchers now believe that more than one type of being may be involved, some of them originating from Outer Space and some of them of an "interdimensional" nature, and consequently possibly from some unknown aspect of our own world. (*FSR* Internet website)

FOLKLORE
(See **psychosocial hypothesis**)

FREDERIC, WISCONSIN
Site of an encounter with a hominid-like creature in December 1974. There have been a number of cases in which hairy humanoid entities (including **Bigfoot**) have been seen in the vicinity of UFOs. On this occasion, a 69-year-old dairy farmer named William Bosak was driving home at 10:30 P.M., when he noticed a disk-shaped object on or very near the ground at the side of the road. Bosak described the

front of the object as being made of glass, through which could be seen a humanoid figure, with its arms raised above its head.

The figure was slim, about six feet tall and covered with reddish fur. Its face was hairless, and its large, humanlike eyes stared out at Bosak as if in extreme fear. The most notable feature of this strange being was its ears, which were long, pointed and projected straight out from the side of the head. Bosak slowed as he passed the object, and as he did so, the lights of his car dimmed slightly. The object then rose into the air with a swishing sound and flew away.

Reports such as this are extremely puzzling, since they describe high technology in the form of apparent craft, in association with beings that give the impression of a primitive stage of evolution. Of course, we cannot know how such evolution would progress on another planet, but since these beings are humanoid in virtually every respect, there is some justification for assuming that a hairy, apelike appearance would imply an early stage of species development—certainly too early for the construction of interplanetary spacecraft.

With regard to the Frederic, Wisconsin, case, however, the description of the entity may hold a clue, albeit an extremely speculative one. Bosak described the creature's arms as being held above its head; in addition, the expression on its face was one of great fear. It is therefore possible that this being was not in control of the craft in which it was seen, but was actually a captive. In view of the hundreds of reports of unknown hominids that have been received from many parts of the world, could it be that this creature was the hapless subject of a zoological specimen-gathering exercise? If so, the origin of the zoologists (and for that matter the reason for the craft landing in Wisconsin) must remain a mystery.

FREEDOM OF INFORMATION ACT (FOIA)

The United States Freedom of Information Act was created in a 1966 Act of Congress with the intention of giving the general public greater access to government records. Despite the assumptions of some people that the FOIA can be used to secure any information of interest, the act has a number of exemptions and amendments, which preclude the release of information deemed to have a bearing on national security. These exemptions include personnel and medical files on government employees; investigatory records, the disclosure of which would interfere with law enforcement proceedings, and so on.

While these exemptions have resulted in the absurd practice of releasing documents that have been almost totally blacked out, much useful information regarding official attitudes to UFOs has been gathered through FOIA requests, not least of which is material proving a government interest in the investigation of UFO events, despite official claims to the contrary.

FRIEDMAN, STANTON

Resident in Frederickson, New Brunswick, Canada, Stanton Friedman is one of the world's best-known ufologists, thanks to his frequent lectures and appearances on television and radio. A former nuclear physicist of 14 years' standing, Friedman is one of the few professional scientists to have openly declared his acceptance of the reality of UFOs, and more particularly of the **extraterrestrial hypothesis**. This is due in large part to his extensive research on the **Roswell** incident, and his conclusion that an alien spacecraft crashed there in July 1947.

Friedman received BS and MS degrees in physics from the University of Chicago, and went on to work on a variety of highly classified projects for such companies as General Electric, General Motors and

Westinghouse. His stance, with regard to the UFO phenomenon, is that some UFOs are extraterrestrial spacecraft, that the U.S. government is in possession of information confirming this fact (but are withholding this momentous knowledge from the people of Earth), and that the arguments put forward by skeptics in favor of a mundane explanation for all UFO sightings are fundamentally flawed, and collapse under serious scrutiny.

FRY, DANIEL

American **contactee** who received several telepathic communications from space beings. Fry was working as a technician at the White Sands missile proving grounds in New Mexico in July 1950, when he watched a UFO land in the desert nearby. A voice then began to speak in his head, warning him to keep clear of the craft, which was still hot.

The telepathic voice introduced itself as "Alan," who apparently was controlling the small, unmanned craft from a mothership orbiting Earth at a distance of 900 miles.

Fry was then invited to climb aboard the saucer, which took him on a trip to New York (the 4,000-mile journey taking about half an hour). During the flight, Alan informed the contactee that the aliens had been living on the mothership for generations. Over the next few years, Alan contacted Fry twice more, transmitting information on various topics and suggesting that Fry write of his experiences, in order to let the world know of the aliens' presence. Fry later wrote a book on his experiences, *The White Sands Incident* (1966), in which he claimed, common with many other contactees, that the aliens were deeply concerned about humanity's misuse of nuclear energy.

GAETANO, PAOLO

Brazilian abductee whose story reveals the complexities inherent in the alien encounter phenomenon. At 9:30 P.M. on November 17, 1971, Paolo Gaetano was driving home from a business meeting in the town of Natividade de Carangola. With him in the car was his colleague, Elvio B. As they were passing the town of Bananeiras, Gaetano felt that there was something wrong with the car's engine. When he mentioned this to Elvio B., the other man merely commented that he was very tired and wanted to go to sleep.

At this point, the car's engine stalled, and Gaetano guided it to the side of the road, from where he watched the arrival of a UFO. The craft fired a beam of red light at the car, which apparently had the effect of causing the driver's door to open. Gaetano was then taken out of the car and into the UFO by a number of small beings, who proceeded to

give him a medical examination with a device that he likened to an X-ray machine. A small incision was also made at his elbow, from which a sample of blood was taken, and which left a scar that was photographed by Brazilian UFO investigators three days later.

In common with many other abductees, Gaetano was then shown some images on monitor screens. On one screen was a map of the Brazilian town of Itaperuna and on the other the image of a nuclear explosion. Gaetano inferred from this that the town faced the threat of atomic destruction for some reason. The next thing he remembered was being helped by Elvio, but he was unable to say how they got home that night.

The most intriguing element of the report was revealed when investigators asked Elvio B. if he had also seen the UFO and its crew. He replied that the only thing he had seen was a bus, which had been driving along the road at a safe distance behind the car. He also mentioned that Gaetano had been frightened by the bus, and had maintained that it was a flying saucer. According to Elvio, the car had come to a halt at the side of the road, and Gaetano had opened his door and fallen to the ground. Elvio had then helped him up, and they then caught a bus (apparently not the same one that had been behind them) to Itaperuna, where Gaetano was examined by a doctor. A police car was sent to the scene of the encounter, and found the car abandoned at the roadside. Neither of the men could explain why they had taken a bus to Itaperuna, rather than driving there.

This case is similar to Maureen **Puddy**'s experience in Australia, in that the principal witness was not alone at the time of the encounter, but was nevertheless the only one to report the presence of nonhuman beings. Jacques **Vallée** has cited the Gaetano case as a possible example of mind control technology, by which images are projected directly into a percipient's consciousness, quite possibly from a human source.

Are we dealing with a terrestrial technology that systematically confuses the witnesses? . . . If certain areas of the human brain can be remotely stimulated, then it is not impossible to think of broadcasts literally saturating large territories with a flood of symbols. Such a device could be a major tool of social change. If disguised under a preposterous or "absurd" appearance, its effects would be undetected for a long time . . . [T]his could be a key to the confrontation with UFOs. (Vallée [1975], p. 130)

Alternatively, it could be that, since the entities had no use for Elvio, they planted a **screen memory** in his mind (disguising the UFO as an ordinary bus), so that he would remain unaware of what really happened.

GAIA HYPOTHESIS

The Gaia Hypothesis was first put forward in the late 1960s by the British atmospheric scientist Dr. James Lovelock, in collaboration with Dr. Lynn Margulis, an American microbiologist. After being approached by NASA to help in the search for life on Mars, Lovelock suggested that the composition of the planet's atmosphere be analyzed. Should the atmosphere be discovered to be in a state of stable chemical equilibrium, Mars would probably be devoid of life. According to Lovelock, if Mars held life, that life would use the atmosphere as a source of raw materials, creating a similar *disequilibrium* to that on Earth.

In 1965, Lovelock began to consider the possibility that the maintenance of the unlikely combination of gases on Earth is the result of a planetary "control system," which might include the life-forms on the surface. Lovelock called this control system "Gaia," after the Earth goddess of the ancient Greeks. (The name was suggested by his neighbor, the novelist William Golding.) The definition of Gaia is as follows: "This postulates that the physical and chemical condition of the surface of the Earth, of the atmosphere, and of the oceans has been and is actively made fit and comfortable by the presence of life itself." This contradicts the orthodox notion that "life adapted to the planetary conditions [as they were] and they evolved their separate ways."

The Gaia Hypothesis has gained great currency in New Age circles, and has been cited as a possible explanation for the existence of **crop circles**. Earth (a conscious being), so the theory goes, is attempting to communicate with humanity through the complex patterns found in fields, and is warning us of the dangers we pose to the biosphere of our world. Of course, it is a short step from this idea to the idea that UFOs and alien beings are themselves projections originating with Gaia, for the purpose of a symbolic form of communication.

GARUDA

In Hindu mythology, a sacred bird that is the mount of the god Vishnu, and which is depicted as a winged humanoid with a face composed of both human and avian features. Garuda shares many traits with the **flying humanoids** that have been sighted across the world, leading to speculation that the beings of mythology may, in some sense, be possessed of an objective reality, and may represent one form of interface between humanity and a nonhuman intelligence that is as yet unacknowledged by orthodox science.

GENETIC ENGINEERING

In the last 20 years or so, the concept of genetic engineering has moved to center stage in the ongoing drama of human/alien encounters. According to many **abduction** researchers, the principal motive for the alien presence on Earth is the hybridization of humans and aliens, with the intention of creating a new species. The reason for this is that the aliens (invariably the **Grays**) have entered a kind of evolutionary cul-de-sac: their genetic material has become irreparably damaged, atrophying their digestive system and threatening the survival of their species. They are therefore coming to Earth to harvest human DNA, which is combined with their own in the form of alien/human **hybrids**, children partially gestated in human females, before being brought to term in artificial wombs.

As a result of examining the claims of abductees (not to mention those of the aliens themselves), many researchers have pronounced themselves satisfied that this is indeed what is happening in these cases: we are experiencing a subtle invasion from another planet, by a dying species certainly hundreds, and perhaps thousands or millions of years, ahead of us technologically. The theory seems to fit the numerous reports, possessing a surface sheen of logic. However, in terms of what we know about biology and genetics, it is found to be seriously wanting.

It is extremely unlikely that alien genetic material would be sufficiently compatible with that of humans to result in reproduction. The great American astronomer Carl **Sagan** once remarked that there was more chance of an elephant mating with a petunia than a human mating with an extraterrestrial. (This analogy is especially apt with regard to the Grays, who are said to possess both plant and animal characteristics.) The problem is that animals derive energy from the oxidization of food, whereas plants derive their energy from photosynthesis. This and other metabolic differences prohibit the production of animal and plant hybrids. In addition, the genetic material found on Earth is the result of evolutionary processes occurring within the isolated biosphere of the planet, and will not be found anywhere else in the Universe (see **extraterrestrial hypothesis**).

Abduction researchers have countered this by saying that the aliens are so technologically advanced that they have developed a way to avoid these difficulties, and are able to control the fusion and reproduction of human and alien genetic material. However, this begs the question: if they are so advanced, why are they apparently unable to secure a few samples of sperm and ova, read the genetic code and manufacture their own copies, without going to the trouble of abducting thousands—perhaps millions—of people?

GIANT BIRDS

Occasionally, areas that have played host to paranormal and UFO activity have also been visited by gigantic birds. On July 18, 1966, residents of Salt Lake City, Utah, were astonished to see a bird "about as big as a Piper Cub [small, single-engine] airplane" circle the city. In December of that year in Gallipolis, Ohio (not far from Point Pleasant, West Virginia, scene of the famous **Mothman** encounters), pilot Eddie Adkins and four friends were standing on the field of the Gallipolis airport, when they saw a large winged creature approaching them along the Ohio River. The pilots estimated that the creature was flying at an altitude of about 300 feet and was moving at about 70 mph. As the creature drew nearer, they could see that its neck was abnormally long, and that its head was swaying from side to side. Its wings did not flap (see **flying humanoids**). One of the men said: "My God! It's something prehistoric!" The creature glided off into the distance and disappeared downriver.

Perhaps a better description of this bizarre creature would have been: "Something mythological." According to researcher Mark Hall, the Allegheny Plateau of Pennsylvania (just north of West Virginia) is one of a number of areas in North America where there was a powerful belief among Native Americans in a species of giant owl. And of course, we must not forget the near-ubiquitous Native American belief in the Thunder Bird, an enormous supernatural winged entity with an eagle's head, whose vast wings were said to produce the rolling of thunder, and whose eyes flashed with lightning bolts.

Although giant birds cannot be considered "alien" in the accepted ufological sense, the fact that they are seen in the 20th century by the comparatively recent descendants of European settlers in America points rather intriguingly to a connection between anomalous beings in general, and human mythology (see **psychosocial hypothesis**).

GILL, FATHER WILLIAM BOOTH

Anglican missionary who, in the company of 37 others, witnessed a disk-shaped UFO and its crew in Papua New Guinea in 1959. There had been several UFO sightings in the area, of which Father Gill was skeptical. Early on the morning of June 21, Gill's assistant, Stephen Gill Moi, saw a disk-shaped object in the sky above the mission at Boianai. At 6:45 on the evening of June 26, he saw a bright white light in the sky to the northwest. As more and more people gathered to watch the spectacle (eventually there were 38), the object became discernible as a disk with four protrusions underneath. According to Father Gill, its size was roughly that of five full moons. On top of the object, partially hidden by the craft's edge, the witnesses could see four humanoid figures, apparently at work on something that could not be seen. Presently, the object began to ascend and became lost in the clouds.

An hour or so later, Gill and the others saw several much smaller UFOs, which he assumed had come from the larger machine. Twenty minutes later, the large UFO returned, and remained until 10:50 P.M.

The following day, Saturday June 27, the UFOs returned to the mission, and the occupants of the large craft could again be seen on its surface. According to Father Gill: "On the large [craft] two of the figures seemed to be doing something near the center of the deck. They were occasionally bending over and raising their arms as though adjusting or 'setting up' something (not visible). One figure seemed to be standing, looking down at us (a group of about a dozen)."

Gill then raised his arms and waved to the figures on the UFO, and was rewarded with a wave from one of them. At that point, dusk was falling, and so Gill asked one of those present to bring him a flashlight, which he used to signal to the UFO. Apparently in response, the craft began to move back and forth, like a pendulum. After several minutes of this, the figures, their work on the craft's hull apparently completed, retreated inside.

Father Gill went into the Mission House for dinner at 6:30 P.M. When he went outside again half an hour later, the UFO had moved off some distance.

Later, it became obscured by low clouds and was not seen again that evening.

The following evening, the UFOs came for the last time. No occupants were visible, although there was a loud metallic bang on the Mission House roof at 11:20 P.M. In his diary, Gill wrote that there was "no roll of 'object' down roof slope afterward," adding that when he went outside to investigate, he saw four UFOs around the mission. When the roof was later examined, no evidence could be found of a heavy object hitting it.

In 1977, Father Gill met Professor J. Allen **Hynek**, who concluded, from the former's descriptions of the smaller objects' positions in the sky during the sightings, that they were most likely stars and planets. However, Hynek dismissed this as an explanation for the large UFO, since it remained stationary for several hours, which would have been impossible for a celestial object, due to the rotation of Earth.

GINA FOIRO

Also known as "the terror that flies at night," the Gina Foiro is a fearsome entity said to haunt Senegal, West Africa. The Mandinka people describe this being as "darkness moving with the face of a man," and maintain that it has the ability to enter locked buildings. The Gina Foiro stands approximately four feet tall, and can appear and disappear at will. It often leaves an extremely unpleasant smell behind. According to Owen Burnham, who grew up in a small village in southern Senegal, and who described the being and its associated legends in the July/August 1997 issue of *UFO Magazine,* "The prognosis for someone who has been visited by 'the terror' is not good and death is regarded as inevitable within a short space of time."

The term "Gina Foiro" is also applied in Senegal to bright, unexplained lights seen in the sky. According to Burnham, the Mandinka are well acquainted with these lights, which are often seen flying in formation, and which flash on and off intermittently.

GRAYS (ALIENS)

Although an enormous variety of alien life forms has been reported by witnesses over the decades since the late 1940s—everything from hairy dwarfs to disembodied brains to one-legged "robots" with tentacles—the Gray has become by far the most commonly reported, and is now as powerful a cultural icon as the flying saucer itself. There seem to be a number of different types of Gray, and abductees and abduction researchers have tried to fit them into categories, based on their reported behavior.

The most commonly reported type are the small Grays, usually about three and a half to four feet tall, and with pasty gray or gray white skin. They have extremely spindly limbs and torsos; some percipients have described an apparent lack of elbow and knee joints, while others have reported the impression that the physiological makeup of these beings is completely undifferentiated—that is, every part of their bodies is made of the same material, as if they had been cut out of dough. Their heads are disproportionately large and hairless, with no nose to speak of (although a subgroup possesses large noses). Likewise, the ears are vestigial or nonexistent, and the mouths are usually described as being no more than a narrow slit. By far the most striking feature of these entities are the eyes, which are almost invariably described as being enormous, almond-shaped and jet-black. It seems that the eyes are the primary channels of communication between the Grays and their percipients (see **abduction**). These short Grays have been described as workers; they seem to have no individuality and have been likened to an insect hive.

The short Grays work in conjunction with another group of similar appearance, who have tan-colored skin and are taller, usually about five feet in height. Abductees tend to assume that these beings are like doctors, since they supervise any physiological procedures that are performed. A third group of Grays are a little taller still—about six feet—and are considered to be the leaders, or "officers."

Finally, there is a kind of 'supreme commander', a very tall being (about seven feet), whose skin is described as either very dark or very pale, and who gives the impression of being female. This being almost always wears a cloak or veil.

The Grays are frequently described as being cold and uncaring toward the people they abduct. Some percipients have suggested that they have no emotions as we would understand the term, and this is why they are intensely curious about ours. Their home world is the subject of much debate, but is generally considered to be in the star system Zeta Reticuli, which is about 37 light-years from Earth. There are two main reasons for Zeta Reticuli being their putative home: firstly, this was the conclusion of Marjorie Fish, who examined the "star map" drawn by Betty **Hill** after the famous abduction of herself and her husband, Barney; and secondly, it is claimed by Robert **Lazar** to be the home of the so-called **extraterrestrial biological entities (EBEs)**.

Although many abduction researchers claim that the similarity in reports of the Grays offers substantial (if not incontrovertible) evidence that alien beings are indeed routinely visiting Earth, other commentators have pointed to the fact that this type of being was originally encountered in the United States, and Grays are still much more often reported there than anywhere else. In addition, now that this type of entity has established itself in our iconography, Grays are being encountered more often in other parts of the world. This implies rather strongly that earlier reports (whether genuine or spurious) have influenced more recent ones, a process known as "cultural feedback." (For an example of this, we can note that after the release of Spielberg's **Close Encounters of the Third Kind**, reports of creatures similar to those depicted in the film increased dramatically.)

Of course, we cannot be absolutely certain that Gray aliens are not really visiting our world. Nevertheless, their reported attributes and behavior force us to consider alternative explanations for their presence among us (see **psychosocial hypothesis**).

(See also **Schwa**)

GREAT AIRSHIPS

At the end of the 19th century, numerous people across the United States reported seeing mysterious dirigible-like aircraft in the skies and sometimes on the ground. Although most of these craft bore scant resemblance to the flying saucers of later decades, ufologists consider these sightings, which occurred between 1896 and 1897, to constitute the first true UFO "flap" (or high concentration of sightings). These flying machines were very similar to the airships that would take to the air a few years later; however, some of them possessed far greater maneuverability, and were also capable of hovering in perfect stillness even in high winds. There was much speculation in the newspapers at the time that they were the creations of mysterious inventors.

According to the American anomalist Jerome Clark, the year 1896 also saw what may have been the first documented UFO **abduction**. At about 6:00 P.M. on November 25, Colonel H. G. Shaw was riding with a companion just outside the town of Lodi, California, when the horse suddenly stopped in its tracks, obviously terrified of something. Shaw and his companion then saw three beings, seven feet tall, very thin and "curiously beautiful." The beings apparently wore no clothes, but were covered with a soft down. They were hairless, with small ears, large, lustrous eyes and a small mouth without teeth.

Evidently, they were not entirely suited to Earth's atmosphere, since each carried a bag with a nozzle attached, from which they periodically inhaled a gas.

The beings then attempted to carry away Shaw and his companion, but found that they lacked the strength to do so. (At one point, Shaw touched one of them under the elbow, and found that the being weighed less than an ounce.) Turning away from the witnesses, the strange people returned to their craft, a 150-foot-long airship which was hovering nearby. They walked with a swaying motion, their feet only touching the ground at fifteen-foot intervals, climbed into the airship and departed rapidly.

Shaw later suggested that the beings might have come from Mars, with the intention of securing a human for study. Jerome Clark writes:

Perhaps it was publicity [Shaw] was seeking, or maybe he just liked a good joke. Whatever the explanation, his story is interesting for what it reveals about another strain of speculation: for all the talk about earthly inventors, there was also some talk about extraterrestrial visitors. Shaw's tale is the first explicitly to link alien beings with unidentified airships. (Clark [1998], pp. 30–31)

Taken as a whole, the subject of mysterious airships contains elements of the mundane and the paranormal in close juxtaposition. Indeed, most of the reports of encounters with airship crews described perfectly normal human beings, most of whom were polite and courteous, and were prepared to chat with witnesses about their marvelous flying machines (which were almost invariably propeller-driven). Although dirigibles would not be produced for several more years, plans for them were already on the drawing boards of numerous inventors, and the idea of routine human flight in such machines was well established in the public's mind. While it is conceivable that one or more unknown

geniuses produced and test flew airships earlier than is commonly acknowledged, it is also very likely that many sightings were hoaxes. As to the reports of airship pilots who were obviously not human, we are again presented with two possible alternatives: one, that these were also hoaxes; and two, that some were genuine encounters with an intelligence that disguised its outward appearance so as to conform more closely to the scientific world view of the time.

(See also **Magonia** and **psychosocial hypothesis**)

GREEN CHILDREN OF WOOLPIT

Over the years, many books on the unexplained have included the story of the green children of Woolpit, citing it as evidence for the existence of a subterranean realm, populated by intelligent beings (see **Hollow Earth Theory**). While the children were probably not from a subterranean realm, the tale serves to remind (and warn) us how such legends can be assimilated into the field of alien encounters, to be recycled as "evidence" that we are "not alone" on Earth.

The story dates from the reign of King Stephen (A.D. 1135–54) and was documented by the English chroniclers William of Newburgh and Ralph, Abbot of Coggeshall. The children (a boy and girl) were discovered one day, wandering lost, weeping and malnourished near the Suffolk village of Woolpit. The villagers were astonished, not only by their strange clothes and stranger language, but also by the fact that their skins were green. The children were taken back to the village, where they were offered food. Still weeping and distraught, they refused everything except green beans, which they ate with relish.

Presently, they were taken to the house of Sir Richard de Calne, a local landowner, who took them in. The boy did not recover from his malnourishment and died some months later; but the girl returned to full health, the greenness of her skin eventually disappearing. She eventually married a man from King's Lynn in Norfolk and apparently lived a long life.

She also learned English, and told the villagers of Woolpit that she and the boy had come from another country where there was no sun, only a hazy light akin to dusk. They had been exploring a system of caves when they had become lost, eventually emerging near Woolpit. So bright was the light compared to that of their own country that they had become frightened and disorientated, and had wandered lost for some time before being discovered.

In his book *The Unexplained,* the American cryptozoologist Dr. Karl Shuker notes that many explanations have been suggested for the story of the green children, including that it is merely a folktale (based on the color of the children's skin and their preference for the "food of the dead," according to Celtic lore). It has also been suggested that they are a variation on the Green Man, a nature spirit personifying fertility. As mentioned above, yet other researchers suspect that they were denizens of some subterranean realm or even from a parallel dimension.

However, folklorist Paul Harris believes that the tale arose from a local legend regarding a medieval Norfolk earl, the guardian of two children who were to inherit an estate. The earl tried to poison them with arsenic, thus ensuring that he was next in line for the estate. But the children survived and wandered for some time through Wayland Wood before being discovered. Interestingly, one of the symptoms of arsenic poisoning is chlorosis, which turns the skin green.

The green children said that they came from a country known as "St. Martin's Land," perhaps a reference to the village of Fornham St. Martin, a few miles to the northwest of Woolpit. To a frightened and disorientated child, a forest might well be seen as a world of perpetual twilight. Karl Shuker reminds us

that in the 12th century, communities tended to be extremely insular, and a person from a distant village might well have spoken a dialect that sounded strange.

A similar green children story emerged from 19th-century Spain, in the Catalonian village of Banjos, the only difference being that both children died within a year of being discovered. However, this story is definitely spurious, since there are no accounts to be found in the newspapers of the time, and there is no such place as the village of Banjos. Also, the nobleman said to have looked after the children was named Señor Ricardo da Calno—a rather obvious variation on Sir Richard de Calne.

GRUDGE (PROJECT)

U.S. Air Force UFO investigation project, the successor to Project **Sign** and forerunner of Project **Blue Book**. Project Grudge was established on February 11, 1949, and followed a policy of total skepticism regarding the possible extraterrestrial nature of some UFOs. Whereas Project Sign had produced the legendary "**Estimate of the Situation**," which had pointed to the likelihood of our having visitors from outer space, Project Grudge embarked on an all-out effort to explain every single case it investigated in entirely mundane terms. According to J. Allen **Hynek**, if a report bore the slightest resemblance to the activities of an aircraft, balloon, etc., the investigation would immediately cease at that point, the sighting officially "explained."

Project Grudge followed another policy which would come to be regarded as most unsatisfactory by researchers. Instead of investigating the reports people made of UFO sightings, Grudge personnel spent much of their time investigating the witnesses themselves, their intention being to demonstrate that any UFO sighting could, if necessary, be explained with recourse to the mental state of the witness. Project Grudge was terminated on December 27, 1949. It was replaced by Project Blue Book in March 1952.

GRUDGE REPORT 13

A legendary document purporting to deal with various aspects of a genuine extraterrestrial presence on Earth, and which first reached the public via Project Stigma, a civilian organization founded in Texas in 1978 by Thomas Adams, with the intention of investigating **cattle mutilations**. In 1981, Project Stigma received in the mail a document entitled "Memorandum." The text of the document was as follows:

An eyewitness has described an official Project Grudge Report Number 13, Top Secret, *Need To Know Only* classification, that was in fact published but then never distributed and was in fact subsequently destroyed. It consisted of 624 pages, typed, offset reproduced on white paper with a gray cover, and included whole pages of print by (name deleted) and Col. Friend. It covered U.S. government Official UFO Procedures, classifications, and all Top Secret UFO activity from 1942 through 1951. Among other information it included the following:

1. (a) Significant UFO sightings.
 (b) UFO landings.
 (c) UFO/Alien Close Approaches, Abductions, Detentions.
 (d) Crashed UFOs and UFO Retrievals.
 (e) Sensitive Military/Industrial Areas where close encounters occurred.
 (f) Technical Details on Dismantled UFOs.
 (g) UFO Physics—Exotic, Nuclear, Weaponry.
   (1) Clean Breeder Reactor size of oval basketball.
   (2) Ultrasonic, Light, Ray and Beam Weapons.

2. Photographic Section—All glossy pages, photos 3½ x 5, 8 x 10.
 (a) Photographs of sensitive UFOs.
 (b) Color photographs of crashed UFOs.
   (1) Three in good condition.
   (2) One dismantled.
 (c) Color photographs of deceased aliens (Averaged 4½ feet).
 (d) Color Photographs of three Living Aliens.
 (e) Color Photographs of Human Mutilations (head, rectum, sex organs, internal organs, blood removal). One military witness observed human abduction, body found a few days later. This case, which had happened in 1958 had been added to the file.

3. Covered Human and Humanoid Aliens.
 (a) Humanoid Species.
 (b) Humanoid Autopsies.
   (1) No indication of age.
   (2) Small species similar to humans, very similar, varied in height a few inches.
   (3) Liquid Chlorophyll Base Nourishment.
   (4) Food absorbed through mouth membrane, wastes excreted through skin. **(5)** Language similar in appearance to Sanskrit, mathematical phrases.
   (6) Live Alien communicated only desired answers to questions. Remained silent on undesired questions.

Classified summary of the report completed the text.

Note: The one copy seen had been annotated and updated by someone.

According to Thomas Adams, the author of the memorandum was one "Captain Toulinet" (real name William S. English) who had worked as an intelligence analyst at RAF Chicksands in Bedfordshire, England. In 1977 he claimed that he was given Grudge Report 13 to read and was instructed to assign a "probability rating" to it. He was subsequently deported from the U.K. and sent back to America. Later, he was contacted by his former base commander at Chicksands, who invited him on an expedition into the New Mexico desert to find a very large alien spacecraft that had been shot down and lay buried somewhere. English accepted the invitation, but while in the desert, their jeep was destroyed by a missile. English survived, but his former commander was killed. English then spent several years "underground," following a nomadic existence in an attempt to avoid the fate of his commander.

William English has since become one of the most controversial figures in the field of **conspiracy theories**, not least because of his claims regarding his service in Vietnam, which included a Special Forces recovery operation in the jungle of Laos. English and his team had located a B-52 bomber that had been attacked by a UFO and set down *completely intact* in the middle of the jungle. The Special Forces team found the bomber's crew dead and horribly mutilated.

The British anomalies researcher Peter Brookesmith conducted his own investigation into English's claims, and the results were presented in a two-part article for the journal *Fortean Times* (numbers 75 and 76). Brookesmith discovered much to indicate that English is, to put it charitably, being economical with the truth:

English's version of his time in Special Forces in Vietnam doesn't hang together . . . He says that he was posted to Vietnam from Fort Davis, Panama, where he was serving with 8th Special Forces Group. His unit was attached to 5th Special Forces in Vietnam. The locations for these Groups are correct, but there is no record of any of 8th SF being attached to 5th SF. Rather odder is English's designation of his unit as "1st Battalion, 5th Platoon,

attached to Operation Phoenix." You would expect at least a company number in between the battalion and the platoon . . . Even in this garbled form, the unit seems not to have existed. (*Fortean Times* Number 76, p. 33)

Brookesmith was also able to establish that U.S. military personnel are exempt from deportation from the U.K. under the Immigration Act 1971. In addition, English's statement that his commander at Chicksands (who he claims died in the rocket attack in New Mexico) was Colonel Robert Black is also erroneous: during the period in question, the commander at Chicksands was Colonel James W. Johnson Jr.

While English's claims may well be an outright hoax, Jacques **Vallée** has suggested in his book *Revelations: Alien Contact and Human Deception* that the Grudge 13 document English says he was given may have constituted a piece of **disinformation** designed to test his analytical skills. Vallée goes on to note wryly that, if this is the case, English failed the test.

GULF BREEZE, FLORIDA

Location of a number of UFO encounters and abductions reported by businessman Edward Walters. The first of these encounters occurred at 5:00 P.M. on November 11, 1987, when Walters was working in his office. After noticing a strange glow outside, Walters went into the front yard and saw a large, circular craft hovering in the air. Walters took several Polaroid photographs of the object, whereupon it fired an intense beam of blue light at him, lifting him off the ground. At that point, he heard a machinelike voice inside his head, which said: "We will not harm you." He was then released by the beam, and the UFO departed.

Walters took his photographs to the *Gulf Breeze Sentinel,* initially claiming that the photographer was an acquaintance of his, who wanted no publicity. The

Sentinel ran the pictures two days later, and presently Walters came into the open as the witness. He and his family proceeded to take more pictures of the UFOs, which were also spotted by other residents of the town.

Walters's claims were accepted by the **Mutual UFO Network (MUFON)**, while being dismissed by the J. Allen Hynek **Center for UFO Studies** (a dispute unfortunately common to ufology). Walters himself underwent several polygraph (lie detector) and psychological tests, the results of which suggested he was not intentionally lying about his experiences.

As to the veracity of the photographs themselves, which have become among the most famous in ufology, opinion is again sharply divided, with some analysts saying they are genuine, while others say that they are of small models double exposed.

Walters's claims were badly damaged when a nine-inch-diameter model of one of the UFOs was discovered in his house after he had moved elsewhere. The house's new owner, Robert Menzer, told a reporter from the *Pensacola News Journal* that, while looking in the attic for the water main shutoff tap, he found the model behind some insulation. The model was constructed from foam plates and a ring of drafting paper on which could be seen parts of an architectural drawing with notes in Walters's handwriting. A resident of Gulf Breeze stated that the drawings were from an unbuilt house that Walters had designed for him in 1989 (the year following the UFO encounters). Walters claimed that the model had been planted in his old house by someone wishing to discredit him, using draft paper stolen from his new home.

Further damaging revelations were to come in the form of a confession from one Tom Smith Jr. that he had watched Edward Walters fabricate some UFO photographs with double-exposure techniques. Smith went on to claim that Walters had asked him to submit some of the faked pictures to the *Gulf Breeze Sentinel*, and say that he (Smith) had taken them. Smith said that he thought about it and then declined to do so, for the sake of his family's reputation.

In spite of these extremely damaging developments, the Gulf Breeze case is still supported by many ufologists, notably the photoanalyst Bruce Maccabee, who maintains that the photographs are of large objects far away from the camera.

HALLUCINATIONS

The idea that hallucinations are the cause of some initially convincing UFO and alien encounter events is a controversial one. Even fervent believers in an extraterrestrial presence will concede that something in the region of 90 percent of UFO sightings can be dismissed as hoaxes, misinterpretations of mundane objects such as aeroplanes, meteors, stars and planets and so on. This still leaves thousands of encounters that are not so amenable to explanation, and it is these that are said to provide impressive evidence of alien visitation. The suggestion that so many people might have hallucinated their experiences is anathema to the ufologist who subscribes to the **extraterrestrial hypothesis**. And yet, it is extremely difficult to deny that hallucinations can account for many such experiences.

In his 1992 book *Fire in the Brain: Clinical Tales of Hallucination,* Ronald K. Siegel of the UCLA School of Medicine's Department of Psychiatry, gives a very good example of how such hallucinations can occur, and how terrifyingly convincing they can be. In a chapter entitled "UFO," Siegel recounts his brief association with a man named Jack Wilson, who had heard him discuss UFOs on a radio program, and who wanted to share a recent abduction experience with him.

Two days previously, Wilson, 52, had been driving to his home in San Diego with his 24-year-old son, Peter. The two men had been visiting relatives in Florida and had been driving all night when they reached Arizona. While driving along an isolated stretch of highway, Wilson and Peter heard a curious, mechanical noise coming from somewhere behind the car. Wilson stopped the car and got out, whereupon he felt a sudden dizziness and saw a blinding light above him. At that point, he saw a gray, humanoid figure with a halo of light around its head. He backed toward the car, and the figure followed him. The next thing he knew, he was being drawn up into the light, which now appeared as a circular UFO. Inside the ship, Wilson floated down a long corridor lined with geometric patterns, and entered a room that reminded him of a hospital operating theater.

Several more gray creatures appeared, and touched his head with something that literally drained his mind of its memories. The memories, which included images from his childhood, his service in the navy and his recent trip to Florida, were displayed on a monitor screen. He was then returned to his car, to find that seven hours had elapsed.

Siegel was naturally intrigued by Wilson's obviously sincere description of the experience, and so decided to concentrate on this case for the next few days. The following day, Siegel took a detailed personal and medical history of Wilson, and arranged for him to have a complete physical examination at the UCLA health sciences complex. While this was being done, Siegel carefully examined Wilson's car (with his permission), but could find no evidence to suggest that it had been involved in any unusual events.

Wilson was given a clean bill of health (the same was true of the many psychological tests, which were also conducted).

By the time all the tests had been completed, Siegel felt he had the answer to the mystery, and, over breakfast in a small family restaurant called Uncle John's, he told Wilson what, in all probability, had really happened on that lonely stretch of highway in Arizona. Wilson and his son had been driving for more than 30 hours, taking turns behind the wheel. At the time of the encounter, Wilson had been driving for about 11 hours. Neither man had been able to sleep particularly well, and so both were extremely tired.

They heard the noise about two hours after sunrise, and when Wilson stopped the car, there was a light mist on the ground.

Mr. Wilson stepped out of the car and quickly stood up. He experienced an immediate dizziness. I reminded him that he had a past history of becoming faint and dizzy whenever he assumed an upright posture after sitting down for long periods of time. The condition, known as orthostatic hypotension, is actually very common. Many people experience it when they stand up after soaking in a hot bath. (Siegel [1992], p. 107)

When Wilson looked east, in search of the source of the noise, he looked directly into the rising sun, and then instinctively turned in the opposite direction, toward what is known as the antisolar point, "a point in space that is directly opposite the sun from an observer." Siegel told Wilson that that was the precise point at which the gray creature appeared.

I drew a diagram showing Wilson, the car, and the sun. Since the sun was above the horizon and behind Wilson, the antisolar point was in front of him, on the ground. Actually the point was marked by the head of his shadow on the ground. When there is mist or dew on the ground, light is focused in such a way as to create a special optical effect called a glory. A glory is a round halo of glowing light that is seen surrounding the antisolar point. When the angles of sunlight and reflected light from the droplets of dew are just right, the glory can sometimes appear as a circular rainbow. Atmospheric physicists call it *Heilgenschein,* a German word meaning "holy light." Glories can be easily mistaken for angels or aliens. (Ibid., p. 108)

The gray creature was, in fact, nothing more than Wilson's own shadow, with the glory forming a shining halo around its head. As Wilson backed away toward his car, the apparition (quite naturally) followed him. Siegel had spoken with Peter, who told him that he saw his father becoming dizzy, and had got out to help, whereupon he also had seen the "gray creature." The extreme fatigue from which both men were suffering resulted in their not recognizing the shadow for what it was. They then returned to the car to discuss what they had seen, and as they talked, they both drifted off to sleep.

Siegel told Wilson that in his opinion, Wilson then entered a hypnagogic state (which is the boundary between wakefulness and sleep—see **bedroom visitors**), in which he "saw" an illuminated circle approaching him. According to Siegel,

This particular image is known as the Isakower phenomenon, named after an Austrian psycho-analyst who first identified it. Isakower claimed the image was rooted in the memory of the mother's breast as it approached the infant's mouth. . . . [H]ypnagogic images can be interpreted in many different ways . . . The drowsy person in the hypnagogic state is just as open to suggestions as subjects in the hypnotized state. As Mr. Wilson and his son continued their drowsy conversation, floating off into sleep, the looming hypnagogic light was subconsciously transformed into the UFO. (Ibid., p. 109)

The two men then slept for the next seven hours, during which Wilson experienced strange **dreams** based upon his conversation with Peter, which included images of tunnels, geometric patterns and memories of their trip to Florida. Peter also dreamed of a tunnel and the trip to Florida. As soon as they woke up, they continued their conversation, telling each other about their strange dreams and "filling in the spaces between the disconnected images with a story line that fit their bedtime discussion about the gray figure."

Siegel then showed Wilson a collection of drawings made by test subjects who had "no significant knowledge of UFOs," and who had been hypnotized and asked to imagine an alien abduction. The drawings "showed little gray men, long corridors, geometric patterns, examinations, and TV screens with memory scenes."

Although Jack Wilson was not entirely convinced by Siegel's explanation for his experience, he conceded that it may well have happened that way, and it is certainly essential to bear in mind that the complexities of human consciousness demand to be carefully considered when searching for answers to the abduction enigma.

However, Siegel adds a wry postscript to his account, which occurred as the two men were in their cars preparing to go their separate ways:

"What caused the mechanical noise?" he shouted as he revved his engine.

"How should I know?" I shouted back. I didn't know.

"Hell, you're the detective," he hollered as he drove off. (Ibid., p. 110)

HANGAR 18
(See **Blue Room**)

HANGAR 18 (FILM)

Made in 1980, directed by James L. Conway and starring Darren McGavin and Robert Vaughn. After a disastrous encounter with a NASA space shuttle in orbit, a UFO crash-lands on Earth, is retrieved and taken to a U.S. government facility for analysis. The film is based on the legends surrounding "Hangar 18" (also known as "Building 18-A") and the **Blue Room** at **Wright-Patterson Air Force Base** near Dayton, Ohio. In these locations it is said that the air force keeps captured alien spacecraft and other artifacts. While the film is an enjoyable enough romp, it is not particularly well written, and does little credit to the legends from which it takes its inspiration.

HANSSEN, MYRNA
(See **Cimarron, New Mexico**)

HEALINGS BY ALIENS
One of the most puzzling and (for those directly involved) frustrating aspects of the alien encounter phenomenon is the ability of the entities to cure humans of a wide range of illnesses. Although the entities seem to possess miraculous medical techniques, as might be expected if we are dealing with some form of technology-based civilization, only a small number of percipients seem to benefit from this; and only 11 percent of UFO-related physiological effects involve healings by nonhuman beings, according to researcher Dan Wright, who is manager of the **Mutual UFO Network (MUFON)** Abduction Transcription Project.

In November 1967 a Danish UFO researcher named Hans Lauritzen, who was suffering from liver hepatitis, was contacted by a Swedish woman who informed him that he was on a list of prospective **contactees**. Intrigued, Lauritzen decided to go on a series of sky watches with four friends, in case there should be something to the woman's claims. On December 7, Lauritzen was sitting with his friends in a damp field; his liver had become enlarged and he was feeling extremely weak. He and the others then spotted two dim yellow globes hovering 100 yards away, whereupon Lauritzen fell into a trance and began to converse telepathically with the beings inside the globes, who told him he had a great power to benefit the human race.

About an hour later, he came out of the trance and ran to his friends. He was astonished to realize that he no longer felt ill. According to Lauritzen: "I ran and ran so fast that my four friends could not follow me. I had to wait for them. I realized that I had been cured of my hepatitis." Lauritzen later went to his doctor for confirmation of the incredible cure. His examination revealed that his previously diseased and enlarged liver had returned to its normal size and was functioning perfectly.

The range of illnesses that have been apparently cured as a direct result of an alien encounter is quite astonishing, and includes arthritis, asthma, heart disease, infertility, multiple sclerosis and tumors. And yet many abductees who suffer from serious, even life-threatening, conditions are not healed. According to the well-known abduction researcher David M. **Jacobs**, one possible reason for UFO-related healings is that the aliens are merely maintaining the condition of their laboratory specimens, although this does not explain why some are not treated.

HIGH STRANGENESS
A term denoting the more bizarre or outrageous aspects of the UFO and alien encounter phenomena. Indeed, high strangeness cases could be seen as constituting a subject in their own right, and constantly point to the immense complexities within the field of ufology, complexities which frequently imply possible explanations other than the widely held belief in the **extraterrestrial hypothesis**.

Although the events reported by UFO and alien witnesses are strange enough in themselves, the reports that can be placed in the category of high strangeness go far beyond the "mere" sighting of unusual flying objects and apparently nonhuman entities. For instance, in France in 1954, a UFO witness was accosted by the humanoid occupant who asked him what time it was. When the man looked at his watch and replied that it was 2:30, the ufonaut sternly told him: "You lie! It is four o'clock!" The being then asked: "Am I in Italy or Germany?" He then returned to his craft and flew away. However, it really *had* been 2:30! In this case, it may be that the occupant was attempting to communicate in a symbolic way regarding the nature of time, whether in terms of relativity or as a variation on the old warning: "It's later than you think!" His question regarding his location is, of course, equally (apparently) absurd, but may have been some arcane reference to human notions of space.

In addition to cases in which the entities do or say bizarre things, there are other cases that are incredibly strange in themselves. The **Mothman** encounters in the late 1960s, for instance, fit particularly well into the category of high strangeness, as do the **evil clowns** and the **Men in Black**.

Some researchers, such as Jacques **Vallée**, who are dissatisfied with the simplism of the extra-terrestrial hypothesis, have suggested that such encounters might be examples of what Vallée has termed **metalogic** ("beyond logic").

If you wanted to bypass the intelligentsia and the Church, remain undetectable to the military system, and leave undisturbed the political and admini-strative levels of a society, and at the same time implant deep within that society far-reaching doubts concerning its basic philosophical tenets, this is exactly how you would have to act [i.e., with apparent "absurdity," on the one hand to impart a truth that lies beyond the human ability to comprehend, while on the other avoiding the serious attention of science, religion and so on]. At the same time, of course, such a process *would have to provide its own explanation* to make ultimate detection impossible. In other words, it would have to project an image just beyond the belief structure of the target society. (Vallée [1975], pp. 36–7) (See also **psychosocial hypothesis**)

HILL, BETTY AND BARNEY

On the night of September 19–20, 1961, Barney and Betty Hill had an experience that would assure them legendary status as the first widely publicized UFO abductees. Returning from a vacation in Canada, the Hills were driving along an isolated section of Highway 3 in the White Mountains of New Hampshire. The vacation had been a spur-of-the-moment decision, and they had not taken quite as much money as they perhaps should, with the result that they decided to forego a motel in favor of a night drive home, which would see them in Portsmouth, New Hampshire, at around 3:00 A.M.

Just south of the town of Lancaster, Betty noticed an unusually bright star, which she pointed out to Barney. It seemed to be following the car, and so Barney pulled over and looked at the star through a pair of binoculars. He could make out a row of windows, and assured Betty that it was just a plane. However, he left the car and walked a little way into a nearby field, trying to get a better look. Moments later, he was running frantically back to the car, shouting that they were about to be captured. Through the binoculars, he had seen a group of strange figures standing at the windows of the craft, and had looked into the eyes of one of them, an experience which terrified him.

The couple drove away, and presently heard a strange beeping sound coming from the rear of the car. They began to feel extremely tired, and then heard another set of beeps. Betty turned to her husband and said: *"Now* do you believe in flying saucers?" Barney replied: "Don't be ridiculous. Of course not."

They finally arrived home just after 5:00 A.M., about two and a half hours later than they expected. As they were about to go into their house, they noticed some shiny spots on the car's paintwork. (Some days later, Betty's sister, who had seen a UFO, suggested they hold a compass next to the spots. When they did so, the needle spun around wildly.)

A week later, Betty began to have vivid nightmares about being captured by strange creatures. So disturbed was she that she decided to write to the **National Investigations Committee on Aerial Phenomena (NICAP)**. Two months later, the Hills were interviewed by NICAP members, one of whom asked them why it had taken them so long to get home. It was only then that they realized how serious the time discrepancy in their journey had been.

Barney was suffering from stomach ulcers, which may have been exacerbated by the stress caused by their UFO sighting and Betty's nightmares, and so they decided to enlist the aid of the noted Boston psychiatrist and neurologist Dr. Benjamin Simon. They also wondered whether there might be a link between the UFO sighting and hidden psychological stresses caused by their interracial marriage (Betty was of European, Barney of African descent).

The Hills were placed in **hypnotic regression**, and the astonishing story that emerged would make headlines all over the world and be the subject of John G. Fuller's 1966 bestseller *The Interrupted Journey*. Both Barney and Betty (who were hypnotized separately) recalled their car being stopped and approached by a group of five-foot-tall, strange-looking **humanoids**, who took them out of the car and into a landed spacecraft. There they were subjected to what would become commonly reported physical examinations, including a pregnancy test administered with a long needle for Betty, and the taking of a sperm sample from Barney. The beings' faces were similar to humans', except that they were completely hairless, and the eyes were somewhat larger, although with pupils and irises. (Some commentators have suggested that these beings were **Grays**, but this does not seem to be the case: artists' impressions of the beings show them to be similar to humans, yet unsettlingly different—in short, too strange to be humans, yet not strange enough to be Grays.)

Betty recalled asking one of the beings, whom she referred to as the "leader," where their home port was. The leader responded by pulling a kind of "star map" out of a wall. On the map were a number of dots, connected by solid and broken lines, representing trade and exploration routes. When Betty asked him which dot represented his home star, he asked her if she knew where she was on the map. She laughingly replied that she knew very little of astronomy. The leader said: "If you don't know where you are, there's no point in my showing you where I am from." (As in many subsequent encounters, the beings communicated with the humans through telepathy and spoke among themselves in their own language.)

The beings showed considerable interest in Barney's false teeth, and asked Betty why hers were not removable. She replied that people sometimes need false teeth when they get older, an answer which surprised the beings considerably, for they had no notion of what "time" is. Betty also asked the leader for some physical evidence of the encounter, and he gave her a book containing a curious script. However, this provoked a heated discussion among the beings, and as Barney and Betty were about to be led out of the craft, the leader said, "Wait a minute"(incidentally, an odd thing to say, for someone with no notion of the concept of time). Apologetically, he took the book back from Betty, saying that it would be better if they had no proof of what had happened to them.

The star map shown to Betty by the leader quickly became one of the most controversial aspects of the case, since her reproduction of it, drawn while under hypnosis, seemed potentially at least to offer some clue as to the origin of the aliens. With this in mind, a schoolteacher and amateur astronomer named Marjorie Fish devoted considerable time and effort to creating, with beads and string, a three-dimensional model of the drawing. Fish's intention was to find a match between the star map and the nearer stars to our Solar System. The astronomer Terence Dickinson examined the model, and concluded that it represented a view from several light-years beyond the binary star system **Zeta Reticuli**, looking toward our own Sun and the star 82 Eridani. The model was subsequently re-created, using a computer program, by another astronomer, Walter Mitchell of Ohio State University, who was "impressed" by it.

While many ufologists, who believed that Earth is being visited by aliens, pointed to the Fish interpretation as offering conclusive proof of their theory, others treated it with much greater caution, suggesting that the large number of stars virtually guaranteed a match of some description. In addition, Jacques **Vallée** questioned the very need for a "star map" on an interstellar spacecraft. Even at our own primitive stage of space exploration, he reasoned, we humans use computer software and telemetry for space navigation, not *maps*. Vallée contends that, if the map really was on the spacecraft, it must have been a prop, placed there for Betty Hill to see.

We can only guess at the purpose of staging such a scene for Betty Hill. Perhaps it served to reinforce her belief that she was dealing with space visitors. Perhaps it diverted her attention away from something else. Perhaps the purpose was to have her convince others that a space invasion was possible. Perhaps, again, it was meant as a symbol of our mistaken understanding of physical dimensions, like the absurd dialogue in other cases [see **high strangeness**]. (Vallée [1990], p. 266)

Although Vallée is critical of some elements in the Hill case (or at least their interpretation by some ufologists), he nevertheless assumes that something extremely unusual, possibly involving a nonhuman

intelligence, did happen to Barney and Betty that September night in 1961. This was not the view taken by Dr. Simon, the Boston psychiatrist who took on their case. His conclusion was that their experience had been entirely subjective, although they certainly believed that what they related had actually occurred. Dr. Simon found several correlations between Betty's experiences and the symbolism commonly found in dreams. The alien book was a case in point. She had asked for proof of the encounter, and had been given a book, which was later taken away from her. Simon discovered that Betty had had an unhappy childhood, and had sought escape in reading, but that her mother had rather cruelly limited the number of books she was allowed to have. Dr. Simon also pointed out some illogicalities often found in dreams, such as the alien leader's saying "just a minute," when he was supposed to have had no notion of time as we know it.

While Barney and Betty were extremely happy together, their interracial marriage was, Dr. Simon suggested, a potential source of great stress (it was not exactly the done thing in 1960s America), and may have resulted in Betty's series of bizarre nightmares, which she related to Barney. Their UFO sighting in the White Mountains (which may have been genuine, or may have been a bright star or planet) could have been the jumping-off point for a waking dream inspired by these stresses.

The Hill case remains the most famous of all alien abductions, with many citing it as the definitive proof of extraterrestrial visitation. However, as anomalist and UFO historian Jerome Clark has written, we will only have the final answer to the Hills' experience when we have the final answer to the UFO mystery itself.

HOAXES

Few things can be more frustrating to the committed UFO researcher than the UFO hoaxer, and it is an unfortunate fact that hoaxes have been perpetrated for as long as UFOs have been seriously studied. In the late 19th century, many spurious tales of **Great Airships** appeared in American newspapers, inspired by the few genuinely anomalous sightings that occurred between 1896 and 1897. The 20th century preoccupation with UFOs and alien visitation has prompted many to toss around hubcaps, garbage can lids and so on and photograph them in flight. Some hoaxers have been a little more sophisticated in their deceptions, attaching circular shaped cutouts to windows and then photographing them. However, such attempts are easily discovered through techniques of photographic analysis.

Some far more imaginative hoaxers claimed ongoing contacts with beings from other worlds, and, while each case should of course be considered on its own merits, a significant number of **contactees** can safely be consigned to this category. One of the most famous contactees was Howard **Menger**, who led one of his followers into a darkened room, telling her that she was about to meet a spacewoman. However, a sliver of light shone briefly through the door, revealing the "spacewoman" to be an associate of Menger's.

Some cases have entered ufological folklore, in spite of being entirely spurious, notably the famous Vidal teleportation case of 1968, in which an Argentine lawyer, Dr. Gerardo Vidal, and his wife were driving from Chascomus to Maipu, when they entered a strange mist covering the road. Both lost consciousness, and awoke to find themselves in an unfamiliar area. Their watches had stopped, and the surface of their car had been scorched. They had somehow been transported 4,000 miles to Mexico City. Subsequent research has revealed that Dr. Vidal and his wife never existed.

Some UFO hoaxes are quite hilarious. In the January 1978 issue of the American magazine *Official UFO*, a report appeared claiming that five months previously, on August 2, 1977, the town of Chester, Illinois, had been obliterated in a UFO attack. When residents of Chester were interviewed by press reporters, they declared that they had no knowledge of such a disaster. The proprietor of *Official UFO*, Myron Fass, responded to this puzzling lack of memory by claiming that the aliens had instantly rebuilt the town and wiped all knowledge of the incident from its citizens' minds.

The **Aztec, New Mexico** case demonstrates how an initial hoax can develop into a complex subgenre within the field of ufology. According to researcher Jerome Clark:

Ufologists' fascination with [**crash-retrievals**] . . . would inspire hoaxers in the 1980s and 1990s to churn out a mass of phony documents, allegedly from official sources, attesting to cover-ups of fantastic secrets. The most notorious of these was a memo attributed to a supersecret group called **Majestic-12**, which directed the study of recovered extraterrestrial vehicles. The identity of the ostensible forger or forgers, still unknown, remains the subject of much speculation, but only a handful of ufologists still hold forth for the document's authenticity. (Clark [1998], p. 301)

A particularly audacious hoax was concocted in England in 1967. On September 4, a paperboy in Clevedon, near Bristol, discovered a five-foot diameter metallic saucer in a field. Over the next few days, five more of these objects (some emitting bleeping sounds) were found in a path stretching 220 miles through the south of England. The police were baffled, and sent the objects to the guided weapons division of British Aerospace, and also to scientists at the Home Office. A bomb disposal team was called out to deal with one saucer, discovered at Chippenham, Wiltshire. Their response to the mystery of the object's nature was to take it to a nearby garbage dump and blow it up! Thankfully, it turned out not to be an extraterrestrial probe (otherwise, who knows what manner of interstellar incident might have been precipitated), but rather a fiberglass model, filled with a noxious-smelling mixture of flour and water. When the truth finally emerged, it was depressingly mundane. The "UFOs" had been manufactured by a group of 15 students from a college in Farnborough as a prank.

The respected British ufologist Jenny Randles makes an interesting and pertinent comment with regard to this case and the worldwide UFO cover-up that is alleged to have been in place for the last 50 years or so.

Had this happened in the U.S., it would have been the "nightmare scenario" for the [U.S. Air Force], where no end of rapid response could have probably succeeded in keeping the lid on what had really happened. The way in which this story appeared in the media across the U.K. within minutes of the first discovery must pose serious questions about the viability of the alleged cover-up. Hiding retrieved spacecraft in the U.S. time after time and year after year seems hard to fit into what took place on this occasion. Also, given that a group of dedicated people with the will and the ability were so readily able to create such a masterful hoax for pure fun, it should make all researchers beware of insisting that a case cannot possibly be a hoax because it is too complex or lacks obvious motivation. (Randles [1995], pp. 110–11)

HOLLOMAN AIR FORCE BASE, NEW MEXICO

Site of an apparent UFO landing and, according to some ufologists, the event which heralded the legendary "secret treaty" between the U.S. government and alien beings. This event is actually no more than a rumor, and, as such, has spawned several alternative scenarios and dates. However, the most reliable one is as follows.

On April 25, 1964, radar scopes at Holloman AFB showed the arrival of three unidentified objects. The craft continued to approach the base, despite being warned to leave the restricted airspace, and presently visual contact was made with the disk-shaped UFOs. One of the craft then broke away from the others and landed on the desert floor. These events were captured on film by two camera crews in the vicinity, which were photographing a missile test launch.

The base commander, along with two officers and two air force scientists, approached the landed UFO as a door in the craft opened and three aliens disembarked. They were a little less than average human height, were dressed in tight-fitting flight suits, and had blue gray complexions, wide-set eyes and prominent noses. Each wore a curious, ropelike headdress. The beings apparently communicated with the humans via telepathy.

After being greeted by the base commander, the visitors were escorted to another part of the base, where they negotiated not only the release of the alien bodies discovered in New Mexico in the **Roswell** Incident but also the exchange of some of their technology in return for the right to experiment on selected human civilians.

In a conversation with Dr. J. Allen **Hynek**, Jenny Randles learned that there had been an alleged plan to release the 16 mm color film of the UFO landing to the public. A film producer was approached by the U.S. Air Force and shown the film in the early 1970s; he was told that it would be part of an "education program," which would culminate in a worldwide announcement of the extraterrestrial presence. However, the producer was subsequently told that the film was a hoax, and that he should forget about it.

Interestingly, UFO and **cattle mutilations** researcher Linda Moulton **Howe** (also a film producer) received a similar promise of UFO footage in 1983, a promise that also was broken.

HOLLOW EARTH THEORY

The Hollow Earth Theory is a very good example of how different elements of the paranormal can shade into one another, the boundaries between them becoming indistinct as old theories and rumors influence more recent ones. This process has proved particularly damaging to modern ufology, where occult imagery and eastern mythology have contaminated what was, at its outset in the late 1940s, essentially a scientific mystery. The great American anomalist Charles Fort said that one may measure a circle beginning anywhere, by which he meant that every aspect of reality is intimately connected to every other aspect. Thus with ufology, one can enter the subject by looking at reports of silver disks flying through the sky, and with unsettling rapidity, find oneself reading of vast kingdoms situated miles beneath the surface of Earth, populated by fabulous superhumans and terrifying monsters.

In the context of alien encounters, the roots of the Hollow Earth Theory can be traced back to a Frenchman named Louis Jacolliot (1837–90), who was a magistrate in Chandernagor, South India. In a series of popular books, including *Le Fils de Dieu* (*The Son of God*, 1873), he told of his experiences with certain Brahmins who passed on to him sacred knowledge of a prehistoric city of incredible splendor, known as Agartha.

In 1886 a Christian Hermetist, Saint-Yves d'Alveydre, published a book entitled *Mission de l'Inde* (*The Mission of India*), based on information revealed to him by his tutor, one Haji Sharif. In his book *Arktos: The Polar Myth in Science, Symbolism and Nazi Survival,* the British author Joscelyn Godwin offers a description of *Mission de l'Inde's* contents:

We learn that it [Agartha] is a hidden land somewhere in the East, below the surface of the earth, where a population of millions is ruled by a "Sovereign Pontiff" of Ethiopian race, styled the Brahmatma. This almost superhuman figure is assisted by two colleagues, the "Mahatma" and the "Mahanga" . . . His realm, Saint-Yves explains, was transferred underground and concealed from the surface-dwellers at the start of the Kali-Yuga, which he dates around 3200 B.C.E. Agartha has long enjoyed the benefits of a technology advanced far beyond our own: gas lighting, railways, air travel, and the like . . . Now and then Agartha sends emissaries to the upper world, of which it has perfect knowledge. (Godwin [1993], p. 84)

The legend of a hollow Earth resurfaced unexpectedly in 1947, with the Arctic expedition of Rear Admiral Richard E. Byrd, who was quoted as saying: "I'd like to see that land beyond the Pole. That area beyond the Pole is the center of the great unknown." Nine years later in 1956, Admiral Byrd led an expedition to Antarctica in which, according to a radio announcement soon afterward, he "penetrated a land extent of 2,300 miles beyond the Pole." Byrd later stated that "the present expedition has opened up a vast new land." There have been persistent rumors that the expeditions discovered gargantuan openings where the North and South Poles should be—entrances, apparently, to the interior of the Earth. However, according to author Ronald D. Story, Byrd's second in command, Dr. Laurence M. Gould, a distinguished geologist at the University of Arizona, denies that any such astonishing discoveries were made. In fact, Gould discussed the subject with Byrd, and both were somewhat bemused by the whole idea of a hollow Earth.

Nevertheless, the rumors have steadfastly refused to go away, and many writers have produced books claiming that our world is indeed hollow, and is home to a highly advanced civilization, which dispatches numerous missions to the surface in flying saucers. One piece of "evidence" they have offered in support of their claims is a series of photographs taken of the North Pole by the satellite ESSA-7. At the time, there was a lack of cloud cover, resulting in an unobstructed view of Earth's surface. The photographs showed a very large, dark, circular area, which was taken to be the northern entrance to the planet's interior. However, the reason for the dark area was rather more prosaic: due to the satellite's orbital trajectory, the area around the pole had not been included in the photomosaic that made up the entire picture: it was dark because it simply had not been photographed (this has not stopped these pictures from turning up regularly in books and magazine articles supporting the Hollow Earth Theory).

Among the purveyors of the hollow Earth notion are Raymond **Palmer**, Richard S. **Shaver** and Brinsley Le Poer Trench. The legend has also given rise to rumors that the Nazis established a secret colony in Antarctica and are the true originators of the flying saucers.

(See also **Deros, Nazi flying saucers, Teros**)

HOLOGRAPHIC THEORY

A theory originally arrived at independently by the University of London quantum physicist David Bohm and the Stanford University neurophysiologist Karl Pribram, in which the Universe is seen as possessing the properties of a gigantic hologram. According to Bohm, who was profoundly dissatisfied with the dual nature (both particulate and wavelike) of matter at the subatomic level, this duality can be explained by recourse to a holographic model, in which the Universe is a unified continuum. In his book *The Holographic Universe,* author Michael Talbot illustrates this in a striking way:

Look at your hand. Now look at the light streaming from the lamp beside you. And at the dog resting at your feet. You are not merely made of the same things. *You are the same thing.* One thing. Unbroken. One enormous something that has extended its uncountable arms and appendages into all the apparent objects, atoms, restless oceans, and twinkling stars in the cosmos. [Original emphasis.] (Talbot [1991], p. 48)

As the name suggests, this theory was inspired by the relatively recent science of holography, in which a three-dimensional image of an object is created by splitting a single laser light into two separate beams. The first beam is pointed at the object, and the reflected light is then made to collide with the second beam. The collision of the two beams of laser light creates what is known as an interference pattern, and this pattern is recorded on film. This film shows nothing more than these interference patterns, which appear as concentric circles and ripples; however, when the film is illuminated by another laser or other light source, the original object can be seen as a three-dimensional image.

Talbot describes a particularly astonishing property of holographic images:

Three-dimensionality is not the only remarkable aspect of holograms. If a piece of holographic film containing the image of an apple is cut in half and then illuminated by a laser, each half will still be found to contain the entire image of the apple! Even if the halves are divided again and then again, the entire apple can still be reconstructed from each small portion of the film (although the images will get hazier as the portions get smaller). Unlike normal photographs, every small fragment of a piece of holographic film contains all the information recorded in the whole. (Ibid., pp. 16–17)

David Bohm maintained that holography supported the concept of the Universe as a projection from a deeper level of reality where everything is connected. (The holographic model can also explain so-called quantum interconnectedness, in which fundamental particles are observed to influence each other instantaneously, in apparent violation of the law prohibiting anything from traveling at faster than the speed of light.)

Karl Pribram also found holography extremely useful in explaining the mystery of the location of memory in the brain. Hitherto, memory had been assumed to reside in a specific location in the brain; however, Pribram found that when he removed various parts of the brains of rats that had learned to navigate a maze, the rats retained the memory of the maze's layout. The implication was that memories are distributed throughout the brain, and do not reside in any one location; moreover, the distribution must be comparable to the information distributed on a holographic film, which remains intact even when parts of the film are removed.

This profound connection between everything that exists, whether matter, energy or thought, has immense implications for the field of "alien" contact. If the holographic model is accurate, contends Talbot, then we live in a Universe where the terms "objective" and "subjective" no longer carry any meaning; rather, the Universe is "omnijective," and what we consider to be "real" external phenomena share a fundamental connection with the internal processes of our minds. It seems significant that so many UFO and alien encounters have a dreamlike quality (so much so that ufologist Jenny Randles has coined a term, the **Oz Factor**, with reference to them).

On this point, Talbot has this to say:

One thing that we do know is that in a holographic universe, a universe in which separateness ceases to exist and the innermost processes of the psyche can spill over and become as much a part of the objective landscape as the flowers and the trees, reality itself

becomes little more than a mass shared dream. In the higher dimensions of existence, these dreamlike aspects become even more apparent, and indeed numerous traditions have commented on this fact. (Ibid., p. 285)

In view of the extremely bizarre nature of many (if not most) nonhuman encounters, which seem to include references to numerous elements in our mythology (which one would expect to be absent from any encounter with a genuine extraterrestrial alien), the Holographic Theory holds much promise for those attempting to understand these events.

HOPKINS, ELLIOTT BUDD

A highly respected professional artist and sculptor who has arguably become the world's foremost investigator of alien **abductions**. Hopkins's interest in UFOs began in the summer of 1964 when, in the company of two other people, he observed an unidentified metallic object in the sky over Cape Cod, Massachusetts. He conducted his first investigation in 1975, when a UFO reportedly landed less than a mile from Manhattan, and was seen by a number of people.

In 1981, Hopkins published *Missing Time*, a groundbreaking comparative study of a number of abduction cases, and which reached the startling conclusion that such cases share a large number of consistent elements, not least the descriptions of the entities involved (which have come to be known as the **Grays**). His second book, *Intruders: The Incredible Visitations at Copley Woods*, was published in 1987 and dealt with one specific case, that of Debbie Tomey (whom he gave the pseudonym "Kathie Davis" in the book). His latest book, *Witnessed: The True Story of the Brooklyn Bridge Abduction*, was published in 1996, and again dealt with a single case, that of Linda **Cortile**.

In 1989, Hopkins founded the Intruders Foundation (IF), a nonprofit research organization dedicated to increasing public understanding of the UFO/abduction phenomenon and to providing support to those who have experienced such phenomena. In 1992 the IF commissioned the Roper Organization to conduct a national survey on the abduction phenomenon in America. The results of the **Roper Poll** have been cited by some researchers as important evidence in favor of the reality of abductions, while others have remained unimpressed. This aside, Hopkins is considered to be one of the most scrupulous and responsible of abduction researchers.

HOWE, LINDA MOULTON

Emmy Award-winning TV producer, reporter and author, and one of the most controversial UFO/alien contact researchers in the field. Her films include *Fire in the Water,* dealing with hydrogen as an alternative energy source; *A Radioactive Water,* which investigated uranium contamination of drinking water in Denver, Colorado; and *A Strange Harvest,* in which she investigated the mystery of **cattle mutilations**. In 1989, Howe self-published a book entitled *An Alien Harvest: Further Evidence Linking Animal Mutilations and Human Abductions to Alien Life Forms.*

Howe has investigated many encounter reports, and has interviewed scientists, civilians and ex-military personnel. The experiences relayed to her have led her to lean away from the **extraterrestrial hypothesis** and more toward alternative theories in which the intelligence encountered is presumed to be inter-dimensional in nature (see **Keel, John A., ultraterrestrials**).

HOYLE, FRED

British astronomer and mathematician, noted for his computations of the ages and temperatures of stars, and the prediction of quasars (quasi-stellar objects), which were subsequently discovered. Hoyle has not been afraid to court controversy, and in partnership with Chandra Wickramasinghe (a former student of Hoyle's and an authority on interstellar material), has suggested that life on Earth may have been seeded by cometary impacts (a process known as "panspermia"). His 1957 novel *The Black Cloud* is based on the intriguing speculation that the building blocks of such space-borne life might be capable of organizing into intelligent, cloudlike entities, an idea also explored by the American writer Philip K. Dick in his novel *VALIS.*

HUMANOIDS

Term denoting a physical configuration comparable to that of a human being, (i.e., two arms, two legs, trunk and head). Some nonhuman entities have been reported with minor differences, for instance the absence of hands or feet, or with more or fewer eyes, etc., but are still referred to as humanoids. Skeptics of alien contact in general, and some researchers who are skeptical of the **extraterrestrial hypothesis** in particular, have cited the preponderance of humanoid reports as strongly implying that we are not dealing with visitors from outer space. The latter group of skeptics are not content to dismiss the entire phenomenon out of hand, but suggest that such encounters may be the result of interaction with a nonhuman intelligence that is presenting itself in a form which we are able to comprehend.

It seems that, while the humanoid form is the optimum configuration for intelligent, technological beings on Earth, it is most unlikely that the same would hold for other planets, which may possess radically different conditions. We may therefore expect genuine extraterrestrial beings to appear strikingly different from ourselves. (For this reason, ironically enough, the more ridiculous-looking a reported "alien" is, the greater the likelihood is of its having come from another planet!)
(See also **psychosocial hypothesis**)

HYBRIDS (ALIEN/HUMAN)

People who claim to have been victims of alien **abductions** have on many occasions reported being shown around the environments into which they have been taken (these are usually described as being spacecraft). Not infrequently, these tours may include a kind of incubatorium containing large numbers of clear vessels, in which float the fetuses of alien/human hybrids. Certain female abductees also visit nurseries containing hybrid infants. These children are described as being rather unhealthy in appearance, and the aliens encourage (and sometimes force) the abductees to hold and nurture the infants. Some researchers have speculated that the aliens understand the need for a young child to experience close contact with a female. Some researchers, notably Budd **Hopkins** and David M. **Jacobs** have suggested that the experiences of some female abductees imply that they have been artificially inseminated by the aliens, only to have the fetuses removed during subsequent abductions.

Taken literally (itself a dangerous course), such reports would seem to indicate that the aliens are engaged in the production of a new species, part human and part alien, for unknown purposes, although abductees who have undergone more positive experiences (they are usually described as terrifying in the extreme) say that the aliens informed them of their intention to populate a distant (unknown) planet with the new race, thus saving humanity from the extinction that would otherwise be its reward for its misuse of Earth's environment. (There is much in the literature on **conspiracy theories** to suggest that the aliens are actually using human genetic material to improve the stock of their dying species.)

HYPNAGOGIC AND HYPNOPOMPIC STATES

(See **bedroom visitors**)

HYNEK, JOSEPH ALLEN

Dr. J. Allen Hynek was highly respected, not only in his chosen field of astronomy, but also in the study of UFOs, which he insisted throughout his life should be conducted on scientific principles. For Hynek, this did not mean dismissing and ridiculing reports of sightings, but rather approaching them with an open but disciplined mind, an admirable stance, which, sadly, he was one of the few ufologists (or scientists) to maintain.

Born in 1910 in Chicago, Illinois, Hynek received a B.S. degree and later a Ph.D. in astrophysics from the University of Chicago, before becoming director of the McMillan Observatory at the University of Ohio. In 1960 he became professor of astronomy at Northwestern University in Evanston, Illinois. By that time, he had spent 12 years advising the U.S. Air Force on its UFO investigations (see Project **Sign,** Project **Grudge,** Project **Blue Book**).

Although during the early years of his UFO involvement Hynek maintained a skeptical attitude toward the phenomenon, he was nevertheless genuinely puzzled by certain reports that refused to succumb to rational explanation (despite the air force's sometimes laughable attempts to explain them), and was intrigued when some of his academic colleagues let him know that they had seen UFOs, but were afraid to say anything officially, for fear of the damage it would cause to their reputations.

In the early 1960s, Hynek met Jacques **Vallée,** then a young graduate student, and was impressed by the Frenchman's highly intelligent attitude to the UFO mystery. He contributed a cover statement and introduction to two books by Vallée (*Anatomy of a Phenomenon* [1965] and *Challenge to Science: The UFO Enigma* [1966] respectively) who argued that UFOs were extraterrestrial in origin (Vallée was later to modify his ideas in favor of the **psychosocial hypothesis**, and to become a vocal critic of the **extraterrestrial hypothesis**).

In March 1966 the state of Michigan played host to a number of UFO events, particularly around the town of Dexter, where strange lights and crafts were seen in the vicinity of a nearby swamp. At the request of the air force, and amid press demands for an explanation, Hynek went to Michigan to investigate. Hynek found himself in a somewhat invidious position, facing intense pressure from the press, while having little quality data with which to form an explanation. Consultation with a University of Michigan chemistry professor led Hynek (as it would have led any good scientist) to decide on the likeliest explanation for the UFO sightings. He told a packed press conference that the Michigan UFO sightings were probably caused by "swamp gas."

Hynek was mercilessly lampooned across the country, and became the personification of the putative air force dishonesty regarding UFOs. This was both unfair and ironic, in view of his changing attitude to the phenomenon. In 1966, Hynek told a House Armed Services Committee hearing on UFOs that the data accumulated through air force investigations deserved to be closely examined by a panel of physical and social scientists. This eventually led to the University of Colorado UFO Project, directed by the renowned physicist and avowed UFO skeptic Edward U. Condon. However, the Condon Report, when it appeared in 1969, recommended that study of the phenomenon should be abandoned, since it offered nothing of scientific value. As a result, Project **Blue Book** was closed down in December of that year, ending official government interest in UFOs.

In 1972, Hynek published *The UFO Experience,* which remains one of the best books on the subject and is still essential reading for anyone with a serious interest in ufology. It was in this book that Hynek defined the six principal types of UFO event: nocturnal lights, daylight disks, radar/visual observations, and the three kinds of **close encounters**. *The UFO Experience* had the additional distinction of being quite favorably reviewed in serious scientific journals, such as *Nature*. In his review, D. G. King-Hele described the cases documented in the book as "cumulatively impressive," while Bruce C. Murray, writing in *Science*, commented that Hynek had "won a reprieve" for UFOs in detailing so many intriguing reports, as well as challenging other scientists to "tolerate the study of something they cannot understand."

In 1973, Hynek founded the **Center for UFO Studies (CUFOS)**, which has become one of the largest and most respected civilian investigative organizations. Hynek and CUFOS were enlisted to provide technical advice by Steven Spielberg for his 1977 film ***Close Encounters of the Third Kind***, in which the veteran ufologist appeared briefly (presumably as himself).

Later years saw Hynek begin to speak more openly of his interest in the occult, and he remained intrigued by Jacques Vallée's exotic theories on the ultimate nature of nonhuman encounters. This point of view did not meet with the unqualified sympathy of his colleagues at CUFOS; nevertheless, it further demonstrated his willingness at least to consider controversial theories that might shed some light on the phenomenon.

After producing two more books, *The Edge of Reality* (1975), which contained transcripts of conversations with Vallée, and *The Hynek UFO Report* (1977) about Project Blue Book, Hynek was diagnosed with a brain tumor, from which he died in Scottsdale, Arizona in 1986.

HYPNOTIC REGRESSION

A highly controversial technique for recovering memories of a past event that are either unclear or have been repressed, usually due to their traumatic nature. Much (though by no means all) material regarding the descriptions and intentions of alien visitors has been recovered through the use of hypnotic regression. Use of this technique has been heavily criticized not only by UFO skeptics but by researchers who rightly claim that it unavoidably distorts recollections to the extent that they are all but useless in understanding the events in question. This is exacerbated by the fact that few abduction researchers are trained in the use of hypnosis, and are prone to ask their subjects leading questions (whether intentionally or not) based on their own beliefs regarding the reality of alien visitation. While in the hypnotic state, a person's mind has a tendency to please the questioner, and this can very easily result in what is known as "confabulation," or the relating of events that did not in fact occur.

This process can result in the creation of false memories of alien abduction (or, in other cases, of childhood sexual abuse—see **False Memory Syndrome**), which can prove extremely damaging to the subject. It is also important to remember that in an experiment with people who claimed no abduction, but who were asked to imagine such an event while under hypnosis, they told stories that matched to a great extent the material retrieved from "genuine" abductees (see **imaginary abductees**).

However, in spite of this, responsible abduction researchers have, in some instances, helped people to come to terms with undoubtedly unusual and traumatic events in their pasts (see **Tomey, Debbie**).

ILKLEY MOOR, YORKSHIRE, ENGLAND

Site of a UFO and alien sighting, which, upon further investigation, turned out to be a full-blown abduction. This is also one of the very rare cases where an alien percipient managed to take a photograph of one of the entities, and for this reason it has become one of the most controversial cases in the field of nonhuman encounters.

At about 7:15 A.M. on December 1, 1987, a former policeman named "Philip Spencer" (pseudonym) left the Yorkshire town of Ilkley to visit his father-in-law, who lived in East Morton on the other side of Ilkley Moor. He took with him a camera to take some shots of the moor, and also a compass (the winter weather in the north of England can be treacherous, and it is easy to lose one's bearings in isolated parts).

Spencer was climbing up a steep hillside, when he became aware of a humming in the air, which he assumed was an aircraft in the overcast sky. He passed a stand of trees and noticed a movement to one side. Turning, he saw a diminutive figure retreating up the side of an overgrown quarry. Spencer shouted to the figure, which was about 50 feet away; it turned and made a gesture as if to wave him away. Spencer was able to take a single photograph of the creature before it disappeared over an outcrop. Giving chase, he rounded the outcrop and was then confronted not with the entity but a large, hovering metallic disk with a boxlike object sliding into the dome on its upper surface. The disk rose quickly into the air and shot away at terrific speed.

Instead of continuing his journey to East Morton, Spencer decided to go back to Ilkley. He was bewildered to see that the shops were open, and that it was now 10 o'clock. Somehow, he had lost one and three-quarter hours. Remembering the photograph he had taken, Spencer went to a one-hour processing shop and had the film developed. During the subsequent investigation by British ufologists Peter Hough and Jenny Randles, the film was analyzed by Peter Sutherst at Kodak, who did not commit himself beyond saying that the film had not been interfered with after processing. Although image enhancement of the photograph was suggested, it was extremely grainy, and Sutherst maintained that there was insufficient detail to justify what is an expensive procedure. Nevertheless, Geoffrey Crawley of the *British Journal of Photography* attempted to computer enhance the image, but failed to reveal any further detail.

Two days after his encounter, Spencer noticed that the polarity of his compass had been reversed, so that the needle now pointed south instead of north. Peter Hough and another investigator, Arthur Tomlinson, took the instrument to Dr. Edward Spooner, head of the Department of Electrical Engineering and Electronics at the University of Manchester Institute of Science and Technology (UMIST). Dr. Spooner succeeded in reversing the compass's polarity, and stated that Spencer could conceivably have accomplished this using equipment in the home (although with considerable risk of electrocution).

Spencer began to have strange dreams of a starry sky, and this, along with his continuing concern over his **missing time**, prompted him to suggest that **hypnotic regression** might help him to remember what had happened to him. A clinical psychologist named Jim Singleton agreed to conduct the regression, during which it was discovered that Spencer was abducted by the occupants of the disk he had seen. Furthermore, he had taken the photograph of the entity at the end of his experience, rather than at the beginning. (This, it seemed, explained a puzzle that had been troubling the researchers, regarding the amount of light in the photograph, which had apparently been taken later in the morning than Spencer initially claimed.)

During his hypnosis session, Spencer described seeing the entity much earlier in his walk, and then being lifted off the ground by some unknown force and into the waiting UFO. Inside the craft, a voice told him not to be afraid. He was taken into a white room and placed on a table. A device resembling a fluorescent tube moved up over his body. He was then shown around the craft, during which he passed what was evidently a porthole. Through it he saw Earth in the distance, and realized he must be in outer space.

He was then shown what was apparently the engine room of the spacecraft, which contained a large gyroscope-like apparatus. At this point, his camera and compass, which were still hanging around his neck, where pulled toward the gyroscope. Spencer was then taken into yet another room, where he was shown two films, one depicting scenes of destruction, pollution and starving people, and the other showing something he refused to talk about, but which he implied had something to do with his relationship with his wife.

Spencer was then released from the craft, and the next thing he remembered, he was watching one of the entities climbing away over the outcrop. In response to Jim Singleton's question, Spencer described the entities as about four feet in height, with rough green skin, large pointed ears and big eyes. They had no noses and their mouths were very small. Their arms were extremely long and ended in large hands. Interestingly, Spencer described their feet as having a V-shape, with two large toes, which is reminiscent of the feet of a chameleon.

During the subsequent investigation of the incident, conducted by a number of researchers, the photograph was again examined, and a square blob was discovered, which roughly corresponded to the position of the UFO's boxlike extension. However, ufologists Philip Mantle and Andy Roberts visited the location of the encounter and established that this blob was an atmospheric phenomenon produced by a combination of lighting conditions and ground moisture.

In the years since Philip Spencer's encounter, it has been suggested that he hoaxed the incident, although the motivation for such a hoax is unclear: Spencer still refuses to allow his real name to be used and has also refused all offers of money for his story. (Of course, quiet satisfaction at having duped the ufology community cannot be ruled out.) Spencer not only remains adamant that the encounter really took place but is also unconcerned whether he is believed or not.

Interestingly, and somewhat ironically, Spencer has become a "much more skeptical person" as a result of his experience. In a letter to Peter Hough and Moyshe Kalman, he wrote:

One thing has changed which I feel might be due to the experience. I now question everything, and every aspect of everything. It has made me a much more skeptical person. I feel I have been dropped into a sea of uncertainty, unable now to have a belief in anything. What happened to me on the moors was "impossible." It throws everything which you think is normal, certain and secure into question. I now exist in a vacuum of disbelief, occasionally reaching out to hold onto something solid, only to discover it is a hologram. (Hough and Kalman [1997], p. 53)

ILLUMINATI

Term denoting any group of adepts possessing, or claiming to possess, secret knowledge (or "light") from a higher spiritual or cosmic source. The term first appeared in Europe in the 15th century, at which time it was associated with occult orders such as the Freemasons and the Rosicrucians. However, the sect with which the term is most commonly associated (thanks, in part, to the novels of Robert Anton Wilson) was the Order of Illuminati, founded in Bavaria on May 1, 1776, by Adam Weishaupt. Weishaupt, then 28, was a professor of Canon Law at the University of Ingolstadt who was accepted into the Masons in 1778, and who incorporated many Masonic elements into his own organization.

Weishaupt's Illuminati attracted many distinguished European figures, such as Goethe and Franz Anton Mesmer; nevertheless, their politics were considered dangerous by the Bavarian government, and the order was suppressed, along with all other secret orders, including Masonry, in the 1780s.

This was far from being the end of Illuminism, however, for the Order was revived in Dresden in 1880 by Leopold Engel, and subsequently taken over in 1885 by Dr. Karl Kellner, who renamed it the *Ordo Templi Orientis* (Order of the Temple of the Orientals), or O.˙.T.˙.O. The O.˙.T.˙.O still exists today, although it split into two organizations after Kellner's death in 1947, one of which is based in England and the other in the United States.

As already mentioned, the American writer Robert Anton Wilson used Weishaupt's Illuminati in *Illuminatus!* the trilogy of novels he coauthored with Robert Shea. One of the most fascinating and entertaining pieces of conspiracy fiction ever written, *Illuminatus!* has also resulted in many claims that the Order still exists, and secretly controls the Earth. Among many other conspiracy theorists, Milton William **Cooper** and Commander X have written a great deal about the true nature of the Illuminati, claiming that the sect was originally an extraterrestrial group who arrived on Earth millions of years ago, and became allied with the Serpent Race. According to Commander X, "the Illuminati are indistinguishable from modern humans, and so are able to pass unnoticed among humanity, believing that it is their 'birthright' to enjoy pleasures and riches that mere mortals cannot possibly be allowed to benefit from." The ever-entertaining Commander continues:

They control the drug trade, allow the free flow of nuclear weapons to underdeveloped countries, put criminal types in power on local, state and federal levels, and basically control the media—permitting only the news they want to be made public. Thus we hear very little of a serious nature about UFOs, alternative energy sources, cures for cancer or AIDS, etc. In addition, we are grossly mislead about a whole barrage of subjects that could be used to turn the tide of human discomfort in our favor. (Commander X [1994], p. 23)

IMAGINARY ABDUCTEES

People who are the subjects of experiments to determine the nature and veracity of alien **abductions**. The best known of these experiments were conducted by Alvin Lawson in California in 1977, in which he gave a brief outline of a hypothetical abduction to a group of people who had not been abducted and had little prior knowledge of the UFO phenomenon. He then performed **hypnotic regression** on them and asked them to fill in the details of what had "happened" to them. Under hypnosis, the subjects provided a large amount of information that had not been divulged to them, but which nevertheless corresponded strikingly to the information given by "genuine" abductees.

Lawson's experiments were criticized by some researchers, who stated that there must have been very few people at that time and in that place who had no significant knowledge of UFOs and aliens. However, as British ufologist John Spencer points out, this statement must also apply to those who claim to have really been abducted. "The study may therefore indicate that while the experience is genuine, detailed recall may be flawed and based on culture and background beliefs." (Spencer [1991], p. 200)

Although skeptics have repeatedly pointed to the imaginary abductee experiments as providing strong evidence that all such experiences are either imagined by sincere individuals or invented by outright hoaxers, there remains an intriguing difference between "true" and "imaginary" abductees: the former invariably display heightened emotions (including blind panic) while under hypnotic regression, while the latter describe their invented experiences with the utmost calm, as if they are perfectly well aware that they are relating a fiction. However, as John Spencer notes, all this really means is that those claiming genuine abductions are genuinely frightened of what they *believe* to have happened, and thus the presence of fear cannot be used as a foolproof indicator of the veracity of an abduction account.

IMJÄRVI, FINLAND

Site of an encounter on January 7, 1970 with a UFO and a short, pixielike being. At 4:45 P.M. two men, Esko Viljo and Aarno Heinonen, were skiing when they heard a buzzing sound. Looking up, they watched the arrival of a bright light, which then transformed itself into a red cloud. The cloud descended toward the ground, whereupon Viljo and Heinonen saw that it contained a metallic, disk-shaped object. As the buzzing sound increased in intensity, the cloud disappeared, and the men could see the craft clearly for the first time. It was about nine feet in diameter, with three hemispheres and a short tube extending from the underside. When the craft had come to within about 10 feet of the ground, a beam of light was projected directly down from the central tube. Heinonen then felt as if someone were pulling him backward whereupon he retreated a little way. At that point, a figure appeared inside the beam of light.

The entity was about three feet tall, thin, and with a pronounced hooked nose, small eyes and ears, and pale skin. It wore light green coveralls, dark green boots and white gloves. It also wore a shiny conical helmet. The little creature was holding a small black box with a circular opening, through which a yellow light could be seen pulsing.

The ufonaut then pointed the box at Heinonen, and instantly the red mist seen earlier returned, accompanied by sparks of red, green and purple light. Although they were struck several times by these sparks, neither Viljo nor Heinonen felt anything.

Presently, the red mist cleared, the light beam and the entity withdrew into the craft, and it departed, leaving Heinonen feeling as if his right side had been anesthetized. This caused him considerable difficulty in walking, and so Viljo helped him back to the cottage owned by Heinonen's parents.

For the next few months, Heinonen felt extremely ill, suffering from headaches, vomiting, loss of memory and breathing difficulties. His urine turned the color of black coffee. Viljo had similar problems, including a red swelling on his face and pains in his eyes. The two men were examined by a doctor, who concluded that they were suffering from a combination of radiation exposure and shock. Later, two independent witnesses were located by a reporter, who claimed to have seen strange lights in the area on the day of the encounter.

Six months after the encounter, Viljo and Heinonen went back to the site with a Swedish journalist, a photographer and an interpreter. All five people suffered red swellings on their hands during the visit.

In the years that followed, Aarno Heinonen reported many encounters with UFOs and alien beings, his descriptions of which were highly reminiscent of the claims of the American **contactees** of the 1950s and 1960s.

IMPLANTS

One of the most intriguing (and potentially verifiable) aspects of alien abduction is the frequent insertion of small devices in the bodies of abductees. Usually, they are inserted into the head, either through the nasal cavity (after which the abductee will experience uncharacteristic nosebleeds) or through the ear, and into the brain. Occasionally, they are inserted into other parts of the body. In some cases, CAT scans have revealed these devices as tiny, bright areas within the brain, which doctors sometimes refer to as "anomalous bright objects." It has been speculated that such implants are used to monitor both the physiological processes in the abductee and his or her movements (in much the same way that human zoologists track the movements of animals in the wild).

According to Harvard psychiatrist John E. Mack:

These so-called implants may be felt as small nodules below the skin, and in several cases tiny objects have been recovered and analyzed biochemically and electromicroscopically. MIT physicist David Pritchard, who has also been analyzing an implant that came out of a man's penis, has written about the criteria for examining and determining the nature of such objects . . . I have myself studied a $\frac{1}{2}$- to $\frac{3}{4}$-inch thin, wiry object that was given to me by one of my clients, a twenty-four-year-old woman, after it came out of her nose following an abduction experience. Elemental analysis and electronic microscopic photography revealed an interestingly twisted fiber consisting of carbon, silicon, oxygen, no nitrogen, and traces of other elements. A carbon isotopic analysis was not remarkable. A nuclear biologist colleague said the "specimen" was not a naturally occurring biological subject but could be a manufactured fiber of some sort. It seemed difficult to know how to proceed further. (Mack [1994], p. 42)

Mack goes on to state that there is no evidence that any recovered implants are composed of rare elements or of common ones combined in unusual ways; nor would it be easy to come to any positive conclusions regarding the nature of an unknown material without having more information on its origin. "Under the best of circumstances it would be difficult to prove, for example, that a substance was not of terrestrial or even human biological origin." (Ibid., p. 42)

Although their composition seems to be rather mundane, holding little hope for a conclusive physical proof of alien origin, the behavior of implants once inside the body is quite interesting. A doctor in Santa Barbara, California, named Roger Leir, has retrieved several unusual objects from patients. He discovered them to be metallic fragments surrounded by a "membrane" that apparently prevents rejection by the body. Although the body will produce similar membranes around foreign objects that have intruded into it, there will always be an inflammatory reaction in the soft tissue around the intrusion. Dr. Leir's patients displayed no such inflammation. Analysis of the membrane revealed its composition as being of protein coagulum (a protein derived from blood), hemosiderin (an oxygen-carrying substance similar to hemoglobin) and keratin (the tough, protective substance that forms the main constituent of skin, hair and nails). According to Dr. Leir, the membrane he discovered in the bodies of his patients could go a long way toward solving the problems of tissue rejection in transplants, if the method of its construction could be determined.

Of course, certain problems do remain with the study of implants. Not only is it accepted, even by abduction proponents, that they are composed of mundane materials, but also very small objects and fibers can become lodged just beneath the surface of the skin, their presence betrayed only by a slight lump or nodule. In addition, many abductees have claimed that, following the revealing of an implant on an X ray or CAT scan, they have been re-abducted and the implant removed before it can be excised by surgeons. It has been suggested that this is further evidence that the aliens are real, and that they do not want us to secure any concrete evidence of their presence. If that is the case, however, why have they allowed any implants to be recovered? Is this just one more example of their apparent incompetence (the propensity of their spacecraft to fall out of the sky being another)?

In view of the nature of UFO and alien encounters in general, it seems unlikely that conclusive proof of their reality will come in the form of recovered implants. As John Mack says, "it may be wrong to expect that a phenomenon whose very nature is subtle, and one of whose purposes may be to stretch and expand our ways of knowing beyond the purely materialist approaches of Western science, will yield its secrets to an epistemology or methodology that operates at a lower level of consciousness . . .

(See also **Sims**, **Derrel**)

INSECTOIDS (ALIENS)

Although many abductees have described the near-ubiquitous **Grays** as being like insects (with their large eyes, quick, efficient movements and hivelike behavior), some people have described encounters with creatures that appeared quite literally to be insects. One such encounter took place on a Friday evening in either 1973 or 1974, when a University of Baltimore law student named Mike Shea was on his way to a bar in Olney to meet a friend. Shea was supposed to be there by 7:00 P.M., and was making good time.

He was about 15 miles from Baltimore, when he glanced through his car window to the left, and saw a beam of light bathing a barn 150 feet from the road.

The beam was coming from a large object hovering silently above, around which a bank of red and yellow lights flickered on and off.

Presently, the beam of light switched off, and as he continued on his way, Shea suddenly had the feeling that he was being followed. When he realized that the UFO was flying above him, he became frightened, his fear made worse by a feeling of an electric current running down his back. However, his fear suddenly left him, and he found himself approaching Olney. Shea could not find his friend at the bar, and then realized that it was 9:00 P.M.—two hours later than he had thought.

Shea went on to become a lawyer in Washington, but the memory of that night, and the fear he had felt just before the period of **missing time**, continued to trouble him. Ten years after the event, he contacted the abduction researcher Budd **Hopkins,** who hypnotically regressed him in an effort to discover what had happened. Shea remembered being terrified of the hovering object, so much so that he could not bring himself to look at it. He then remembered seeing four figures standing by the roadside.

He described them as being dressed in a black armor; their heads were also black, and they had large eyes. The creatures had six bowed legs and a carapace on their backs, making them look like nothing so much as grasshoppers. At that point, Shea unaccountably brought his car to a halt and climbed out. He could now see two UFOs: the large one he had seen earlier hovering above, and a smaller one on the ground. Shea then recalled being taken into one of the craft and undergoing a physical examination, during which various samples were taken from his body.

In examining cases such as this, proponents of the **extraterrestrial hypothesis** have reached something of an impasse, brought about by the controversial nature of reports of nonhumanoid entities associated with UFOs. Indeed, it has been suggested by some that the more outlandish reports (such as Mike Shea's) be dismissed, for no other reason than that they conflict with the "standard" alien bodily configuration (i.e., the Gray). This is unfortunate, since, if we are being visited by one or more extraterrestrial civilizations, we should not be surprised if they appear strikingly different from us (a virtual certainty if their home planet is in any way different from Earth); and the dismissal of such data can only do a disservice to the extraterrestrialists' cause.

INTEGRATRON

An alien-designed electrical rejuvenation machine, partially built by UFO **contactee** George Van Tassel, but never completed. After his encounter on August 24, 1953, with a spaceman named Solganda, Van Tassel began to receive much information from the **Space Brothers** via their ESP-based "omni-beam." Included with all the usual material concerning cosmic philosophy and advice for saving Earth, Van Tassel received plans for the Integratron, the purpose of which was to reverse ageing in the elderly and prevent it in the young.

Over the next five years, Van Tassel threw himself into the construction project with the utmost enthusiasm, working hard to raise the funds necessary for its completion. He claimed to his many followers that, once operational, the machine would be able to rejuvenate up to 10,000 people per day. (Interestingly, and perhaps conveniently, he added that the bodies of his older devotees would not alter in outward appearance, but their cells would be regenerated.)

By 1959 the Integratron had begun to take shape in quite an impressive way. The outer structure was a four-story-high dome 55 feet in diameter, gleaming pure white in the fierce heat of the desert near Giant Rock, California. It was constructed primarily of wood, without the aid of nails or screws. While he was working on the Integratron, Van Tassel made the marvelous discovery that the structure was also a time machine, capable of displaying images from other eras in its interior.

For the next 25 years, Van Tassel worked on his wondrous device, appealing for more funds whenever he ran out of money, which happened often. However, the Integratron had still to be completed when he died of a heart attack in 1978. The following year, Van Tassel's wife, Dorris, experienced a financial crisis and was forced to sell the land around Giant Rock to a real estate developer from San Diego. When the developer announced his intention to turn the Integratron into a disco, Van Tassel's indignant followers raised enough money to buy back the land in 1981. The Integratron remains unfinished and, as British anomalies researchers Janet and Colin Bord muse, is perhaps best seen as a "fitting monument to all the contactees, whose faith in the Space Brothers has never quite been justified."

INTERIORS OF UFOs

One of the most intriguing questions in the field of UFO/alien encounters has to be: what is it like inside a UFO? While the **contactees** enthused incessantly about being given guided tours of alien spacecraft, most victims of modern alien **abductions** have slightly less to say about conditions throughout the UFO as a whole. Part of the reason for this is, presumably, the purpose behind their being abducted in the first place: unlike the contactees, who almost invariably claimed friendly encounters, the abductees are taken into UFOs against their will and are subjected to various (usually unpleasant) medical procedures, in the manner of laboratory animals. It is therefore rather unlikely that the **Grays** will be too anxious to show off their pride and joy, when there is work to be done.

However, abduction researchers, notably David M. **Jacobs**, have gathered a certain amount of information on UFO interiors. Due to the efficient, businesslike behavior of the aliens, abductees are almost invariably only allowed to see those parts of the ship in which the various procedures take place (and are very rarely allowed to see such things as engine rooms, flight decks, etc.).

According to Jacobs, an abductee can enter a UFO one of two ways: either up a retractable stairway and in through a hatch if the craft is on the ground; or up through a beam of (usually) blue light and into the underside if the UFO is hovering in the air. (Some have displayed what is known as "doorway amnesia"; in other words, they are aware of a doorway or entrance hatch, but cannot remember actually going through it.) Once inside, they find themselves in a corridor, which apparently curves around the perimeter of the craft. They are then led down another corridor, which leads deeper into the interior, to one or more of the examination rooms. These are also described as being circular, with domed ceilings and a diffuse light, which has no clearly defined source. Throughout the ship, the walls are white or gray, and everything is kept exceptionally clean.

These rooms contain a great deal of medical equipment, either attached to the walls or ceiling, in various drawers, or on wheeled trolleys. The centerpiece of the examination room is the table on which the abductee is compelled to lie. This table is frequently described as resting on a pedestal, which rises smoothly from the floor, as if everything is constructed from a single piece of metal (or whatever it is that the aliens use to build their ships). From its sides extend armlike appendages, containing lights and other equipment.

Other rooms described are also circular, and are lined with benches, which, like the examination table, extend smoothly from the fabric of the bulkhead. Some abductees have recalled seeing other humans sitting here, as if waiting for their turn on the table. Elsewhere in the UFO is a room sometimes described as the "incubatorium," containing numerous glass vessels in which human/alien **hybrids** float in a clear liquid. From here, female abductees are often taken into a kind of visiting room, in which they are encouraged to interact closely with sickly-looking hybrid infants and older children.

Although, as mentioned above, it is a very rare occurrence, abductees will sometimes describe rooms not directly associated with the purpose behind their abduction. The flight decks of the UFOs are invariably described as being extremely simple, with very few of the trappings of **science fiction**, containing no more than a single control console and a seat.

There is an interesting absence of what might be called "creature comforts," such as personal accommodations or living quarters. Likewise, aliens are never seen eating or drinking, or performing any other recreational activities that might be considered natural for a crew on active duty. However, as Jacobs points out, this does not necessarily mean that such things do not happen on board UFOs, it merely indicates that abductees have not seen them.

INTERPLANETARY PARLIAMENT
(See **King, George**)

INTERPLANETARY PHENOMENON UNIT (IPU)

A legendary military unit, which was part of the Scientific and Technical Branch, Counterintelligence Directorate, Department of the Army. According to some researchers (particularly those specializing in UFO **crash-retrievals**), the IPU was (and perhaps still is) a quick-response team operating out of Camp Hale, Colorado, and was responsible for securing the area around UFO crash sites, collecting the debris and delivering it to various secret locations.

The existence of this unit, with its extremely provocative name, has tantalized UFO researchers for some time. On May 25, 1997, the Computer UFO Network (CUFON) posted a page on the Internet, detailing its attempts to secure information on the IPU, through the U.S. **Freedom of Information Act**. According to CUFON member Jim Klotz, the group filed a request for documents relating to the IPU in 1992. This resulted in more than 40 items of correspondence, which "produced absolutely no records of the IPU," in spite of an official admittance that the unit did indeed exist. Klotz describes how CUFON contacted the U.S. Army Intelligence and Security Command (INSCOM), IACSF-FI (Intelligence Activity, Central Security Facility—Freedom of Information) at Fort George G. Meade, Maryland, requesting "copies of all records pertaining to the Interplanetary Phenomenon Unit (IPU) of the Scientific and Technical Branch, Counterintelligence Directorate, Department of the Army."

The response, quoted on the CUFON website, was as follows:

Please be advised that the Interplanetary Phenomenon Unit of the Scientific and Technical Branch, Counter Intelligence Directorate, Department of the Army, was disestablished during the late 1950's and never reactivated. All records pertaining to this unit were surrendered to the U. S. Air Force Office of Special Investigations in conjunction with operation "Bluebook."

We regret that we are unable to be of more assistance concerning this matter.

Another CUFON request met with this response:

Records of the Interplanetary Phenomenon Unit no longer are maintained by the Department of the Army. Once surrendered, the records become the property of the gaining office (U. S. Air Force Office of Special Investigations) and their disposition would not be monitored by the army. Consequently, the information you seek is not available through this office.

Further responses from U.S. Army INSCOM alerted the CUFON researchers that certain phrases they had used might have been standardized, a suspicion that was later borne out, after an appeal to the secretary of the army. In 1993, CUFON received copies of two pages of the U.S. Army Intelligence and Security Command's FOI/PA SOP (Freedom of Information/Privacy Act Standard Operating Procedure document), which included the following rather interesting instructions for dealing with certain requests for information:

23. Unidentified Flying Objects
(UFOs)/Interplanetary Phenomenon Unit
(IPU)/Bluebook.
a. Periodically this office will receive requests concerning an activity described as the "Interplanetary Phenomenon Unit" and for information on UFOs.
b. When replying to requests for UFO records, our reply should be as follows: "This is in response to your letter of——under the Freedom of Information Act, 5USC 552, requesting information concerning Army Intelligence records relating to UFO encounter reports.
"To determine the existence of Army Intelligence investigative records responsive to your request, we have conducted an indepth check of the files and indices maintained by this office.
"We regret to inform you that there is no record concerning UFOs within this office and the Department of the Army."

c. If asked about the IPU, the reply is as follows:
"Please be advised that the Interplanetary Phenomenon Unit of the Scientific and Technical Branch, Counterintelligence Directorate, Department of the Army was disestablished during the late 1950's and never reactivated. All records pertaining to this unit were surrendered to the U. S. Air Force Office of Special Investigations in conjunction with operation 'Bluebook.'
"There is no record system maintained within the Department of the Army to catalog, process, index or otherwise evaluate UFO information. We regret that we are unable to be of more assistance concerning this matter."
d. If there is a follow-on request concerning the IPU, our reply should be as follows:
"As stated in our letter of ——, records of Interplanetary Phenomenon Unit no longer are maintained by the Department of the Army. Once surrendered, the reports become the property of the gaining office (U. S. Air Force, Office of Special Investigations) and their disposition would not be monitored by the Army. Consequently, the information you seek is not available through this office."
e. If we are questioned further concerning this unit, our reply should be as follows:
"As stated in our previous letters of —— and——, the Department of the Army is no longer in possession of the records you seek and we cannot locate any information on the unit. Unfortunately, for that reason alone, we are simply unable to answer your questions."

The CUFON investigators realized that they had indeed been receiving "canned responses," taken from the SOP document, "without any supporting documentation, and, we suspect, without valid records searches being made." According to Jim Klotz:

FOIA requests to the Air Force Office of Special Investigations (AFOSI), to which the Army IPU records were supposedly "surrendered," resulted in denials that AFOSI was maintaining any IPU records or had any record of the files transfer. Finally, after several queries, AFOSI responded that the material had been destroyed, but could not, or would not produce any authority for such a statement.

Klotz believes that the SOP document and its use in the responses CUFON received with regard to the Interplanetary Phenomenon Unit, is evidence of "active management of UFO information." It is also further evidence that secrets can be kept over long periods of time, despite the assertions of debunkers, who claim that any significant government knowledge of UFOs (with its potentially shattering implications for humanity) would have leaked out long ago.

INTRUDERS (TV MINISERIES)

Made in 1992, directed by Dan Curtis and starring Richard Crenna, Mare Winningham, Susan Blakely, Ben Vereen, Steven Berkoff and Daphne Ashbrook. A rather loose adaptation of Budd **Hopkins**'s second book *Intruders: The Incredible Visitations at Copley Woods* (1987). A housewife in Nebraska and an art gallery owner in California suffer periods of **missing time** and undergo **hypnotic regression** by an initially skeptical psychiatrist, who gradually becomes convinced of the authenticity of alien abduction.

Despite its tenuous relationship to the original book, this is one of the most intelligent and sympathetic portrayals of alien encounters yet made. The acting is uniformly excellent (the always-

entertaining Steven Berkoff appears as a manic amalgamation of Hopkins, David **Jacobs** and John **Mack**) and the special effects subtle and convincing. Interestingly (and rather amusingly), while the series was in production, there was some concern among its makers and some ufologists that a nationwide, televised portrayal of alien abduction might result in thousands of people suddenly retrieving repressed memories of being taken by aliens. In the event, this did not happen.

INVADERS, THE (TV SHOW)

American science-fiction series, which ran for 43 episodes from 1967 to 1968. It starred Roy Thinnes as an architect named David Vincent who witnesses the landing of a flying saucer and subsequently discovers that a secret invasion of Earth is under way. The invaders of the title are highly intelligent amorphous **blobs**, which have taken on human form, so that they may pass unnoticed in our world. Their only imperfection, a ridiculously clumsy plot device enabling the hero to recognize them, is a little finger that cannot be bent. In addition, the aliens' bodies are instantly incinerated when they are killed, thus leaving no evidence of their existence.

Although it is difficult to see how this basic scenario could have held viewers' interest for much longer than its 43-episode run, *The Invaders* did make amusing use of some of the elements of UFO conspiracy theory, such as the secret presence of an alien civilization, the abduction and murder of human beings and a paranoid assertion, based on unverifiable information, that Earth is under threat from an inimical alien intelligence. A two-part miniseries, based loosely on the original, was aired in 1995.

INVADERS FROM MARS (FILM)

Made in 1953 and directed by William Cameron Menzies. A young American boy witnesses the arrival of a flying saucer near his home. The craft buries itself under a sandpit, which the Martians use as a headquarters for their invasion plans.

This film, perhaps more than any other, puts to rest the repeated assertions by **abductions** researchers that there is no provenance in **science fiction** for the elements repeatedly found in accounts of alien encounters. For instance, in one memorable scene, one of the female characters is abducted by the Martians, who place her on an operating table. A long, metal probe is then inserted into the back of her head, and she is implanted with a small mind-controlling device. In addition, while the Martians do not correspond physically to the **Grays** in abduction accounts, they nevertheless display the same hive mentality, acting as "soldiers" under the command of a diminutive being with a large head.

Interestingly, the confusion between dream and reality inherent in abduction accounts (see **hallucinations**) is also provenanced at the end of the film. Just as all seems lost, the boy wakes up to discover that the Martian invasion has been no more than a nightmare; however, just as he is about to relax, he sees a flying saucer coming in to land in exactly the same place as in his dream!

INVISIBLE COLLEGE

An unofficial group of professional scientists whose aim is to conduct serious research into the true nature of the UFO phenomenon, and especially to establish whether it has an intelligent origin. The term was originally used in the early 17th century. In an article entitled "The UFO Mystery." published in the *FBI Bulletin* (Vol. 44, no. 2, February 1975), Dr. J. Allen **Hynek** wrote:

Way back in the "dark ages" of science, when scientists themselves were suspected of being in league with the Devil, they had to work privately. They often met clandestinely to exchange views and the results of their various experiments. For this reason, they called themselves the Invisible College. And it remained invisible until the scientists of that day gained respectability when the Royal Society was chartered by Charles II in the early 1600s.

Although modern punishments for departing from conventional wisdom are not quite as severe as those of four centuries ago, a scientist declaring him- or herself in favor of UFO research can expect a certain amount of damage to be done to their reputations— not to mention their funding. For this tragic and rather disgraceful reason, scientists with an interest in the phenomenon have decided to follow it in strict privacy, away from the scrutiny of other scientists who feel it necessary to "destroy, distort, or simply ignore the very facts they are supposed to investigate" (Vallée [1975], p. 15).

JACOBS, DAVID MICHAEL

American **abductions** researcher, and the first academic to attempt a serious study of the experience. His longtime interest in ufology began in 1966, when he read an article in the April issue of *Life* magazine about a UFO "flap" that was occurring at the time. Jacobs's interest became deeper when he read John G. Fuller's book *The Interrupted Journey*, which detailed the famous **Hill** abduction. Although he had his doubts about the likelihood that the Hills really had encountered aliens, Jacobs nevertheless felt that the subject deserved serious study, and in 1973 he completed his Ph.D. thesis on the subject, which was published in revised form in 1975 as *The UFO Controversy in America*.

Jacobs joined the History Department at Temple University in Philadelphia, Pennsylvania, and now teaches the only university-level course on the UFO phenomenon. In 1982 he met Budd **Hopkins** and

read his groundbreaking book *Missing Time,* and was impressed by the similarities in detail between the abduction accounts Hopkins investigated. He nevertheless felt some confusion, since he was well aware of the rich provenance of alien encounters (meetings with angels and demons, contact with the spirit world, memories of past lives and so on); he therefore decided to begin investigating abductions himself.

The results of this research were published in the book *Secret Life: Firsthand Accounts of UFO Abductions* in 1992. Based on data from approximately 300 regressions and interviews with 60 abductees, the book describes a number of phases through which an abduction experience commonly moves.

Although Jacobs initially stated his belief in the possibility of a psychological explanation for abductions, he has subsequently become a leading proponent of the **extraterrestrial hypothesis**, a view which he consolidated in 1998 with the publication of his third book, *The Threat*. In this book he paints a rather gloomy picture of humanity's future, in which Earth will be dominated by aliens, whose program of creating alien/human **hybrids** is the prelude to their colonization of our planet.

J. ALLEN HYNEK CENTER FOR UFO STUDIES

(See **Center for UFO Studies**)

JANAP (JOINT ARMY/NAVY/AIR FORCE PUBLICATION) 146

A directive issued by the Joint Chiefs of Staff in December 1953, which set down the correct procedures for reporting information considered by the observer to require "very urgent defensive and/or investigative action." This information pertained to intelligence sightings, including hostile or unidentified aircraft, missiles, UFOs, submarines, ships and unidentified personnel on the ground. The directive forbade both military personnel and civil airline pilots from discussing such sightings with the media or the general public, under penalty of a prison term of one to 10 years and/or a fine of $10,000.

Many ufologists have pointed to JANAP 146 as evidence of the U.S. government's desire to suppress UFO-related information (which may have included knowledge of the interplanetary nature of the phenomenon). However, UFO skeptic have rightly pointed out that reports of activities that might have national security implications are protected by the U.S. Communications Act of 1934, and the U.S. Espionage Act, which prevent them from being discussed publicly. In his criticism of the stance taken by Major Donald E. **Keyhoe** and others in the 1950s, aviation historian Curtis Peebles states that: "Believers used these penalties [imprisonment and/or fines] to put a more sinister meaning on JANAP 146. The provisions for reports of airplanes, missiles, submarines, ships, and ground parties were ignored. UFOs were depicted as its only interest." (Peebles [1995], p. 112) However, contemporary researchers have refined this position, pointing to the fact that UFOs occupy a category *entirely separate* from the other, more mundane sightings, implying government acceptance of the fact that some UFOs, while being of vital defense interest, are not man-made machines.

JANOS PEOPLE

Alien race supposedly from the doomed planet Janos, who came to Earth in a colossal spacecraft carrying the remnants of their civilization, and abducted a British family in June 1978.

During a trip to Gloucester, the family saw a UFO and experienced an hour of **missing time**. Under **hypnotic regression**, they recalled being taken from their car into the UFO by tall, human-looking aliens, who conducted physical examinations of the family, before telling them that their home planet had been destroyed by its moon, and that they were looking for a new place to live. In common with many other abduction accounts, the family said that they had been asked to drink a fluid that would make them forget the encounter, a motif familiar in **folklore**, and which has been commented upon by those who favor the **psychosocial hypothesis** for nonhuman encounters.

The current whereabouts of the aliens are unknown, since their open letter to the people of Earth (published in Frank Johnson's 1980 book *The Janos People*) unfortunately went unheeded.

JASON SOCIETY

An elite group of scientists, which plays a central role in the more paranoid UFO **conspiracy theories**, especially those presented by Milton William **Cooper** and John **Lear**. In 1955 the Eisenhower government in the United States realized that the treaty they had forged with an alien race (in which the aliens would be allowed to abduct humans in exchange for items of their technology) had been broken. In Cooper's version of this legend, the aliens came from a dying planet orbiting the star Betelgeuse, and had arrived in our Solar System in 1953. The secret treaty, which had been signed at Edwards Air Force Base in California the following year, included an exchange program in which 16 aliens would stay on Earth, while the same number of humans would travel to the aliens' planet, in order to exchange knowledge of each other's culture. However, the aliens quickly violated the treaty by murdering numerous humans, killing livestock (see **cattle mutilations**) and using the tissues to repair their damaged genetic stock.

According to Cooper, the aliens were also manipulating human society through occultism and black magic and (perhaps even worse) conspiring with the Soviet Union. In an attempt to regain control of the situation, President Eisenhower ordered the formation of an ultrasecret study group, the Jason Society, composed of 35 members of the Council on Foreign Relations, to examine every aspect of the alien situation, and to formulate adequate responses to it.

Over the course of several meetings held at the Quantico Marine Base, the Jason Society decided that the alien presence posed such a threat to Earth's established political, economic, social and religious orders that it had to be kept absolutely secret, and that even incoming presidents should be vetted by the society, which would decide whether they should be told of the real situation. In addition, the society suggested that the Soviet Union be approached and an alliance forged against the aliens (making the entire cold war, in effect, a colossal smoke screen). Securing funding for their ultrasecret operations was obviously a serious problem, which they overcame by cornering the multibillion-dollar international drugs market.

The Jason Society also infiltrated the Vatican and learned the secret of the **Fatima** prophecy, which had been jealously guarded by the Catholic Church since 1917. According to the prophecy, in 1992 a child would unite the world under a false religion. Three years later, he would be revealed as the Antichrist, which would lead to World War III and nuclear destruction. In 2011, Christ would return and the Millennium would commence. The Jason Society took this information to the aliens, who confirmed that it was true, since they had already visited the future in time machines, and had seen it for themselves. When the U.S./Soviet alliance developed their own method of time travel, they also saw that the Fatima prophecy had been accurate.

According to Cooper, the Jason Society met again in 1957 and formulated three alternatives to deal with the double problem of nuclear destruction and environmental collapse (see **conspiracy theories**). The third alternative was for the Earth's elites to colonize the Moon and Mars. This was swiftly put into effect, with the aid of alien space technology and chemically subdued human slave labor.

JERSEY DEVIL

A hideous, demonic entity, which terrorized eastern Pennsylvania and southern New Jersey in 1909. Whether or not such a creature ever existed is open to debate; however, the hysteria it provoked in some 30 towns was real enough, and demonstrates how an initial sighting of a (perhaps) genuine anomaly can generate a climate of extreme fear in which many subsequent sightings are reported by otherwise sane, well-balanced and trustworthy people.

The origin of the Jersey Devil legend can be traced back to Leeds Point, New Jersey, where, in 1735, a Mrs. Leeds became pregnant for the 13th time. This inauspicious number prompted her to say that the child might well turn out to be a devil. She was right. Her offspring was a monstrosity with a horse's head, bat's wings, cloven hooves and a tail. It is said to have flown away into the forests of southern New Jersey. Since then, it has made its loathsome presence known by crying out eerily in the night, leaving footprints and occasionally killing livestock.

The Jersey Devil would undoubtedly have become a minor footnote in the annals of American folklore, were it not for the sightings of 1909, when more than a 100 people claimed to have seen the thing. At 2:00 A.M. on January 17, 1909, a postmaster named E. W. Minister of Bristol, Pennsylvania, saw a glowing, ram-headed creature flying over the Delaware River. Two other people saw the creature, one of them a police officer who fired at it.

Over the next few days, a weird flying entity was sighted by many more people, and strange tracks were found in the snow. However, descriptions of the "Devil" varied considerably, implying that hysteria had taken hold over the New Jersey and Pennsylvania communities. Some people described a creature with a ram's head, while others saw a horse's head, while still others reported a creature that breathed fire and had an alligator's skin. In Salem, New Jersey, a police officer encountered a "devil bird" with one foot resembling a horse's and the other a mule's. Then, in Moorestown, Pennsylvania, a fisherman saw a three-foot-high creature with a dog's face.

The last sighting took place on February 24, 1909, when Salem County farmer Leslie Garrison saw a six-foot-long bird with human feet fly past. Soon after, the Arch Street Museum in Philadelphia held an exhibition, which included a "genuine" Jersey Devil that had been captured alive. Unfortunately (and perhaps unsurprisingly), it turned out to be a hoax: a stuffed kangaroo had been painted with bright green stripes, and a pair of fake wings attached to its shoulders. The real Jersey Devil, if the legend is to be believed, is still out there, somewhere.

(See also **flying humanoids** and **giant birds**)

JESSUP, MORRIS K.
(See **Philadelphia Experiment**)

JOHANNIS, PROFESSOR RAPUZZI

Writer, artist and geologist who experienced one of the earliest recorded encounters with nonhuman entities. At 9:00 A.M. on August 14, 1947, Johannis, a keen hiker, was climbing up a valley near Mount Carnico del Col Gentile near the town of Villa Santina, to the north of Venice, Italy.

Presently, Johannis became aware of a reddish object on the ground. He put on his spectacles and saw that it was actually a metallic, lens-shaped machine about 30 feet wide. Johannis was unaware of the UFO phenomenon (as were most people at that time), and assumed it must be some kind of secret aircraft, perhaps Russian. The professor, who was alone in the valley, glanced around, hoping that there might be some other people nearby who might corroborate his sighting. He was relieved when he spotted two boys standing at the edge of a nearby wood, and he shouted at them to come and have a look at the curious machine.

He began to walk toward them, but stopped in his tracks when he realized that they were not boys, but strange humanoid creatures, about three feet tall. The two little entities began gingerly to move toward the geologist, at which point he felt a strange weakness and light-headedness come over him, as if he were having a dream. This is a frequently reported element in **close encounters**, and British ufologist Jenny Randles has called it the **Oz Factor**.

As the entities approached, Johannis saw that they were dressed in tight-fitting blue suits. Their heads were disproportionately large and hairless, and they wore dark skullcaps. Their noses were long and their slitlike mouths opened and closed in the manner of a fish's gills. Their eyes were very large, and were dark purple in color. Their skins had a slight greenish tinge to them (this feature has led Jenny

Randles to speculate that this may have been the origin of the phrase "little green men," much despised by ufologists).

After some moments spent staring at each other, the professor decided to try to communicate with the creatures. In what he hoped was a friendly way, he raised his geologist's pick and shouted: "Who are you?" Unfortunately, the entities evidently took this to be a threatening gesture; one of them raised its claw-shaped hand to its belt, whereupon a flash of light hit Johannis on the arm, knocking him to the ground and momentarily robbing him of his senses. His pick was snatched away by some unseen force and landed about six feet away.

As the professor lay partially paralyzed on the stony ground, the beings walked over to the pick and carefully examined it, before returning to their craft and climbing aboard. The object then swiftly rose into the air, showering the valley floor with small stones, before it rapidly dwindled in size and disappeared.

It was not until several hours later that Johannis recovered enough strength to get up and make his way painfully to the village of Raveo. When his disheveled appearance prompted concerned questions from those at the inn where he was staying, the professor explained that he had fallen off a rock face.

JUNG, CARL GUSTAV

(See **collective unconscious**)

KAREETA

In 1946, there were numerous sightings in North America of an extremely large, winged object flying at high altitudes. A multiple-witness sighting occurred over San Diego, California, between 7:25 P.M. and 9:00 P.M. on October 9, while many people were out watching a meteor shower. Although UFO reports made during such events are considered by many to be potentially very unreliable (as are those made near large airports), the descriptions of the object in this case are intriguing. One group of witnesses said that it looked like an extremely long plane, with two reddish lights. It traveled across the face of the Moon at high speed. In his book *Flying Saucers on the Attack,* Harold T. Wilkins quotes a female witness as saying:

The strange object was certainly no airplane. The wings, which moved, were too wide for any bird. Indeed, they were rather like the wings of a butterfly. The whole object emitted a red glow. (Wilkins [1954], p. 39)

Wilkins continues:

Another woman and a man say the object looked like a bat, hooked, weird, and very large. One woman saw it from between two houses, and it took at least 80 seconds to cross that space; so that, at that time "it must have changed speed from very fast to slow." Two other witnesses who saw the same weird object from different parts of South California, say it was stationary for some time. "Then it moved slowly, accelerated, and left a trail of luminosity behind it. At that time its motion was very slow." A woman, who is a professional astronomer, took a time exposure of the moon, and says that the film, when developed, showed a strange effect of smoke rings, or halations seen on films and plates, as if fire were coming out of the moon, or as if a passing object had left a vapor trail.

The sum total of the eye-witnesses' evidence is that this strange object, which had the appearance of a space ship, remained far overhead all night, considerably varied its rate of speed, and was alternately brilliantly illuminated and dark. There was also an occasional emission of a flash of light, or a luminous jet of gases. (Ibid., pp. 39–40)

Another witness, Mark Probert, was contacted by an unnamed psychic in California, who offered information—apparently acquired through **channeling**—about the UFO, and claimed that the bat-shaped object came from "some planet west of the moon"—a rather vague (not to mention scientifically illiterate) statement, since compass references are only applicable on the surfaces of planets, and cannot be used to locate points in outer space. Wilkins quotes Mark Probert as saying:

The strange machine is called the *Kareeta* . . . it is attracted at this time because the Earth is emitting a column of light which makes it easier of approach. The machine is powered by people possessing a very advanced knowledge of anti-gravity forces. It has 10,000 parts, a small but very powerful motor operating by electricity, and moving the wings, and an outer structure of light balsam wood, coated with an alloy. The people are non-aggressive and have been trying to contact the Earth for many years. They have very light bodies. They fear to land, but would be willing to meet a committee of scientists at an isolated spot, or on a mountain top. (Ibid., p. 42)

Wilkins wisely refrains from commenting on this rather suspect information. Indeed, the naïveté it demonstrates is quite breathtaking, especially the reference to the Kareeta having "10,000 parts." Also, the idea of an interplanetary spacecraft using antigravity propulsion, yet being made of "balsam wood," is, to put it mildly, ludicrous (see **Loka**). (Although it may be churlish to mention it, one cannot help but be reminded of the reported construction of the spacecraft claimed to have crashed near **Roswell**, New Mexico, in 1947.) Nevertheless, the notion of a colossal wooden spaceship plying the celestial oceans between worlds does have a certain Fortean charm!

KEEL, JOHN ALVA

New York-based journalist and paranormal investigator, who has become one of the most controversial and influential writers in the field, thanks to several classic books, among them *UFOs: Operation Trojan Horse* (1970) and *The **Mothman** Prophecies* (1975).

In the late 1960s, Keel secured a fairly lucrative book contract and spent several months in the Ohio River valley, investigating reports not only of UFOs but also of poltergeists, **Men in Black** and monstrous beings of various kinds. As a result of his research, he broke away from mainstream ufology, which largely accepted the **extraterrestrial hypothesis** as being the likeliest explanation for genuine UFO activity, and developed his theory of **ultraterrestrials**. These ultraterrestrials, Keel claimed, are malignant intelligences from another dimension of existence, who are able to enter our reality at will and pursue their favorite pastime—namely, subjecting humanity to terror and misery. To realize these sinister aims, the ultraterrestrials have used various disguises over the centuries—disguises which are conducive to the world view prevalent at the time, and that have included angels, demons, fairies and other beings of folklore, anomalous animals such as **Bigfoot** and sea monsters, and, in the 20th century, space travelers from other worlds.

Keel expounded his unorthodox views with considerable passion, and a not inconsiderable contempt both for scientific debunkers and ufologists who considered the phenomenon to be essentially scientific in nature. In this regard, as UFO historian Jerome Clark states, Keel must be considered more a demonologist than a ufologist; however, his influence in broadening the UFO debate to include its frequent transcendental aspects (which the extraterrestrialists tend to view with distaste) is undeniable.

Unlike the majority of researchers, Keel claimed to have had numerous paranormal and nonhuman contact experiences himself, particularly while investigating the Mothman encounters in Point Pleasant, West Virginia, in the late 1960s. For instance, he claimed many telephone contacts with a "Mr. Apol," an ultraterrestrial who was trapped in our "time frame," and who frequently could not tell the past from the future.

Keel also had much to say on the Men in Black, claiming that they, as ultraterrestrials, have been present throughout human history, and have frequently intervened to influence its course. They are the origin of the Grim Reaper figure and the widespread legends of vampires. According to Keel, a man in a dark cloak and hood gave Thomas Jefferson the design for the Great Seal of the United States (the eye-in-the-pyramid motif so beloved of conspiracy theorists). Indeed, Keel went so far as to equate the Men in Black with the minions of the King of the World, the legendary figure who resides in Earth's interior, and who controls the course of human history (see **Hollow Earth Theory**).

In spite of his eccentricities, Keel has contributed an enormous amount to the study of anomalous phenomena, and while he still belongs firmly at the outlandish fringes of ufology, his bizarre speculations have at least opened the minds of some to the possibility that UFOs and associated phenomena may represent a far more complex reality than is generally supposed. As Jerome Clark states:

Even his admirers were sometimes willing to acknowledge . . . that his conclusions outdistanced his evidence by some considerable margin, that his historical, psychological, and social analysis was amateurish, that many of the reports he cited were questionable, that the extreme kinds of experiential claims on which he was fixated were hardly characteristic of the UFO phenomenon as a whole, and that his speculations were laced with paranoia. Yet no one denied that as a teller of scary stories he could be wonderfully entertaining. (Clark [1998], p. 495)

(See also **psychosocial hypothesis**)

KELLY, KENTUCKY

Site of one of the most famous nonhuman encounters of the 1950s. Kelly is a tiny hamlet a few miles from the town of Hopkinsville, Kentucky, and was the home of the Sutton family. On the evening of August 21, 1955, the Suttons were entertaining a relative, Bill Taylor. At about seven o'clock, Taylor went outside to get some water from the Suttons' well, and saw a saucer-shaped object with a glowing, multicolored exhaust, descend into a nearby field. Taylor ran back into the house and excitedly told the others what he had seen. Not surprisingly, they had trouble believing him, and he was trying to convince them that he was not joking, when they were all alerted by the sound of a dog barking in the yard.

Elmer Sutton and Bill Taylor went to the kitchen window to see what was causing the commotion, and watched in astonishment as a three-foot-tall creature approached the house with its long, almost apelike arms raised in the air. The entity had a large, hairless head and huge, batlike ears. Its eyes were also large and situated on the sides of its head, and its mouth was a wide slit extending from ear to ear. More frightening still, the thing appeared to be self-luminous, and cast a weird silvery glow across the yard.

Presently, the creature was joined by several others, and the strange visitors began to wander around outside the house. At one point, they climbed a tree next to the house and dropped onto the roof. Now terrified, the people inside armed themselves with shotguns and fired at the creatures, hitting them several times; however, whenever a creature was struck, there was a metallic sound, and the entity would roll over and scurry away on all fours, apparently unharmed. When Bill Taylor attempted to leave the house, his hair was grabbed by one of the entities sitting on the roof.

As with the first creature, whenever the beings approached the house, they would raise their arms above their heads. Bud Ledwith, who worked at radio station WHOP in Hopkinsville and who later investigated the encounter, suggested that this may have been a friendly gesture, although the Sutton family were understandably in no mood to accept such overtures.

The encounter lasted for most of the night, with the creatures wandering around the yard, climbing trees and so on. Whenever they were struck by bullets, they would float gently to the ground, rather than jump. At no time did they attempt to enter the house. In the early hours of the morning, the Suttons decided they would have to make a run for it, and managed to get into their car. They then drove into Hopkinsville and reported what had happened to Deputy Sheriff George Batts, who drove out to the house with two Kentucky state policemen, but could find no trace of the creatures or the UFO in which they had apparently arrived.

Although the authorities could have been forgiven for assuming that the whole episode had been a hoax, Chief of Police Greenwell concluded that the Suttons and Bill Taylor had been genuinely frightened by something. No motive for a hoax was found, and Bud Ledwith quickly realized that the last thing the Suttons wanted was publicity.

Dr. J. Allen **Hynek** became marginally involved with the case when he inquired as to whether there had been a traveling circus in the area at the time of the encounter, from which some monkeys might have escaped. He did accept, however, that the Suttons claimed to have shot several of the creatures, and if that were true, then at least one body should have been found, but none were.

KEYHOE, MAJOR DONALD EDWARD

One of the most outspoken proponents of the **extraterrestrial hypothesis**, Donald Keyhoe was the originator not only of the idea that the U.S. Air Force was (and is) covering up its knowledge of the interplanetary origin of some UFOs but also of the idea that there are two factions within the military and intelligence communities: one which believes that information proving UFO reality should be gradually released to the general public, in preparation for a full disclosure at some future date; and another which believes that human society would collapse under the weight of such an announcement, which should therefore never be made.

Keyhoe was born on June 20, 1897, in Ottumwa, Iowa. He attended the Naval Academy Preparatory School in Annapolis, Maryland, and then the Naval Academy. He was commissioned as a lieutenant in the Marine Corps in 1919. His military career was interrupted by injury, but he returned to active duty in the Second World War, achieving the rank of major by the time he finally retired from the marines.

His involvement with the UFO phenomenon came about in 1949 as a result of a commission from the popular magazine *True* to write an article on flying saucers (Keyhoe was by that time a successful freelance writer). His research for the article, subsequently entitled "Flying Saucers Are Real," led him to conclude that they were indeed spacecraft from other planets, and that the air force knew this and was covering up the facts.

Keyhoe expanded his article into a book entitled *The Flying Saucers Are Real*, which was enormously popular, selling 500,000 copies in paperback. He not only originated the idea that the air force was covering up the facts about UFOs but also that the government was gradually releasing UFO-related information to the public, in preparation for the day when a full disclosure would be made, an idea which still has many supporters today, in spite of the fact that the long-awaited disclosure has yet to come. He also drew attention to the apparent correlation between the development of atomic weapons in 1945, and the upsurge in UFO sightings from 1947 onward, suggesting that this dangerous technology had forced the aliens to pay much closer attention to humanity. Keyhoe followed *The Flying Saucers Are Real* with *Flying Saucers from Outer Space* (1953), *The Flying Saucer Conspiracy* (1955), *Flying Saucers: Top Secret* (1960) and *Aliens from Space* (1973).

In January 1957, Keyhoe became director of the **National Investigations Committee on Aerial Phenomena (NICAP)**. Unfortunately, his directorship saw severe financial problems emerging for the organization, partly due to Keyhoe's lack of managerial experience, and partly due to a drop in membership (from 12,000 to 4,000) resulting from declining public interest in UFOs. In 1969, Keyhoe was asked by the Board of Governors to resign; he did so.

Keyhoe then retired to write his final book, *Aliens from Space*. In 1981 he was invited to join the Board of Directors of the **Mutual UFO Network (MUFON)**, but advancing years prevented him from contributing a great deal to the organization.

He died on November 29, 1988.

KING, GEORGE

Contactee who founded the **Aetherius Society** after a disembodied voice said to him: "Prepare yourself! You are to become the voice of the Interplanetary Parliament." The intention of the society was (and is) to pass on to humanity telepathically relayed wisdom from the "Great Ones," benign space intelligences based in our Solar System and living comfortably on every planet except Mercury, which is uninhabitable (King's one and only acknowledgment of current astronomical knowledge).

King has claimed to have had numerous adventures in outer space, including a battle with a malevolent dwarf armed with a ray gun on Mars. During these astonishing escapades, he learned the secret history of the Solar System, which he published in books such as *You Are Responsible* (1961), *The Nine Freedoms* (1963) and *Life on the Planets* (1966). According to the Great Ones, humanity's original home was the planet Maldek, which was blasted to fragments when an experimental nuclear explosion turned out to be rather more powerful than planned. The remains of Maldek became the asteroid belt between Mars and Jupiter. However, it was decided that the "lifestreams" of the Maldekians should be reborn on Earth (the other planets of the Solar System already having advanced civilizations).

The first great civilization of Earth arose on the Pacific continent of Lemuria. Unfortunately, the Lemurians also experimented recklessly with atomic power, and blew themselves up. Next came Atlantis, in the Atlantic Ocean. Once again, however, the Atlanteans unleashed the power of the atom and destroyed themselves. This is apparently why the **Space Brothers** are so concerned by modern humanity's flirtation with nuclear energy and weapons, although, according to King, if we suffer the same self-inflicted fate as our ancestors, we will be reborn on a new planet following the same orbit as Earth, but on the far side of the Sun, and therefore not visible to us.

King (who now lives in Santa Barbara, California, and runs the still-thriving Aetherius Society) also claims that several times a year, a gargantuan spacecraft known as the "Third Satellite" orbits 1,550 miles above Earth. Invisible to sight and radar, this colossal vehicle beams positive energies from the Sun, via pyramid-shaped crystals, toward the people of Earth.

Although George King and the Aetherius Society are dismissed, along with the other **contactees** of the 1950s and 1960s, by most ufologists, such people are nevertheless worthy of study in a sociological context, as purveyors of alternative religious systems. In their 1997 book *UFOs and Ufology: The First Fifty Years,* Paul Devereux and Peter Brookesmith have this to say:

While it is perfectly plain that King's cosmology is a mishmash of pseudoscience, mythology and elements taken from earlier self-appointed seers and would-be messiahs, his basic message is closely allied to that promulgated by many other contactees of the 1950s. It is also a perfect expression of Jung's dictum that: "Anything that looks technological goes down without difficulty with modern man"—King cannot resist justifying his religion through technical marvels, the modern equivalent of biblical miracles. (p. 79)

KLARER, ELIZABETH

One of the earliest of the **contactees**, and one of the few women to have claimed encounters with the **Space Brothers**, Elizabeth Klarer saw her first UFO, which flew over her home in Natal, South Africa, in 1917, when she was seven. After one or two more sightings of strange craft when she was an adult, Klarer had the first of her **close encounters** of the third kind on December 27, 1954. At the time, she was living in a farmhouse in the Drakensberg Mountains, when she saw the handsome occupant of a 55-foot-diameter craft that was hovering nearby, a sight that alarmed her somewhat.

Nearly a year and a half later, on April 7, 1956, Klarer again encountered the handsome ufonaut in the same place. This time, however, she had no fear, and rushed to meet him as he stood beside his craft. He immediately took her by the waist and swung her up onto the UFO's hull, both of them laughing as he did so. He then said to her in perfect English: "Not afraid this time?" To which she replied: "I have known your face within my heart all my life." (The reader may be excused for feeling a little nauseous at this point; however, worse is to come.)

The spaceman's name, it turned out, was Akon, and he hailed from the planet Meton in the Alpha Centauri star system (which, along with its companion, Proxima Centauri, is the nearest star system to Earth, at 4.2 light-years). Akon invited Klarer into his ship, and together they flew off into space. He told her: "We rarely mate with Earth women; when we do, we keep the offspring to strengthen our race and infuse new blood." This was probably just as well, since Klarer, who was married at the time, would soon take Akon as her lover and bear him a child.

Their child, who was delivered on Meton by Akon himself, was named Ayling, and stayed with his father on their planet, which was, apparently, free from hunger, war and disease—not to mention politics and money. They did, however, visit her occasionally at her home in South Africa.

In 1977, Klarer published a book detailing her relationship with Akon, entitled *Beyond the Light Barrier*, an account that contradicted her original statements, made soon after her first contact in 1956, and published in *Flying Saucer Review*. In the earlier reports, she claimed that Akon was from Venus, and that the Venusian air inside the craft was most pleasant to breathe; whereas in her book, she maintained that she could not remain on Meton (not Venus) due to the difficulty she had in breathing the atmosphere.

KLASS, PHILIP JULIAN

The most famous and vocal of UFO **debunkers**, Philip Klass has become an almost demonic figure to those who maintain that UFOs represent a genuine mystery, which science has yet to explain (those who subscribe to the **extraterrestrial hypothesis** in particular consider him their arch nemesis). An electrical engineer by profession, Klass first became intrigued by the UFO phenomenon in the wake of the sightings around Exeter, New Hampshire, in 1965. He came to the conclusion that, although a fascinating phenomenon worthy of scientific investigation, UFOs were actually little-understood meteorological events, such as ball lightning and plasma discharges. He published his theory in his first book, *UFOs: Identified* in 1968.

However, the plasma/ball lightning theory was discredited by atmospheric physicists, prompting Klass to maintain subsequently that all UFO and alien encounters were and are the result of hoaxes, misidentification of mundane phenomena, and so on. This line of reasoning would be continued in his other books, *UFOs Explained* (1974), *UFOs: The Public Deceived* (1983), *UFO Abductions: A Dangerous Game* (1989) and *The Real Roswell Crashed-Saucer Coverup* (1997).

An active member of the **Committee for the Scientific Investigation of Claims of the Paranormal (CSICOP)**, Klass has investigated and cast serious doubt on numerous cases of UFO/alien encounters. While he is to be congratulated on some of his debunking missions, he nevertheless has drawn fire from UFO believers and agnostics alike for his occasional neglect of data that would otherwise prove troublesome to his contention that there is absolutely no evidence whatsoever to suggest that Earth is being visited by spacecraft from other planets.

KRASPEDON, DINO

Brazilian **contactee** who encountered a UFO and its pilot while driving through the mountains near Paranã, in São Paolo state, Brazil. Not long after, in March 1953, Kraspedon (whose real name was Aladino Felix) answered his door to find the spaceship captain on the doorstep. There followed a long series of meetings and discussions between Kraspedon and the alien, who was from Venus, in which the latter held forth on various topics, including UFO propulsion, theology and astronomy. Kraspedon subsequently published his notes on these conversations in a book entitled *My Contact with Flying Saucers* in 1959.

Kraspedon made a number of prophecies, including natural disasters, political assassinations and terrorist attacks in Brazil. Later, police stations and public buildings in São Paolo were indeed attacked. However, the leader of the terrorist gang turned out to be none other than Dino Kraspedon. Upon his arrest in August 1968, he said: "I was sent here as an ambassador to the Earth from Venus. My friends from space will come here and free me and avenge my arrest. You can look for tragic consequences to humanity when the flying saucers invade this planet."

Unfortunately for Kraspedon, his "friends from space" apparently decided against both freeing him from prison and invading Earth.

KRLL, O. H.

Alien being, who was among the crew of the spacecraft that landed at **Holloman Air Force Base**, New Mexico, in April 1964. The being's name has a number of variations, including "Krill," "Krlll" and "Crill." The "O. H." is said to stand for "Original Hostage," implying that Krll was obliged to remain on Earth, although, in view of other allegations that there is an ongoing ultrasecret exchange program between Earth and Krll's planet, he may not be a prisoner (he is said to be still here).

The main source of information on O. H. Krll is Milton William **Cooper**, who maintains that the alien supplied the U.S. government with a huge amount of scientific information, which was published in various journals under the name O. H. Krill. However, as Jacques **Vallée** states, the byine "O. H. Krill" has never been spotted in any scientific journal.

LANDING TRACES

However fascinating reports of encounters with aliens and other nonhuman creatures may be, the most important reports of UFO activity, from a scientific standpoint, are undoubtedly those in which physical traces are left behind by the objects. As the anomalist and UFO historian Jerome Clark states: "Landing-trace incidents . . . ought to have the potential to settle the issue of whether UFOs exist as extraordinarily anomalous phenomena. At least in theory, they take UFO experiences out of the realm of anecdotal testimony and into the laboratory, where hard evidence can be scrutinized and documented." (Clark [1998], p. 83)

Clark, however, goes on to describe a problem that has been lamented by more than one ufologist in the past—namely, the refusal by the majority of scientists to consider UFOs as worthy of serious investigation, even when they have the chance to analyze physical traces left behind after a UFO has departed. The proper analysis of a material sample requires the use of expensive and complicated equipment by scientists from several different disciplines. Thus, any interested scientists are forced to conduct such analyses alone, on their own time, during the hours in which the laboratories where they work are closed. As a result, they cannot hope to do the kind of work that could be done by a large, well-coordinated team. In addition, such is the general antipathy to UFOs in the scientific community that those with a genuine interest are forced to maintain anonymity, for fear that their reputations (not to mention the reputations of the establishments employing them) will suffer, should their interest be discovered.

As a result of this situation, there have been a number of lost opportunities, as well as some very intriguing cases where a highly anomalous event was proved to have taken place (see **Trans-en-Provence**). One of the more unfortunate cases was the encounter at Delphos, Kansas, on November 2, 1971. At about 7:00 P.M., 16-year-old Ronald Johnson was tending sheep with his dog near the family home, when he heard a rumbling sound and saw a large object with shining blue, red and orange lights. Similar to a mushroom in shape, the UFO hovered about two feet above the ground as the sheep bleated in panic.

Presently, the object flew away and Ronald Johnson rushed into the house to tell his parents what he had seen. Initially skeptical, his parents went outside with him, and together they watched the UFO, now merely a bright light in the sky, move off towards the horizon.

The family inspected the area of ground above which the object had hovered, and discovered an eight-foot-diameter circle of glowing, gray soil. Ronald's parents touched the circle, and found that, contrary to their expectations, there was no heat. However, their hands became numb after coming into contact with the affected soil, a condition that persisted for several weeks.

The Johnsons reported their sighting to the *Delphos Republican*. After initially meeting with indifference, they persuaded a reporter from the paper, Thaddia Smith, to take a look at the ring. When Smith arrived, she also noted that a tree stump had been crushed flat, as if something very heavy had landed on it (see **Quarouble, France**). She also noted that the limb of a live tree had been snapped as if it had been dead for some time, although it was still green beneath the bark. In addition, the lower part of the limb had a whitish tinge, and appeared to be blistered in places.

According to Jerome Clark:

Seven separate soil analyses conducted by university and other laboratories sought to compare control samples with samples taken from within the ring. The latter were found not to absorb water, had a higher acid content, and contained more soluble salts as well as two to two and a half times more calcium. They also produced less seed growth and were coated with a hydrocarbon of low molecular weight that various analysts were able to remove only by heating to 100 degrees C. or washing with ethyl alcohol. Embedded in the ring soil samples was a second unusual organic material of higher molecular weight. This second substance was composed of white, crystal-like fibers. In other words, the results of the tests performed at the time were interesting but inconclusive, leaving several mysteries in their wake. (Clark [1998], p. 171)

Unfortunately, this was as far as the analyses went; due to a lack of support from a skeptical scientific community, the research was not carried to its conclusion, and the ultimate nature of the processes that had produced the "Delphos ring" has not been established.

(See also **Rendlesham Forest**)

LARGE GRAYS

A variation on the **Grays**, most of which are short—about three-and-a-half to four-and-a-half feet tall—and are now by far the most commonly reported alien type. The large grays are probably of the same species as the shorter version (they possess the same spindly limbs and oversized heads), but invariably perform a different function: whereas the short grays are usually seen as "workers" or "drones," with little to differentiate them from each other, the larger grays are often described as "leaders" or "doctors." Usually dressed in robelike garments, they can be anything from five to eight feet in height, and if any communication with the percipient takes place, it will be with these beings. Any physical or mental procedures that are performed on the percipient are performed by the large grays (see **abduction**).

LAZAR, ROBERT SCOTT

American scientist who claims to have analyzed alien spacecraft at the top secret S-4 site, near **Area 51** in Nevada. Originally an informant of John **Lear**, Lazar subsequently abandoned his pseudonym "Dennis" and went public in an interview with reporter George Knapp on the Las Vegas TV station KLAS in March 1989.

According to Lazar, he was approached in December 1987 by representatives of Naval Intelligence, who offered him the opportunity to work on a highly classified research project based at Groom Lake in the Nevada desert. Between December 1988 and March 1989, he worked on a **reverse engineering** project, the purpose of which was to discover the engineering principles of a number of spacecraft kept at S-4.

Lazar, along with other personnel, would be taken to the facility in a bus with blacked out windows. While at the base, numerous physical tests were conducted on him, and at one point, he was made to drink a glass of yellow liquid. He was also hypnotized several times, which he thinks may have interfered with his memory.

While working at S-4, Lazar concentrated his efforts on reverse engineering the systems on one particular craft, which he nicknamed the "sports model," due to its sleek, low-profile appearance. He was told that the UFOs were propelled by gravity amplification, and were partly fueled by the superheavy **Element 115**, of which each craft needed 7.8 ounces to operate. On one occasion, Lazar was allowed to enter the "sports model," and noted that the 35-foot-diameter craft contained three levels (the uppermost of which he was never allowed to see). The middle level contained three seats (clearly designed for very small people), a few panels and a central column extending up from the reactor, which was about the size of a basketball. The lower level contained the gravity amplifiers, which powered the ship.

During one of his trips to the S-4 installation, Lazar claims to have watched a brief test flight of the "sports model," in which the craft briefly rose several feet above the ground, its underside glowing blue. Indeed, it is alleged that many of the frequent UFO sightings around Area 51 and S-4 are actually alien spacecraft on test flights.

Eventually, Lazar gave in to temptation and took his wife and some friends, including John Lear and a real-estate appraiser named Gene Huff, to the perimeter of Area 51. They managed, on several occasions, to see some astonishing aerobatics displays, but one night they were finally caught by a security patrol. Although there were no direct repercussions for his wife and friends (apart from a 50-minute detention), Lazar himself was summoned on the following day to Indian Springs Air Force Auxiliary Field, 35 miles northwest of Las Vegas. During his debriefing, he was threatened with death, but was nevertheless instructed to return to S-4 and continue with his work. He refused.

One of the reasons Lazar decided to go public with his information was that he considered it "a crime against the American people" for the government to withhold its UFO- and alien-related information. In addition, he became increasingly concerned that he might be killed, and concluded that the only way to stay alive would be to tell the media everything he knew about Area 51 and S-4. The military, he decided, would not take the risk of killing him and raising suspicions about the installations.

Subsequent research into Lazar's past by Stanton T. **Friedman** and others revealed serious discrepancies between his claims about his education and previous employment, and documented facts. For instance, he claims to have obtained a master's degree in physics from the Massachusetts Institute of Technology (MIT), and a master's in electronics from the California Institute of Technology (Caltech). No evidence for either has been found.

Although a number of attempts were made to discredit him (involving malicious rumors that he was involved in the illegal drugs trade and other nefarious activities), Lazar did admit that he and his first wife had owned a legal brothel in Nevada in the early 1980s. As a result of this, and the fact that he had done some freelance computer work for the current owner of the brothel, Lazar was arrested and charged with pandering. At his attorney's suggestion, Lazar pleaded guilty and was sentenced to three years suspended and 150 hours of community service.

Whether his claims are true or not, Robert Lazar has become one of the most famous and controversial figures in modern ufology, with as many supporters as detractors.

(See also **Aviary**; **Bennewitz, Paul**; **conspiracy theories; propulsion of UFOs**)

LEAR, JOHN

American pilot and son of William P. Lear, the inventor of the Lear Jet. John Lear was the first of the so-called whistleblowers, a group claiming to have secret knowledge of the alien presence on Earth (see **Aviary**), and was instrumental in the formation of current UFO **conspiracy theories**. According to Lear, the U.S. government has forged a secret treaty with malevolent extraterrestrials from a number of star systems, including Betelgeuse and Barnard's star, whereby they are allowed to abduct selected humans in exchange for items of their technology.

The aliens, however, have reneged on their part of the deal, and have been abducting large numbers of people and implanting them with electronic mind-control devices. This resulted in the Pentagon's obsession with the Strategic Defense Initiative ("Star Wars"), which is actually a research effort to produce weapons capable of defeating the aliens.

Lear has also linked this basic scenario with other right-wing conspiracy theories regarding a "secret government" bent on world domination and the subjugation of humanity.

LEÓN, DR PADRÓN

Spanish doctor who encountered one of the most bizarre and astonishing UFOs in the history of the subject. The location was the Grand Canary Islands; the date June 22, 1976. Just before 9:30 P.M., Dr. León was riding in a taxi with the son of a woman he had been called out to treat. As the car rounded a bend, the witnesses saw a transparent sphere about 200 feet ahead of them, hovering just above the ground. At that moment, the taxi's occupants felt an intense cold, accompanied by the failure of the car's radio.

In his report to the Spanish Air Ministry, Dr. León described the object as being like a gigantic soap bubble, with a diameter comparable to a two-story house. Inside the UFO could be seen a long, vertical tube and a horizontal platform, on top of which were three large panels. On this platform stood two extremely tall (about 10 feet) beings with spindly limbs and disproportionately short legs. They appeared to be wearing tight-fitting suits, of a shade of red Dr. León had never seen, and black "divers" helmets.

The tube then began to exude a blue gaslike substance, perhaps in response to the taxi driver switching on the car's headlights. The gas quickly filled the sphere, which, astonishingly, began to swell to 10 times its original size, as if being literally inflated. It then rose into the air. Fear-stricken, the witnesses drove to a nearby house and sought refuge inside. Together with the house's occupants, they watched through a window as the UFO shot away into the sky with a whistling sound. When some distance away, its shape changed to that of a spindle surrounded by a white halo.

This is clearly a far cry from the classic disk and cigar shapes commonly reported, and for that reason the Grand Canary sighting is among the most intriguing on record. Indeed, it is difficult to see how a mundane phenomenon could have been misidentified as this strange object and its crew. If Dr. León and his companions (not to mention the people in the house) did not hoax the encounter, and did not suffer from an unlikely shared hallucination, there seems little to say other than that what they saw was a genuinely anomalous phenomenon.

LEYS

Invisible lines of energy running across the landscape, and connecting ancient sites of mystical significance, such as stone circles, megaliths, burial sites, holy wells and so on. According to Alfred Watkins, an amateur antiquarian who first conducted research into the subject in the 1920s, the leys represent ancient trade routes, astronomical and holy sites.

In recent years, New Age philosophy has maintained that the powerful earth energy concentrated in leys (and which is particularly powerful at ley intersections) is utilized by UFOs. This energy has been compared to the Chinese *ch'i*, or universal life force, and ley intersections are frequently the sites of paranormal activity, such as poltergeist phenomena.

LIBERTY, KENTUCKY

Scene of a UFO abduction in 1976. At 11:15 P.M., Mona Stafford, Louise Smith and Elaine Thomas were returning home, after dining out, to Liberty from Lancaster. They were traveling southwest along Route 78, when they saw a red glow in the sky to the east. The glow quickly approached the car, and presently the three friends saw that it was actually a large (100-foot-diameter), disk-shaped object, circled by windows, around which red lights flickered. The disk also had a blue dome that shone brightly.

The UFO then projected three blue white beams of light on to the ground, one of which hit the car, illuminating the interior and causing the passengers to experience tingling on the skin and headaches. Louise Smith stopped the car and climbed out in a state of abject fear, before Mona Stafford pulled her back.

At that point, the encounter entered a phase of **high strangeness**. Silence fell about the car, as all three women started to cry. The car's engine seemed to have cut out, and yet it was moving at 85 mph along a perfectly straight road (there are no straight sections on Route 78).

In the next instant, everything had returned to normal, and the women drove to Smith's trailer home without further incident. When they arrived, they noticed that the time by the kitchen clock was 1:25 A.M.—about an hour and a half later than it should have been. When Smith looked at her wristwatch, she saw with disbelief that the minute hand was moving with the speed of a second hand. All three women continued to experience physical problems, including serious headaches and burning eyes.

The case was investigated by the **Mutual UFO Network (MUFON)**, who suggested that **hypnotic regression** might reveal what had happened to the women during their period of **missing time**. University of Wyoming psychologist Dr. Leo Sprinkle conducted the sessions, which were financed by the *National Enquirer*. James Young, a detective with the Lexington, Kentucky, police department, performed polygraph (**lie-detector tests**) on the women and concluded that they were not lying about their experiences.

During her regression, Mona Stafford recalled being held down on a table in a hot room, and examined with an eyelike instrument. Elaine Thomas spoke of being in a room with a single window, surrounded by four-foot-tall beings with gray skin and large dark eyes. A kind of brace was fastened around her neck, which tightened whenever she tried to speak or even think. Louise Smith remembered being doused with a scalding liquid.

Six months after the initial encounter, on July 29, 1976, Smith told researcher Leonard H. Stringfield that she had been awakened the previous evening by a disembodied voice that had told her to drive to the scene of the abduction. Against her will, she had complied. While there, she had felt someone or something tugging at her hands, and she later discovered that three of her rings were missing (they were tight-fitting and could not have simply slipped off). In September, two of the rings appeared near the door to her trailer home.

In the months that followed, the women remembered their abduction in greater detail, and Mona Stafford spoke of being taken to an underground place (see **Cimarron, New Mexico**). Stafford also had a subsequent encounter with an alien being in her own trailer home. The being, dressed in a shimmering robe and with red hair and beard, said to her: "Buree, the mind is still hungry." He then vanished.

LIE-DETECTOR TESTS

Many people claiming to have had encounters with UFOs and nonhuman entities have undergone lie-detector tests, frequently at their own request, in an effort to prove that they are not intentionally fabricating their experiences (a favorite charge of skeptics and **debunkers**). If these people fail their tests, it is immediately assumed by many that they are indeed lying; and if they pass, it is assumed that their encounters were objectively real events. However, there are serious problems with these interpretations, due to the fact that polygraphs are not 100 percent infallible. An accomplished liar can fool the machine with ease, and it must be said that there has been more than one accomplished liar active in ufology over the years.

In addition, even if a person is able to pass a polygraph test, administered by an experienced operator, this does not necessarily mean that their experience was objective, that is, that it happened in the external world. A person experiencing a vivid hallucination might well assume that it represents a real, external event, and this belief would enable him or her to pass a polygraph test. In other words, if one *believes* that something has happened—even if it was only a hallucination—he is telling the truth when he says that it happened. This means that lie-detector tests, like **hypnotic regression**, are of very limited use in establishing hard facts about the UFO phenomenon, as experienced by percipients.

LIMINAL ZONES

Term coined by the anthropologist Victor Turner to denote zones or regions of transition, or threshold. A liminal zone can be a place, such as a road or crossroads, a river, a seashore, a bridge or the outskirts of a town or other settlement. It can also be a certain time, such as dawn or dusk.

Liminal zones also exist within the minds of human beings, particularly on the boundary between sleep and wakefulness (see **bedroom visitors**). According to the British author Patrick Harpur:

Caravan sites or trailer parks often become especially haunted by UFOs or by strange creatures, perhaps because they are liminally situated between town and country, habitat and wilderness . . . Here, the laws of time and space, matter and causality seem attenuated; and we glimpse for an instant the unseen order of things. (p. 53)

When human beings enter a liminal zone, a zone of threshold or transition, a subtle yet profound alteration can occur within the psyche, resulting in a sudden ability to apprehend what Harpur calls "daimonic reality," the realm of myth and the supernatural.

(See also **Oz Factor**)

"LIZARD MAN" (ALIEN)

In recent years, there have been increasing reports of humanoid alien beings resembling reptiles. One of the most striking of these cases occurred in July 1983 in Mount Vernon, Missouri. The case is also notable for the fact that the witnesses observed no fewer than three different types of entity in the vicinity of a landed UFO, a somewhat unusual occurrence even for the field of ufology.

On the morning in question, farmer Ron Watson and his wife Paula noticed some silvery flashes coming from a pasture adjacent to their farmhouse. Ron took a pair of binoculars, peered into the pasture and saw two silver-suited figures. Passing the binoculars periodically to each other, the couple watched in disbelief as the two entities moved their hands over the prone form of a black cow. Then, as the beings began to jerk their hands upward, the cow rose up from the ground, as if being levitated by some unseen force. The unfortunate animal was then floated into a cone-shaped UFO that stood nearby. The craft had a highly polished, mirrorlike surface, which made it virtually invisible due to the reflection of its surroundings.

The Watsons then noticed two more entities standing beside the UFO. One of them was about six feet tall, with a green skin and a distinctly reptilian appearance. Its eyes were large, unblinking and contained vertical pupils. Its hands and feet were webbed. Even more bizarrely, the other entity appeared to be a **Bigfoot**-type creature.

His curiosity overcoming his fear, Ron Watson told his wife that he was going to get closer to the otherworldly group in the pasture. Paula, however, managed to persuade him not to leave the house. Presently, the beings entered the UFO, which then disappeared.

Subsequently, the Watsons learned from the farmer who owned the pasture that one of his black cows was missing. Not surprisingly, the farmer refused to believe the Watsons when they tried to tell him what had happened to his animal, which was not seen again.

(See also **Bigfoot, cattle mutilations, Reptoids**)

LOKA

The Loka is a gigantic mothership containing numerous smaller UFOs, according to information received by psychics in the United States in the 1940s and 1950s. The mothership is said to come from an "Etherian World" and is driven by atomic engines operating a "screw mechanism." The unmanned smaller UFOs are observation devices, which transmit information back to the Loka.

Harold T. Wilkins, in his 1954 book *Flying Saucers on the Attack*, states:

The world from which they come is beyond the normal spectrum of visibility, or any tangibility, or the wave frequencies of color, or sound as we know them on earth. The satellite disks are small, but the "brain ship" which directs them, may be up to half a mile wide! This "Etherian World" is alleged to be inhabited by men of very advanced scientific knowledge, and they are alleged to use nuclear energies derived from fissioning the atom by chain reactions. They are said to be *not* hostile, but will attack if they deem themselves menaced. (p. 43)

As with the information concerning the spacecraft known as the **Kareeta**, which Wilkins also mentions, the material concerning the Loka is characterized by extreme naïveté, particularly with regard to the "Etherians'" use of "nuclear energies derived from fissioning the atom." One would expect a highly advanced interplanetary civilization to have moved on from nuclear fission, just as humanity is struggling to perfect nuclear fusion.

With regard to the Etherians themselves, Wilkins quotes a statement from "the mystic quarters in the U.S.":

If there is another world war, using nuclear energies, these mysterious cosmic craft may be forced to intervene; for the release of radioactive forces from atomic bomb explosions has rather seriously disturbed the universe. These etherian beings are up to fifteen feet tall. Any intervention would be impersonal and impartially directed. No sides would be taken. Why do they now appear in the skies of Earth? They come always when a civilization has reached a peak and seems destined to collapse, Their purpose is to collect, examine and record the achievements of that culture and civilization, and its scientific discoveries, much as the anthropologist concerns himself with the culture of primitive tribes and vanishing races. All past civilizations on earth have had their day and perished. (Ibid., p. 44)

Although the Etherians seem to share their main concerns regarding humanity's misuse of nuclear energy with the **Space Brothers** of **contactee** lore, they appear to have more in common with John **Keel's ultraterrestrials**, in that they hail from some rarefied, invisible world that is all around us. It is therefore puzzling that they should need to build solid, "nuts-and-bolts" spacecraft like the Kareeta and the Loka, which are powered by a nuclear technology that humanity itself now possesses.

LURE, OPERATION

A somewhat naive project designed to coax aliens to land openly on Earth, so that contact with humanity might be officially established. Operation Lure was first suggested by Robert Spencer Carr, a former Director of Educational Research at Walt Disney Studios, who later served with the U.S. Army Orientation Service, and who was a special adviser to the **National Investigations Committee on Aerial Phenomena (NICAP)**. The project was based on an earlier attempt to construct a top secret UFO landing field by the Canadian Defense Research Board in 1958, which failed, apparently, because there was nothing interesting enough to attract the aliens' attention. Operation Lure was wholeheartedly endorsed by Donald E. **Keyhoe**, who described it at length in his 1973 book *Aliens from Space*. According to Keyhoe:

The Lure will be an isolated base with unusual structures and novel displays, designed to attract the UFO aliens' attention. The space beings' curiosity has been demonstrated hundreds of times in their close approaches to cars, trains, ships and aircraft, also in their repeated hovering over outdoor theaters, power stations and unusual buildings.

The Lure will have three or more dummy UFOs, disk types with domes, built of aluminum. Each one will have glass panels to show that no one is hiding inside. There will be no attempts to capture aliens or UFOs. The base will be unmanned, and the nearest humans will be stationed at hidden observation posts over a mile distant. No aircraft or ground traffic will be allowed near the Lure, and all interceptor chases will be ended. (Keyhoe [1973], pp. 270–1)

Not surprisingly, Operation Lure has never been put into practice. Even if there really are extraterrestrial aliens out there who are monitoring activities on Earth, it seems unlikely that their curiosity would be at such a childish level that they could be coaxed into landing by the presence of a few model flying saucers. In addition, it must be said that if they had any intention whatsoever of establishing open contact with humanity, they would have done so already. If, on the other hand, they do intend to make open contact at some future date, their agenda is unlikely to be influenced by our efforts to encourage them to land *en masse.*

MACK, PROFESSOR JOHN E.

Harvard University psychiatrist and alien **abduction** researcher, John Mack is one of the very few academics prepared to talk openly about the possibility that such events might represent the activities of a genuine nonhuman intelligence (a position for which he has been trenchantly criticized more than once).

Initially a skeptic with regard to the whole idea of UFOs and aliens, Mack became intrigued by the subject after meeting Budd **Hopkins** in January 1990. Impressed with Hopkins's research, Mack stated in his 1994 book *Abduction: Human Encounters with Aliens:*

What Hopkins had encountered in the more than two hundred abduction cases he had seen over a fourteen-year period were reports of experiences that had the characteristics of real events: highly detailed narratives that seemed to have no obvious symbolic pattern; intense emotional and physical traumatic impact, sometimes leaving small lesions on the experiencers' bodies; and consistency of stories down to the most minute details. But if these experiences were in some sense "real," then all sorts of new questions opened up. How often was this occurring? If there were large numbers of these cases, who was helping these individuals deal with their experiences and what sort of support or treatment was called for? What was the response of the mental health profession. And, most basic of all, what was the source of these encounters? (p. 2)

In an effort to address these questions, Mack began to conduct his own sessions with abductees, and reached conclusions that are somewhat at odds with those of other abduction researchers. Whereas the most popular assumption is that the aliens represent a callous, militaristic culture intent on using humanity as cattle for their own genetic (and, according to some, nutritional) purposes (see **conspiracy theories**, Milton William **Cooper**, and John **Lear**), Mack sees them as having humanity's best interests at heart. Indeed, their concerns seem to echo those of the **Space Brothers** of the 1950s and 1960s, the main difference being that Mack's **Grays** are more concerned with ecological damage through pollution, than with the cold war threat of nuclear annihilation.

The information retrieved from Mack's subjects is a good deal more complex than the "average" scenario of physical examination and genetic manipulation, and includes memories of past lives, both on Earth and on other planets. Mack's conclusions lean more toward the **psychosocial hypothesis** than the **extraterrestrial hypothesis**, since he suspects that what we commonly call "aliens" are actually a manifestation of a "divine source or *anima mundi*," in other words, a powerful nonhuman intelligence that has always existed alongside humanity.

MAD GASSER OF MATTOON

Bizarre, possibly nonhuman entity that terrorized the small Illinois town of Mattoon during a two-week period in the summer of 1944. The first attack came on the night of August 31, 1944, when a resident of Mattoon suddenly awoke feeling extremely ill. He got out of bed, rushed to the bathroom and vomited. His first thought was that the gas must have been left on in the house, and, on returning to bed, he asked his wife if she had done so. She replied that she had not, but decided to get up just to make sure. She found, however, that she was unable to move.

The following evening, another Mattoon resident, Mrs. Betty Kearney, awoke in her bedroom to find a sickeningly sweet smell suffusing the room. In a subsequent interview with a local newspaper, Mrs. Kearney said: "At the time I thought it might be from flowers outside the window. But the odor grew stronger and I began to feel a paralysis of my legs and lower body. I got frightened and screamed." She was alone in the house: her husband was working late, and when Bert Kearney returned home about one and a half hours later, he discovered a dark figure standing at the bedroom window.

For the last 90 minutes, police and other residents, alerted by Mrs. Kearney's screams, had been searching the area for the culprit, without success. The prowler had obviously not gone very far, and Kearney immediately gave chase. The prowler, however, easily evaded him and disappeared into the night.

Kearney described the prowler as being tall, and dressed in dark clothing, which included a tight-fitting cap. Although it seems clear enough that these witnesses actually experienced something extremely unusual, the waters became muddied considerably when the *Mattoon Journal-Gazette* became involved with the case. As Jerome Clark notes in his highly informative 1993 book *Unexplained!*, the newspaper did no one any favors when it referred to Mrs. Kearney as the "first victim," which was itself untrue. The use of the word "first" implied that there would be more victims. "As it happened, other alleged attacks did follow, all reported in the kind of overwrought prose that frightened more than informed." (p. 237)

In all of the reports, the subsequently named "Mad Gasser" followed the same *modus operandi,* which consisted of squirting a sickly and nauseating vapor into his victims' homes. The victims would then suffer paralysis lasting for up to an hour, accompanied by painful swelling on the face.

On the evening of September 5, Mrs. Beulah Cordes returned home with her husband to find a piece of cloth on their front doorstep. Curious, Mrs. Cordes picked up the cloth, which was soaked in a strange liquid, and sniffed it. She later said: "I had sensations similar to coming in contact with an electric current. The feeling raced down my body to my feet and then seemed to settle in my knees. It was a feeling of paralysis." She quickly began to experience burning pains and bleeding in her mouth, and she was physically sick. The police were called, and they searched the area around the house, discovering a skeleton key and an empty lipstick tube nearby. Although the liquid-soaked cloth was sent for examination, no firm conclusions as to its composition were reached.

Partly due to events such as this, and partly due to the sensationalistic treatment of the visitations in the newspapers, hysteria spread through the town. One woman called the police in a panic, saying that a man answering the Mad Gasser's description was trying to break into her house. As Clark states, this may or may not have been a genuine Gasser visitation.

The citizens decided that they were not going to stand for this situation, and, in spite of pleas for calm by the police, organized a number of vigilante groups, which patrolled the streets of Mattoon throughout the night. The police commissioner stated that some kind of "gas maniac" was indeed in the area, but "many of the attacks are nothing more than hysteria. Fear of the gas man is entirely out of proportion to the menace of the relatively harmless gas he is spraying."

The Mad Gasser's busiest night was on September 10, during which five people fell victim to his strange fumes. However, the following morning, the police began to adopt a policy of total skepticism toward his antics. On the morning of September 12, the chief of police held a press conference at which he stated: "Local police, in cooperation with state officers, have checked and rechecked all reported cases, and we find absolutely no evidence to support stories that have been told. Hysteria must be blamed for such seemingly accurate accounts of supposed victims."

The evening of September 13 saw the Gasser's final visit, in which a witness reported a "woman dressed in man's clothing" spraying gas into the home of Bertha Burch. Mrs. Burch searched around the house the next morning, and discovered several footprints apparently made by high-heeled shoes.

While many of the Mad Gasser's "attacks" were almost certainly the result of the mass hysteria that gripped Mattoon during those two fraught weeks, the first two visitations could not have been caused by this, since at that point, no one had heard of such a thing, and the nickname "Mad Gasser" had yet to be coined. Also, contrary to what the chief of police claimed, there *was* physical evidence, in the form of the liquid-soaked cloth, skeleton key and lipstick tube discovered by Beulah Cordes, not to mention the shoe print found by Bertha Burch.

Jerome Clark finds this latter evidence significant in the light of an earlier "gasser" case, which occurred in Botetourt County, Virginia, in 1933. The *modus operandi* of the Botetourt Gasser was virtually identical to that of the Mad Gasser of Mattoon. The county's residents likewise armed themselves and went out into the night, searching for the gas-spraying miscreant.

A farmer named F. B. Duval experienced a gassing and, on his way to fetch the police, saw a man making his escape in a car. An examination of the area a short while later revealed prints of a woman's shoes. According to Jerome Clark:

One of the last gassings was reported near Lithia in nearby Roanoke County. Afterward the victim found discolored snow with a sweet-smelling, oily substance in it. When analyzed, it turned out to consist of sulfur, arsenic, and mineral oil— something like the components, authorities thought, of insecticides. A trail of footprints led from the house to the barn, but none away from the barn. They were, according to press accounts, a "woman's tracks." (Clark [1993], p. 241)

Like their English cousin **Springheel Jack**, the American Mad Gassers remain as enigmatic today as they did at the time of their attacks. It is virtually certain that some attacks did take place, although they undoubtedly gave rise to spurious reports inspired by mass hysteria. Their motives are unclear, and seem characterized by absurdity; equally absurd is the fact that the attacks ceased as suddenly as they had begun.

MAGONIA

The name used by Jacques **Vallée** and other ufologists who subscribe to the **psychosocial hypothesis** to refer to the supernatural realm in which paranormal phenomena such as UFOs, nonhuman entities, folkloric beings and Marian apparitions originate. The name itself has its origin in a medieval French folk belief in a magical land beyond the sky, whose denizens sometimes came to Earth in "cloud ships." In his 1988 book *Dimensions: A Casebook of Alien Contact*, Vallée quotes a manuscript by Agobard (A.D. 779–840), Archbishop of Lyons, France, which describes the capture of beings from the sky. Agobard himself witnessed the parading through the streets of four people who, it was claimed, had become stranded on Earth, and were about to be executed, only being saved by the bishop's intervention. His manuscript is entitled *Liber contra insulam vulgi opinionem*, and is basically a tract against superstitious and non-Christian beliefs.

We have seen and heard many men plunged in such great stupidity, sunk in such depths of folly, as to believe there is a certain region, which they call Magonia, whence ships sail in the clouds, in order to carry back to that region those fruits of the earth which are destroyed by hail and tempests; the sailors paying rewards to the storm wizards and themselves receiving corn and other produce. Out of the number of those whose blind folly was deep enough to allow them to believe these things possible, I saw several exhibitions in a certain concourse of people, four persons in bonds—three men and a woman who they said had fallen from these same ships; after keeping them for some days in captivity they had brought them before the assembled multitude, as we have said, in our presence to be stoned. But truth prevailed. (p. 16)

The concept of Magonia can be taken as a metaphor for the origin of paranormal phenomena, although it must be said that that origin is still a profound mystery. According to Vallée:

Magonia, as it appears in such tales, is sometimes a remote country, an invisible island, some faraway place one can reach only by a long journey. Indeed, in some tales, it is a celestial country . . . This parallels the belief in the extraterrestrial origin of UFOs so popular today. But a second—and equally widespread—theory, is that *Magonia constitutes a sort of parallel universe, which coexists with our own. It is made visible and tangible only to selected people, and the doors that lead through it are tangential points . . .* (Ibid., p. 128)

(See also **liminal zones, ultraterrestrials**)

MAJESTIC 12 (MJ-12)

An ultrasecret U.S. government research and development/intelligence agency whose function was to analyze and respond to UFO and alien activity. On December 11, 1984, Jaime Shandera, a 45-year-old Los Angeles-based film producer, received a package in the mail. The package contained a roll of exposed but undeveloped Tri-X 35 mm film. When Shandera, together with his friend William **Moore**, developed the film, they found that it contained seven pages of a typewritten document. Dated November 18, 1952, the document purported to be a briefing paper for

President-elect Dwight D. Eisenhower, and explained how the Majestic 12 organization had been created by President Harry Truman after the UFO crash at **Roswell**, New Mexico, in 1947. In part, the document read:

On July 07, 1947, a secret operation was begun to assure recovery of the wreckage of this object for scientific study. During the course of this operation, aerial reconnaissance discovered that four small human-like beings had apparently ejected from the craft at some point before it exploded. These had fallen to earth about two miles east of the wreckage site. All four were dead and badly decomposed due to action by predators and exposure to the elements during the approximately one week time period which had elapsed before their discovery. A special scientific team took charge of removing these bodies for study. (See Attachment C.) The wreckage of the craft was also removed to several different locations. (See Attachment B.) Civilians and military witnesses in the area were debriefed and news reporters were given the effective cover story that the object had been a misguided weather balloon.

According to the briefing document, the original members of Majestic 12 were: Admiral Roscoe H. Hillenkoetter, the first director of the **Central Intelligence Agency (CIA)**; Dr. Vannevar Bush, who organized the Office of Scientific Research and Development, and was thus instrumental in the establishment of the Manhattan Project to develop the first atomic bomb; Defense Secretary James V. Forrestal, who had a nervous breakdown and committed suicide in 1949; General Nathan F. Twining, commanding general of Air Matériel Command at Wright Field (now **Wright-Patterson Air Force Base**) in Dayton, Ohio; General Hoyt S. Vandenberg, who had ordered the Air Technical Intelligence Center to destroy its "**Estimate of the Situation**," which had concluded that UFOs were probably interplanetary; Dr. Detlev Bronk, chairman of the National Research Council and a member of the Medical Advisory Board of the Atomic Energy Commission, who performed the autopsies on the bodies discovered at Roswell; Dr. Jerome Hunsaker, who was appointed chairman of the National Advisory Committee on Aerospace around the time of Majestic 12's formation; Rear Admiral Sidney W. Souers, executive secretary of the National Security Council; Gordon Gray, special assistant to President Truman on National Security and Director of the Psychological Strategy Board; Dr. Donald Menzel, chairman of the Department of Astronomy at Harvard, an expert cryptographer and, ironically enough, officially an avowed UFO skeptic. Menzel's skepticism is troubling with regard to the authenticity of the Majestic 12 briefing document; however, Stanton **Friedman** has uncovered evidence that Menzel, aside from his academic work, was also a consultant to the **National Security Agency (NSA)** and the CIA, and was regarded as being outstandingly discreet with regard to classified material. The last two members of Majestic 12 were General Robert M. Montague, director of the Anti-Aircraft and Guided Missiles Branch of the U.S. Army Artillery School and commanding general of the Atomic Energy Commission installation at Sandia Base, Albuquerque, New Mexico; and Dr. Lloyd V. Berkner, executive secretary of the Joint Research and Development Board.

In December 1994, UFO researcher Don Berliner received a package, mailed from Wisconsin, which contained a roll of 35 mm film. Once developed, the film revealed more pages referring to Majestic 12, and which were entitled: *Majestic 12 Group Special Operations Manual: Extraterrestrial Entities and Technology, Recovery and Disposal*. As the title suggests, the document contains exhaustive instructions on how to retrieve, pack, transport and store alien hardware and aliens themselves.

Majestic 12 remains one of the most controversial elements in the field of ufology, with many (if not most) ufologists maintaining that the various documents relating to the group are fakes. Much of the debate has centered on the typographical conventions used in the documents, with the skeptics claiming that they do not conform to the conventions in use at the time the documents were allegedly written, while the defenders of Majestic 12 claim that those conventions were not always strictly adhered to.

Another bone of contention is the signature of Harry Truman on the document known as the "Truman Memorandum." Dated September 24, 1947, the memo reads:

MEMORANDUM FOR THE SECRETARY OF DEFENSE
Dear Secretary Forrestal,

As per our recent conversation on this matter, you are hereby authorized to proceed with all due speed and caution upon your undertaking. Hereafter this matter shall be referred to only as Operation Majestic Twelve.

It continues to be my feeling that any future considerations relative to the ultimate disposition of this matter should rest solely with the Office of the President following appropriate discussions with yourself, Dr. Bush and the Director of Central Intelligence.

[Signed] Harry Truman

For the skeptics, notably Philip **Klass**, Truman's signature ironically gave the lie to this document, since it was established that it matched perfectly an earlier signature on a letter to Vannevar Bush, dated October 1, 1947. Since no one ever duplicates his or her signature exactly, Klass reasoned, the signature on the Truman Memorandum had to have been photocopied; in other words, the document was a fake. However, the fact is that people do sign their names identically over a given period, and so this criticism loses credibility.

Arguments over the authenticity of the Majestic 12 documents—and hence the reality of the agency itself—continue to fly back and forth, ensuring them mythological status in the fields of ufology and conspiracy theory, at the very least.

MARTIAN MEDIUMS

In the late 19th century, four women claimed to have made contact with the inhabitants of the planet Mars through the process of **channeling**. They were Helene Smith, whose real name was Catherine Elise Muller; Mrs. Smead, the wife of an American clergyman; Miss "S. W.," who was a patient of the great Swiss psychologist Carl G. **Jung**; and "Mireille," whose case was investigated by the French researcher Colonel de Rochas.

Helene Smith was an amateur Spiritualist medium who not only claimed to have had numerous adventures on Mars while in a psychic state outside of her body but also had learned and could speak the Martian language. Her case was investigated by the eminent Swiss psychologist Theodore Flournoy, who concluded that Helene was, basically, fantasizing about Mars in order to escape from the depressing parochialism of her everyday life (she also claimed to have been Marie Antoinette in a previous life). Although Flournoy, from a purely psychological point of view, was fascinated by the detail contained in Helen's visions of Mars, which included the way the Martians spoke, acted, dressed, worked, traveled and so on, he was most intrigued by the Martian language she spoke. In his examination of the cases of the Martian Mediums in *Fortean Times* Number 76, the folklorist Hilary Evans describes how, shortly after experiencing a vision of a house and a Martian flying through the air with a kind of jet pack, Helene received the message: *"Dode ne chi haudan te meche metiche astane ke de me veche."* Six weeks later it was explained to her that this message meant that the house she had seen in her vision belonged to a Martian named Astane, who had been the man flying through the air with the jet pack.

Flournoy was also interested to observe that this language, apparently no more than gibberish, was actually internally consistent, with its own grammar and syntax, and that Helene would always use the same words with the same meanings. Flournoy came to the conclusion that the Martian language was actually a coded version of French, since it seemed to obey the same linguistic rules. Evans writes: "If anything, this made it even more of a marvel: it meant that Helene had by some unconscious process invented a new language and committed it to memory."

The case of Mrs. Smead was investigated by the American researcher Professor James Hyslop at the suggestion of her husband. Like Helene Smith, Mrs. Smead was no stranger to psychic experiences, having seen apparitions on many occasions. She was also proficient in the use of the planchette (a device used to receive written messages from the spirit world). Mrs. Smead at first received messages from her three dead children, who informed her that many spirits of the dead resided on other planets. Later, she received messages from another daughter who was living on Mars, and who described the canal network covering the planet. (At the time, there was much speculation regarding the astronomer Percival Lowell's observations of linear features crisscrossing the red planet.)

After a hiatus (for reasons which are unclear) of five years, Mrs. Smead's Spiritualist sittings were resumed, as were the messages from Mars. According to Hilary Evans:

More details of places on Mars and the lifestyle of the Martians, along with specimens of their language, were communicated: "Mare" = man, "Maren" = men, "Kare" = woman, "Karen" = women, for example, suggesting that the language of Mrs. Smead's Martians, like that spoken by Helene Smith, was similar in structure to Earth languages. But the two Martian languages were not the same. Maybe the messages came from two different Martian races? (*Fortean Times* Number 76, p. 25)

Like Helene Smith, Mrs. Smead gave detailed descriptions of the Martians' way of life, their architecture and modes of travel (which included electrically driven airships). Hyslop's investigation led him to conclude that the information on Mars came from a secondary personality, which had for some reason split off from Mrs. Smead's main personality. Evans quotes him thus:

We find in such cases evidence that we need not attribute fraud to the normal consciousness, and we discover automatic processes of mentation that may be equally acquitted of fraudulent intent while we are also free from the obligation to accept the phenomena at their assumed value. Their most extraordinary characteristic is the extent to which they imitate the organizing intelligence of a normal mind, and the perfection of their impersonation of spirits, always betraying their limitations, however, just at the point where we have the right to expect veridical testimony from their claims. (Ibid., p. 25)

Miss S. W. was a rather disturbed and moody 15-year-old, whose father had recently died, and whose mother seems to have been somewhat unbalanced.

S. W. was also a talented medium, who was able to perceive noncorporeal beings, and who frequently entered trance states in which she traveled to other worlds of the spirit. These "spirit worlds" included Mars, whose inhabitants, according to S. W., are considerably ahead of humanity in the "technical arts," although they do not possess "godlike souls" as humans do. Once again, S. W. referred to the planet-wide canal system on Mars, which was used for irrigation.

Eventually, S. W. became much less truculent and found a job, which she enjoyed doing. All in all, her general character improved drastically, and Jung concluded that the Spiritualist material she had produced represented the development of her adult personality.

The case of "Mireille" was investigated by Colonel de Rochas, who had known her and her family for many years. During several hypnosis sessions, Mireille, 45 years old, described floating up into space and encountering what she described as "phantoms." She made many visits to other planets, including Mars, and it was on one of these psychic voyages that she encountered Victor, an old friend who had been dead for 10 years. It seems that Victor was acting as Mireille's guide during her otherworldly sojourns, and presently he began to use her as the channel for his own communications. According to Victor, the people on the planet where he lived (which may or may not have been Mars: he was rather vague on this) used their arms to express emotions. As a result, their arms were extremely prominent, to the extent that visionaries on Earth mistook them for angels' wings.

Like Hyslop, de Rochas concluded that such communications represented the activity of a secondary personality; de Rochas even said as much to Victor, who was rather amused at this expression of skepticism, replying that "your doubts as to whether I exist don't prevent me from existing!" Victor later added (quite cleverly): "I am sure you have earthly friends whose existence you never question, even though you know them only by the letters you exchange with them."

Although it is extremely unlikely (to put it mildly) that these four women were communicating with civilizations on Mars, their cases are nevertheless remarkable in their demonstration of the power of the unconscious mind. In these cases, the raw material was the planet Mars, the focus of much speculation on the possibility of extraterrestrial life at the end of the 19th century. As Hilary Evans states in the conclusion to his article in *Fortean Times*:

The form that psychodrama takes will depend partly on the individual's interests and preoccupations, partly on the acceptable "myths" of his or her cultural environment. It is not surprising that for many of us today, this should take a space-age form in which we believe we are involved in alien-contact adventures. What is fascinating is to see the same "acceptable myth" being resorted to in the 1890s by four women of different ages, nationalities and circumstances—and all within a few years of one another. (Ibid., p. 28)

MARZANO, GENOA, ITALY

Scene of an alien abduction, which occurred around midnight on December 6, 1978. Twenty-six-year-old night watchman Fortunato Zanfretta noticed four suspicious lights, apparently from torches, in the courtyard of an unoccupied summer house. The lights were moving about three feet above the ground and, thinking that intruders might be present, Zanfretta tried to radio his headquarters. However, both the radio and his car's headlights failed. Zanfretta then took his gun and a torch, left his car and walked slowly up to the courtyard's gate. At that point, the lights moved out of sight behind the house.

Zanfretta approached the house and peered around the corner. At that moment, something pushed him to the ground, and Zanfretta looked up to see a 10-foot-tall humanoid being. The creature appeared to be dressed in a suit composed of horizontal tubes, much like the "Michelin man." Its eyes were enormous illuminated triangles, and on each side of its wide head protruded three long spines. It had another sharp protrusion on each side of its forehead, which may have been ears, or perhaps horns.

The terrifying apparition suddenly vanished, and Zanfretta felt a wave of heat accompanied by a loud whistling noise. A large triangular object ascended into the air from behind the house and flew away at high speed. Zanfretta ran back to his car and called his headquarters, frantically shouting that the intruders were not men. Before fainting, he looked at his wristwatch; the time was 12:16 A.M., about 15 minutes later than he expected.

Zanfretta's colleagues searched for him and only found him about an hour later in the middle of a field some distance from his car. Nearby there was a depression, shaped like a horseshoe and about 25 feet wide.

The night watchman later suffered severe headaches, and these, along with his experience of **missing time**, prompted him to undergo **hypnotic regression**. According to his recovered memories, he was abducted by the hideous beings and taken to an uncomfortably hot, round room, where a device was placed over his head, causing him severe pain.

MEIER, EDUARD ALBERT "BILLY"

Born in Buelach, Switzerland, in 1937, Eduard "Billy" Meier has come to be regarded as the preeminent prophet of the ufological New Age, as a result of his claims to have had hundreds of contacts with beings residing in the Pleiades star cluster. According to Meier, the Pleiadians first made contact with him in 1942, when he was five years old. A Pleiadian man named Sfath began to prepare Meier for his mission in life, followed by **Asket**, a beautiful woman from another universe.

Early in the afternoon of January 28, 1975, Meier (who had become a farmer and odd-job man, and had lost an arm) was out walking near his home in Hinwil, Switzerland, when he witnessed the arrival of a Pleiadian spacecraft (known as "beamships"). The craft landed about 100 yards from him, and a figure emerged. The being was Semjase (pronounced sem-yah-see), an astonishingly beautiful woman who was to be the third of Meier's teachers. Over the next 15 years or so, Meier would meet Semjase and other Pleiadians (such as **Ptaah**, **Quetzal** and Plaja), and would take over 1,000 photographs of their elegant beamships. He would also produce more than 3,000 pages of notes detailing the Pleiadians' philosophy and science.

The Pleiadians claimed to come from a planet called Erra in the star system Taygeta, having moved there from a planet in the constellation Lyra several million years previously. However, like so much of the information relayed to **contactees**, the aliens' pronouncements sound more like badly researched science fiction than anything we could accept at face value. For one thing, the Pleiades, which are about 430 light-years from Earth in the constellation Taurus, are composed of approximately 500 "B" type stars (of which seven are visible to the naked eye). These are hot blue stars, about 150 million years old, and with a very short (in cosmic terms) life span, due to the speed with which they consume their hydrogen fuel. A stellar environment such as this would be utterly inimical to humanoid life; were a planet such as Erra to exist in the Pleiades, nothing could survive on it (see **Pleiadians/Plejarans**).

Nevertheless, Meier's photographs of the Pleiadian beamships are extremely impressive; indeed, they are among the clearest ever to have been produced by a UFO witness. Researchers sympathetic to Meier's claims have suggested that they would have taken considerable technical and financial resources to produce . . . by a virtually penniless farmer with only one arm. Two such researchers in the United States, Wendelle Stevens and Jim Dilettoso, subjected the photographs to computer analysis in the late 1970s, and concluded that they are genuine (i.e., that they show large objects far from the camera, rather than small models close to the camera). However, the Arizona-based research organization Ground Saucer Watch (GSW) also analyzed the photographs and pronounced them fakes.

Meanwhile, Meier and his followers (of which there was a considerable number) established the Semjase Silver Star Center in Switzerland, to which all were free to travel and learn of the Pleiadian philosophy. In 1991 skeptical researcher Kal Korff, who had already produced a book that had demolished many of Meier's claims, infiltrated the group and managed to obtain numerous photographs, which he later analyzed and discovered to be fakes.

As it turned out, Korff was taking something of a risk in entering the 50-acre compound of the Semjase Silver Star Center, even with an assumed name. When he asked some of Meier's followers how they would take to a visit from the despised Korff, one replied that he would not be allowed to enter . . . and that if he did enter, he would not be allowed to leave.

For Meier's part, the claims of extraterrestrial adventures have grown ever more outlandish. He maintains, for instance, that he has been taken on numerous trips through time with his Pleiadian friends; on one such trip he met Jesus Christ and was inducted as the 13th disciple. He has also produced photographs of dinosaurs, at least one of which bears an uncanny resemblance to an illustration in a magazine. While on a trip into deep space, Meier was able to take a snapshot of the "eye of God," which turned out to be a poor reproduction of a photograph of the Ring Nebula in the constellation Lyra.

MENGER, HOWARD

One of the best known **contactees** of the 1950s, Howard Menger was born in New Jersey in 1922 and encountered his first extraterrestrial when he was 10 years old. He was out walking in woodland when he came upon an incredibly beautiful woman with golden eyes, who smiled at him and said that she had come a long way to speak to him. The woman, who came from Venus, told Menger that her people would visit him many times, and that he would fulfil a hugely important purpose on Earth.

During his time as a soldier in the Pacific in the Second World War, Menger received a number of telepathic messages from the Venusians, and would occasionally meet with them at various locations. After the war, he set up a sign writing business, and was able to scrape a living for himself, his wife and their son. The Venusian contacts continued, and one of the ways in which Menger was able to offer help was by procuring Earth clothing for them to wear, so that they could pass unnoticed while on our planet. On one occasion in 1956, he photographed an arriving spacecraft, but due to the radiation produced by the vessel, the result was little more than a hazy blob.

According to the Venusians, there were civilizations scattered all over the Solar System, all of them perfectly human-looking. In 1959 he published a book entitled *From Outer Space to You*, which detailed his adventures, including a trip to an alien base on the Moon. Menger also managed to procure some alien food, a piece of processed potato, which contained five times more protein than an Earth potato, and which formed part of the aliens' highly nutritious vegetarian diet. According to Menger, this diet enabled them to live much longer than Earth people. Their technology was approximately 2,500 years in advance of our own.

Menger and his second wife, Connie, claimed to have lived earlier lives (in which they were lovers) on other planets in the Solar System, he on Saturn, she on Venus (species on different planets apparently being genetically compatible). Connie wrote her own book, entitled *My Saturnian Lover* (1958), in which she described her relationship with Menger, who was a spiritual teacher named Sol da Naro.

Oddly, in the early 1960s, Menger performed an abrupt about-face and claimed that he had been working for the CIA in an experiment to test public reaction to claims of extraterrestrial civilizations. A few years later, he retracted these statements and maintained that his own contacts had been genuine.

MEN IN BLACK (FILM)

Made in 1997, directed by Barry Sonnenfeld and starring Tommy Lee Jones, Will Smith, Linda Fiorentino, Rip Torn and Vincent D'Onofrio. A hugely entertaining piece of comic-book science fiction (not to mention comic-book ufology), *Men in Black* follows the activities of an ultrasecret organization with the responsibility of maintaining order among the roughly 1,500 aliens currently residing on Earth (mostly in Manhattan). The plot is somewhat flimsy and seems to have something to do with an attempt to steal a miniature galaxy floating within a glass charm, which the eponymous heroes, Kay and Jay (Jones and Smith) must foil before Earth is blown to pieces by an alien spacecraft.

The film is exciting, funny and extremely cool; however, as might be expected, it pays little attention to genuine **Men in Black** lore, preferring to assume that the MIBs are human secret agents. This is understandable, since the legends surrounding the MIBs in the UFO literature are rather complex, contradictory and confusing.

MEN IN BLACK (MIB)

Mysterious personages who have, on numerous occasions, visited witnesses to UFO- and alien-related events and warned them not to discuss their experiences with anyone. Much debate has centered around the true identity of the MIBs, especially in view of their frequently bizarre appearance and behavior. MIBs are typically (although not invariably) described as wearing immaculate black suits, white shirts and black ties, hence their name. Occasionally, they wear old-fashioned Homburg-style hats. Indeed, there is a general air of the old-fashioned about them. They are frequently seen to drive large black cars, which, although appearing to be brand new, are nevertheless many years out of date. Although this in itself would seem strange enough, MIB percipients also report feelings of other-worldliness on many occasions, as if their unwanted guests are not quite human (see **Oz Factor**).

One of the most intriguing examples of an MIB encounter occurred on the evening of September 11, 1976. The percipient was Dr. Herbert Hopkins, a physician living in Orchard Beach, Maine. Dr. Hopkins had been involved in the investigation of a UFO encounter reported by a man named David Stephens, and had been conducting **hypnotic regression** on the witness (see **Norway, Maine**). On the evening in question, Dr. Hopkins was alone in the house, his wife and son having gone out to see a film, when he received a telephone call from a man claiming to be a representative of the New Jersey UFO Research Organization. The caller asked if he might come over to discuss the Stephens case, to which Hopkins readily agreed.

No sooner had this short conversation ended than he saw a man approaching the house. He later commented that there was no way the man could have arrived from the nearest public phone in that short time. (This was, of course, in the days before mobile cell phones were easily available!) As he showed his guest in, Hopkins noticed a number of other strange things about the man. He was dressed entirely in black, and when he took off his hat, Hopkins saw that he was completely bald; in fact, he was completely *hairless,* with no eyebrows or eyelashes. At one point in their conversation, the MIB drew his gloved hand across his deathly-pale face, and smeared the lipstick that he was wearing. Hopkins was astonished to realize that the makeup had been intended to give the impression of lips: the MIB actually had none.

Sitting perfectly still, the strange visitor asked Hopkins a number of questions about the Stephens case, speaking in a curious, expressionless monotone (a mode of speech often described in such cases). Presently, the MIB said that Hopkins had two coins in his pocket, which was true. He asked him to remove one, hold it in the palm of his hand and watch it. According to Hopkins:

It suddenly began to develop a silvery color—and
the silver became blue, and then I had trouble
focusing. I could focus on my hand perfectly well—
that was my reference point—but the coin was
simply gone. Not abruptly. It simply slowly
dematerialized—it just wasn't there anymore. I
didn't smell anything. I didn't feel anything. I didn't
hear anything. (Jenny Randles [1997], p. 165)

The MIB concluded this demonstration by stating: "Neither you nor anyone else on this plane will ever see that coin again." (Note he said "plane" rather than "planet," an intriguing touch which has prompted some researchers to suggest an extra-dimensional origin for the MIB.) The visitor then asked Hopkins if he knew how Barney **Hill** had died. Hopkins replied that, to the best of his knowledge, Hill had died of a stroke. The MIB disagreed. "No, Barney died because he had no heart, just as you no longer have your coin." This statement, understandably, chilled Hopkins to the bone, and when the MIB then instructed the physician to destroy all of his materials pertaining to the Stephens case, he subsequently complied.

However, as British ufologist Jenny Randles reminds us, the facts of the case were already public knowledge, and so it is difficult to see how any purpose could be served by this instruction.

At this point, the MIB's voice began to slow down dramatically, and he said: "My energy is running low . . . must go now . . . good-bye." He then stood up with great difficulty and left the house, walking even more stiffly and unsteadily than he had before. As soon as he had walked around the corner of the house, there was a bright flash of blue light. Hopkins searched for the man, but he had apparently vanished.

When the physician's wife and son returned home later, they found Hopkins sitting at the kitchen table with a gun and with all of the lights in the house switched on. Later inquiries revealed that there was no New Jersey UFO Research Organization. Not only had the MIB lied about this, but also about Barney Hill's death: he *had* died of a stroke, and not because his heart had disappeared from his chest!

One of the earliest encounters with an MIB occurred in 1952, after Carlo Rossi saw a strange flying object while fishing in the Serchio River, near San Pietro a Vico, Italy. Although he told no one of his encounter, when he returned to his fishing spot some weeks later, Rossi was approached by a man with extremely angular features, and who was dressed in a dark blue suit. Speaking Italian in a heavy Scandinavian accent, the man asked Rossi if he had seen any unusual flying objects in the area recently. Fearing the man's menacing demeanor, Rossi denied having seen anything, whereupon the stranger offered him a cigarette. Rossi described the cigarette as having a rather unusual gold mark on it. As soon as he began to smoke it, he felt nauseous, and the stranger instantly took it away from him, tore it to pieces and threw it away. He then left the puzzled fisherman alone on the riverbank.

Kenneth Arnold stands beside his private aircraft, which he was flying when he had his landmark sighting over the Cascade Mountains on June 24, 1947 (*Mary Evans Picture Library*)

Above Project Blue Book, U.S. Air Force UFO investigation project headed by Major Hector Quintanilla, established by the Pentagon in March 1952 and based at Wright-Patterson Air Force Base in Dayton, Ohio *(Mary Evans Picture Library)*

Left French-born computer scientist and UFO researcher Jacques Vallée *(Mary Evans Picture Library)*

Above Professional artist and sculptor Budd Hopkins, who has arguably become the world's foremost investigator of alien abductions *(Mary Evans Picture Library)*

Left Contactee Orfeo Angelucci, who wrote a book about his experiences entitled *Secret of the Saucers (Fortean Picture Library)*

Left A Martian encountered by Cedric Allingham on Februar[y] 18, 1954, while walking along the Scottish coast between Lossiemouth and Buckie *(Mary Evans Picture Library)*

Below Two of several photographs taken in 1967 of a UFO sighted in San José de Valderas, a suburb of Madri[d]. The sightings were part of an extremely elaborate hoax centering on an alleged planet called Ummo *(Fortean Picture Library)*

Above In southern Puerto Rico, 1980, two youths were waylaid in the mountains by a group of diminutive humanoid creatures, one of which was killed by one of the boys in a skirmish. They took the corpse back to Salinas and gave it to the owner of a funeral parlor, who preserved it in a glass jar of formaldehyde *(Quest Picture Library)*

Right Some time between September 21 and October 2, 1989, a UFO landed in front of numerous witnesses in Voronezh, 300 miles south of Moscow, Russia. The first witnesses to the landing were children, and these are some of the pictures they drew of what they saw *(Quest Picture Library)*

cвет
(light)

"кнопки"
(control-
buttons)

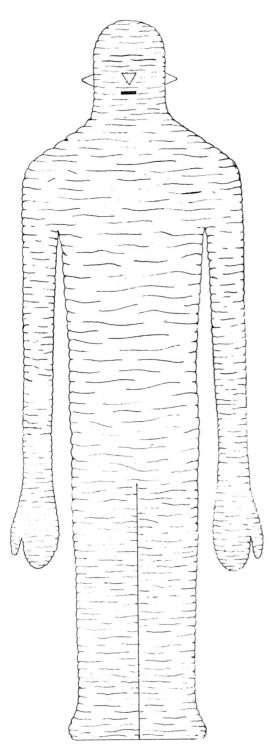

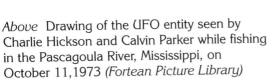

Above Drawing of the UFO entity seen by Charlie Hickson and Calvin Parker while fishing in the Pascagoula River, Mississippi, on October 11, 1973 *(Fortean Picture Library)*

Above Artist's impression of the humanoid creature seen in a park in the Jardim Andere district of Varginha, Brazil, in January 1996. Varginha was host to a great deal of UFO and alien-related activity at this time *(Quest Picture Library)*

Below Unmarked black helicopters have frequently been seen in connection with UFO/alien activity. Their origin and purpose remain shrouded in mystery *(Quest Picture Library)*

Above In July 1965, Valensole, France, farmer Maurice Masse was working on his lavender field when he encountered a UFO and its occupants. The illustration is superimposed on a photograph of the site *(Mary Evans Picture Library)*

Above The "scow" — an alien spacecraft from the planet "Clarion" — with whose occupants Truman Bethurum became quite friendly in 1952, in Nevada *(Mary Evans Picture Library)*

Left Aura Rhanes, captain of the "scow" *(Mary Evans Picture Library)*

Mawnan "Bird Man" based on
sketch by Juni Melling, witnessed
and drawn 17/4/76

I saw this monster
bird last night. It
stood like a man
then it flew up
though* the trees.
It is as big as a man. Its eyes are red an
shine brightly. Sally Chapman 4/7/76

Birdman monster. Seen on 3rd July, quite late at
night but not quite dark. Red eyes. Black mouth.
It was very big with great big wings and black claws.
Feathers grey
B. Perry 4th July 1976

Children's eyewitness drawings of the
Owlman, a flying humanoid that has
periodically terrorized the southwest of
England for some years, apparently
concentrating its activities around the
village of Mawnan, Cornwall (Fortean
Picture Library)

Left A frame from a movie film of Bigfoot (known as Sasquatch in Canada), taken by Roger Patterson, October 20, 1967, at Bluff Creek, northern California *(René Dahinden/ Fortean Picture Library)*

Right The Chupacabras, an extremely violent and dangerous anomalous animal, which made its first appearance in the years following an unexplained subterranean explosion in the Cabo Rojo area of Puerto Rico in 1987 *(Quest Picture Library)*

Left Mothman was seen by more than 100 people in Point Pleasant, West Virginia, 1966–67 *(Fortean Picture Library)*

Right The Yeti, also known as the Abominable Snowman, is an apparently nonhuman biped whose natural habitat is the Himalayas *(Fortean Picture Library)*

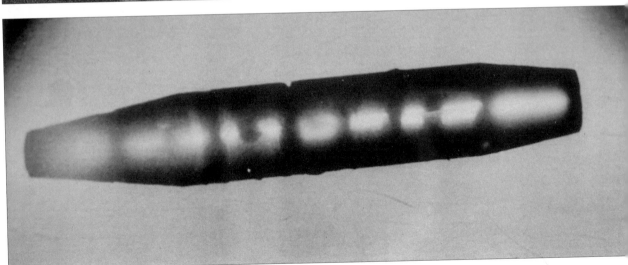

Top UFO contactee George Adamski (left) being interviewed on television by Long John Nebel *(Fortean Picture Library)*

Bottom The gigantic cigar-shaped Venusian interplanetary carrier photographed by Adamski over Palomar Gardens, California, 1952 *(Mary Evans Picture Library)*

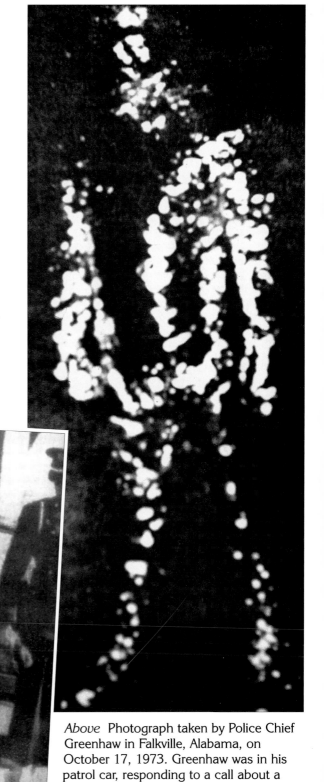

Above This famous picture allegedly depicting an alien was, according to German researcher Klaus Webner, produced as a joke for the April 1, 1950 edition of the newspaper *Wiesbadener Tagblatt* by its editor William Sprunkel and a photographer named Hans Scheffler. Scheffler's five-year-old son Peter *(right)* acted as a template for the alien, which was painted in by Scheffler later *(Quest Picture Library)*

Above Photograph taken by Police Chief Greenhaw in Falkville, Alabama, on October 17, 1973. Greenhaw was in his patrol car, responding to a call about a landed UFO, when he came upon the entity *(Quest Picture Library)*

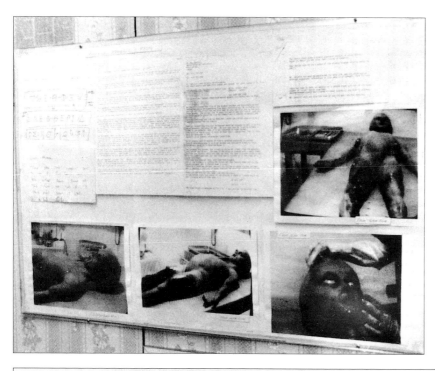

Left This display at the UFO museum at Roswell, New Mexico, shows stills from the controversial footage of an alien autopsy *(Fortean Picture Library)*

Below Front page of *Roswell Daily Record*, July 8 and 9, 1947 *(Fortean Picture Library)*

Leased Wire
Associated Press

Roswell Daily Record

RECORD PHONES
Business Office 2288
News Department 2287

VOL. 47 NUMBER 99 ESTABLISHED 1888   ROSWELL, NEW MEXICO,   TUESDAY, JULY 8, 1947   5c PER COPY

Movies as Usual

GRAND

Claims Army Is Stacking Courts Martial

Indiana Senator Lays Protest Before Patterson

Washington, July 8 (AP)—Senator Jenner (R-Ind.) contended today that "the high command in the European theatre is stacking courts against defendants in court martial."

In a letter to Secretary of War Patterson demanding a full investigation of army military trial procedure. Jenner offered what he said was documentary proof that

1 "Prisoners are not being permitted to employ either civilian or military counsel of their own choice in the preparation and presentation of their defense"

2 "Every effort is being made to prevent attorneys who were

RAAF Captures Flying Saucer On Ranch in Roswell Region

House Passes Tax Slash by Large Margin

Defeat Amendment By Demos to Remove Many from Rolls

Washington, July 8 (AP)—The house passed today the Republi-

Security Council Paves Way to Talks On Arms Reductions

Lake Success, July 8 (AP)—The United Nations security council today approved an American blueprint for arms reduction discussions despite a Russian warning that the plan would bring about a collapse of arms regulation efforts.

The vote was 9 to 0, with Russian and Poland abstaining

No Details of Flying Disk Are Revealed

Roswell Hardware Man and Wife Report Disk Seen

The intelligence office of the 509th Bombardment group at Roswell Arms Air Field announced at

Ex-King Carol Weds Mme. Lupescu.

Leased Wire
Associated Press

Roswell Daily Record

RECORD PHONES
Business Office 2288
News Department 2287

Vol. 47 NUMBER 100 ESTABLISHED 1888   ROSWELL, NEW MEXICO,   WEDNESDAY, JULY 9, 1947   5c PER COPY

Gen. Ramey Empties Roswell Saucer

Lewis Pushes Advantage in New Contract

Southern Mines Only Hold-outs In New Contract

Washington, July 9 (AP)—The odds lengthened today that John L. Lewis would play his new, ace-studded contract into a grand slam.

With 75 per cent of the soft

Sheriff Wilcox Takes Leading Role in Excitement Over Report 'Saucer' Found

Arrest 2,000 In Athens in Commie Plot

Revolution Was Set to Be Pulled Off Thursday

Athens, July 9 (AP)—The Greek government announced that more than 2,000 persons were arrested in the Athens area early today in raids aimed at stamping out a Communist plot to stage a revolu-

Send First Roswell Wire Photos from Record Office

Ramey Says Excitement Is Not Justified

General Ramey Says Disk Is Weather Balloon

Fort Worth, July 9 (AP)—The flying saucer fever spread to Iran today.

From reports from Zabool Shoorf and Sarbisheh near the Afghan frontier said residents there had observed strange satellite bodies" in the sky

Above The shack on the Foster Ranch (now the Bogle Ranch), near Corona, New Mexico, where rancher Mac Brazel and U.S. Army Air Force intelligence officers Major Jesse Marcel and Captain Sheridan Cavitt allegedly spent the night of July 6 or 7, 1947 before Brazel led the latter two to the "debris field" *(Karl Pflock/Fortean Picture Library)*

Right Marcel holds the tattered remains of a "flying disc" found that summer some 75 miles from Roswell. Marcel maintained that the material seemed "not of this Earth," but it was probably the remains of a weather balloon *(Fortean Picture Library)*

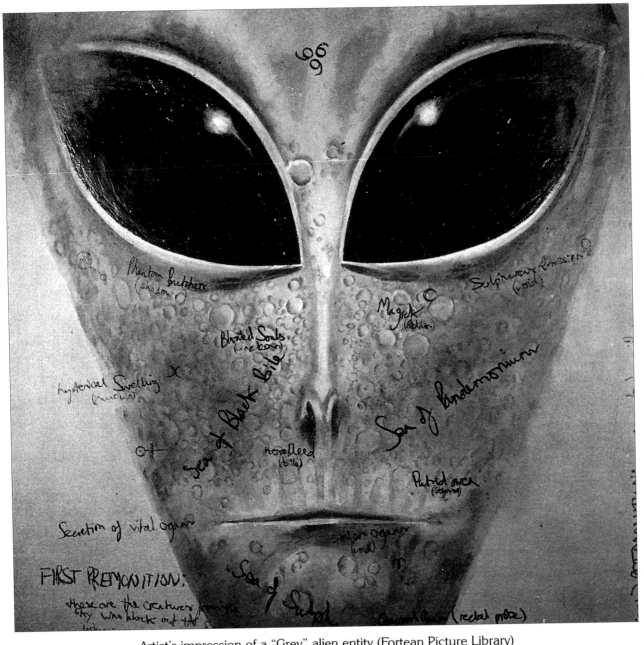

Artist's impression of a "Grey" alien entity (Fortean Picture Library)

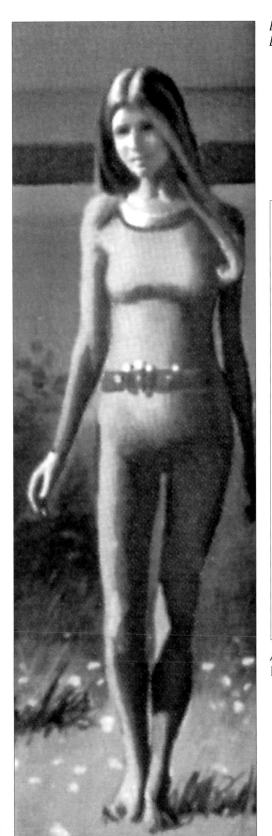

Left Artist's impression of a "Nordic" alien entity *(Quest Picture Library)*

Above An example of "Martian medium" Hélène Smith's Martian handwriting *(Fortean Picture Library)*

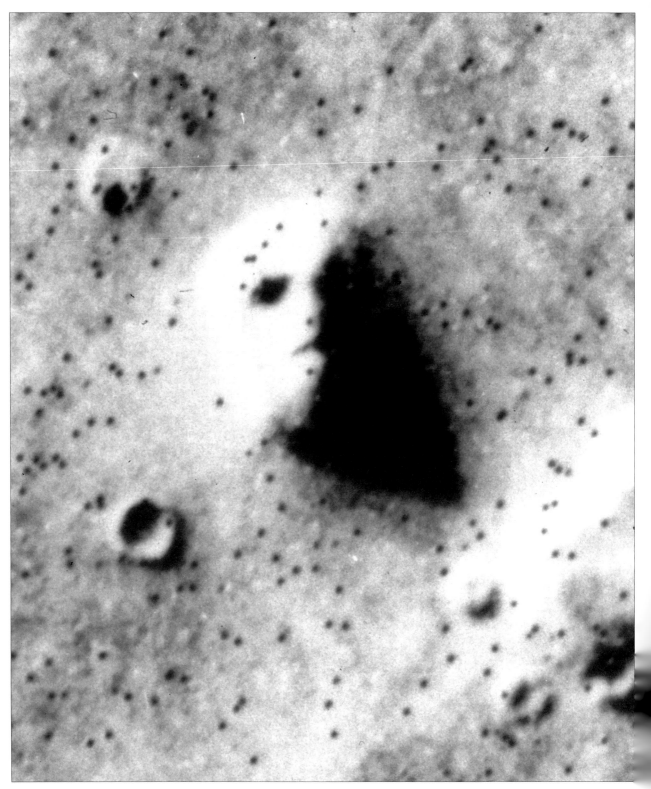
The "Face on Mars" or the "Martian Sphinx," which was photographed during the Viking missions to Mars in 1976 (Science Photo Library)

Typically, MIBs claim to represent either the government, the military or a civilian UFO group, although none of them have ever been traced to these origins. On the occasions where a witness thinks to note down the registration numbers of their cars, it is later discovered that no car has ever been registered with these numbers. Not all MIBs are bizarre in appearance: there are many cases in which they have appeared perfectly normal, although they are almost invariably described as being rather menacing and intimidating. Curiously, many of their victims later comment that it never occurred to them to ask their visitors to leave their homes, as they surely would have done on any other occasion. It seems that they are subdued through subtle but unknown means during the MIB visit, and fail to react in any significant way, even when their interrogators seem not to be human.

While some MIBs are apparently not human, others give no indication of anything other than an earthly origin, and may well be genuine government agents keeping an eye on UFO witnesses. Indeed, Jenny Randles has suggested that these human agents may be using MIB mythology to cover their tracks, even going so far as to behave in bizarre or ridiculous ways, thus ensuring that their activities are reported in trashy tabloids instead of responsible newspapers. This idea has been supported (after a fashion) by William **Moore**, who alleges that MIBs are indeed government agents in disguise. According to Moore, these agents work for a "bizarre" unit of U.S. Air Force intelligence, called the Air Force Special Activities Center (AFSAC) headquartered at Fort Belvoir, Virginia. Moore maintains that this unit was inspired to use the MIB disguise by the **Bender** case, which was the subject of Gray Barker's seminal 1956 book *They Knew Too Much About Flying Saucers,* the first book to address the mystery of the Men in Black.

Although many UFO researchers have suggested that some MIBs may indeed be alien beings disguised

(albeit rather ineptly) as humans, they seem to have more in common with ghosts and specters than aliens. Their appearance and behavior suggest that they are somehow dislocated in time; even their manner of expression owes something to the B-movies of the 1940s and 1950s. (One MIB told a witness not to report a UFO encounter "if you want your wife to stay as pretty as she is.") While the entirely normal-looking MIBs may well be human beings following their own obscure agendas, the more bizarre specimens could conceivably be psychic manifestations of the paranoia that gripped America in the 1950s. During these nightmare years, many innocent people were ruined as a result of allegations of Communist sympathies or affiliations. It could be that the more outlandish MIBs represent a psychic "echo" of that past national trauma, in a similar way to that in which certain houses and places are the sites of more traditional hauntings, resulting from violent or tragic events. In this respect, they may be similar to the **tulpas** of Tibetan mysticism. However, this would seem to fall short of explaining the encounters with MIBs that occur outside the United States. And yet, paranoia is not a psychological phenomenon exclusive to America; and, in a global context, MIB manifestations could represent the externalization of a common, deeply rooted fear and mistrust of authority.

The anomalist Jerome Clark has an alternative suggestion, although one still based on this psychic component:

One provisional interpretation, more descriptive than explanatory, might be that such occurrences take place in an "experiential reality"—a kind of subjective state that, at least in its ostensible physical setting, is indistinguishable from event-level reality; yet within this seemingly familiar environment, unearthly entities of various kinds appear and interact with the experient. They may be no more "real" than figures in unusually vivid dreams; thus, for example, they leave no footprints when they are seen to cross a muddy field. (Clark [1998], p. 384)

(See also **Keel, John Mothman, psychosocial hypothesis, ultraterrestrials**)

METALOGIC

A word suggested by ufologist Jacques **Vallée** to describe the strangeness inherent in many UFO and alien encounters. In such **high strangeness** cases, the behavior of the entities involved is characterized by absurdity, whether in their dress, speech or other activities. It has been suggested by Vallée and others that this behavior militates against an extraterrestrial origin for UFOs and "aliens," at least in terms of their being explorers from another planet. Nevertheless, such behavior does imply an advanced intelligence—so advanced, in fact, that its activities extend far beyond human concepts of rationality and logic.

The statements and activities of aliens encountered by both **contactees** and victims of **abductions** are examples of metalogic. Vallée gives the example of a man who was taken into a UFO in South America. During his experience, he saw the alien entities consulting an instrument that looked exactly like a clock, except that it had no hands. In another case, a UFO pilot asked a witness if he was in Italy or Germany. The now ubiquitous **Grays** have a habit of performing medical procedures that one would expect to be utterly unnecessary for a highly advanced civilization.

According to Vallée:

Situations such as these often have the deep poetic and paradoxical quality of Eastern religious tales ("What is the sound of one hand clapping?") and the mystical expressions of the Cabala, such as

references to a "dark flame." If you strive to convey a truth that lies beyond the semantic level made possible by your audience's language, you must construct apparent contradictions in terms of ordinary meaning. (Vallèe [1975], p. 36)

"MICHELIN MAN" (ALIEN)

Although a bewildering variety of aliens have been encountered over the last five decades or so, one particular feature has cropped up again and again in reports from all over the world, and that is the tubular, Michelin-man-type space suit. One such encounter occurred in La Plaine des Cafres, on Réunion Island in the Indian Ocean.

On July 31, 1968, a 31-year-old farmer named Luce Fontaine was picking some grass for his rabbits in a forest, when he saw a classic disk-shaped UFO hovering in the air about 80 feet away. Two glasslike cylinders protruded from the upper and lower surfaces of the object. Fontaine could make out two figures in the transparent center section of the craft. The entities were approximately three feet tall and were dressed in suits composed of horizontal tubes or folds. Each wore a dome-shaped helmet with a transparent visor, through which Fontaine could just discern their humanoid faces.

At that moment there was a blinding flash of light, which Fontaine likened to a welding arc, accompanied by a blast of heat and wind. By the time Fontaine had regained his senses, the craft and its occupants had vanished. When the police investigated the scene 10 days later, they discovered increased radioactivity in the area of the landing. Fontaine's clothes were similarly affected.

(See also **Holloman AFB** and **Marzano, Genoa, Italy**)

MILLER, RICHARD

American contactee who met alien beings on numerous occasions in the 1950s. His first encounter came in 1954, when he succeeded in contacting the extraterrestrials through the remarkably straightforward means of shortwave radio. He was told to drive to an isolated area near Ann Arbor, Michigan, where he waited for about 15 minutes before witnessing the arrival of a disk-shaped spacecraft. A hatch opened and a staircase was lowered to the ground. A young man, entirely human-looking and dressed in a brown single-piece suit, then emerged from the hatch and beckoned Miller to enter the craft.

He climbed the staircase and found himself in an entrance chamber that apparently circled the entire craft. The ufonaut "radiated a kind of friendliness," which put Miller completely at ease. He was then taken to the flight deck of the ship, where he met the commander, who spoke fluent English and introduced himself as Soltec. Soltec told Miller that the aliens came from the planet Centurus, in the Alpha Centauri star system. Why "Centurus" should sound so similar to "Centauri," a human word, was apparently not explained. Equally curious is the name of the Centuran craft: *Phoenix*, a creature of human mythology.

Soltec said that Centurus belonged to a "Universal Confederation" of more than 680 planets. Membership was allowed only when a civilization had reached a certain evolutionary level. In common with many other **contactees**, Miller was told that Earth was still quite a way from being granted membership of the wider galactic community, due to the warlike ways of humanity. According to Miller, the aliens had already contacted the governments of Earth with an offer of friendship, but had been turned away. The reason, unsurprisingly, was that those in power wanted to maintain their hold over the rest of humanity, and had subsequently covered up the alien presence. The Centurans had therefore decided to contact the people of Earth on an individual basis, in the hope that their existence would eventually become undeniable, even by those in authority.

Equally unsurprisingly, Soltec then went on to give a pseudo-history lesson, describing how the ancient civilizations of Atlantis and Lemuria had fought a nuclear war and destroyed each other, and adding that there were safer ways of utilizing the power of the atom than smashing it to pieces.

It is slightly odd that Richard Miller is nowhere near as famous as other contactees, such as Eduard **Meier**, since his own encounters continued for more than 20 years, and he produced a vast amount of written material on the Centurans.

"MINES" (ALIENS)

On November 9, 1979, Bob Taylor, a 61-year-old forestry foreman was inspecting some trees in a clearing near Livingston, Lothian, Scotland, when he became aware of a large, gray spherical object hovering nearby. The object was Saturn-shaped, with a wide rim around its equator and a number of dark openings. Taylor later suggested that the object might have been trying to camouflage itself, since it appeared to become unfocused as he watched it.

At that point, the object disgorged two smaller spheres, each about the size of a basketball. The spheres had six rodlike protuberances, which gave them the appearance of "sea mines." As they rapidly approached the witness, they made a sucking noise, and produced an odor so intense that Taylor lost consciousness.

He awoke about 20 minutes later to the sound of his dog barking. His left thigh was itching, and his chin felt as if something had burned it. In addition, his trousers were torn, and he felt nauseous. There was no sign of the large sphere, or the two "mines." Taylor staggered back to his truck and tried to radio for help, but the instrument would not work. He tried to drive away, but his disorientation was too severe and he was unable to avoid getting the vehicle stuck in mud. Eventually, he gave up trying to drive and walked home unsteadily.

The police were called in to investigate, and were sufficiently puzzled to treat Taylor's experience as an assault. They examined the scene of the encounter, and discovered an imprint apparently left by the large sphere, as well as smaller holes in the ground where the "mines" had rolled along.

While it is, of course, probable that something happened to Taylor while he was unconscious, no further investigation seems to have been carried out.

MISSING TIME

A principal element in some, although not all, alien **abductions**, missing time refers to the period of time within which an encounter with nonhuman entities occurs, and which the percipient is later unable to recall. Periods of missing time vary greatly in length, ranging from a few minutes to several days, as in the Travis **Walton** case. There are a number of theories to account for missing time; for instance, some researchers have suggested that it is the mind's own way of suppressing memories of traumatic events (many abduction experiences being of an extremely unpleasant nature). Others have suggested that it is the aliens themselves who erase the percipients' memories of what has happened to them. Many abductees have corroborated this, claiming that the aliens told them that they would be made to forget their experiences, although the apparent ease with which such memories can be retrieved by means of **hypnotic regression** makes one wonder why they would bother.

Skeptics have suggested that missing time is actually a perfectly normal occurrence, pointing out that most people perform mundane or repetitive tasks without much thought, and this can make time appear to pass more quickly than normal. However, it is difficult to see how this could account for experiences in which percipients lose several hours in the blink of an eye, finding themselves in a completely different location from the one occupied just before the missing time period.

It is also unclear why some percipients experience missing time, while others do not, and encounter nonhuman entities in full consciousness, remembering every detail of what occurred without the aid of hypnosis.

MJ-12

(See **Majestic 12**)

MOCA VAMPIRE

Possible forerunner to the **Chupacabras** or "Goatsucker." In the mid-1970s, Spanish researcher Salvador Freixedo investigated a number of unexplained animal deaths in and around the Puerto Rican town of Moca. According to Freixedo:

During an evening in which UFOs were sighted over the town of Moca, two ducks, three goats, a pair of geese, and a large hog were [slain and were found] the following morning on a small farm. The owner was going insane, wondering who in the world could have visited this ruin upon him. The animals betrayed the wounds that have become typical of this kind of attack [i.e. by the Chupacabras], and of course, they were all done with incredible precision . . . [T]here wasn't a trace of blood in any of the animals, and in spite of the fact that the dead geese had snow-white feathers, upon which the slightest speck of blood would have shown up immediately.

. . . I visited the rural areas on various occasions to investigate the events firsthand and found that the farmers were as intrigued by their animals' deaths as they were by the enigmatic lights that could be seen in the nocturnal skies. (Quoted in Internet article by Scott Corrales)

Freixedo also investigated the death of a cow found mutilated in a farmer's field. The skin had been pulled back from its head, and part of its nose was missing, "although there was no indication of rending." Unlike the Chupacabras, no sightings were made of the "Moca Vampire," although it seems extremely likely that the earlier attacks are linked to the now world-famous "Goatsucker."

(See also **cattle mutilations**)

MONTAUK PROJECT

Astonishingly bizarre conspiracy, which draws together a number of diverse elements, including UFOs, alien contact, time travel, psychic espionage, secret science and the clandestine exploration of other planets. The Montauk Project has its roots in the infamous **Philadelphia Experiment** of October 1943.

In the early 1970s, Preston Nichols, an electronics engineer and resident of Long Island, New York, had been experimenting with parapsychology, when he discovered that the psychics with whom he was working seemed to lose their ability at the same time every day. Subsequent research revealed that the psychics' abilities were being undermined by transmissions on the 410–420 MHz wavelength. Nichols pinned down the source of these transmissions to the U.S. Air Force Base just outside the town of Montauk, at the easternmost end of Long Island. The base had been officially decommissioned in 1969; however, when Nichols paid a visit, he found it to be very much active and tightly guarded.

In 1984, Nichols was informed by a friend that the Montauk base had once again been abandoned, and when he returned, he discovered large amounts of abandoned electronic equipment. In one of the buildings, he found a man living rough, who claimed to have been a technician on the "Montauk Project," which was apparently abandoned after the arrival of a strange and terrifying "beast." The vagrant also claimed to recognize Nichols as his erstwhile boss on the project. This was later corroborated when a stranger arrived at Nichols's house, claiming that Nichols had worked as assistant director on the project.

At that time, Nichols was employed at a defense contractor on Long Island and, following a hunch, he went to the basement of the building in which he worked. The basement contained a high security area, which was guarded by security personnel. Nichols walked up to one of the guards and handed him his low-level security pass; he was surprised when, without comment, the guard gave him a high-level pass in return. Once inside the area, Nichols entered a certain office. On the desk was a name plate with his name and the title "Assistant Project Director."

Later, Nichols experienced a flood of hitherto-suppressed memories concerning his work on the Montauk Project. Subsequent research and investigations revealed that the main intention of the project had been to manipulate time, using technology provided by aliens from the Sirius star system. The focus of these experiments was the "Montauk Chair," which was connected to a series of powerful computers. A psychic would sit in the chair, and his thoughts would be amplified by the computers to create a tunnel through hyperspace, connecting the Montauk base with different times and places.

The Montauk controllers then began to explore time and space via the hyperspatial tunnel, sending personnel through to observe their surroundings and report on what they found. According to Nichols, the Montauk controllers returned again and again to a ruined square in an unknown city in the year A.D. 6037. At the center of this square was a golden statue of a horse, surrounded by hieroglyphic inscriptions. Everyone who was sent through the tunnel was required to look at these inscriptions, apparently because the statue contained some form of technology, which the controllers wanted to investigate.

Nichols also maintains that a secret human colony on Mars had been trying to find a way into the derelict alien city in the Cydonia region (see **artifacts (alien)**) but had been unable to do so. The Montauk controllers then decided to open up a hyperspace tunnel to the region directly underneath the large, five-sided DiPietro-Molenaar Pyramid at the center of the city. An expedition was sent, and a technology was discovered, which came to be known as the "Solar System Defense." The alien equipment was interfering with an unspecified experiment being conducted on Mars, so it was shut off "retroactive to 1943." This, apparently, had the effect of allowing hostile UFOs into the Solar System (the modern era of UFO sightings has been dated to the mid- to late-1940s).

As the Montauk controllers became increasingly cavalier in their attitude to time exploration, even attempting the manipulation of the past on occasion, Nichols and certain of his colleagues decided to sabotage the project. Duncan Cameron, the most gifted of the psychics used in the Montauk Chair, was given a secret signal, whereupon he conjured up a terrifying monster from his unconscious mind, which proceeded to smash up the base. The controllers immediately ordered all the generators on the base to be shut down, which apparently banished the "beast" from normal space-time. This marked a suspension of the Montauk Project, although Nichols claims that it has since been resumed.

Preston Nichols, along with writer and advertising executive Peter Moon, has published a number of books about the project, including *The Montauk Project: Experiments in Time* (1992), and *Montauk Revisited: Adventures in Synchronicity* (1994). Among the strange claims of teleportation, time travel and mind control experiments, there is also an element of occultism and magic. In *Montauk Revisited*, Nichols and Moon describe a magical operation that was conducted in 1946 by the rocket scientist John

Whiteside, "Jack" Parsons and L. Ron Hubbard, founder of the Church of Scientology. The operation was called the Babalon Working, and was intended to open a doorway between dimensions, through which the goddess Babalon (meaning "understanding") might manifest. According to Nichols and Moon, the Babalon Working succeeded, allowing inimical forces from another dimension access to Earth. (Whether it was the Babalon Working or the deactivation of the DiPietro-Molenaar Pyramid that allowed these sinister Lovecraftian forces to manifest is not made clear.)

Interestingly (and perhaps uniquely), the authors of the Montauk books say that they are an "exercise in consciousness," and may be read as science fiction, if the reader so chooses. They also make the distinction between "hard facts," which are backed up by physical evidence or documentation; "soft facts," which are not untrue, but which cannot be verified; and "gray facts," which are merely plausible. The confusion between plausibility and fact is characteristic of the entire field of ufology. **Conspiracy theories** such as the Montauk Project can be seen as symptoms of a wide-spread apprehension regarding the ethical dangers arising from the advancement of science and technology.

MOORE, WILLIAM LEONARD

Highly controversial American UFO researcher and advocate of the **Majestic 12** documents. Moore was one of the first researchers to conduct an in-depth investigation of the apparent UFO crash near **Roswell**, New Mexico, in July 1947. While on a promotional tour for the book he coauthored with Charles Berlitz, *The Roswell Incident* (1980), Moore was telephoned by a man claiming to be a U.S. Air Force colonel, who requested a meeting to discuss Moore's findings. Moore would later call his contact "Falcon" (see **Aviary**), and would release information regarding the nine extraterrestrial races currently visiting Earth, one of which is the Gray race, from the **Zeta Reticuli** star system.

Falcon (real name Richard C. Doty) claimed to represent the U.S. Air Force Office of Special Investigations (AFOSI), who were very interested in the activities of Dr. Paul **Bennewitz**. In return for UFO-related information, Moore agreed to spy on Bennewitz for AFOSI, supplying him with **disinformation** in an attempt to confuse him and draw him away from sensitive lines of inquiry. Bennewitz was told of the secret treaty between the U.S. government and a race of evil aliens who needed to ingest animals and even humans to maintain their atrophied digestive systems. According to this disinformation, the aliens were also abducting humans and implanting them with mind control devices, as well as creating android beings from human and animal body parts (an activity reminiscent of the "underpeople" in the science-fiction stories of Cordwainer Smith). As these revelations pushed him closer and closer to a nervous breakdown, Bennewitz informed other UFO researchers (including John **Lear**) of the dreadful situation, thus creating a powerful mythology that has become deeply entrenched in ufology.

At a **MUFON** conference in Las Vegas, Nevada, in 1989, Moore delivered a lecture in which he confessed to working for AFOSI and supplying Bennewitz with disinformation. Moore stated that the disinformation program in which he was involved "gave every appearance of being somehow directly connected to a high-level government UFO project." In spite of the audience's anger at these revelations, Moore took no questions from the floor and exited the building as soon as he had finished.

According to Moore:

I would play the disinformation game, get my hands dirty just often enough to lead those directing the process into believing that I was doing exactly what they wanted me to do, and all the while continue to burrow my way into the matrix so as to learn as much as possible about who was directing it and why. (Quoted in Clark [1998], p. 164)

MOTHMAN

A large, headless, winged nonhuman entity that terrorized the community of Point Pleasant, West Virginia, U.S. in 1966–7. During a 13-month period, Mothman was seen by more than a 100 people, virtually all of whom described a creature seven feet tall, dark gray in color, with large wings and huge, brightly glowing red eyes that shone from the upper part of its torso.

Mothman was seen most often around the "TNT area," a disused explosives factory near Point Pleasant, although it was encountered by many more people throughout that area of the Ohio River valley. Interestingly, when witnesses reported sightings of the entity in flight, they maintained that its wings remained perfectly still. Even when it was seen to take to the air, Mothman's wings did not flap, as would be expected of an avian animal.

The Point Pleasant encounters were extensively investigated by New York journalist John A. **Keel**, who published his fortean classic *The Mothman Prophecies* in 1975. Keel's description of the period from late 1966 to late 1967 contains numerous elements of **high strangeness**, including **cattle mutilations**, UFO sightings, encounters with alien beings (see **Derenberger, Woodrow**) and visits from **Men in Black**.

There has, of course, been much speculation as to the significance of the strange events in and around Point Pleasant (which ceased as suddenly as they had begun). Keel himself blamed the weird manifestations on what he calls **ultraterrestrials**, malicious beings from another dimension of space-time. (See also **flying humanoids** and **Owlman**)

MUTUAL UFO NETWORK (MUFON)

International organization, based in Seguin, Texas, devoted to scientifically based study and research into the UFO phenomenon. Founded in May 1969, MUFON is a nonprofit corporation, which maintains that "a concentrated scientific study by dedicated investigators and researchers will provide the ultimate answer to the UFO enigma [MUFON website]."

MUFON is currently the largest UFO organization in the world, with some 5,000 members, and representatives in many countries. In North America, individual field investigators are supervised by state directors, and the entire organization is governed by a Board of Directors comprising 21 men and women. The current international director is Walter H. Andrus. MUFON also produces the monthly *MUFON UFO Journal*, which includes articles on every aspect of ufology, as well as the findings of recent investigations.

Like the J. Allen **Hynek Center for UFO Studies** in Chicago, MUFON is notable for the emphasis it places on rational, scientific investigation. As a result, its membership includes many representatives of academia, such as physicists, chemists, historians and engineers.

NATIONAL AERONAUTICS AND SPACE ADMINISTRATION (NASA)

On a list of people who might be expected to encounter UFOs on a more or less regular basis, astronauts must surely come somewhere near the top. For this reason, ever since its creation in 1958 to coordinate and direct U.S. aeronautical and space research activities, NASA has come under the scrutiny of the UFO community, and it seems that ufologists have been justified in this.

During their Gemini V flight, on August 24, 1965, Gordon Cooper and Charles Conrad were asked by the flight director, Christopher Kraft, if they could see anything flying near their capsule. Kraft said: "We have a radar image of a space object going right along with you from 2,000 to 10,000 yards away. The radar return is approximately the same magnitude as Gemini V."

The following is a transcript of an exchange between Mission Control and the crew of Gemini VII, Jim Lovell and Frank Borman:

SPACECRAFT: Bogey at 10 o'clock high.

CAPCOM: This is Houston. Say again 7.

SPACECRAFT: Said we have a bogey at 10 o'clock high.

CAPCOM: Gemini 7, is that the booster or is that an actual sighting?

SPACECRAFT: We have several, looks like debris up here. Actual sighting.

CAPCOM: Estimate distance or size?

SPACECRAFT: We also have the booster in sight . . .

By far the most famous sightings were allegedly made by the crew of Apollo 11, while in transit to the Moon and on the lunar surface. The first sighting occurred after only one day in space, when the crew (comprising Neil Armstrong, Edwin "Buzz" Aldrin and Michael Collins) spotted an unusual object ahead of them. The UFO seemed capable of altering its shape, appearing first as a pair of hollow cylinders, and then as an "open book."

According to rumors that have continued to circulate despite vehement denials from NASA, almost as soon as the Lunar Excursion Module *Eagle* made its historic landing in the Sea of Tranquillity on July 21, 1969, a number of large alien spacecraft landed nearby. Dr. Vladimir Azhazha, professor of mathematics at Moscow University, maintains that all messages referring to UFO activity in space and on the Moon were censored by NASA, a claim that, once again, has been dismissed by the agency. NASA's chief spokesman, John McLeaish, stated that the only delays in the transmission of messages from the Moon occurred as a result of normal processing through equipment.

Some of these rumors are rather wilder than others. According to one, several alien beings disembarked from one of the UFOs and stood on the lunar surface, apparently carefully watching the *Eagle.* Mission Control was apprised of the situation and ordered Neil Armstrong and Buzz Aldrin to remain inside the module until the alien spacecraft had departed. As history shows, they disobeyed this order (although it seems more likely that they would have obeyed it, in view of the aliens' unknown intentions).

The British researcher Timothy Good asked Dr. Paul Lowman of NASA's Goddard Space Flight Center whether the rumors regarding the cover-up of UFO-related messages was feasible. He quotes Lowman's reply in his book *Beyond Top Secret: The Worldwide UFO Security Threat*:

Most of the radio communications from the Apollo crew on the surface were relayed in real time to earth. I am continually amazed by people who claim that we have concealed the discovery of extraterrestrial activity on the Moon. The confirmed detection of extraterrestrial life, even if only by radio, will be the greatest scientific discovery of all time, and I speak without exaggeration. The idea that a civilian agency such as NASA, operating in the glare of publicity, could hide such a discovery is absurd, even if it wanted to. One would have to swear to secrecy not only the dozen astronauts who landed on the Moon but also the hundreds of engineers, technicians, and secretaries directly involved in the missions and the communication links. (Good [1996], p. 453)

NATIONAL INVESTIGATIONS COMMITTEE ON AERIAL PHENOMENA (NICAP)

NICAP grew from humble beginnings to be perhaps the most influential of UFO organizations. Its origins were in a small monthly discussion group run by Clara L. John, editor of a minor flying saucer newsletter called *Little Listening Post.* These informal meetings were held in Washington, D.C., in 1956, and were attended by physicist T. Townsend Brown. Brown was interested in the **propulsion of UFOs**, and was convinced that a prolonged scientific investigation into the phenomenon would yield useful insights into the problems surrounding human interstellar flight.

The need for a serious scientific investigation of UFOs was voiced by many people, and so, on August 29, 1956, Brown founded the National Investigations Committee on Aerial Phenomena, which was officially incorporated on October 24. NICAP's Board of Governors boasted several highly respected citizens, including Rear Admiral Delmer S. Fahrney, who had directed the U.S. Navy's guided missile program, and retired Marine Corps major Donald E. **Keyhoe**.

However, NICAP got into financial trouble almost immediately. Keyhoe blamed Brown (who was director) for inefficient management and demanded his resignation. Brown complied, and Keyhoe was asked to replace him. He agreed.

Keyhoe was not much better than Brown at managing the organization; despite his grand prediction of 100,000 members by the end of 1957, NICAP could only claim 5,000 members a year later. Funding was a constant problem. Keyhoe not only asked members for donations, he put a good deal of his own money into the beleaguered organization. In spite of these tribulations, NICAP retained its credibility as a serious UFO investigation group.

In the mid-1960s, NICAP's membership increased to 14,000 as a result of numerous UFO reports. The organization also supported the University of Colorado UFO Project, under the direction of physicist Edward U. Condon, but when it became clear that Condon had no intention of examining the phenomenon impartially, NICAP announced its intention to "do all that the Colorado Project was supposed to do."

These noble intentions were scuppered, on the one hand by Keyhoe's lack of management skills, and on the other by the Condon report, *The Scientific Study of Unidentified Flying Objects*, which concluded that UFOs were not worthy of serious scientific investigation. The resulting decline in public interest (exacerbated by a fall in the number of reports) hit NICAP hard, and its membership fell to below 5,000. Keyhoe was fired in December 1969, and Joseph Bryan III became acting director until a permanent replacement could be found. John L. Acuff took over the leadership but resigned in 1978. Although rumors abounded (and still abound) that NICAP was infiltrated and undermined by the **CIA**, UFO historian Jerome Clark maintains that the agency's influence was not nearly as pernicious as some people have suggested.

NICAP was disbanded in 1980, and its files were turned over to the J. Allen **Hynek Center for UFO Studies**.

NATIONAL SECURITY AGENCY (NSA)

The National Security Agency was founded in 1952 by President Harry Truman with the purpose of planning, coordinating and directing signals intelligence and information in support of United States defense. According to the NSA website:

The ability to understand secret foreign communications while protecting our own—a capability in which the United States leads the world—confers a unique competitive advantage. The skill to accomplish this is cryptology, the fundamental mission and core competency of NSA. NSA is charged with two complementary tasks: exploiting foreign electromagnetic signals and protecting the electronic information critical to U.S. national security. "Exploiting" is referred to as signals intelligence; "protecting" is known as information systems security. Maintaining this global advantage requires preservation of a healthy cryptologic capability in the face of unparalleled technical challenges.

In the signals intelligence (SIGINT) role, NSA intercepts and analyzes foreign electromagnetic signals—many of them protected by codes, ciphers, and complex electronic countermeasures—to produce intelligence information for decisionmakers and military commanders. The focus is on interpretation of three broad types of signals: communications, such as telephone or teleprinter messages; non-communications signals, such as radars; and telemetry, the signals associated with missiles, weapons systems and space vehicles.

According to some conspiracy theorists within the ufology field, there is a top secret project, known as Sigma, which oversees electronic communications with extraterrestrial groups. This project is run through the National Security Agency.

NAZI FLYING SAUCERS

A highly controversial alternative to the **extraterrestrial hypothesis**, the theory of Nazi flying saucers grew out of the very real development of advanced flying machines by the Third Reich during the Second World War. According to researchers such as Renato Vesco and W. A. Harbinson, in addition to the well-known Messerschmitt ME-262, the first fully operational jet fighter, Nazi scientists had also made significant advances in the development of radically new, high-performance aeroforms.

The first of these was known as the *Feuerball*, a small (about five feet) spherical aircraft, called the "Foo Fighter" by the Allied air crews who encountered them during bombing runs over Germany. The basic flight principles of the *Feuerball* were later incorporated into a larger, more advanced, disk-shaped machine called the *Kugelblitz* (Ball Lightning Fighter). W. A. Harbinson's researches yielded the name Rudolph Schriever, a former *Luftwaffe* aeronautical engineer who had allegedly designed, built and test flown the *Kugelblitz* between 1941 and 1943.

In his introduction to *Man-Made UFOs 1944–1994: 50 Years of Suppression* by Renato Vesco and David Hatcher Childress, Harbinson outlines one of the many newspaper clippings, dating from the 1950s, which he uncovered:

Flugkapitan Schriever, with "three trusted colleagues," had actually constructed, in August 1943, a "large specimen" of his original "flying disk," but . . . in the summer of 1944, in the East Hall of the BMW plant near Prague, he had redesigned the original model, replacing its former gas turbine engines with some highly advanced form of jet propulsion. (x–xi)

Apparently, the *Kugelblitz* had a diameter of 137.76 feet, a height of 104.96 feet, and was capable of reaching 1,250 mph at an altitude of 40,000 feet.

When it became clear that Germany would lose the war, Schriever destroyed the *Kugelblitz* prototype. The best Nazi scientists and engineers were then evacuated to a secret underground base in an area of Antarctica, which had been stolen from Norway, and whose name had been changed from Queen Maud Land to *Neuschwabenland*. Safely ensconced in the icy fastness of Antarctica, the Nazis continued to develop their technology, which has been responsible for most of the genuine UFO sightings since the war.

According to Harbinson and others, the renegade Nazis have met on many occasions with administrations in both America and the former Soviet Union, and have traded obsolete items of their technology for essential materials. In the 1950s and 1960s, both superpowers used this technology in their own research into disk-shaped aircraft design, and were able to develop their own vehicles. However, since the Nazis in Antarctica have always managed to remain several steps ahead, their position remains unassailable, and they remain in Antarctica.

NEAR-DEATH EXPERIENCES (NDEs)

There are a number of striking parallels between encounters with apparent alien beings, and near-death experiences. The NDE is a puzzling and potentially hugely significant event, which can occur when a person has sustained a life-threatening injury or is on the point of death for other reasons. Thousands of people have reported NDEs, and the basic elements are remarkably consistent; these include the sudden awareness that one is "outside" of one's body, followed by travel through a long, dark tunnel, at the end of which is an incredibly bright light, which, nevertheless, is easy to look at. Once "inside" this light, the experiencer frequently meets friends and family members who are dead. At that point, however, another presence makes itself known. This presence is almost always described as sublimely compassionate, and will make it known to the experiencer that it is not yet time to enter the afterlife, whereupon he or she will then return to the physical body.

In a typical alien abduction, the experiencer also has a feeling of floating and approaching a bright light. Instead of friends and loved ones, however, the abductee will find himself in the company of celestial beings of a different kind. Usually these are seen as cold and malevolent (or, at the very least, disinterested in the well-being of the experiencer). Although the two experiences are characterized by different emotions (NDEs produce feelings of extreme happiness, while abductions are frequently terrifying), they are nevertheless profoundly similar in terms of a journey to another "reality" (see **Oz Factor**).

Dr. Kenneth Ring, professor of psychology at the University of Connecticut, has made an in-depth study of the parallels between NDEs and alien encounters, which are reproduced in his book *The Omega Project: Near-Death Experiences, UFO Encounters and Mind at Large* (1992). Dr. Ring suggests that the journey into another "reality" (which is common to both scenarios) is a manifestation of **encounter-prone personalities**, in which a high degree of spiritual sensitivity is evident.

NIAGARA FALLS, NEW YORK

Scene of a very strange encounter in January 1958. At 1:30 A.M., a woman (whose anonymity has been maintained) was driving along the New York State Thruway near Niagara Falls. There was a violent snowstorm, and the woman was driving extremely carefully, looking for an exit from the thruway. In the distance, she could just about make out what she took to be a plane crash on the center section of the road.

As she drew closer, she saw what appeared to be a narrow, illuminated rod, approximately 50 feet high, which was apparently sinking into the ground. At that point, the car's engine and lights died, sending the woman into something of a panic. She then became aware of two shapes rising around the pole, which continued its apparent descent into the ground. "They seemed to be like animals with four legs and a tail but two front feelers under the head, like arms. Then, before I could even gasp the things disappeared and the shape rose and I then realized it was a saucer, it spun and zoomed about ten feet off the ground and went up into the air and I could not even see where it went." (Vallèe [1990] pp. 22–3)

NORDICS

A race of extraterrestrial beings first reported by the **contactees** of the 1950s and 1960s. The Nordics are so called because of their Scandinavian appearance. They are invariably described as being tall and strikingly attractive, with blond or sandy-colored hair, which they frequently wear fairly long, and blue (sometimes catlike) eyes. They are usually described as wearing tight-fitting, single-piece ski-type suits.

Encounters with the Nordics were the first to be widely reported, and occurred early in the modern era of ufology. At this stage, alleged encounters with aliens were entirely pleasant affairs: the visitors would greet the witnesses politely, and would frequently offer guided tours of their spaceships. On many occasions they would offer trips to the Moon and other planets in the Solar System. These beings usually claimed to be natives of Venus and Mars; some claimed to have come from worlds slightly farther afield, such as Saturn and Uranus.

Although the contactees were primarily American (George **Adamski**'s early encounter in 1952 with a man from Venus occurred in California), reports of Nordics became a particularly European phenomenon in the following decades. Their attitude toward humans was much more civilized than that subsequently displayed by the fascist-like **Grays**; indeed, in the years since the Grays made their appearance, the Nordics have told those whom they contact that they are aware of the Grays' activities, and that humans should be aware of those diminutive miscreants. As far as the Nordics are concerned, humanity should be nurtured and guided toward a more enlightened way of living. They are very fond of warning us about our misuse of technology (particularly nuclear energy), although they never seem to come up with any useful alternatives.

Throughout the 1960s, '70s and '80s, the number of encounters with Nordics steadily declined, and now their position as the main species visiting Earth has been almost totally usurped by the ubiquitous Grays, although they are still sometimes reported in the United Kingdom and continental Europe. There have even been reports from several abductees of Nordics and Grays working together, although this is rather rare. For the most part, the Nordics, although apparently in retreat, prefer to maintain their policy of observation rather than direct interference in the affairs of humanity.

(See also **Meier, Eduard "Billy"**)

NORWAY, MAINE

Scene of an extremely strange UFO encounter in 1975. At 3:00 A.M. on October 27, two shift workers, 21-year-old David Stephens and 18-year-old Glen Gray, were playing music in their trailer home when a terrific explosion brought them hurrying outside. They were unable to see anything that might have caused the noise. They then decided, for some reason they were unable to fathom, to go for a drive up to Lake Thompson, about 12 miles away.

They had driven about a mile along Route 26, when the car suddenly turned into a lane. Despite his best efforts, Gray could not regain control of the vehicle, which gradually picked up speed. As the lane became a rough track, the men realized that the ride was inordinately smooth.

Events then took an even stranger turn, as the car passed a field and the two men saw a group of cows shaking their heads from side to side. Presently, the car came to a stop near another field containing two bright lights. At first, Stephens and Gray assumed that the lights belonged to a truck. When the lights ascended into the air, they decided it must be a helicopter, and so they switched off the engine and wound down the windows, listening for the sound of its engine. They were greeted only with silence, and as the lights approached them, they saw that the "helicopter" was actually a metallic cylinder.

Gray discovered that the car was once again under his control. He and Stephens closed their windows, locked their doors and drove away as fast as they could. The car had barely driven a mile when it was enveloped in a blinding white light, and the men lost consciousness. They awoke to find themselves another mile down the road, with their windows open and the doors unlocked. They were also shocked to discover that their eyes were glowing orange!

Looking into the early morning sky, they again spotted the UFO, which was drifting away to the east. They continued on for another couple of miles, whereupon the UFO vanished. Gray was then somehow forced to turn onto another road leading to Tripp Pond, at the southern end of Lake Thompson, whereupon the UFO reappeared, and the car engine died. The UFO then ascended farther into the sky and remained motionless until it was joined by two other objects, which were disk-shaped and displayed red, blue and green lights. These smaller UFOs proceeded to dart over the surface of the pond.

At that point, Stephens and Gray noticed a thick fog rising from the waters. The pond also seemed, incredibly, to increase in size until it appeared as vast as an ocean. As the two men gazed in bewilderment at the scene before them, an island appeared in the center of the "ocean," above which one of the disk-shaped UFOs hovered.

At 6:30 A.M., the car's engine started again, and Stephens and Gray drove home, with the cylinder-shaped UFO still hovering overhead. In his examination of this weird case, the anomalist Mike Dash has this to say:

The bizarre recollections of Stephens and Gray mark their encounter as a "**high-strangeness**" case—a report characterized by its essential illogicality, the dreamlike quality of its imagery and the unlikelihood that its events actually occurred as described. Such reports often have psychical components, and because their complexity makes them difficult to evaluate and their content means that they are hard to believe literally, they have often been ignored by mainstream ufologists. (Dash [1997], p. 158)

(See also **Men in Black**)

OAKENSEN, ELSIE

British abductee. On November 22, 1978, Oakensen was driving home from work, and was on a road approaching the village of Church Stowe, Northamptonshire, when she saw a dumbbell-shaped UFO hovering about 100 feet above the road. There were two lights, one red and one green, on the smooth, gray surface of the object. Unwilling to stop on the busy road (no one else seems to have seen the UFO), she drove underneath it and continued toward Church Stowe. Suddenly, her car lost power. She was enveloped in a pulsating light, and recovered a little farther down the road. However, she realized that 15 minutes had passed, which she could not account for.

After a single unsuccessful attempt to recover her **missing time** through the use of **hypnotic regression**, Oakensen was encouraged to try creative visualization at the scene of her UFO sighting by the British ufologist Jenny Randles. As a result, she was able to recall being led to a place where she was "scanned" with a bright light by shadowy, gray shapes. Apparently, Oakensen was not quite satisfactory, and she had the feeling that she had been "rejected" by the entities, who returned her to her car.

Interestingly, Randles states that there was an independent sighting less than two hours after Oakensen's encounter, about four miles away.

Four women, younger than Mrs. Oakensen but who did not know of her or her story (and vice versa), were driving through the village of Preston Capes. They saw similar colored lights to those which first alerted Elsie Oakensen and then parallel beams shot from a cloud. Their car began to lose power and the object paced them, until they entered the village lit by street lamps and the car returned to normal. The

UFO lights now merged into one and vanished. (Randles [1994], p. 159)

Since no clear link between the two encounters had been established at the time, there was no follow up on the other witnesses to establish whether they, too, experienced missing time.

O'BARSKI, GEORGE

American UFO witness. O'Barski, a liquor store manager in New York City, was returning home after work in the early hours of a January morning in 1975. He was driving through North Hudson Park on his way to an all-night diner, when his car radio crackled with static and then died. At that point, he heard a strange noise and saw a disk-shaped UFO descending into the park.

As O'Barski watched in amazement, the UFO landed and 10 small figures, dressed in uniforms, disembarked. The beings proceeded to dig up pieces of turf with small shovels, and placed the pieces in bags, before climbing back into their craft. The object then took off and flew away.

The ufonauts left behind approximately 15 triangular holes in the ground, which were still visible some months later. When investigators tried to locate other witnesses to the event, they were contacted by William Pawlowski, the doorman of an apartment block overlooking North Hudson Park. Pawlowski claimed to have seen a disk-shaped object flying over the park on the night in question.

OLD SAYBROOK, CONNECTICUT

Scene of a relatively uncommon close encounter in which nonhuman entities were seen *inside* a UFO. Early on the morning of December 16, 1957, a former teacher named Mary Starr was awakened by a bright light shining into her bedroom. Going to the window, she saw a cylindrical UFO hovering above her garden. The object was between 20 and 30 feet long and contained several openings or portholes. There were also a number of smaller lights around the rim.

The portholes apparently extended to the deck of the craft, for through them Starr could clearly see two figures moving past each other, in their entirety. Starr described the figures as being approximately four feet tall and dressed in a single garment that flared out into a bell shape from the neck. Each entity had a transparent, orange, cube-shaped "helmet," through which could be seen a bright red, perfectly spherical "head." Both entities had their right arms raised, as if in some kind of salute. Neither seemed to have hands.

As Starr continued to watch, a third entity appeared, and at this point the craft began to glow brightly. This had the effect of obscuring the portholes and the interior. An antenna briefly appeared from the upper surface of the craft, then withdrew as the UFO moved off into the distance. It then tilted upward and flew away at terrific speed.

ORANG BATI

A flying humanoid indigenous to the Indonesian island of Seram. In his book *The Unexplained* (1996), cryptozoologist Karl Shuker describes a visit to Seram by the tropical agriculturist Tyson Hughes in June 1986. According to the local people, the orang bati live inside the extinct volcanoes in Seram's largely unexplored interior.

The orang bati inspire abject terror in the indigenous population, who describe the creatures as man-shaped, about five feet tall and with red skin. They have large, black, batlike wings and a long, thin tail. The "islanders" fear seems to be well-founded, for they told Hughes that at night the orang bati leave their volcanic homes amid Seram's rain forest and fly out to the human settlements along the coast. There they occasionally abduct a child and carry it back to their volcanoes, from which it never returns.

(See also **flying humanoids, Mothman, Owlman**)

ORANGES (ALIENS)

A group of nonhuman, or perhaps semihuman, entities associated with alien activity in a number of locations, notable the underground alien **bases** said to be located at various points throughout the world, but especially in the western Unites States. The Oranges are said to be quite similar to humans in appearance, although their hair is red, their skin has an orange tone, and there is something of the reptilian in their faces.

It has been suggested that the Oranges are a hybrid race (see alien/human **hybrids**), but one that has been produced through the fusion of humans and **Reptoids**, rather than humans and **Grays**. People who have encountered these beings in the environment of an underground base report that they seem to perform the tasks of servants or menials.

(See also **Dakelia Barracks, Cyprus**)

ORLAND PARK, ILLINOIS

Location of a close encounter with nonhuman entities that contains some elements of **high strangeness**. At eleven o'clock on the morning of September 24, 1951, a 24-year-old steelworker named Harrison Bailey was walking through some woods near Orland Park, when he suddenly felt a burning sensation on his neck. Turning, he saw a large, gray, oval object at the edge of a nearby field. At one of the object's windows, Bailey could see two humanoid figures, with helmets and tinted visors, watching him. The entities asked him, apparently through telepathic means, where he came from and where he was going. Bailey then walked away from the craft, feeling incredibly fatigued. He also suffered cramps throughout his body. There then followed a lengthy period of **missing time**, since the next thing Bailey knew, it was late afternoon.

Interestingly, this part of his experience was corroborated in a rather unsettling way. Bailey, a black man, had told no one of his strange encounter, and yet the following day he was stopped by a threatening group of white men, who demanded to know if he had "come out of a flying saucer yesterday." Bailey denied knowing anything about it.

Over the years that followed, Bailey suffered numerous health problems, which he attributed to his encounter with the UFO and its occupants. In 1975 he decided to undergo **hypnotic regression** in an effort to discover what had happened during those missing hours in September 1951.

Under hypnosis, he recalled the woods being invaded by numerous diminutive creatures that looked like frogs, but which walked upright. The frog-beings were about one and a half feet tall, with large eyes that wrapped around the sides of their heads; their mouths were no more than slits. Their hands were tiny, as were their feet, which had three toes. Their skin was smooth, brown and striped.

Most oddly, the frog-beings were accompanied by hundreds of dark, inch-long insects, which bore some resemblance to ladybirds, and which moved quickly in all directions. The frog-beings communicated with each other in high-pitched squeaks as they jumped up and down around Bailey, repeatedly touching his hips.

As his hypnosis revealed, it was only upon running away from these strange creatures that Bailey came upon the landed UFO on the edge of the field. At that point he lost consciousness, and awoke inside the craft. He was approached by two of the helmeted humanoids, who once again communicated with him telepathically, telling him that their intentions were entirely peaceful, and that they wanted to establish open contact with humanity. As Bailey tried to avoid looking at their faces, which were strange and flattened, and only partially hidden by the visors, they continued that he had been chosen as spokesman for them.

However, for some reason, Bailey never achieved anything approaching the fame experienced by the like of George **Adamski**, despite giving up his job and becoming a preacher. He received only limited further visits by the aliens, in 1977 and 1978.

(See also **contactees**)

OVERLORDS

A mysterious and little-known group of aliens who contacted a Swedish man in 1965. On December 9, "Helge" (pseudonym) was out walking on a frozen lake near his home. He had recently been diagnosed with a kidney stone, and would be operated on in a few days' time. As he continued his walk, he came upon a UFO that had landed on the ice. The ship's crew were humanoid, with no hair, pointed ears and slanted eyes. They passed a cylindrical instrument over his body, which had the effect of dissolving the kidney stone (the following day, Helge's doctor was astonished to find that the stone had vanished). The alien commander told Helge that his race would soon arrive at Earth with a vast fleet of spacecraft. When it began to grow dark, the aliens climbed aboard their saucer and left.

Helge did not encounter the aliens again until August 1966, when he returned to the now thawed lake and saw a UFO hovering overhead. As the craft descended toward the water, he rowed out onto the lake in a dinghy. One of the ufonauts then gave him a small sheet of metal containing strange symbols, told him to keep it on his person at all times, and then instructed him to go to the Bahamas. For some reason, Helge decided to bury the metal plate.

Neither Helge nor his wife were sure what to do about their odd instructions. Eventually, however, they decided to follow them, and flew to the Bahamas in March 1967. They had received further instructions (presumably through telepathic means) to go to the island of Little Exuma. Unfortunately, however, they forgot to retrieve the metal plate from its hiding place, and so their trip was without incident.

On the return flight to Sweden, Helge noticed that there were 14 Catholic priests on the plane, one of whom, Father Rapas, told Helge that he worked as an agent for the aliens, whom he referred to as the Overlords.

Helge then became involved with a UFO research group in Stockholm. In January 1968 the group received a letter from Father Rapas, telling them that the Overlords wanted them to start a peace organization, which would be called the New Generation and which would follow 65 rules, called the "Rapas Rules." This split the UFO group, some of whose members did not like being told what to do. However, the New Generation grew eventually to include some 600 members, and apparently received its funding from the Overlords themselves.

Once again, Helge was instructed to go to Little Exuma, which he did, this time remembering to bring the metal plate. From there he was taken by two Overlord agents to a nearby island containing an alien base beneath a mountain. According to conspiracy researcher Jim Keith, in his *Casebook on the Men in Black*:

There were a number of entities resident in the mountain, including giants, dwarves, and hermaphrodites. Helge also met members of the group who had originally contacted him, and other individuals conforming to the **MIB** description, who had thin pointed features, were deeply tanned and Oriental-looking, and had long fingers and dark eyes. (Keith [1997], p. 71)

Helge was shown a three-dimensional record of Earth's history, and an armory containing many high-tech weapons, and one of the Overlords' cars—a self-steering Cadillac! He was told that the underground base was the training center for the New Generation. Apparently, while Helge was in the Bahamas, another Overlord agent, an American named Loftin, notified the **CIA** of the aliens' presence. He was later murdered, albeit in a mundane way, with a bullet to the head.

Helge continued his association with the Overlords for the next 20 years, only breaking with them when he began to suspect that they were merely mercenaries who would ally themselves with whomever best served their interests. As Jim Keith comments, there is a close parallel between the Overlords and the equally bizarre communications from the planet **UMMO** that occurred around the same time.

OWLMAN

A flying humanoid that has periodically terrorized the southwest of England for some years, apparently concentrating his activities around the village of Mawnan, Cornwall. The first encounter occurred on April 17, 1976, when two sisters, 12-year-old June and nine-year-old Vicky Melling saw a large man with wings hovering over the village church. Nearly three months later, on July 3, two teenage campers, Sally Chapman and Barbara Perry, heard a strange hissing noise in the surrounding woods. They then saw a humanoid figure standing among the trees about 20 yards away. Sally Chapman described the entity as being like a huge owl, with fierce, brightly glowing red eyes, adding that the two girls assumed someone had dressed up and was playing a joke on them . . . until the creature flew up into the air.

The following morning, another young girl on vacation saw the same (or a similar) creature. In their book *Alien Animals*, Janet and Colin Bord quote a letter Jane Greenwood wrote to the local newspaper, the *Falmouth Packet*, describing her encounter:

It was Sunday morning and the place was in the trees near Mawnan Church, above the rocky beach. It was in the trees standing like a full-grown man, but the legs bent backward like a bird's. It saw us and quickly jumped up and rose straight up through the trees.

My sister and I saw it very clearly before it rose up. It has red slanting eyes and a very large mouth. The feathers are silvery gray and so are his body and legs. The feet are like big, black crab's claws.

We were frightened at the time. It was so strange, like something in a horror film. After the thing went up there was [sic] crackling sounds in the tree tops for ages.

Later that day we spoke to some people at the camp-site, who said they had seen the Morgawr Monster [a sea serpent occasionally sighted off the coast of Cornwall] on Saturday, when they were swimming with face masks and snorkels in the river, below where we saw the birdman.

. . . Our mother thinks we made it all up just because we read about these things, but that is not true. We really saw the bird man, though it could have been someone playing a trick in very good costume and make-up.

But how could it rise up like that? If we imagined it, then we both imagined the same thing at the same time. (Bords [1980], p. 137)

There were several more Owlman sightings between 1977 and 1978 in the vicinity of Mawnan Church. Janet and Colin Bord visited the church in April 1978, searching for clues to the possible identity of this mysterious interloper. During their visit, they noticed

one significant feature: that Mawnan church is built in the middle of a prehistoric earthwork.
This led us to speculate whether the church was on a ley [see **leys**], and indeed we have found several alignments passing through Mawnan church . . .

There may well be more [undiscovered] alignments . . . However, we are not claiming that these map alignments do definitely constitute leys. To establish that will involve time-consuming fieldwork. But we feel we have established that some research of this kind would be fruitful. The repeated appearances of the Owlman by Mawnan church and the synchronistic sighting of Morgawr in the sea below suggest to us that here is a powerful earth energy center. (Ibid., pp. 138–9)

(See also **flying humanoids, Mothman, ultraterrestrials**)

OWLS

Owls are occasionally associated with the presence of alien entities (usually **Grays**). In the time immediately prior to or following an abduction, the percipient will notice a large owl in or near his or her home. The animal is usually described as being somewhat larger than normal, and the percipient is somewhat unnerved by the intensity with which it watches him. It has been suggested that the presence of owls (and other animals notable for their dark eyes) are actually **screen memories** of the aliens themselves.

OZ FACTOR

Term coined by the British ufologist Jenny Randles to denote an apparent alteration in consciousness experienced by some witnesses to UFO events. The Oz Factor usually involves feelings of timelessness, coupled with a preternatural stillness in the environment. For instance, an encounter occurring in a rural area will be preceded by a total cessation of all natural sounds, such as the chattering of insects or the rustling of leaves. At this stage, the percipient has the feeling that he or she has somehow departed from normal reality, and has entered a realm that is similar to our own, but in which subtly different physical laws apply.

It is difficult to assess the significance of the Oz Factor with regard to the ultimate origin of **close encounters**. Proponents of the **extraterrestrial hypothesis** contend that this altered state of consciousness is instigated by the aliens themselves, as a method of subduing their intended victims prior to abduction. An alternative, though related, theory is that the Oz Factor represents an unavoidable human psychological response to being in close proximity to these creatures.

A radically different explanation has been put forward by researchers who subscribe to the **psychosocial hypothesis** for UFO encounters. They suggest that the Oz Factor offers support to the theory that witnesses to such events are actually experiencing visions, which represent highly symbolic communications, possibly originating within the human psyche, or which may have an external source. In support of this contention, the psychosociologists point to the fact that the vast majority of "alien" encounters are not corroborated by other people present, who should experience exactly what the percipient does. One of the best examples of this is the experience of Maureen **Puddy**. It also seems significant that many such encounters occur when the percipient is in bed, on the edge of sleep, or driving on an isolated stretch of road, an activity known to result in a shallow hypnotic state on occasion.

(See also **bedroom visitors, high strangeness**)

PACIENCIA, RIO DE JANEIRO, BRAZIL

Location of an encounter with some of the strangest UFO entities on record. At 2:20 A.M. on September 15, 1977, a 33-year-old bus driver named Antonio La Rubia was on his way to work when he saw a disk-shaped object hovering over a nearby football field. As he made to run away, he was struck by a blue beam from the 200-foot diameter craft, which paralyzed him. Three figures then materialized around him; one of them pointed a small, cylindrical instrument at him, and he suddenly found himself inside the UFO, which then took off (he could see the ground falling away through the transparent walls).

The ufonauts were incredibly bizarre. Each had a football-shaped head with a long, rapidly spinning antenna extending from the top. Around the middle of the head was a ring of blue-tinted mirrors. Their egg-shaped torsos were covered with aluminum-colored scales, and their two arms were like a cross between an elephant's trunk and a tentacle. They each wore a kind of utility belt, from which hung more of the cylindrical instruments that had been used to transport La Rubia aboard the craft. Most oddly of all, the entities had only one leg, a narrow column about a foot long, terminating in a small, circular "foot."

La Rubia was taken into a large chamber, where he encountered about 24 more entities. He was subjected to a physical examination, during which blood was drawn from one of his fingers. The entities then proceeded to show him a series of pictures, first of himself (both dressed and naked), then of a horse and cart, then of traffic in a city, and then of a dog attacking one of the entities. The creatures evidently knew how to defend themselves, for the dog promptly turned blue and melted! Finally, La Rubia was shown a kind of spacecraft assembly plant, with countless robots working on the ships.

The very next moment, La Rubia was on Earth once again, standing on the street opposite the bus station where he was employed, with one of the entities beside him. The ufonaut instantly vanished, leaving him alone to watch as the craft flew away. He checked the time, and realized that he had spent about 35 minutes on board the UFO. In common with many (but by no means all) alien percipients, La Rubia suffered from various health problems in the weeks following his encounter; these included nausea, diarrhea and fever.

PALMER, RAYMOND A.

Science-fiction writer, pulp-magazine editor and founder of *Fate* magazine, the world's longest-lived paranormal journal. Born in Milwaukee, Wisconsin, in August 1910, Ray Palmer became one of the founding fathers of modern ufology—or, perhaps more accurately, of UFO mythology. As a child, Palmer was involved in a tragic accident which badly injured him and left him with a hunchback. As if that were not unfortunate enough, he also suffered from a severe growth-hormone deficiency, reaching an adult height of only four feet. As a result, he found himself in dire need to escape his deeply unsatisfactory life and found solace in the pulp magazines of the 1920s and 1930s (the term "pulp" came from the low-quality pulpwood paper used). Palmer wrote science-fiction stories for the pulps, selling his first, "The Time Ray of Jandra," to *Wonder Stories*, which published it in the June 1930 issue. Palmer went on to publish numerous stories in a variety of genres, including westerns and even pornography.

In 1938, Palmer was chosen as the new editor of *Amazing Stories,* the most famous and successful of the pulps produced by the Ziff-Davis publishing group. He quickly became aware of a fascination among his readers with the idea of lost civilizations, in addition to their fascination with another staple of early science fiction: the scantily clad, unfeasibly curvaceous spacewomen who regularly cavorted on the lurid covers of the pulps. It seemed to Palmer that his readers' hunger for sexual imagery was equally matched by a hunger for mysticism and cosmic revelation, a suspicion reinforced by the increase in circulation every time *Amazing Stories* published anything to do with Atlantis or Lemuria.

In late 1943, while wondering how best to capitalize on this interest, Palmer received a letter from a man named Richard S. **Shaver**, who claimed to have had numerous surreal and terrifying adventures in a vast cavern system miles beneath the surface of Earth. Shaver's stories were subsequently published in the magazine as true recollections. The result was a huge increase in the circulation of *Amazing Stories*: within two years it had climbed to an astonishing 250,000 per month. The so-called "Shaver Mystery" would come to exert a profound influence on both the occult and conspiracy aspects of ufology over the following decades.

PALOS VERDES, CALIFORNIA

Location of an encounter with humanoid entities and large, disembodied brains, which occurred in August 1971. The exact date of the encounter is unclear: it may have been August 17 or 31. At 2:00 A.M. on the morning in question, two men in their late 20s were driving home from a friend's house, when they came upon two unusual objects on the highway. In the car's headlights, they saw that the objects were actually brains, each about the size of a basketball. Shocked, the two men slowed down and regarded the brains for some moments through the car's windows, before continuing on their journey.

After dropping off his friend, the driver continued on to his own house. Although he lived only 10 minutes away, the drive home actually took him two and a half hours. He was utterly unable to recall what had happened during this period of **missing time.**

When investigator Ann Druffel looked into the case, she gave the driver the pseudonym "John Hodges," and arranged for him to undergo **hypnotic regression**. He recalled that after dropping his friend off, he had been taken into a room, where he communicated with one of the brains through telepathy. He also recalled the presence of a number of seven-foot-tall, gray-skinned **humanoids** with webbed hands and feet (which led Hodges to conclude that their natural habitat was aquatic).

The brains then proceeded to show Hodges a series of three-dimensional holographic images of nuclear explosions, and explained to him that humanity was misusing its power over nature. It was then that Hodges realized that the gray-skinned humanoids were actually in control. They informed him that the brains were actually biomechanical translation devices. Later in the encounter, the beings inserted a "translator cell" into his brain (see **implants**), through which they would be able to contact him in future. They then took him back to his car.

For several years after the encounter, Hodges received a number of prophetic messages through his translator cell. The messages referred to a war that would begin in the Middle East and then spread to Europe around the year 1983. Nuclear weapons would be used, and afterward the aliens would make open contact with humanity in 1987. Needless to say, none of these predictions proved to be accurate.

PASCAGOULA, MISSISSIPPI

Location of one of the most famous and hotly debated UFO **abductions** in the history of the subject. The encounter occurred on October 11, 1973, when Charlie Hickson, 45, and Calvin Parker, 18, went fishing in the Pascagoula River. Their experiences were reported in the press the following day:

PASCAGOULA, Miss. [UPI] Two shipyard workers who claimed they were hauled aboard a UFO and examined by silver-skinned creatures with big eyes and pointed ears were checked today at a military hospital and found to be free of radiation.

. . . Jackson County chief deputy Barney Mathis said the men told him they were fishing from an old pier on the west bank of the Pascagoula River about 7 P.M. Thursday when they noticed a strange craft about two miles away emitting a bluish haze.

They said it moved closer and then appeared to hover about three or four feet above the water, then "three whatever-they-weres came out, either floating or walking, and carried us into the ship," officers quoted Hickson as saying.

"The things had big eyes. They kept us about twenty minutes, photographed us, and then took us back to the pier. The only sound they made was a buzzing-humming sound. They left in a flash."

"These are reliable people," Sheriff Diamond said. "They had no reason to say this if it had not been true. I know something did happen to them."

The sheriff said the "spacecraft" was described as fish-shaped, about ten feet long with an eight-foot ceiling. The occupants were said to have pale silvery-gray skin, no hair, long pointed ears and noses, with an opening for a mouth and hands "like crab claws." (United Press International)

The younger man, Parker, promptly fainted at the sight of the entities, and remained unconscious throughout the abduction; while Hickson described being placed in a horizontal position, floating in midair, and being examined by an instrument that reminded him of a huge eye.

The case was investigated by Dr. J. Allen **Hynek** and investigative journalist Ralph Blum, who were told by Sheriff Diamond that Hickson and Parker had requested a polygraph test (see **lie-detector tests**) to prove that they were not lying about their experience. The police even tried to trick the witnesses into giving themselves away by leaving them in a room with a hidden tape recorder. Hickson and Parker spoke to each other, with awed and frightened voices, about the encounter, and made no mention whatsoever of a hoax.

The men were later hypnotized by UFO researcher James Harder, who concluded that the alien encounter had been real. Hynek was more cautious, and said that while the men had definitely been badly frightened by *something,* it was too early to say exactly what that something had been.

The Pascagoula case was also investigated by arch debunker Philip J. **Klass** and a *Rolling Stone* reporter named Joe Eszterhas. These investigators quickly located a bridge attendant and two toll booth operators who had had a clear view of the scene of the encounter on the evening in question, and yet had seen nothing unusual. In addition, they pointed out that the encounter had occurred only a few hundred yards from Highway 90, a busy road from which many motorists should have been able to see the arrival of the UFO. Sheriff Diamond responded to this by saying that three (unnamed) motorists had indeed witnessed the UFO's approach.

Klass was rightly unimpressed by mention of unnamed witnesses, and turned his attention to the lie-detector tests the two men had passed, discovering that the operator had not completed his training course, and had thus not been certified by his training school. Klass then asked a licensed operator how long such a test would take to administer, who replied that it would take a whole day. The test conducted on Hickson and Parker had lasted barely 20 minutes.

Joe Eszterhas discovered that Hickson was not quite as reliable as Sheriff Diamond had maintained. On several occasions, he had borrowed money from his coworkers at the Ingalls shipyard, and had repaid them by trying to get them promotions. He had subsequently been fired for "conduct unbecoming a supervisor."

These findings, however, have done nothing to quell the debate concerning the veracity of the Pascagoula encounter.

PHILADELPHIA EXPERIMENT

Legendary U.S. Navy experiment in invisibility, supposedly conducted in the Philadelphia Navy Yard in 1943. The forerunner to the notorious **Montauk Project**, the experiment involved making the ship USS *Eldridge* invisible to radar through manipulation of electromagnetic energy in accordance with Einstein's Unified Field Theory. The experiment succeeded beyond the navy's wildest dreams: not only did the *Eldridge* become invisible to radar, it literally became *invisible.* It also teleported to the navy yard at Norfolk, Virginia, several hundred miles away.

However, the experiment exacted a terrible cost in terms of human life. When the ship reappeared in the Philadelphia yard, several crew members had become fused with the decks and bulkheads of the ship, while the rest had been driven hopelessly insane. Some crewmen subsequently burst into flames spontaneously, while the survivors babbled about encountering strange alien beings in the "hyperspace" between the two navy yards.

In 1955 the noted astronomer Morris K. Jessup published his classic *The Case for the UFO,* a copy of which was mailed anonymously to the chief of the Office of Naval Intelligence in Washington in July of the same year. The book had been heavily annotated in three different colors, by someone who apparently knew the secret of the UFOs.

Three officers, Major Darrell Ritter, Captain Sidney Sherby and Commander George Hoover, were sufficiently intrigued by the book and its annotations to contact Jessup and suggest a meeting in Washington. Jessup agreed, read the annotations and was shocked to discover that one of them referred to the Philadelphia Experiment. He had already been told of the experiment in a series of letters he had received from a mysterious man calling himself Carlos Miguel Allende (aka Carl M. Allen).

Commander Hoover asked to see the letters, and Jessup complied. Hoover and Sherby then arranged for the Varo Manufacturing Company of Garland, Texas (a military research contractor), to print the annotated version of *The Case for the UFO* in a private, 127-copy edition. According to Jacques **Vallée**:

The Varo document played the same role for UFO buffs in the Sixties as the **MJ-12** documents and the Dulce papers [see alien **bases**] played in the Eighties: it was supposed to contain the absolute final truth about the nature of flying saucers, their pilots, and even the secret of gravity. And it seemed to confirm the fact that there were high-level government scientists who were deeply involved in UFO research. (Vallée *Revelations: Alien Contact and Human Deception*, New York, Ballantine Books [1991], pp. 200–201)

These revelations had much the same effect on Jessup as the **disinformation** received by Paul **Bennewitz** had on him. Jessup was shocked, depressed and terrified by the information contained in the annotations to his book, which had been made, clearly, by Allende. Jessup's depression intensified as he became obsessed with the bizarre material to which he had been exposed. His emotional problems were exacerbated by marital difficulties and, tragically, he committed suicide in Florida in 1958.

The Philadelphia Experiment is believed by many serious ufologists to be entirely apocryphal; Vallée goes so far as to suggest that it, along with the MJ-12 documents, may have been created with the express purpose of diverting attention away from reports of genuine UFO activity.

According to a statement on the Department of the Navy website, posted on September 8, 1996 in response to the numerous inquiries it has received regarding the Philadelphia Experiment:
Personnel at the Fourth Naval District believe that the questions surrounding the so-called Philadelphia Experiment arise from quite routine research, which occurred during World War II at the Philadelphia Naval Shipyard. Until recently, it was believed that the foundation for the apocryphal stories arose from degaussing experiments, which have the effect of making a ship undetectable or "invisible" to magnetic mines. Another likely genesis of the bizarre stories about levitation, teleportation and effects on human crew members might be attributed to experiments with the generating plant of a destroyer, the USS *Timmerman*. In the 1950s this ship was part of an experiment to test the effects of a small, high-frequency generator providing 1,000 hz instead of the standard 400 hz. The higher frequency generator produced corona discharges, and other well-known phenomena associated with high frequency generators. None of the crew suffered effects from the experiment.

ONR [Office of Naval Research] has never conducted any investigations on invisibility, either in 1943 or at any other time (ONR was established in 1946). In view of present scientific knowledge, ONR scientists do not believe that such an experiment could be possible except in the realm of science fiction.

PHOTOGRAPHS OF ALIENS

In view of the large number of UFO photographs in existence, and the similarly large number of reported encounters with alien beings, one might expect there also to be plenty of photographs of aliens. Unfortunately, this is not the case: there are several such photographs, but (with one notable exception, to be discussed later) they fail to come anywhere near offering convincing evidence of alien presence, and the ones that manage to avoid being risible are invariably so blurred as to be absolutely useless.

One of the most pitiful attempts was made by one Gianpietro Monguzzi, who claimed to have witnessed the arrival of a disk-shaped UFO in the Berina Mountains in Italy in July 1952. Monguzzi captured an image of a mountain backdrop, with the UFO in the middle distance and a squat, space-suited figure (complete with antenna) standing beside the craft. However, it is clear, even from a cursory examination of the photograph, that it is of two small—and not particularly well-made—models.

American contactee Howard **Menger** also managed to snap one of his Venusian friends (in view of the nature of their encounters, the **contactees** have produced remarkably few photographs of aliens). The result is less than impressive, and shows a person completely in silhouette (and thus unidentifiable) standing in front of what looks like a cardboard cutout of an **Adamski**-type "scoutship."

Slightly more impressive (but still highly dubious) is the photograph taken by Police Chief Jeffrey Greenhaw in Falkville, Alabama, on October 17, 1973. Greenhaw was in his patrol car, responding to a call about a landed UFO, when he came upon a six-foot-tall figure in a silvery spacesuit, similar to a fire-fighting suit. As the creature approached him, Greenhaw took a photograph of it, and then switched on his car's rotating red light, causing the entity to flee. Although he gave chase in the patrol car, he could not catch up with the spaceman.

Marion Webb, an investigator with the **National Investigations Committee on Aerial Phenomena (NICAP)** put on a firefighter's suit and had some photographs taken. The results were virtually identical to Greenhaw's photograph. It was then suggested that Greenhaw had faked his photograph in an attempt to gain publicity following the recent **Pascagoula** abduction. Greenhaw, however, maintained that he had not hoaxed his photograph.

One of the most famous photographs allegedly depicting an alien being was taken in West Germany in the late 1940s, bought by an unnamed GI and then passed on to John Quinn on May 22, 1950. It shows a diminutive humanoid, apparently the survivor of a UFO crash, being escorted by two military personnel, one of whom is carrying a piece of breathing apparatus connected by a long tube to the creature's mouth. The alien has only one leg and a circular foot, which apparently rotated. Once again, this was later revealed to be a hoax. According to German researcher Klaus Webner, the photograph was produced as a joke for the April 1, 1950, edition of the newspaper *Wiesbadener Tagblatt* by its editor William Sprunkel and a photographer named Hans Scheffler. Scheffler's five-year-old son Peter acted as a template for the alien, which was painted in by Scheffler later.

Another German hoax, also produced in 1950, involved the supposed capture of a diminutive man from Mars, who is shown in the photograph between two trench-coated "secret service agents." According to the story circulated at the time, the UFO pilot, whose craft had crashed near Mexico City, was sent to Germany for study (why he should have been sent to Germany was never made clear). The Danish journal *UFO-Nyt* carefully examined the photograph, and concluded that it was fraudulent, drawing attention to the way in which the alien's tiny hands were held in the agents' closed fists, rather than their thumbs and fingers, as would have been expected. According to *UFO-Nyt,* the two men were actually holding a carriage, which had then been painted out of the photograph, to be replaced by the image of the small alien.

The rather gruesome photograph (rather gruesomely known as "Tomato Man") is an example of what may well have been a genuine incident that has been misrepresented as extraterrestrial in nature. The photograph, apparently showing the burned and mangled victim of an aircraft crash, was released in 1978 by Williard McIntyre, Charles Wilhelm and Dennis Pilchis, who belonged to an organization called the Coalition of Concerned Ufologists of America. The story that accompanied the photograph was that a young naval photographer, based at White Sands Missile Range in New Mexico, was ordered over the border from Laredo, Texas, into Mexico on July 7–8 1948, to photograph a UFO that had crash-landed in the area. Photographic analysis by Kodak suggested that the picture probably had been processed in the late 1940s. Although it has been suggested by some that Tomato Man was actually a monkey used in an experimental V-2 rocket flight, the twisted pair of spectacles that can be seen near to the body would suggest that it is actually a human being, perhaps the pilot of an experimental aircraft that suffered a disastrous malfunction during a test flight.

Occasionally, a photograph surfaces, which is so obviously a hoax that one wonders what certain ufologists must have been thinking when they cited it as evidence of alien reality. In 1990 a photograph came to light that was described by some researchers as a "legitimate photo of an alien body recovered at the site of the **Roswell** UFO crash and stored in '**Hangar 18**' at **Wright-Patterson Air Force Base**." The "alien," apparently dead, was dressed in a silver jumpsuit and was strapped to a table. It was completely hairless and had large, slanted eyes. However, strong evidence of a hoax was present in the form of an entirely terrestrial zip fastener on the being's suit. The photograph's provenance was rather intriguing: at a UFO conference in Munich, Germany, in 1970, ufologist Marina Popovich displayed a black-and-white version, claiming to have discovered it in the files of the eminent Russian scientist, the late Felix **Zigel**. Apparently, the photograph had been given to Zigel by Dr. J. Allen **Hynek** at a secret conference in Canada in the 1960s. The actual origin of the photograph was later revealed to be an exhibit at the "Man and His World" exposition in Montreal, Canada, which was closed in the 1980s.

(See also **Roswell autopsy footage, Salinas corpse**)

PLEIADIANS/PLEJARANS

Highly advanced, space-faring civilization encountered on many occasions by the contactee Eduard "Billy" **Meier**. According to information available on the Billy Meier Webpage, the Pleiadian/Plejaran (pronounced "play-yar-en") star system exists in a space-time dimension that is a fraction of a second ahead of our own space-time. The Pleiadian/Plejaran system is several million years older than the Pleiades star cluster known to astronomers on Earth, and is approximately 500 light-years away (about 70 light-years farther away than "our" Pleiades).

In February 1995 the Pleiadians withdrew all of their bases from Earth, and allowed Billy Meier to reveal their real name, "Plejarans." Their intention had been to expose all those fraudulently claiming to be in contact with "Pleiadians" (presumably, the hoaxers would reveal themselves by omitting to mention the name "Plejarans").

The Pleiadians/Plejarans are virtually identical to humanity, since we share a common ancestry among the stars, specifically in the "Lyra-Vega Star Systems." They have been visiting and influencing Earth for the last 28 million years, and some of their interventions have been "disastrous." The Pleiadians/Plejarans feel obligated to assist us in our journey toward enlightenment and truth; however, they respect our freedom to accept or reject their help.

(See also **Asket, Ptaah, Quetzal** and **Semjase**)

POP MUSIC AND UFOLOGY

The world of pop and rock music has enjoyed a lengthy flirtation with UFOs and alien encounters. Ever since the king of rock 'n' roll himself, Elvis

Presley, spotted a UFO over his Bel Air home in 1966, musicians and songwriters have been fascinated by the phenomenon. According to the British writer Andy Roberts: "Exactly *why* rock 'n' rollers choose to take UFO imagery to their hearts is hard to pin down but from what they say, the implication seems to be that the UFOs represent the *ultimate* nonhierarchical power, accessible to all [original emphasis]."

In the late 1960s and 1970s, the psychedelic counterculture found the perfect expression of its nonmaterialistic ideals in the (then) peaceful and spiritually oriented activities of the saucer people. The very title of Pink Floyd's second album, *A Saucerful of Secrets*, hinted at the fantastic knowledge apparently waiting for us just beyond the horizon of our tiny world. Across the Atlantic, the Byrds sang about "Mr. Spaceman" who left glowing footprints in the dark, while Neil Young gave us "After the Gold Rush" with its silver spaceships and redemption on new worlds. Jimi Hendrix was also passionately interested in ufology, and read widely in the booming literature at the time.

Back in England, bands such as Steve Hillage's Gong and Hawkwind threw themselves headlong into the mythology of extraterrestrial civilizations and travel to other planets. In the early 1970s, such imagery grew a little more sophisticated and began to include Celtic mysticism (in Hawkwind's "Assault and Battery," Dave Brock sang of making our lives sublime and leaving footprints in the sands of time).

One of the best-known exponents of extra-terrestrial intelligence was, of course, David Bowie, whose classic "Space Oddity" expressed humanity's burgeoning desire to leave its planetary cradle, while "Starman" invoked images of friendly aliens watching us from a distance, afraid that open contact might "blow our minds." Bowie played an alien visitor in what is widely regarded as his most accomplished performance in Nicolas Roeg's 1976 film *The Man Who Fell to Earth*.

Interestingly, while the fantasy-inspired musical excesses of the 1970s (with their 20-minute songs and airbrushed album sleeves) were blasted unceremoniously away by the punk and new-wave movements, UFO imagery remained firmly in place, perhaps because the phenomenon itself has refused to leave the public imagination. Performers such as Debbie Harry and Poly Styrene (of X-Ray Spex) maintained an interest in the subject, while the Stranglers recorded an album entitled *Themeninblack* (see **Men in Black**).

In the 1980s and 1990s, popular culture has followed the resurgence of interest in ufology and the paranormal, with pot-smoking **Grays** turning up on posters, rave music fliers and T-shirts with rather tedious regularity. With regard to the contemporary counterculture interest in UFOs, Andy Roberts states:

The fact that this resurgence of interest . . . among the young groovers has arisen at the same time as a huge growth in the use of LSD and Ecstasy may help shed some light on the connection between UFO experiences and altered states of consciousness. Dancing under the influence can create trance-like states and this may well be the window through which UFO imagery shines. ("Rocking the Alien," *Fortean Times* Number 88, pp. 37–8)

PROPULSION OF UFOs

As might be expected, much effort has been devoted over the years to determining precisely how UFOs (assuming that they are alien spacecraft) are powered, and what principles they utilize to enable faster-than-light interstellar travel. Equally un-surprisingly, in those instances where communication with ufonauts has been established (see **contactees**), the aliens have proved less than helpful in explaining the engineering behind their spacecraft.

Perhaps ironically, given the rather dubious status he holds in the eyes of many ufologists, Robert

Lazar is the only UFO experient whose information on ET spacecraft propulsion comes anywhere near to making sense in terms of orthodox science. According to Lazar, the alien spacecraft he examined while working at S-4, the companion site to **Area 51** in Nevada, operate through the use of gravity amplifiers. In an article posted on the Internet, Lazar states:

We know that the shortest distance between two points is a straight line, so in our universe we've always assumed that the fastest way from Point A to Point B was to travel in a straight line between the two points at the speed of light ... [T]he fact is that when you are dealing with space/time and you enjoy the capability of generating an intense gravitational field, the fastest way from Point A to Point B is to distort, or warp, or bend the space/time between Points A and B, bringing Points A and B closer together. The more intense the gravitational field, the greater the distortion of space/time and the shorter the distance between Points A and B.

In his fascinating book *Alien Liaison: The Ultimate Secret,* British ufologist Timothy Good quotes **NASA** physicist Alan Holt's *Field Resonance Propulsion Concept* thus:

If the speed of light is a true limit of velocity in space-time, then the potential extraterrestrial visitors must utilize a form of transportation which transcends space and time to keep the trip times short. UFOs are often observed to disappear instantaneously. In a subset of these cases, the UFO later appears at a nearby location, implying a disappearance from and a reappearance into space-time.

The high-speed, right-angle turns, abrupt stops or accelerations of UFOs, and the absence of sonic booms despite calculated speeds of 22,000 mph or more, suggest that UFOs may generate an artificial gravitational field or otherwise use properties of space-time which we are not familiar with. UFO propulsion systems appear to involve electromagnetic or hydromagnetic processes, as evidenced by radiative effects on the environment, such as burns, dehydration, stopping of automobile engines, TV and radio disruptions, melting or alteration of ground and road surfaces, power disruptions, and static electricity effects . . . (Good [1992], p. 160)

According to Lazar, the UFOs he examined did indeed operate on principles of gravity generation, utilizing the so-called strong magnetic force that holds atomic structures together, but which we cannot yet access. In this way, the alien ships are able to focus their gravity amplifiers on a particular point in space; when the amplifiers are switched on, the space-time between the ship and its destination is "folded," so that the intervening distance becomes negligible. The ship then moves the shortened distance between points, the amplifiers are switched off and space-time instantly reverts to its normal shape. In effect, the ship has traveled a great distance virtually instantaneously without violating the universal limit of the speed of light (186,000 miles per second).

PSYCHOSOCIAL HYPOTHESIS

The seeds of the psychosocial hypothesis were sown by the great Swiss psychologist Carl G. Jung in his book *Flying Saucers: A Modern Myth of Things Seen in the Sky*, which appeared in English in 1959. In this book, Jung suggested that UFOs represent the archetypal "mandala," or circle, a universal image residing in the **collective unconscious** and which in turn represents unity, wholeness and harmony. To Jung, the appearance of disks in the skies, while essentially a psychological phenomenon, nevertheless was a significant expression of human apprehension and uncertainty in the face of the dangers inherent in modern life (in reference to the cold war, he said that our world "is dissociated like a neurotic"). However, Jung stressed that while his theory suggested a possible *reason* for UFO sightings, it did not explain what UFOs actually *are*. Indeed, the UFOs' ability to leave physical traces on the ground, and the fact that they are detectable with radar, left Jung as puzzled as any ufologist. At the end of *Flying Saucers,* he admitted the possibility that UFOs are real objects, which afford "an opportunity for mythological projections."

Ufologists were not terribly impressed by Jung's talk of the collective unconscious and psychic materializations: at the time, the consensus was that genuinely anomalous UFOs were spacecraft from other worlds—the so-called nuts-and-bolts interpretation. It was not until 10 years after the appearance of *Flying Saucers* that a serious ufologist, the French-American astronomer and computer scientist Jacques **Vallée**, returned to Jung's seminal ideas and expanded them into what would come to be known as the psychosocial hypothesis (also called, occasionally, the "new ufology").

Although Vallée's first two books, *Anatomy of a Phenomenon* (1965) and (with his wife, Janine) *Challenge to Science: The UFO Enigma* (1966) had advocated the **extraterrestrial hypothesis**, his 1969 book *Passport to **Magonia**: On UFOs, Folklore and Parallel Worlds* was every bit as radical as Jung's *Flying Saucers* had been a decade earlier. In this book, Vallée offers a completely new way of looking at the mystery of UFOs and nonhuman entities. Comparing the central elements of modern UFO contacts with those of encounters with supernatural beings in folklore, he suggests that they are manifestations of the same underlying phenomenon, adding that the surface details correspond to the world view prevalent at the time of the encounters. In other words, the fairies, goblins and demons encountered

in medieval times have become the alien explorers encountered in the late 20th century, in what Vallée calls a "morphology of miracles." In later books, such as *Dimensions: A Casebook of Alien Contact* (1988), Vallée suggests that the underlying cause of these multifaceted phenomena may well be an unseen and extremely powerful nonhuman intelligence, whose intention is to guide the psychic evolution of humanity.

Passport to Magonia proved extremely influential on ufological thinking, prompting other respected researchers, such as Jerome Clark and Loren Coleman, to address the possibilities it raised. In their book *The Unidentified* (1975), Clark and Coleman examined the apparent correlations between ancient and modern encounters uncovered by Vallée, concluding that "UFO visions are the psyche's attempt to escape the stranglehold that strict rationalism has on 20th-century humanity [and to] restore what is seen as the natural balance between the mind's thinking and feeling aspects." (Clark [1998], pp. 497–8) Ironically, while Clark and Coleman subsequently abandoned these speculations in the face of the physical traces UFOs proved capable of leaving behind, their thoughts nevertheless proved influential in ufology, consolidating the position of the psychosocial hypothesis as a useful tool with which to address the UFO mystery.

Interestingly, the psychosocial hypothesis is much more sympathetically regarded in the United Kingdom and continental Europe than in the United States, where the **extraterrestrial hypothesis** is still very firmly adhered to (although there are, of course, many psychosociologists in America and many extraterrestrialists in Europe). The reasons for this are unclear, but may well have much to do with America's numerous successes in the field of space exploration, and the resulting (and quite understandable) fascination of the population with such endeavors.

(See also **abduction, imaginary abductees, ultraterrestrials**)

PTAAH

One of the **Pleiadians/Plejarans** in contact with Eduard "Billy" **Meier**. Ptaah is the father of **Semjase**, Pleja and a son, Jucata, who died when his spacecraft suffered a navigational malfunction and hit a star. Ptaah is 770 Earth years old, and is the commander of the Pleiadian spacecraft fleet. He holds the rank of JHWH (pronounced "ish-wish"), a person who has attained the highest level of knowledge and wisdom possible in the material universe. JHWH is, of course, the Tetragrammaton (also YHWH), the unmentionable name of God. Ptaah at present oversees the spiritual development of his home world, Erra, and our Earth, although he avoids direct intervention in the affairs of humanity.

PUDDY, MAUREEN

Australian UFO percipient whose case has been frequently cited as evidence that such encounters are more subtle and complex than the straightforward **extraterrestrial hypothesis** would suggest. At 9:15 P.M. on July 3, 1972, Mrs. Puddy, then 37 years old, was returning to her home in Rye, Victoria, from a visit to her son, who was in the hospital. The road on which she was traveling suddenly became flooded with an intense blue light (the precursor of many UFO events), and she looked up to see a disk-shaped object, which paced her car for several miles, emitting a hum similar to an elevator. Presently, the object flew away.

Three weeks later, on July 25, Mrs. Puddy was again driving on that stretch of road, when the UFO returned, this time apparently causing the vehicle's engine to stall. When the car had glided to a halt, she heard a disembodied voice say: "All your tests will be negative. Tell the media, do not panic, we mean no harm. You now have control." The

car's engine started, and the UFO departed once again.

Mrs. Puddy reported her encounters to the Royal Australian Air Force (RAAF) who, understandably, could do little more than send her the requisite forms to fill in.

In February the following year, 1973, Mrs. Puddy felt a strange, invisible presence in her house, accompanied by the voice she had heard in her car, which told her to "go back to the same meeting place." Being somewhat apprehensive about going there alone, she contacted the Victorian UFO Research Society. Two VUFORS investigators, Judith Magee and Paul Norman, agreed to meet her at the scene of her first two encounters.

As Mrs. Puddy was on her way to meet the investigators, however, one of the "aliens" decided to put in an early appearance, materializing on the front passenger seat beside her. The entity looked somewhat like those encountered by the **contactees** of the 1950s and 1960s: he had long, blond hair and was wearing a single-piece ski-type suit. He vanished almost immediately, and Mrs. Puddy was able to continue to her rendezvous with the two ufologists.

When she arrived, Magee and Norman sat with her in her car, until she realized that the entity encountered earlier was standing outside. Although she pointed him out to her companions, they could see nothing. The entity beckoned to her, but she remained in the car.

At that point, Mrs. Puddy suddenly seemed to faint; nevertheless, she continued to describe what she was experiencing. As Magee and Norman listened in astonishment, she began to describe a circular, windowless room, at the center of which was a mushroom-shaped object covered with hieroglyphs. The entity was now in the room with her, and asked her to continue her description. However, Mrs. Puddy grew deeply frightened at the thought that there was no apparent means of escape from the room, and she started to cry. She then regained consciousness, but had no memory of what had just occurred.

About a week later, the entity appeared again in the front seat of Mrs. Puddy's car while she was driving. It had been raining heavily, and visibility was extremely poor, but while the "spaceman" was in the car, the weather suddenly improved dramatically. He vanished again after a few moments, and the poor weather conditions quickly resumed.

This case would seem to indicate that some UFO and alien encounters, at least, do not occur in so-called objective reality. The fact that Mrs. Puddy's body remained in the car during her "abduction" implies either that her consciousness was somehow taken into the UFO, leaving her corporeal being behind; or that the entire abduction was essentially a psychological event.

(See also **encounter-prone personalities, fantasy-prone personalities** and **psychosocial hypothesis**)

QUAROUBLE, FRANCE

Scene of an encounter with a landed UFO and alien beings in September 1954. The Quarouble encounter is one of the most impressive examples of a UFO leaving landing traces on record. The events were described in *France-Soir,* September 15, 1954.

Three investigators for the air police arrived at Quarouble Nord yesterday to interview M. Marius Dewilde, the man who saw two "Martians" near his back-yard gate. They left the village convinced that during the night of Friday to Saturday, a mysterious craft had indeed landed, as claimed by M. Dewilde, on the tracks of the Saint-Amand-Blanc-Misseron railway line, near crossing No. 79.

Their inquiries seem, in effect, to confirm the statement made by the metalworker. The witness declared that on Friday, about 10:30 P.M., he had seen a machine of an elongated shape, three meters high, six meters long, sitting on the tracks a few meters away from his house. Two beings of human appearance, of very small height and apparently wearing diving suits, could be seen nearby. M. Dewilde walked toward them, but at that moment a beam of greenish light was focused on him from the craft and he found himself paralyzed. When he was able to move again the machine had started to rise and the two beings had disappeared.

. . . The ground, examined meter by meter, shows a trace of footsteps . . . [T]here are traces on the sleepers that could have been made by a machine landing on [them]. In five places the wood of the sleepers is compressed over an area of about four square centimeters. These markings all have the same appearance and they lie symmetrically, on one line. Three of them—those in the middle— are 43 centimeters apart. The last two are 67 centimeters away from the preceding ones.

A craft landing on legs instead of wheels like our own aircraft would leave just such traces, one of the inspectors of the air police has declared.

M. Dewilde's story is also confirmed by several inhabitants of the region. In Onnaing, at about 10:30 P.M. (the time indicated by M. Dewilde), a young man called M. Edmond Auverlot and a retired man, M. Hublard, saw a reddish light traveling in the sky. The same light was seen from Vicq by three young men.

The air police concentrated their investigations on the markings found on the railway sleepers, and consulted several railway specialists, who concluded that an object exerting a pressure of 30 tons had been present. Examinations were also made of the gravel of the railway bed, which revealed calcination of the stones. They had become brittle, indicating the presence of intense heat, which had raised their temperature to just below melting point. Whatever had landed on the railway line had caused oxidation in the gravel.

QUATERMASS AND THE PIT (FILM)

Made in 1967, directed by Roy Ward Baker, written by Nigel Kneale and starring Andrew Keir, James Donald, Julian Glover and Barbara Shelley. A highly enjoyable (if somewhat quaint) thriller, which has much in common with UFO lore. A buried alien spacecraft is discovered during excavations in the London Underground. The army is called in to clean up and examine the ship, and a soldier working alone inside it is driven half insane by something he glimpses. Soon afterward, the cordoned-off tube station is beset by violent poltergeist phenomena, and the spacecraft breaks open to reveal a number of long-dead, three-foot-long insects.

Professor Quatermass (Keir) and his assistant Barbara Judd (Shelley) are enlisted to help figure out what it all means. They discover that the surrounding area of London has for years been prey to similar psychical phenomena. Their colleague, Dr. Matthew Roney (Donald), brings along his "optiencephalograph," which translates thoughts to visual images displayed on a monitor screen. The device is placed on Judd's head and, accessing archetypal imagery, displays Earth's prehistory. The spacecraft, it seems, came from the planet Mars 5 million years ago. The **insectoid** Martians instigated a kind of genetic engineering experiment on early humanity, boosting the intelligence of our ancestors, and killing those who did not make the grade.

The evil-looking, horned heads of the Martians gave rise to later images of Satan, while the killing of substandard human specimens became the legendary "Wild Hunt." As the hidden energies of the spacecraft are released through the army's examination of it, a hideous force erupts into the streets of London, causing the population to begin a Wild Hunt of their own. The spacecraft's energies combine with the other psychic disturbances and coalesce into a gigantic, white-hot electric Devil that towers above the city. When all seems lost, Roney sacrifices himself by climbing a crane and swinging it directly into the entity, instantly earthing its electrical power and destroying it.

Although the film is **science fiction**, and was not ostensibly inspired by ufology, there are some striking and interesting parallels; for instance, the crashed spacecraft motif, the presence of aliens in prehistory (see **ancient astronauts**), the genetic breeding program (a favorite theme in **abduction** and **conspiracy theory** literature), and the notion that alien activity in the past is profoundly connected with our folkloric and religious beliefs.

QUAZGAA

Leader of the alien race known as the "Watchers," who have maintained contact with Betty **Andreasson** since her childhood. It was through Quazgaa (perhaps the most communicative of all the Gray-type creatures encountered by humans) that Betty learned of the Watchers' plan to intervene in the affairs of humanity, in order to protect Earth from the ravages of pollution. According to Quazgaa, the human race is in grave danger of becoming sterile in the near future, and it is for this reason that the aliens are harvesting human genetic material, which they intend to use in the creation of a new species.

(See also **abductions, Grays**)

QUETZAL

A Pleiadian space commander who was stationed in Earth's Solar System for 11 years between 1975 and 1986. According to Eduard "Billy" **Meier**, Quetzal is a distinguished scientist and inventor, is 464 years old, has four beautiful wives and six children. His wives are very close friends of another Meier contact, **Semjase**, and they have often asked her if she would like to join their "marital unit," an idea that apparently does not appeal to the spacewoman.

He is also said to have given Billy Meier and his followers a number of highly advanced technological devices, which "have been of great help in the fulfillment of their mission," although precise details on the workings of these instruments are not easy to establish.

(See also **Asket, Pleiadians/Plejarans, Sfath**)

QUEZET, MEAGAN

South African victim of an attempted alien abduction, which was only later revealed through the means of **hypnotic regression**. On January 3, 1979, Quezet was out for a walk with her son André near their home in Mindalore, Johannesburg, when they both noticed an unusual object on the road ahead. The object was shaped like an egg, and stood upright on its undercarriage.

As Quezet and her son approached the object, a hatch opened and five entirely human-looking people with dark hair, beards and coveralls climbed out and began to speak to the witnesses in an odd accent. At this point, Quezet began to grow nervous, and told André to run home and fetch his father. As soon as the boy started to run, the ufonauts turned on their heels and hurried back into their craft, which immediately took off. André, who had watched this happening, stopped running and waited for his mother to catch up with him, and together they went home.

News of the encounter eventually reached the United States, where a tabloid newspaper offered to pay for Quezet and her son to undergo hypnosis (ironically, the rather dubious tabloid press in America often contributes to the expensive business of in-depth UFO investigation). During one of the subsequent hypnosis sessions, Quezet recalled being persuaded by the ufonauts to enter their craft, where they grabbed her, apparently intending to give her one of the standard physical examinations. However, she managed to wrestle free of their clutches and jump out of the UFO, shouting at André to get his father (André himself has never agreed to undergo hypnosis, preferring to try to forget about the whole incident).

The behavior of the ufonauts is rather interesting, since "human" aliens rarely show such aggression towards their percipients (leaving that sort of thing to the callous **Grays**), and are much more likely to give people a pleasant tour of the ship than to force them to undergo humiliating physical probings.

RAINBOW CITY

An ancient and deserted center of alien culture said to lie beneath the South Pole. According to the redoubtable Commander **X** in his book *Underground Alien Bases,* Rainbow City was built by colonizers from outer space about 2.5 million years ago, and was discovered by a man named Emery during an Antarctic expedition in 1942.

Emery's group found their way into a great central plaza dominated by a pyramidal temple. Inside this temple, they found themselves in a colossal library lined with books that spoke their alien texts when opened. Also in the library was a "huge chairlike thing with great arms, with what appeared to be keyboards covered with queer characters set into the arms." The chair also had a large, caplike extension that fit over the sitter's head.

The great library was also lined with numerous gigantic pillars. Commander X writes:

Upon the first [pillar] was carved a representation of the Solar System, with the third and fourth planets in colors—the third green and the fourth red. Leading from the red planet was a group of elongated dots, and other marks, that looked like pointers headed toward the base of the green planet. On the same pillar was series [sic] of markings (straight lines) in arithmetical order; after each group appeared a character evidently depicting the numeral system. There were circles divided into different ways and characters in relation to them. There were squares and triangles and cubes with different sets of characters following. (Commander X [1990], p. 124)

The expeditionary party discovered another set of books, which were apparently language primers, and little by little, they were able to build up a limited knowledge of the strange alien tongue, aided in their pronunciation by the books' vocal capability. Eventually, they discovered an instruction manual for the "chair," which they were able to read.

They each sat in the chair, with hands fastened down on the arms. The huge cap was lowered over the head, and the power turned on. This machine sent a gentle vibration through the brain and nerves. They found that later they could continue the learning of the language with greater ease and flexibility in speech. Also that their comprehension of the contents of the books was greater. (Ibid., p. 125)

After leaving the library, the Emery expedition explored other parts of Rainbow City and discovered museums, hospitals, living quarters, laboratories, shops and gardens, as well as enormous centers of heavy industry in the city's lower levels. Everything in the city was somewhat larger than the human scale, suggesting that the original inhabitants were somewhere in the region of eight feet in height.

Commander X also reminds us that "the legendary" T. Lobsang Rampa visited Rainbow City, and told of his experiences with Venusian Masters in his book *My Visit to Venus* (although Rampa is perhaps not the most trustworthy of sources). It must also be said (without wishing to be churlish) that Rainbow City as described by Emery via Commander X, sounds rather a lot like the fabulous underground city of the "Krel" in the 1956 film *Forbidden Planet*. Even more striking is the parallel between the learning chair in Rainbow City and the Krel device used by Professor Morbius, with which he inadvertently boosts his own IQ, enabling him to learn the Krel language much more quickly than would otherwise have been possible.

(See also alien **bases, Hollow Earth Theory**)

RAWLINS, WYOMING

Location of an encounter with a humanoid being, which resulted in a brief trip to another planet allegedly 163,000 light-years away. On October 25, 1974, an oil driller in his early 40s named Carl Higdon was on a hunting trip by himself in the Medicine Row National Forest, near Rawlins, Wyoming, when he spotted a group of elk. He raised his rifle, took aim and fired . . . but the bullet stopped after about 50 feet and dropped to the ground, as if it had hit an invisible wall. As he was trying to figure out what had happened, Higdon heard a twig snap behind him, spun around, and saw a rather odd-looking man standing nearby.

The man was tall, about six feet two inches, and was of medium build. He was dressed in black, with a double sash across his chest and a wide belt with a starlike symbol on the buckle. His face was broad, his nose flat and his chin nonexistent; his hair was short and stood straight up. Most unusual, however, was the man's lack of hands: his left arm ended in an apparent stump, while his right ended in a device shaped like a narrow cone about 12 inches long.

The strange entity introduced himself as "Ausso" and, apparently as an offering of friendship, gave Higdon a packet of four pills, each one of which, said Ausso, was equivalent to four days' food. When Higdon had taken one, Ausso made a gesture with his cone-tipped right arm, and in the next instant Higdon found himself strapped into a chair in a small room with transparent walls. There was another being like Ausso, sitting in one of four chairs. The room also contained a control panel, a mirrorlike device and a cage containing the five elk Higdon had been hunting, which had been subdued somehow.

Ausso's cone-arm seemed to be an all-purpose tool: when he waved it at the control panel, the alien ship took off, and Higdon saw first the ground and then Earth itself fall away. A few moments later, the ship landed on a planet wreathed in darkness. Ausso told Higdon that they were now 163,000 light-years from Earth. This figure is a little puzzling, since it would put Ausso's planet well outside our galaxy. In fact, there is a strong implication that the alien planet was in the Large Magellanic Cloud, which is about 50,000 parsecs (163,000 light-years) away. (The Large and Small Magellanic Clouds are small, irregular satellite galaxies in the southern sky.)

The ship landed near a colossal building, on top of which was a bright light, and which generated a loud electrical hum. Standing near the base of the building were five human beings talking together. From his position in the ship, Higdon could make out three teenage girls, a teenage boy and a man in his 40s.

Once again, Ausso gestured with his cone-arm, and, this time, Higdon found himself instantly transported to a room apparently inside the huge building, where he was examined by a metallic device. When the examination was finished, Ausso told Higdon that he was not what they were looking for, and would be taken back to Earth immediately. (This perhaps implies that the people Higdon had seen outside really were human beings.) The pills Higdon had been given then floated out of his pocket (evidently to deny him any proof of his adventure).

In the next moment, Higdon found himself on Earth once again. Unprepared for the rocky slope on which he was positioned, he immediately fell, injuring himself. He looked at his wristwatch and saw that only two and a half hours had passed. He then searched for his truck, and found it in terrain that was impossible to drive through, so he called for help on his CB radio. He was rescued shortly afterward and taken to a nearby hospital, where he related his experience, which he had no trouble in recalling.

RENDLESHAM FOREST, SUFFOLK, ENGLAND

Location of the most famous and impressive UFO incident to occur in the United Kingdom. The Rendlesham Forest incident is significant not only because the percipients were highly trained military personnel but also because both alien entities and physical traces were involved.

In the early hours of December 27, 1980, two U.S. Air Force security guards were patrolling the East Gate sector of RAF Woodbridge, which, along with its companion base, Bentwaters, was owned by the British Ministry of Defense (MoD) but staffed by U.S. Air Force personnel, and formed an important component of NATO's European defenses. The two security guards spotted a light moving through the trees in nearby Rendlesham Forest. Thinking that it might have been an aircraft in difficulties, they informed their superiors of the situation by radio.

The Woodbridge control tower and the radar defense unit at RAF Watton had already locked on to a target approaching from the north, in spite of the fact that no military aircraft were flying that night. Three more security personnel were sent out to the East Gate sector to investigate. After spending some time searching the dark forest, the security team came upon a wide clearing, at the center of which stood a glowing object. Standing on three short struts arranged in an equilateral triangle, the object was of a metallic appearance, with a curious "quilted" or "patchwork" surface texture. At its apex shone a bright red light, while around the base was a bank of intense blue lights.

Tentatively, the security guards approached the object, which began to glide away across the clearing, as a group of nearby farm animals were thrown into panic and nearly stampeded out of their field.

The site of the encounter was examined the following day. Lieutenant Colonel Charles Halt, who was the deputy base commander of RAF Bentwaters at the time, submitted his now famous memorandum to his superiors describing the investigation. Dated January 13, 1981, the memorandum reads:

SUBJECT: Unexplained Lights

TO: RAF/CC

1. Early on the morning of 27 Dec 80 (approximately 0300L), two USAF security police patrolmen saw unusual lights outside the back gate at RAF Woodbridge. Thinking an aircraft might have crashed or been forced down, they called for permission to go outside the gate to investigate. The on-duty flight chief responded and allowed three patrolmen to proceed on foot. The individuals reported seeing a strange glowing object in the forest. The object was described as being metallic in appearance and triangular in shape, approximately two to three metres across the base and approximately two metres high. It illuminated the entire forest with a white light. The object itself had a pulsing red light on top and a bank(s) of blue lights underneath. The object was hovering or on legs. As the patrolmen approached the object, it maneuvered through the trees and disappeared. At this time the animals on a nearby farm went into a frenzy. The object was briefly sighted approximately an hour later near the back gate.

2. The next day, three depressions 1½" deep and 7" in diameter were found where the object had been sighted on the ground. The following night (29 Dec 80) the area was checked for radiation. Beta/gamma readings of 0.1 milliroentgens were recorded with peak readings in the three depressions and near the center of the triangle formed by the depressions. A nearby tree had moderate (.05–.07) readings on the side of the tree toward the depressions.

3. Later in the night a red sun-like light was seen through the trees. It moved about and pulsed. At one point it appeared to throw off glowing particles and then broke into five separate white objects and then disappeared. Immediately thereafter, three star-like objects were noticed in the sky, two objects to the north and one to the south, all of which were about 10° off the horizon. The objects moved rapidly in sharp angular movements and displayed red, green and blue lights. The objects to the north appeared to be elliptical through an 8–12 power lens. They then turned to full circles. The objects to the north remained in the sky for an hour or more. The object to the south was visible for two or three hours and beamed down a stream of light from time to time. Numerous individuals, including the undersigned, witnessed the activities in paragraphs 2 and 3.

CHARLES I. HALT, Lt Col. USAF
Deputy Base Commander

Although Halt was not aware of any alien beings associated with the objects, Airman Lawrence Warren, who was also present, subsequently claimed that entities were visible inside a number of smaller objects that broke off from the triangular object. He also stated that in the immediate vicinity of the UFO, time seemed to slow down. According to Warren, Colonel Gordon Williams, overall base commander, entered the clearing at that point and attempted to communicate with the entities inside the smaller UFOs, by holding up his arms. The entities responded by holding up their own arms.

Warren also claimed to have suffered damage to his retinas as a result of looking at the bright lights of the UFOs. The activity in the clearing was recorded by a large number of military personnel (Warren estimated about 80). In an interview with British ufologist Timothy Good, he said that during his debriefing, he and the other security police were shown some film of UFOs taken during the Second World War, and the Korean and Vietnam conflicts, apparently in order to make them understand why a cover-up was necessary.

The Rendlesham Forest incident has been most extensively investigated and documented by ufologist

Jenny Randles, who has written several books on the encounter, the latest of which is *UFO Crash Landing? Friend or Foe?: The Full Story of the Rendlesham Forest Close Encounter,* published in 1998. Randles notes that events such as this are covered up by the authorities, citing her attempts to retrieve the Halt memorandum as an example. The memorandum was sent to the MoD by Squadron Leader Donald Moreland, commander of RAF Bentwaters. However, he told Randles that he knew nothing of any UFO incident in Rendlesham Forest, and it was not until 1983 that the memorandum was released in America under the **Freedom of Information Act**. According to the MoD, no further action was taken regarding the UFO landing at RAF Woodbridge; the reason given, apparently (and rather incredibly), was that the UFO activity was not considered to be of defense significance.

It has been suggested by skeptics and **debunkers** that the Orford Ness lighthouse, about five miles away, was responsible for the UFO sightings in Rendlesham Forest. However, they do not explain how highly trained military personnel, who had seen the lighthouse on many previous occasions and had thus dismissed it as a possible cause, could have mistaken it for a large, triangular, metallic object standing in a forest clearing. In addition, the lighthouse explanation cannot account for the increased levels of radioactivity that were subsequently recorded.

REPEATER WITNESSES

Term denoting people who claim to have had numerous UFO sightings or contacts with alien beings throughout their lives. In the early years of modern ufology (post-1947), repeater witnesses were **contactees** who claimed ongoing and friendly relationships with the **Space Brothers**. Since serious ufologists at the time considered such people to be "crackpots," and their claims to be unworthy of study, the term "repeater witness" was synonymous with "untrustworthy publicity-seeker."

However, in the late 1970s and throughout the 1980s, it became clear that victims of alien **abductions** could also be placed in the category of repeater witnesses, since they, too, claimed ongoing contact with aliens, albeit of a rather less pleasant kind. It has been suggested that those who experience UFO events throughout their lives are somehow psychically attuned to the phenomenon, whereas those who refuse to believe in the reality of such things are much less likely to encounter them. While this is an interesting theory, it is somewhat undermined by the many cases in which people with no previous interest in UFOs, and who did not believe in the phenomenon, have subsequently been contacted on many occasions. Indeed, there is another theory that the more sympathetically one regards the UFO enigma, the less likely one is to encounter it. This has led to the notion that UFO and alien activity is a kind of mind-expanding process, designed (by who or what is unclear) to increase certain people's awareness of a wider and more profound reality.

REPTOIDS (ALIENS)

Extremely hostile, technologically advanced beings said by some to be already residing on Earth, and by others to be on their way to our planet inside a gigantic planetoid starship. Either way, the Reptoids apparently consider Earth to be their property, perhaps due to their occupation of the planet many millennia ago. Reptoids are frequently described as tall and powerful, with lizardlike facial features and green, scaly skin, although some variations have been reported, implying either natural subgroups or genetic alteration of some kind.

The Reptoids appear to be the masters of the **Grays**, which perhaps accounts for their being seen far less often. Their attitude to humanity is not a pleasant one: they consider us to be little more than a resource to be exploited and, on occasion, consumed. Some commentators, such as Commander X, have stated that life in the universe is basically divided into beings possessing souls (such as humanity and the more friendly alien races) and those, such as the Reptoids and the Grays, who are soulless, and thus inherently evil.

REVERSE ENGINEERING

A process by which unfamiliar technology is dismantled and examined with the intention of applying its basic principles to one's own related projects. Although frequently associated with UFOs and alleged **crash-retrievals** of alien spacecraft, reverse engineering is a common practice among military and industrial organizations when securing items of foreign technology, such as enemy aircraft and weapons systems.

(See also **Area 51; Element 115; Lazar, Robert**)

RHANES, AURA

(See **Bethurum, Truman**)

RIGEL–PROCYON WAR

According to information received from an unnamed abductee by the American researcher George C. Andrews, Earth is a battleground being fought over by two powerful extraterrestrial civilizations: the Rigelians and the Procyonians. Although it is generally accepted by researchers who accept the various **conspiracy theories** associated with UFOs and alien activity that the species known as the **Grays** come from the **Zeta Reticuli** star system, Andrews's source claims that they actually come from Rigel, about 800 light-years from Earth in the constellation Orion. Due to the fallout from a nuclear war, which nearly decimated their civilization several thousand

years ago, the Rigelians' sebaceous glands have been genetically damaged, making the digestion of food extremely difficult.

It is the Rigelians who have forged a secret treaty with the U.S. government, whereby they allow limited access to their weapons technology (resulting in the Stealth and SDI—Star Wars—programs) in return for the right to abduct and experiment upon certain humans.

According to Andrews:

Working under the instructions of the humanoids from Rigel, CIA and former Nazi scientists have developed and deployed malignant strains of bacteria and viruses, including AIDS. The rationale from the fascist point of view is to exterminate portions of the population considered to be undesirable. The rationale from the Rigelian point of view is to decimate the human population to such an extent that the survivors would accept open control by the Rigelians. (Andrews [1993], p. 143)

Although they themselves have no emotions, they are able to experience ours through telepathy (see **abductions**), and pay special attention to sexual emotions.

Standing against this dangerous species are the Procyonians, tall, attractive, entirely human-looking beings from the star system Procyon, about 11.4 light-years from Earth in the constellation Canis Minor. The Procyonians bear a striking resemblance to those beings claiming to have come from Venus, who met the **contactees** in the 1950s and 1960s. It was the Procyonians who experimented with the artificial insemination of primitive humanity, and who were thus responsible for the development of human intelligence.

Their motivation for breeding with humans [which is apparently ongoing] is to tune up the frequency of our species, in order to help us to help ourselves. Their concern is for the well-being of all forms of life, not just humanity. The entire biosphere will benefit if we fulfil our positive potential, instead of self-destructing and destroying our planet's biosphere in the process. (Ibid., p. 144)

Also known as Blonds or **Nordics**, these beings are totally benign with regard to humanity, although they dislike intensely our frequently violent attitude to each other. They are also saddened by our governments' secret alliance with the Rigelians (the Procyonians originally offered an alliance with humanity, but since they refused to share their weapons technology, our leaders declined their offer). Their level of technology is far beyond that of the Rigelians: they are even capable of traveling through time and between dimensions, and teleportation.

According to Andrews's source, the Rigelians were originally tall and beautiful Nordics, who ruled a vast galactic empire and colonized the uninhabited planets in the Procyon system. There followed a cataclysmic civil war on Rigel, known as "the Great War," which virtually destroyed the Rigelian civilization and hideously warped the beautiful Nordics, turning them into genetically damaged Grays. As soon as they had rebuilt their industries, the Grays launched an attack on the Procyon colony, although the Rigel–Procyon War has now entered a state of uneasy truce.

RIRIE, IDAHO

Location of an alien encounter that was extremely unusual, in that one of the entities reportedly drove the witnesses' car. The incident occurred at 9:30 P.M. on November 2, 1967, just outside the town of Ririe, Idaho. Two young Navajo Indians, Guy Tossie and Will Begay, were driving along a highway, when they saw a sudden flash of light, accompanied by the

appearance of a domed, disk-shaped object eight feet in diameter. The object apparently materialized out of nowhere, in common with many other UFOs.

As the object hovered in front of them, about five feet above the road, the green and orange lights around its rim casting an eerie glow over the scene, Tossie and Begay looked into the transparent dome, and saw two small figures inside. The dome then opened and one of the occupants floated down to the road. The creature was humanoid, about three and a half feet tall, and was wearing a tight-fitting, single-piece suit with a large backpack. Its hairless head was covered in curious, horizontal wrinkles, and its large, staring eyes contained vertical, catlike pupils. It had virtually no nose to speak of, and its large, pointed ears were situated high up on its head. Its mouth was little more than a horizontal slit.

The creature approached the car, opened the driver's door and climbed in behind the steering wheel. Not surprisingly, Tossie and Begay slid as far over to the right as they possibly could. The UFO then apparently applied some unseen force to the vehicle and towed it, with the entity steering, into a nearby field. When the car finally came to a halt, Tossie opened the passenger door and made a run for it, while a terror-stricken and trembling Begay stayed in the car. The entity then turned to him and began to speak in a strange, chirping language, while the other creature exited the craft and shone what seemed to be a searchlight on the fleeing figure of Tossie. The second entity then approached the car, doubtless to Begay's utter dismay. However, the first creature climbed from the vehicle and together they returned to their craft, which then ascended into the air and departed.

Meanwhile, Tossie had made it to a nearby farmhouse, where he blurted out what had just happened to him and Begay to the family. He managed to persuade the farmer to return with him to the field, where they found the car, with its lights on and engine running, and Begay sitting in the front seat with his eyes tightly shut, apparently in a state of shock.

Not long after Tossie and Begay had reported their encounter to the state police, other people in the area corroborated their story to a certain extent, claiming to have seen strange lights in the sky, while some farmers stated that something had panicked their animals on the night of the encounter.

RIVERSIDE, CALIFORNIA

In the early afternoon of August 22, 1955, a group of children were playing in the garden of the home of the Douglas family. One of the children (who were aged between four and 15), Kermit Douglas, noticed a bright object hovering over the house. This object disappeared, to be replaced by a metallic disk. Other disks began to appear and disappear with odd, belllike sounds, and then one of them landed in an adjacent field.

A bizarre entity emerged from the UFO. The entity was about three and a half feet tall, with a perfectly spherical head, large, square red eyes, a large, open mouth and four diamond-shaped features instead of a nose.

Two of the children saw a translucent being, similar to the first, floating in front of a neighbor's house, while another boy reported seeing a disembodied arm beckoning to him. One of the entities then spoke to another boy. This creature was different from the others: it had four legs hanging below its narrow torso; even more curiously, while it had two arms, it also had *two forearms* extending from each elbow. The entity said to the boy that if he climbed into a nearby tree, they would give him a ride in one of their ships in 15 minutes. In spite of the general fear among the children, the boy and a friend climbed the tree; however, the other children turned a garden hose on them and forced them back to the ground.

True to the entity's word, one of the disks presently approached the tree, waited a moment and then flew away, accompanied by the other UFOs. Although it would be easy to dismiss this case as a product of overactive young imaginations, the children's parents noted that they were very frightened for days after their encounter. Of course, it must be borne in mind that children can and do convince themselves that their fantasies are real, and thus it would not be surprising that they frightened themselves so considerably.

ROBERTSON PANEL

Soon after the great wave of sightings across the United States in 1952, during which a large number of UFOs were seen and tracked on radar in the restricted airspace over Washington, D.C., the **CIA** indicated its concern over such sightings. Not only was the agency afraid that enemy agents might try to clog military communications channels with spurious reports, it was also deeply concerned that if it became routine for the military to dismiss UFO reports, a genuine enemy missile attack might also be dismissed as "UFOs," with disastrous consequences for the United States.

Therefore, on December 4, 1952, the Intelligence Advisory Committee recommended that the CIA should commission a group of selected scientists to review the evidence for genuinely anomalous UFOs. The Robertson Panel was convened under the chairmanship of the respected physicist Dr. H. P. Robertson of the California Institute of Technology. The panel, while ostensibly convened to assess the evidence for UFOs, had a hidden agenda: to defuse the growing public concern over the phenomenon.

The panel opened on January 14, 1953, and was adjourned four days later, after examining the 75 best-documented cases from 1951 and 1952. The conclusions of the Robertson Panel were as follows:

2. As a result of its considerations, the Panel concludes:

a) That the evidence presented on Unidentified Flying Objects shows no indication that these phenomena constitute a direct physical threat to national security.

We firmly believe that there is no residuum of cases which indicates phenomena which are attributable to foreign artifacts capable of hostile acts, and that there is no evidence that the phenomena indicate a need for the revision of current scientific concepts.

3. The Panel further concludes:

a) That the continued emphasis on the reporting of these phenomena does, in these perilous times, result in a threat to the orderly functioning of the protective organs of the body politic.

We cite as examples the clogging of channels of communication by irrelevant reports, the danger of being led by continued false alarms to ignore real indications of hostile action, and the cultivation of a morbid national psychology in which skillful hostile propaganda could induce hysterical behavior and harmful distrust of duly constituted authority.

4. In order most effectively to strengthen the national facilities for the timely recognition and the appropriate handling of true indications of hostile action and to minimize the concomitant dangers alluded to above, the Panel recommends:

a) That the national security agencies take immediate steps to strip the Unidentified Flying Objects of the special status they have been given and the aura of mystery they have unfortunately acquired;

b) That the national security agencies institute policies on intelligence, training and public education designed to prepare the material defenses and the morale of the country to recognize most promptly and to react most effectively to true indications of hostile intent or action.

We suggest that these aims may be achieved by an integrated program designed to reassure the public of the total lack of evidence of inimical forces behind the phenomena, to train personnel to recognize and reject false indications quickly and effectively, and to strengthen regular channels for the evaluation of and prompt reaction to true indications of hostile measures.

The Robertson Panel Report effectively dictated the policy of the U.S. Air Force Project **Blue Book** from then on until the project's demise in 1969. After the report's release, Blue Book was to become embattled on two fronts: first, it was now required to prove that UFOs did not exist, no matter how impressive the evidence it received; and second, the assertion that UFOs did not represent a threat to national security meant a sharp decrease in the project's already meager resources.

ROERICH, NICHOLAS

Poet, artist, mystic and member of Madame Blavatsky's Theosophical Society, Nicholas Roerich had a lifelong fascination for Eastern mysticism, specifically the legends surrounding the hidden kingdom of Shambhala, a paradise of universal wisdom, peace and enlightenment, located somewhere in the region of Tibet, perhaps in the interior of the planet (see **Hollow Earth Theory**).

It was during an expedition through China and Mongolia toward Tibet in 1925–8 that Roerich and his party saw a UFO. The date was August 5, 1927, the location, the Kukunor district. In his 1930 book *Altai-Himalaya: A Travel Diary*, Roerich describes the encounter thus:

We all saw, in a direction from north to south, something big and shiny reflecting the sun, like a huge oval moving at great speed. Crossing our camp this thing changed in its direction from south to southwest. And we saw how it disappeared in the intense blue sky. We even had time to take our field glasses and saw quite distinctly an oval form with shiny surface, one side of which was brilliant from the sun. (Quoted in Godwin [1993], p. 102)

According to Roerich, the lama accompanying the party said that the object was a very good sign, meaning that they were protected by Rigden-jyepo, the King of the World who resides in the fabulous realm of Shambhala, and who is preparing an invincible army with which he will one day conquer all nations.

ROPER POLL

A highly controversial poll conducted by the Roper Organization in the United States in 1991, which has been cited by **abductions** researchers Budd **Hopkins**, John **Mack** and others as indicating that a huge number of Americans have been abducted by nonhuman entities. The Roper Organization questioned 5,947 respondents, asking them such yes or no questions as: have you ever awoken paralyzed with a sense of a strange person or presence in the room?; have you experienced a period of an hour or more in which you were apparently lost, but did not remember where or why?; have you ever felt yourself to be flying through the air without knowing how or why?; have you ever found puzzling scars on your body without remembering how you sustained them? and so on.

Roper found 18 people out of the 5,947 who replied yes to all of the five key questions (and who thus were possible victims of alien abduction), representing 0.3 percent of the sample. However, the margin for error in the poll was ±1.4, meaning that the number of abductees could, statistically, very well be zero. According to Paul Devereux and Peter Brookesmith in their 1997 book *UFOs and Ufology: The First Fifty Years*: "To find out if this number is representative, you would need to question at least five times as many people as Roper did, and probably many more, in order to overcome a law of diminishing returns." (p. 170)

In their interpretation of the Roper Poll results, published in their 1992 pamphlet entitled *A Report on Unusual Experiences Associated with UFO Abductions, Based on the Roper Organization's Survey of 5,947 Adult Americans*, Hopkins, David M. **Jacobs** and Ron Westrum stated that if a person replied yes to four out of the five key questions, it would imply a possible abduction. As a result of this, the number of such people revealed by the poll increased from 18 to 119, representing 2 percent of the sample, or 3.7 million of the U.S. population.

Devereux and Brookesmith attack the logic in such an assumption, and quote the market researcher James R. Adams as saying:

What they are saying is, if abduction, then all of these other symptoms. All these other symptoms (or some of them, even), therefore abduction. This does not follow; the logic has what is known as an "undistributed middle." If it is raining, the pavements are wet. But, the fact that the pavements are wet does not mean that it is raining. (Quoted in Devereux and Brookesmith [1997], p. 170)

ROSWELL AUTOPSY FOOTAGE

Early in 1995, a piece of film footage surfaced purporting to show an autopsy being conducted on an extraterrestrial cadaver. The discovery was reported throughout the world, initiating a controversy that still rages to this day. The man who brought the film to the world's attention was an independent film producer named Ray Santilli, who had initially spoken with a former military cameraman regarding some 1950s footage of Elvis Presley. The cameraman had then mentioned that he had some other film, which Santilli might find interesting. This proved to be something of an understatement.

The cameraman, now in his 80s, explained that he had always processed his own film, and for this reason had kept a copy of the film he had taken just after the UFO crash near **Roswell**, New Mexico, in 1947. When asked why he wanted to sell the footage, he replied that he wanted to buy a wedding present for his granddaughter.

Santilli was contacted by Stanton T. **Friedman**, who had spent considerable time and effort in researching the so-called Roswell Incident. According to Santilli, President Harry Truman was easily recognizable in the film. The autopsy on the alien being had been conducted in Dallas, Texas, near the 8th Air Force Headquarters in Fort Worth. Santilli also claimed that his research at the Truman Library had established that Truman had been in Dallas at the time of the autopsy. However, Friedman decided to do some checking for himself: when he went to the library, he could find no documentary evidence that Harry Truman had been in either Texas or New Mexico in the relevant period. This raised Friedman's suspicions, since it meant that Santilli had not, after all, verified Truman's presence in Dallas.

The footage was screened at the Museum of London on May 5, 1995, before an audience of UFO researchers and journalists. No introduction or explanation was given regarding the film's contents, and Santilli left immediately afterward without answering any questions (which the audience found irritating, to say the least). Santilli had assured researchers that they would be given access to the mysterious cameraman himself, whose name was apparently "Jack Barnett," although this name did not appear in the lists of cameramen serving with the armed services in 1947. In any event, the promised access to "Barnett" did not happen.

Stanton Friedman was invited to the London screening of the autopsy footage; oddly, however, he did not receive his invitation until 24 hours before, and found it impossible to make the trip from his home in Canada in time. Friedman had sent a fax to Santilli on May 3, challenging him to produce the information necessary for a proper evaluation of the film's authenticity. The list of this information was as follows:

1. The make and model of the film camera used.
2. The type of film used and the dates of the filming.
3. Evidence in the form of a written report from Kodak or whoever supposedly determined the vintage of the film.
4. J. B.'s [Jack Barnett's] military discharge papers—DD 124.
5. A set or two of military orders from the right time frame indicating where J. B. was assigned, names of associates, etc.
6. A receipt for the $100,000 [which Barnett was allegedly paid for the film].
7. Some kind of withdrawal slip showing from whence cometh the $100,000. Your small office gives no indication that you would find it easy to lay your hands on that amount of cash [Friedman had visited Santilli at his office in London on April 4].
8. Evidence of a supposed showing to supposed religious leaders.
9. Any evidence that BBC had ever intended to show the footage.
10. Evidence that there had been contact with the Truman Library and any indication that Truman was in Dallas any time in the period July 1–September 30, 1947. They tell me he wasn't in Texas.
11. Any evidence that your effort is other than an attempt to spread disinformation to discredit Roswell . . . similar to the U.S. Air Force attack on Roswell in September, 1994 . . . similar to the Doug and Dave Faked Crop Circle nonsense of several years back. [Douglas Bower and Dave Chorley claimed to have hoaxed many British **crop circles**.]

Friedman received a prompt (if rather unsatisfactory) response the very next day: "None of the above is of interest to me."

Even the dating of the film spools proved controversial: when the Kodak office in Copenhagen, Denmark, was asked to date the manufacture of the film stock, through reference to the square and triangular code markings on the spool edge, they concluded that it had been manufactured in 1947. However, the people at the Copenhagen office were apparently inexperienced, and did not realize that these particular symbols were repeated every 20 years.

Santilli had used Kodak's name while promoting the footage, and this prompted Peter Milson, Marketing Planning Manager with Kodak in England, to issue the following statement:

ROSWELL FOOTAGE:
Comments from Kodak

The possibility of life-forms on planets other than Earth has always fired the imagination. This has been particularly true in the movie business and Kodak has been involved in supplying camera negative to such films, e.g. *E.T.* and ***Close Encounters of the Third Kind.***

More recently, we have become involved in a more complex situation, namely, we have been asked to confirm the age of a piece of film known as "the Roswell Film," which allegedly shows alien life-forms.

We have seen sections of either the film or its projection leader in 3 Kodak locations: U.K., Hollywood and Denmark. The following outlines the conclusions of our examinations:

1. In our manufacturing process we put a code on the edge of the film which repeats every 20 years.

2. The symbols we have seen on the Roswell film samples suggest the film was manufactured in either: 1927, 1947 or 1967.

3. We are, therefore, unable to categorically confirm when the film was manufactured.

4. It should also be remembered that even if the age of the film manufacture is confirmed, this does not necessarily indicate that the film was shot and processed in the same year.

So, the bottom line is, that although we would like to know if aliens actually exist, Kodak cannot categorically confirm either the age of the film or when it was shot and processed.

Friedman eventually managed to view the film, along with Dr. Bruce Maccabee, an experienced analyst of UFO photographs. It immediately became clear to them that there were a number of discrepancies between what they saw on the autopsy footage, and the testimony from eyewitnesses that had been gathered over the years. The creature lying on the autopsy table bore little resemblance to the ufonauts described at Roswell; for instance, the "alien" in the film had six fingers and toes, while the Roswell entities allegedly had four long fingers, without opposable thumbs.

Neither did the wreckage displayed in the film look much like descriptions of the Roswell wreckage. The famous "I-beams," which witnesses described as being made of a balsalike substance, with purplish symbols on them, were clearly metallic in the film, with the symbols stamped onto them. In addition, while the Roswell symbols were described as being a little like pictograms or hieroglyphics, the ones in the film looked suspiciously like Roman letters. Indeed, the word "VIDEO" was even present, partially disguised by additional lines and the mirroring of some letters. (One is reminded here of Billy **Meier** showing his followers a picture of the Ring Nebula and saying it is the eye of God.) When these discrepancies were mentioned to Santilli, he responded by claiming several different dates and locations for the UFO crash.

The autopsy itself poses further serious problems. For one thing, it proceeds far too quickly, with the examiners discovering almost immediately that the creatures eyes are covered with jet-black contact lenses. They then pull them out without any thought as to the damage this might cause to the eyes themselves. The examiners then cut open the body and remove the internal organs, dropping them into specimen dishes without any attempt to note their supporting structures. In fact, the whole operation is conducted in an incredibly ham-fisted manner, in view of the apparent uniqueness of the specimen with which they are dealing. Indeed, it looks as though the entire autopsy was performed in a matter of a couple of hours, instead of the weeks of careful, step-by-step procedures one would expect.

The Roswell autopsy film has been shown to a number of special-effects experts, almost all of whom have stated that, in their opinion, the "alien" is a manufactured dummy.

ROSWELL, NEW MEXICO

By far the most famous of all UFO events, the Roswell Incident occurred on the Independence Day weekend, 1947. On July 1, a number of unknown targets appeared on radar screens at the White Sands Proving Grounds. The following evening, Mr. and Mrs. Dan Wilmot were sitting on their porch in Roswell, when they saw a glowing object pass overhead, headed in a northwesterly direction. On the evening of July 4, during a violent thunderstorm, rancher W. W. "Mac" Brazel heard a loud explosion more powerful than the thunderclaps.

At about 11:30 P.M., an object on the White Sands radar screen disintegrated in a "starburst," indicating that it had crashed. Meanwhile, Roswell resident Jim Ragsdale and his girlfriend, Trudy Truelove, were on a camping trip north of Roswell, when they saw a glowing object hurtle overhead before hitting the ground about a mile from their campsite. Ragsdale

persuaded Truelove to go with him in search of the downed object. Driving across the rough terrain, they eventually came upon the crash site and saw a strange object lying against the side of a cliff. At that point, their flashlight failed, so they decided to return to their camp.

The following day, Saturday, July 5, a group of archaeologists working in the area discovered the crash site, and one of them went back into town to inform the sheriff, George Wilcox, who in turn notified the fire department. Military personnel were also sent to the scene (guided there by their tracking of the object in its final moments of flight). On discovering the archaeologists, they escorted them away from the object and swore them to secrecy. The bodies of five crew members were discovered and taken away.

Ragsdale and Truelove had already been back to the site, had seen the bodies and had even managed to retrieve a few pieces of wreckage. They then watched the arrival of the military, and decided to throw away the pieces of wreckage, for fear of discovery and arrest.

While out inspecting his pastures, "Mac" Brazel discovered a large field of debris, composed of what looked like metal foil, balsalike I-beams and parchment with curious, flowerlike designs printed on it. Brazel collected some of the debris and took it to his neighbors, Floyd and Loretta Proctor, who suggested he hand it in to Sheriff Wilcox in Roswell.

At 1:30 P.M., Glenn Dennis answered the phone at the Ballard Funeral Home in Roswell. It was the mortuary officer at Roswell Army Air Field (RAAF). He asked Dennis if Ballard's had any four-foot-long, hermetically sealed caskets. Dennis only had one, and asked if there had been an accident at the base, to which the mortuary officer replied that this was just for their future reference. He called back shortly afterward, asking how to handle bodies that had been exposed to desert conditions (once more, just for their information).

Later that day, Dennis picked up an injured airman in the Ballard ambulance (the funeral home had a contract to provide ambulance services for RAAF) and took him to the base hospital. When he arrived, he saw three field ambulances. On his way into the emergency room, he glanced into one of the ambulances and saw some strange wreckage, shaped like the front portion of a canoe.

Inside the emergency room, one of the nurses spotted Dennis and told him he had better leave if he wanted to avoid trouble. An officer also spotted him, and an ugly scene ensued in which Dennis was threatened with dire consequences if he ever spoke about what he had seen.

On Sunday, July 6, Brazel took some of his wreckage into Roswell, where Sheriff Wilcox notified RAAF. Colonel William Blanchard, commanding officer of the 509th Bomb Group (the only atomic bomber group in the world at that time), ordered intelligence officer Major Jesse A. Marcel to interview Brazel and examine the material. He concluded that he should visit the debris field in Brazel's pasture, which he did the following day in the company of Brazel and counterintelligence agent Captain Sheridan Cavitt. Blanchard obtained some of the debris from Wilcox and had it flown to Washington, D. C. via Fort Worth Army Air Field.

On July 7, Dennis asked one of the nurses from the base out to lunch at the officers' club. In a state of obvious distress, she told him that she had been asked to assist in the preliminary autopsy of several small bodies, which had exuded such a horrific stench that even the doctors had been forced from the room. According to the nurse, the beings had large heads, large, deep-set eyes, noses that were concave and thin, slitlike mouths.

The nurse was later transferred to England, and Dennis never saw her again. There is a rumor that she died in a military aircraft accident, although there is no corroborating evidence for this.

Marcel and Cavitt loaded two cars with material from the debris field, which was about three quarters of a mile long and 200 to 300 hundred feet wide. At 2:00 A.M., Marcel arrived home with some of the debris and awoke his wife and young son, Jesse Jr, so that they might take a look at the strange, incredibly tough and amazingly light material.

At 11:00 that morning, 1st Lieutenant Walter Haut took the press release he had been told to write into Roswell, giving it to the two radio stations and two newspapers. By 2:30 P.M., the story had been picked up by the AP wire, and would shortly be known all over the world.

Jesse Marcel was ordered to fly the debris to Wright Field (now **Wright-Patterson Air Force Base**), Dayton, Ohio, for analysis. During a stopover at Fort Worth AAF, General Roger Ramey took charge of the material and ordered a press release stating that it was actually nothing more unusual than the wreckage from a weather balloon. To back up this claim, he arranged for parts from such a device to be displayed at a press conference. Marcel was sent back to Roswell, while the genuine wreckage continued its journey to Wright Field. For his part, Marcel would later maintain that what he found in Brazel's pasture was not a weather balloon, and researchers have frequently commented that he would surely be expected to know the difference between a weather balloon and the exotic material that was found.

Brazel was then interrogated by the military for a week, an experience that caused him to change his story concerning the strange attributes of the wreckage. He remained silent on the subject for the rest of his life.

The U.S. Air Force has since come up with several explanations for what happened at Roswell, including that the material recovered was from a then top-secret Project Mogul balloon (Mogul was designed to detect Soviet atomic bomb tests). With regard to the small bodies also allegedly recovered, the air force explains that they were actually artificial human dummies, which were dropped from high altitudes in human-endurance experiments. However, this does not explain the small stature of the bodies recovered at Roswell. In addition, such dummies were not used until the mid-1950s.

ROSWELL: THE UFO COVER-UP (FILM)

Made in 1994, directed by Jeremy Paul Kagan and starring Kyle MacLachlan, Martin Sheen, Dwight Yoakam, Kim Greist and Xander Berkeley. A made-for-television drama, based on the events surrounding the alleged UFO crash near **Roswell, New Mexico.** The film is engaging and wellmade, following an ageing Marcel (MacLachlan) as he attends an air force reunion while searching for answers to the mystery that has haunted him all his life. The crash and retrieval of the UFO is shown in several flashbacks, and there is much material concerning a ufonaut who survived for some time in a top-secret hospital.

RUPPELT, EDWARD J.

(See Project **Blue Book**)

SAGAN, CARL EDWARD

Born in New York in 1934, Carl Sagan was Professor of Astronomy and Space Sciences and Director of the Laboratory for Planetary Studies at Cornell University. The world's greatest popularizer of science, he played a crucial role in the U.S. space program, briefing the *Apollo* astronauts for their flights to the Moon and contributing greatly to the *Mariner, Viking, Voyager* and *Galileo* expeditions to Mars and the outer planets.

Sagan wrote a number of best-selling books on science and astronomy, including the Pulitzer Prize-winning *The Dragons of Eden* (1977) and *Cosmos* (1980), which became the best-selling science book in history. Its companion television series was watched by more people than any other ever made. He received 22 honorary degrees from various universities for his contributions to science, education and the consequences of nuclear war.

His novel *Contact* (1985) was filmed in 1997, directed by Robert Zemeckis and starring Jodie Foster, Matthew McConaughey, James Woods, Tom Skerrit and John Hurt. It tells the story of a young radio astronomer, Ellie Arroway (Foster), who is obsessed with the search for extraterrestrial intelligence (see **SETI**), and who discovers a signal originating near the star Vega. The message is deciphered, and is revealed to be a set of instructions for an interstellar vehicle.

Although an enthusiastic advocate of the possibility of extraterrestrial civilizations, Sagan irritated many ufologists with his 1997 book *The Demon-Haunted World: Science as a Candle in the Dark*, in which he pointed out many of the absurdities and unfounded assertions associated with all aspects of the paranormal. However, in spite of his good-natured skepticism, Sagan was a hero to millions of people for the ease with which he explained difficult concepts, opening the layperson's mind to the wonders and mysteries of the universe.

Carl Sagan died in December 1996, at the age of 62, from bone marrow cancer.

SALINAS CORPSE

One of the most intriguing cases of nonhuman (though not necessarily extraterrestrial) contact in recent years occurred in southern Puerto Rico in 1980. The story has it that a youth named José Luis "Chino" Zayas had been in the mountains behind a National Guard's camp with a friend, when the two boys were waylaid by a group of diminutive, humanoid creatures 12 to 14 inches in height, with large, hairless heads, large almond-shaped eyes and pointed ears. One of the creatures grabbed Chino's leg, and the youth, seized with panic, picked up a piece of wood and killed the creature with a single blow to the head.

Chino took the corpse back to Salinas and gave it to Wito Morales, the owner of Monserrate Funeral Parlor. Morales placed the corpse in a glass jar and filled it with formaldehyde, to preserve it. The specimen was later confiscated by Officer Osvaldo Santiago of the Salinas police, for further investigation. According to the respected UFO researcher Jorge Martín:

Days later, Osvaldo returned without the jar and told his wife not to discuss the subject since his superiors had ordered no further investigation into the matter. Apparently the military had taken over and would deal with the case. ("The Salinas 'ET Corpse'", *UFO Magazine* March/April 1998, p. 25)

Corroboration came from Calixto Pérez, a professor of chemistry at the University of Puerto Rico and resident of Salinas, who also examined the creature in the jar:

I can tell you it wasn't a fetus. I've seen too many baby fetuses in different stages of development at the University of Puerto Rico, and that thing didn't look like a baby in the least . . .

That thing had glossy, rough skin and with a color like our own, but mixed with clear greenish tones. Let me clarify that this wasn't a side-effect from the formaldehyde.

That was the color of its skin. It only had four fingers and its arms were very long. It wasn't human. In my opinion, it was something extraterrestrial.

Its skull, its head, was too large for the body, which was thin, and its eyes were much too large. Regarding its nose, it had no nose as such, because it would have entered a decomposition stage and the skin would have fallen off. It simply lacked a nose. That's how it was. (Ibid., pp. 25–6)

According to British ufologist Timothy Good in his book *Alien Base: Earth's Encounters With Extraterrestrials* (1998), the police informed the military authorities in the United States, and the jar, with its bizarre contents, was taken away by representatives from **NASA**.
(See also **Caspar Mummy, Chupacabras**)

SALZBURG, AUSTRIA

Location of an encounter with a bizarre and extremely uncommon Gray-type entity with compound eyes (see **Grays, insectoids**). The encounter occurred at 11:00 P.M. on May 15, 1951; the witness was a soldier with the U.S. Army occupation force, and has always maintained his anonymity. The soldier was on his way home, when the entity moved into view from behind some bushes, pointed a long, thin device at him and paralyzed him. The entity was about five feet tall, and was wearing a transparent, near-spherical helmet. Its short arms ended in long, graceful, four-fingered hands. It was dressed in a two-piece suit, the legs of which were tight-fitting and merged into its shoes, while the body appeared to be rigid and cylindrical. Its cranium was also slightly cylindrical, extending up and back from a wide, heart-shaped face. The most striking feature was the eyes, which were large and compound, like an insect's. It had no ears or nose to speak of, and its mouth was a very small horizontal slit.

The entity then did something that is most interesting, in the context of the **extraterrestrial hypothesis**: in order to make the soldier light enough to pull into its nearby craft, the entity strapped a black, square device to his chest. The soldier, now virtually weightless, was pulled toward the UFO, which was sitting in a nearby field. He and the entity floated up to the top of the 150-foot-diameter disk, where a hatch opened and they entered. If the entity was indeed an extraterrestrial, we can speculate that the black square represented a slightly cruder form of the technique used by the **Grays** in their modern **abductions**, whereby victims are floated out of their normal environment.

Once inside, the soldier watched Earth fall away through the UFO's transparent walls. The craft hurtled past the Moon and on to Mars, where it landed on a raised platform, which was surrounded by other spacecraft. The entity then left the craft, while the soldier looked out through the walls, and saw other human beings leaving two of the other saucers.

Presently, the entity returned to the craft, which flew back to Earth. Once again, the square, black device was strapped to the soldier's chest, and he was floated to the ground. The UFO then departed.

It was six years before the soldier felt able to share his experience with anyone. In December 1957 he went to *The Citizen* newspaper in British Columbia, where he told a reporter what had happened to him in Austria. Although the reporter tried on several occasions to trick the soldier into contradicting himself, he did not, and the reporter was greatly impressed by his apparent truthfulness.

SAUCER SMEAR (PUBLICATION)

Described by John **Keel** as a "boil on the ass of ufology," *Saucer Smear* is the official publication of the Saucer and Unexplained Celestial Events Research Society (SAUCERS). The newsletter is edited by veteran UFO researcher and commentator James W. Moseley, who has been involved in ufology since the 1950s.

Saucer Smear is a free "trade journal," consisting primarily of UFO-related humor and gossip. The November 15, 1997, issue (the journal is published sporadically) included the following "position statement":

. . . [T]here is no scientific proof (as opposed to mere *evidence*) that **anything** strange is going on. In particular, fifty years of the so-called modern flying saucer era have produced no hard evidence that we are being visited by spacecraft from another planet, or that the [U.S.] Government is conspiring to keep us in the dark about same.

In our opinion, strange things are indeed going on, but because they are not *reproducible,* the evidence is largely anecdotal. We believe that there is a definite link, or overlap, between UFO phenomena and psychic phenomena. Your editor has personally experienced several examples of both, from time to time during his life.

To us, the most likely answer to all of this is that we share this planet with another Intelligence, whatever it may be, and that this situation has existed throughout recorded history, if not longer [see **psychosocial hypothesis, ultraterrestrials**]. There is no need to assume we are being invaded by spaceships. If we ever are so invaded, we believe the evidence for it will be far more clear-cut than anything we have seen so far.

SCAPE ORE MONSTER

One of several hostile, reptilian humanoid creatures said to haunt the swamps and bayous of the southern United States. The Scape Ore Monster caused fear and consternation during the summer of 1988, in the area around Scape Ore swamp in South Carolina. Following several encounters and other odd events reported in the press, including one in which a car belonging to the Waye family was discovered one morning to be covered with scratches and teeth marks, a 17-year-old youth named Christopher Davis decided to come forward with his own report of a terrifying encounter with the Scape Ore Monster.

On June 29, 1988, Davis was driving home to the tiny village of Browntown. While he was crossing Scape Ore, his car suffered a puncture, and so he pulled over to the side of the road to repair it. The time was about 2:00 A.M. when he finished the job and put his tools away. At that point he glanced into an adjoining field, where he saw a weird, humanoid creature running at full speed across the field toward him. The creature was huge, perhaps seven feet tall, and its eyes were glowing bright red in the darkness.

Seized with terror, Davis jumped into his car and drove off, just as the creature reached him. As Davis struggled to get the car back onto the road, the hideous, reptilian creature thrust its hands through the wound-down window. Before accelerating away, the youth caught a glimpse of three long fingers, black nails and green skin. Although he left the creature behind, this was not the end of Davis's dreadful experience. Looking in the rear-view mirror, he saw the thing running after the car.

In the next moment, there was a heavy thud above him, and Davis realized in horror that the creature had jumped onto the roof of the car. He could see its long, thick fingers at the top of the windscreen, as if it were struggling to keep its grip. As the car increased speed, the creature either jumped

or fell off the car, and Davis fled home. When he arrived, he would not leave the car until his father came out of the house.

The encounter was reported to the local sheriff, who was impressed by Davis's apparently genuine terror. Commenting on this case in his book *Borderlands* (1997), the anomalist Mike Dash notes that all but two of the 20 or so reports of what John **Keel** calls "abominable swamp slobs" were made after the release of the horror film *The Creature From the Black Lagoon* (1954).

SCHIRMER, HERBERT

American abductee. In the early hours of December 3, 1967, Patrolman Schirmer was on the outskirts of Ashland, Nebraska, when he had a sudden feeling that something was not quite right. At that moment, he saw a bull charging the gate of its corral, as if frightened by something. Schirmer stopped his patrol car and went to the gate to make sure it was shut properly.

Continuing with his patrol, Schirmer was heading southwest at 2:00 A.M. when he noticed the lights of what he assumed to be a truck. However, as he approached, he realized that the "truck" was actually a disk-shaped object, which ascended into the air. Returning to the police station, he noted his observation of a "flying saucer," and also realized that it was about an hour later than it should have been. The following day, Schirmer began to suffer from headaches and nausea, and also discovered a red welt on his neck.

Schirmer's sighting came to the attention of the University of Colorado UFO Project, a high-profile, air force-sponsored investigation under the direction of Dr. Edward U. Condon that would subsequently dismiss UFOs as unworthy of serious scientific attention. On February 13, 1968, Schirmer was hypnotically regressed by University of Wyoming psychologist Dr. Leo Sprinkle, and related how a blurred object had come out of the UFO toward him. His car engine had died, and he had been somehow prevented from drawing his gun.

The Colorado investigators concluded that Schirmer's experiences had not been objective, but that he had suffered a delusion of some kind. However, Schirmer himself, unsurprisingly, was not satisfied with this interpretation of his experience. His performance at work suffered, and he subsequently resigned. Anxious to find out what had happened during his hour of **missing time**, he contacted an Iowa-based writer on UFOs named Warren Smith. Researcher Loring Williams was also recruited to conduct another **hypnotic regression**.

A considerably more detailed experience emerged during hypnosis by Williams, in which a number of humanoid beings came out of the UFO, one of whom sprayed a green gas over Schirmer's patrol car, before pointing a device at him. Schirmer briefly lost consciousness, and awoke to find one of the beings touching his neck. The patrolman then opened his door and climbed out as the being asked: "Are you the watchman over this place?" The being then pointed to a nearby power plant and asked if it was the only source of power humans had.

The beings then took Schirmer into their ship through a hatch in the underside. They entered a room about 26 by 20 feet, which contained chairs and various instrument panels. Communicating in a mixture of telepathy and English, the beings then took Schirmer on a tour of the craft, during which he saw a number of other computer-like instruments and devices. The alien leader said that they came from a nearby galaxy, and had established secret bases at various locations throughout the world. Their ships were sometimes disabled by earthly radar, but were destroyed by their mother ships before they could crash on Earth.

According to the information Schirmer was given, the alien spacecraft were powered by "reversible electromagnetism," and were capable of drawing additional energy from both electrical power lines and reservoirs on Earth. The aliens claimed that they were planning to contact many more people, but followed no particular pattern (this to confuse governments as to their activities). Their intention was, in effect, to allow humans to get used to the idea of their presence before revealing themselves openly.

The aliens themselves were between four and a half and five feet tall, with gray skin and narrow heads. Their unblinking eyes were catlike, their noses were flat and their mouths little more than horizontal slits. They wore soft, balaclava-style helmets with a small antenna over the left ear. Each of them wore a curious insignia of a winged serpent on the chest.

After telling Schirmer that he would remember the landing of the UFO and nothing more, the alien leader said that they would return to see him two more times. The patrolman was then returned to his car, and the UFO departed.

(See also **abductions,** Barney and Betty **Hill, humanoids**)

SCHWA

A mysterious "corporation" created and run by Bill Barker, an artist based in Nevada. The Schwa Corporation (whose motto is STAY AWAKE) produces a wide range of spoof "alien defense" equipment, designed to protect the owner against **abductions**. The word "schwa" actually refers to an unstressed syllable, the phonetic symbol for which is an inverted *e*, which also frequently appears on Schwa merchandise.

Schwa products, which range from alien-invasion survival cards, to T-shirts, to bumper stickers and key rings, are coated with a mysterious substance known as "Xenon," which reacts to the presence of aliens, thus alerting the owner that an abduction or other type of encounter may be imminent. For instance, the corporation logo, a Xenon-coated head of a Gray alien, appears on Schwa coffee mugs; should a Gray be in the vicinity, the head will disappear. However, the Xenon process has not quite been perfected, and placing hot liquid in the mug will also make the head disappear! This wry and astute humor, coupled with Barker's familiarity with the more bizarre fringes of ufology, have made Schwa products hugely popular.

SCIENCE FICTION

While there have been many science-fiction stories, novels and films that have been inspired by the UFO phenomenon, there is also evidence to suggest that the reverse is also true, with a number of reported encounters with UFOs and supposedly alien beings having been heavily influenced by exposure to science-fiction imagery. In the former case, we can look at films such as *The Day the Earth Stood Still* and *Invaders from Mars*, and easily discern the influences ufology had upon them. However, in the latter case, the connections become somewhat more nebulous and harder to define.

In his *UFO Encyclopedia*, British ufologist John Spencer notes that the interior of the flying saucer in *The Day the Earth Stood Still,* with its circular outer corridor, central control room and sophisticated medical equipment, has been described frequently in subsequent years by many UFO percipients, notably Betty and Barney **Hill** and Antonio Villas **Boas**. It seems that cases such as these, with an apparent input from science fiction, can be divided into two categories: outright hoaxes, and cases in which a genuinely anomalous event may have occurred.

Hoax cases can be very easy to spot indeed, so obvious is the science-fiction imagery. For instance, in an encounter that occurred in Argentina in 1957, the witness reported a tall being in an armored suit with stiff limbs, no hands and a bulbous metal helmet. The creature itself strongly resembled a Gray. However, this description was identical in every detail to the aliens in the 1956 film *Earth vs. the*

Flying Saucers. In another case from Argentina, the monstrous creature reported was seven feet tall, with huge, circular eyes, an external brain and enormous pincers instead of hands. This being is also instantly recognizable as one of the "mutants" used for manual labor on the planet Metaluna, in the 1954 film *This Island Earth.* In the latter case, we can see how a kind of cultural feedback loop can sometimes be created, with UFO imagery (the Metalunans' spacecraft was a classic flying saucer) inspiring science fiction, which in turn inspires subsequent UFO reports. This can also be seen in ***Close Encounters of the Third Kind***, in which the diminutive aliens were clearly inspired by previous humanoid reports, and yet which resulted in a considerable jump in Gray-type reports after the film's release.

The cases in which some anomalous event seems to have occurred are much harder to explain, in spite of the evidence for contamination by science-fiction imagery. Many people have come to accept that something rather strange is happening in cases of alien **abductions**, even if they are radically opposed in their opinions as to the cause. A number of abduction researchers have steadfastly maintained that the Gray alien has no provenance in the history of science fiction, an assertion that is patently false (one need only watch *Earth vs. the Flying Saucers* again to establish this). Abductionists also claim that the medical procedures carried out on board Gray spacecraft (such as the insertion of tiny implants into abductees' bodies) cannot be found in science fiction. They obviously had the good sense not to watch *Invaders from Mars*!

The problem with contamination of alien encounter reports by science-fiction imagery arises from the apparent veracity of so many percipients. Even those ufologists, such as Jacques **Vallée**, who cannot accept that the entities come from another planet (see **psychosocial hypothesis**) agree that such encounters represent interaction between human beings and some kind of powerful intelligence. John Spencer suggests that the similarity between science-fiction imagery and UFO reports may be due to the percipient experiencing an event, which is utterly beyond his or her comprehension. Since the human brain does not like to deal with such events as they are, and struggles to place them within a familiar frame of reference, it is perhaps to be expected that it will choose the context of science fiction as an appropriate "lens" through which to experience the events. As Spencer states: "This is not to suggest that the event is unreal or inspired by science fiction, only that the report may be distorted by the imagery of science fiction." (Spencer [1991], p. 346)

SCREEN MEMORIES

According to **abductions** researchers, when a person is taken by aliens against his or her will, a screen memory will be superimposed over the memory of what actually occurred. Thus, the percipient will recall a spacecraft as a large vehicle such as a bus, or even an oddly shaped house, while the aliens themselves will become large-eyed animals such as deer or **owls**. The reason why screen memories occur is unclear: some have suggested that this is merely the way in which the human mind disguises memories of a particularly unpleasant or traumatic nature, making them easier for the person to deal with; others suggest that it is the aliens themselves who plant these memories, either out of concern for the mental well-being of the abductee or as a precaution against too many people becoming consciously aware of their presence.

Screen memories are usually uncovered through the use of **hypnotic regression**, itself a highly controversial and by no means foolproof method of recovering information regarding past events. Indeed, there is a very real danger that in the hands of an unscrupulous or inexperienced practitioner,

hypnosis can actually insert spurious screen memories into the consciousness of a person who *thinks* he or she *might* have encountered aliens at some stage in their lives.

SEARCH FOR EXTRATERRESTRIAL INTELLIGENCE (SETI)

The brainchild of American astronomer Frank Drake, who conducted the first modern radio search for intelligent extraterrestrial signals, Project Ozma, at Green Bank Observatory, West Virginia, in 1960, the Search for Extraterrestrial Intelligence (SETI) project was originally called Communication with Extraterrestrial Intelligence (CETI). It became SETI in the mid-1970s because of the arrogant tone of the word "communication," and the fact that no one had been found to communicate *with*.

The rationale behind SETI is, first, that intelligent life elsewhere in the universe is a virtual certainty and, secondly, that such civilizations will almost certainly use radio transmissions as a method of interplanetary communication. Interestingly (and rather ironically), some SETI scientists have speculated that our first radio contact with extraterrestrials will be via robot probes in our own Solar System. It has been suggested that ancient, highly advanced space-faring civilizations may well have placed such probes in the vicinity of stars with potentially life-bearing planets, monitoring their development over millions of years, and then contacting their home worlds in the event that intelligent life arises in the systems under observation. We should therefore not be surprised if we eventually detect signals from these robot probes. However, when faced with the possibility that these probes (whether manned or unmanned) are actively monitoring our planet at close range, the vast majority of SETI advocates do not react sympathetically, citing (quite reasonably) the absence of absolute proof (as opposed to evidence of varying quality).

SEMJASE

The best known and most frequently mentioned of the **Pleiadians/Plejarans** who have been in contact with Swiss contactee Eduard "Billy" **Meier** for a number of years. Semjase (pronounced "sem-yah-see") is 344 Earth years old, slim, blue-eyed, fair-skinned and strikingly attractive. She is utterly humanlike in appearance, apart from her elongated earlobes. She is also extremely intelligent, even for a Pleiadian, and holds the rank of demi-Jshrjsh (pronounced "ish-rish"), which means demi-queen of wisdom.

Semjase knows more about life on Earth than any other extraterrestrial on the planet. Her first contact with Billy Meier occurred in January 1975, and she confined her activities exclusively to Europe, learning German as her first Earth language (there are other Pleiadians working in America and Asia). In December 1977, Semjase had a serious accident at the Semjase Silver Star Center in Hinterschmidrüti, Switzerland, and was immediately taken to her home planet, Erra, in the Pleiades (which, apparently, are not the same Pleiades known to astronomers on Earth).

She returned to Earth in May 1978, and contacted Meier for the last time in February 1984. In the same year, she suffered a "cerebral collapse" as a result of her earlier accident, and was taken to the DAL universe (parallel with our own DERN universe), where she is now being nursed back to health with the help of her friend **Asket**. According to her father, **Ptaah**, the regeneration of her brain and mental faculties will take about 70 Earth years.

SFATH

The grandfather of **Semjase**, Sfath was the first **Pleiadian/Plejaran** to contact Eduard "Billy" **Meier**, when the **contactee** was five years old. In 1942, Sfath took the boy on a flight in his beamship, during which he placed a helmetlike learning device on his head and transmitted a vast amount of knowledge to him. This education continued for several years, and was continued by **Asket**. Sfath died soon afterward.

SHAMANIC HYPOTHESIS

According to those ufologists who subscribe to the **psychosocial hypothesis**, the UFO phenomenon has always shared the planet with humanity, appearing in various guises over the millennia. Our ancestors saw flaming shields in the sky, globes of light that danced among the clouds and were interpreted as the work of either God or the Devil. We, on the other hand, when faced with similar phenomena, frequently assume that they are spacecraft piloted by beings from other worlds, beings who are perhaps similar to ourselves, with a similar curiosity and desire to explore the cosmos.

The shamanic hypothesis takes into account the apparent historical ubiquity of UFO and nonhuman encounters, with regard to the human capacity for myth-making, or the use of the imagination as a tool with which to apprehend reality. Shamanism is an ancient practice that results in contact with spirits residing in the natural world, in the pursuit of sacred knowledge and powers of healing. There are several ways in which a person may become a shaman, such as through injury or serious illness. When this happens, and the prospective shaman is close to death, contact is established with the spirit world, which contains entities from the underworld or the sky. Frequently, the souls of dead ancestors will also be encountered, as will the spirits residing in trees, rocks and animals.

During their encounters with the "otherworld," prospective shamans are forced to undergo incredibly harrowing experiences, such as being cut open by the spirits and having their internal organs ripped out and replaced with new ones, pieces of quartz (which enable them to fly) and "iron bones." A celestial journey is also undertaken, in which the shamans converse with the spirits of their ancestors.

When the initiation is over and the life-threatening crisis past, the shaman goes on to fulfil a vital function to his society. This includes asking permission from various spirits to hunt and kill their animals, and the performing of healing rites on members of the society who have become injured or ill.

The parallels with modern UFO experients are striking. For instance, the extreme operations conducted on the shaman's "body" while in the spirit world are also frequently conducted on the bodies of UFO **abductees**. In one case in 1975, a woman from North Dakota was taken from her car into a UFO, where the entities opened her skull, removed her brain and replaced it with another! Other abductees recall being taken to underground caverns, a familiar motif in shamanism. The British anomalist Patrick Harpur suggests that the tiny pieces of quartz that are inserted into the shaman's body are equivalent to the **implants** placed in the bodies of abductees.

There is, however, a puzzling discrepancy between the profound and detailed communication that ensues between the shaman and the spirits of the otherworld, and the frequently reported *lack* of communication between abductees and the taciturn "aliens." A possible reason for this could be our lack of awareness of the spiritual world, resulting from our increasingly materialistic and technology-based mind-set. It could also be that UFO and nonhuman encounters represent an attempt by the "consciousness of the universe" (for want of a better term) to reestablish contact with those humans who have turned their backs on spiritual reality.

SHARD

(See **artifacts (alien)**)

SHAVER, RICHARD SHARPE

Born in 1910, Richard Shaver became a legend in fringe ufology through his alleged adventures in alien-controlled realms far beneath the surface of Earth. While working as a welder in a Detroit factory, Shaver began to hear voices coming from his welding gun, telling him to do evil things. As a result, he soon found himself in prison, a victim of the hideous underground race known as the **Deros**, whose habit it was to focus harmful, deleterious rays on the people of Earth, thus causing all the strife that has plagued our world over the centuries. However, Shaver was rescued from prison by a beautiful woman named Nydia, a member of another group called the **Teros**, who were the sworn enemies of the Deros.

Nydia took Shaver into the fabulous underworld, to Tero-controlled territory, where he learned the history of the subterranean races in a vast library of telepathic microfilms. Shaver later wrote up his experiences in the "thought records" in a rambling, 31,000-word document entitled "I Remember Lemuria," which was published as nonfiction in Ray **Palmer**'s *Amazing Stories* magazine in 1943. Other stories followed, such as "Cave-City of Hel," "Quest of Brail" and "Mer-Witch of Ether-18." Their popularity was enormous and unprecedented and, before long, other people began to write to Ray Palmer with their own experiences with the Deros and Teros.

When people across the country started to report strange flying objects in the sky in the late 1940s, Shaver and Palmer pointed to this as proof that Shaver had been telling the truth: the flying saucers, they said, were craft piloted by the denizens of the inner earth, and by alien beings related to them.

Although Shaver claimed to have spent many years in the caves of the Deros and Teros, Palmer subsequently discovered that these missing years had actually been spent in a mental hospital. However, officially at least, he maintained that Shaver's experiences must have occurred in a psychic or astral realm, and that what Shaver perceived as the evil Deros were actually dark spirits, or the souls of the dead. Richard Shaver died in 1975.

SIGN (PROJECT)

The U.S. government's first UFO investigation project, which was established in 1947 as a result of a letter from Lieutenant General Nathan F. Twining, commander of the Air Materiel Command, to Brigadier General George Schulgen, commander of the air force. Schulgen had requested a preliminary study of flying disk reports and received the following letter, dated September 23, 1947:

1. As requested by AC/AS-2 there is presented below the considered opinion of this Command concerning the so-called "Flying Disks." This opinion is based on interrogation report data furnished by AC/AS-2 and preliminary studies by personnel of T-2 and Aircraft Laboratory, Engineering Division T-3. This opinion was arrived at in a conference between personnel from the Air Institute of Technology, Intelligence T-2, Office, Chief of Engineering Division, and the Air Craft, Power Planet and Propeller Laboratories of Engineering Division T-3.

2. It is noted that:

a) The phenomenon reported is something real and not visionary or fictitious.

b) There are objects probably approximating the shape of a disk, of such appreciable size as to appear to be as large as man-made aircraft.

c) There is a possibility that some of the incidents may be caused by natural phenomena, such as meteors.

d) The reported operating characteristics such as extreme rates of climb, maneuverability (particularly in roll), and action which must be considered evasive when sighted or contacted by

friendly aircraft and radar, lend belief to the possibility that some of the objects are controlled either manually, automatically or remotely.

e) The apparent common description of the objects is as follows:

(1) Metallic or light reflecting surface.

(2) Absence of trail, except in a few instances when the object was apparently operating under high performance conditions.

(3) Circular or elliptical in shape, flat on bottom and domed on top.

(4) Several reports of well kept formation flights varying from three to nine objects.

(5) Normally no associated sound, except in three instances a substantial rumbling roar was noted.

(6) Level flight speeds normally above 300 knots are estimated.

f) It is possible within the present U.S. knowledge—provided extensive detailed development is undertaken—to construct a piloted aircraft which has the general description of the object in subparagraph (e) above which would be capable of an approximate range of 7,000 miles at subsonic speeds.

g) Any developments in this country along the lines indicated would be extremely expensive, time consuming and at the considerable expense of current projects and therefore, if directed, should be set up independently of existing projects.

h) Due consideration must be given to the following:

(1) The possibility that these objects are of domestic origin—the product of some high security project not known to AC/AS-2 or this Command.

(2) The lack of physical evidence in the shape of crash recovered exhibits which would undeniably prove the existence of these objects.

(3) The possibility that some foreign nation has a form of propulsion, possibly nuclear, which is outside of our domestic knowledge.

3. It is recommended that:

a) Headquarters, Army Air Forces issue a directive signing a priority, security classification and Code Name for a detailed study of this matter to include the preparation of complete sets of all available and pertinent data which will then be made available to the Army, Navy, Atomic Energy Commission, JRDB [Joint Research and Development Board], the Air Force Scientific Advisory Group, NACA [National Advisory Committee on Aeronautics—the forerunner of **NASA**], and the RAND and NEPA [Nuclear Energy for Propulsion Applications Program] projects for comments and recommendations, with a preliminary report to be forwarded within 15 days of receipt of the data and a detailed report thereafter every 30 days as the investigation develops. A complete interchange of data should be effected.

4. Awaiting a specific directive AMC will continue the investigation within its current resources in order to more closely define the nature of the phenomenon. Detailed Essential Elements of Information will be formulated immediately for transmittal thru channels.

It is interesting to note the reference made in this letter to the "lack of physical evidence in the shape of crash recovered exhibits," a reference that is seen by skeptics as proof that no UFO crashed at **Roswell**, New Mexico, two months or so earlier. Roswell advocates respond that the Twining letter is classified Secret, whereas information on the Roswell UFO crash was classified above Top Secret, and for that reason could not have been referred to in a Secret document.

On December 30, 1947, approval was given for the establishment of Project Sign, with the lowest security rating: Restricted. As soon as Project Sign was up and running, it was deluged with UFO reports, which led to fears that an enemy could use such reports to clog up military communications channels (see **Robertson Panel**).

The following year, Project Sign and the U.S. Air Force Air Technical Intelligence Center (ATIC), both based at **Wright-Patterson Air Force Base** in Dayton, Ohio, produced the Top Secret **Estimate of the Situation**, which admitted the probability that UFOs were interplanetary. When General Hoyt S. Vandenberg, the air force chief of staff, ordered the Estimate of the Situation to be destroyed (on the grounds that the evidence did not warrant the radical conclusions), the personnel at Project Sign split into two groups, those who accepted the extraterrestrial origin of UFOs, and those who maintained that they could be explained in mundane terms.

On February 11, 1949, Project Sign was renamed Project **Grudge**.

SIMONTON, JOE

American farmer who encountered a UFO and its occupants on his property near Eagle River, Wisconsin. At 11:00 A.M. on April 18, 1961, Simonton heard a rumbling noise coming from outside his house and went to investigate. He was confronted by a silvery, disk-shaped object 30 feet in diameter and 12 feet high, hovering a few feet above the ground.

A hatch opened on the upper surface of the object, and Simonton saw three people inside. Only slightly smaller than average humans, the occupants were dressed in black two-piece suits with turtle necks. Simonton described them as being very nice-looking, a little like Italians, with dark hair and olive complexions. One of the men showed Simonton a jug, and through gestures made him understand that they needed water, which Simonton provided.

The farmer then noticed that one of the occupants was cooking something on a pan over a "flameless grill." Seeing Simonton's interest, another ufonaut handed him three pancakes before closing the hatch. The object then ascended into the air and flew away to the south.

Simonton contacted his old friend, Sheriff Schroeder, who sent two deputies to the farm. Although the pancakes were the only evidence of the encounter, it was generally felt that Simonton had not lied about his experience. The case was investigated by Dr. J. Allen **Hynek**, who passed on one of the pancakes to the U.S. Air Force for analysis (Simonton had eaten one and found it unappetizing, tasting of cardboard).

According to the results of the air force analysis:

The cake was composed of hydrogenated fat, starch, buckwheat hulls, soya bean hulls, wheat bran. Bacteria and radiation readings were normal for this material. Chemical, infrared and other destructive type tests were run on this material. The Food and Drug Laboratory of the U.S. Department of Health, Education and Welfare concluded that the material was an ordinary pancake of terrestrial origin.

The absurd, pancake-frying behavior of the ufonauts has led some ufologists to suggest a parallel with traditional folktales, in which supernatural beings often gave humans small items of food, in return for minor services or favors.
(See also **folklore, psychosocial hypothesis**)

SIMS, DERREL

American **abductions** researcher, ex-**CIA** agent and self-proclaimed "alien hunter." Sims is a rising star in the field of abductions research and claims to have been involved in the removal of numerous alien **implants** from the bodies of abductees. The chief investigator for the Houston UFO Network (HUFON), Sims also claims to be fighting an ongoing battle with an alien warlord called "Mondoz."

However, while many researchers are impressed with Sims's credentials and the results he has obtained in his research (he has a large and growing collection of alleged implants), others have criticized his methods heavily, while a few have accused him of outright charlatanism. One of these, a real-estate agent and paranormal researcher named Rebecca Schatte (who had a **missing time** episode in 1983), is convinced that Sims is a "fraud," and has made it her business to watch his activities carefully.

SKY-BEAST HYPOTHESIS

A radical and highly controversial suggestion to account for the appearance of UFOs throughout history. According to the sky-beast hypothesis, UFOs are actually living entities native to Earth—or, rather, to the skies above Earth. They are capable of spending their entire lives in the upper atmosphere, only occasionally descending toward the ground, where they are spotted by humans. Although this theory sounds outrageous, Dr. Karl Shuker has commented on how every other ecological niche has been colonized, with the exception of the skies (known flying animals are left aside in this context, since they do not spend their entire lives in the sky):

As a zoologist, I had always been perplexed by the absence of exclusively sky-dwelling life-forms on our planet, especially given the incredible ingenuity demonstrated by evolution in successfully populating everywhere else with living things. If [the proponents] of the sky-beast scenario are correct, however, perhaps I no longer need to be perplexed—merely frustrated that I have yet to glimpse any examples of evolution's best-kept but most amazing secret of all. (Shuker [1996], p. 137)

The sky-beast hypothesis was extensively investigated by a radio officer in the U.S. Merchant Marine named Trevor James Constable, according to whom these creatures can attain truly gigantic sizes, from a few centimeters in length to half a mile. Constable suggests that the reason the sky beasts are not seen more frequently is that they reflect infrared light, which is invisible to humans. Like the octopoids of the oceans, the sky beasts can change color, and when they do, they occasionally reflect visible light . . . and are seen as UFOs.

Constable also believes that sky beasts may have been responsible for the so-called Foo Fighter sightings during the Second World War. These small, spherical UFOs frequently buzzed aircraft on bombing runs over Europe, displaying behavior that some pilots likened to curiosity. Constable suggests that these may have been more primitive cousins of the larger sky beasts seen in the years since the end of the war.

"SLABS" (ALIENS)

Perhaps the strangest of all aliens reported over the years are the slablike beings encountered near the town of Prospect, Kentucky, in 1977. At about 1:00 A.M. on January 27, 19-year-old Lee Parrish was driving home in his jeep, when he noticed a large, rectangular UFO, glowing red-hot, hovering over some nearby trees. Suddenly, the car radio died, and the jeep was drawn directly underneath the UFO, which shot away into the sky after a few moments. However, when Parrish arrived home, he discovered that it was about half an hour later than it should have been. In addition, his eyes were painful and bloodshot.

Parrish subsequently underwent **hypnotic regression** to retrieve the **missing time**, during which he recalled that his car had been pulled up into the air by an unseen force, and he himself had been instantaneously transported into a circular room aboard the UFO. There he encountered the bizarre beings. There were three of them, one of which was no less than 20 feet tall and shaped like a suitcase, with a semicircular raised section on top. It was black, with a rough texture, and a single jointed arm extending from it. The second creature was about six feet tall, red, and also with an arm (not jointed), while the third was white, also six feet tall, with a wedge-shaped "head" and a curved, parabolic profile.

Parrish had the impression that the second entity was afraid of him. Nevertheless, it slowly approached the youth and touched him with its arm, which made him feel cold. At that point, the three beings merged into one another and disappeared, and Parrish was instantly returned to his jeep. After the encounter, Parrish felt that the beings would contact him again one day, although there is no record of any subsequent encounters.

SLEEP PARALYSIS
(See **bedroom visitors**)

SOCORRO, NEW MEXICO

Location of one of the most famous and impressive close encounters with a UFO and associated entities. At 5:45 P.M. on April 24, 1964, Patrolman Lonnie Zamora was chasing a speeding motorist south of Socorro, when he heard a sudden roar and witnessed the descent of a strange, egg-shaped object, which emitted a bright, rocketlike exhaust from its underside. The UFO landed near a dynamite shack, and Zamora was afraid that the exhaust might cause an explosion, so he abandoned his pursuit of the motorist and headed for a nearby ridge and a good vantage point.

From the top of the ridge, Zamora could clearly see the metallic object, which had landed on four diagonal legs. On the side of the machine was a curious red insignia, consisting of an upward-pointing arrow, with a semicircle above and a horizontal bar below. Beside the object stood two small humanoid figures dressed in white coveralls. One of them noticed the policeman's presence and jumped, as if startled. The two figures then moved behind the object. After radioing in to his headquarters and informing them of a possible aircraft accident, Zamora drove slowly toward the UFO and then left his car, whereupon he heard a slamming sound, followed by the roar that had signaled the object's arrival. Zamora, who had walked to within about 50 paces of the object, dived for cover as it took off and flew away over a nearby mountain range.

A few moments later, Sergeant Sam Chavez arrived on the scene, and together the two policemen inspected the landing site, where they discovered four depressions, about two inches deep, and four burn marks in the brush.

The case was investigated by Dr. J. Allen **Hynek**, then a consultant to Project **Blue Book**, who concluded that Zamora and Chavez were sincere, honest and reliable. Zamora especially was hoping that Hynek would be able to explain the encounter for him in conventional terms, a trait the astronomer had noticed in many other witnesses. The Socorro landing was the case that finally convinced the initially skeptical Hynek that some UFOs represented a genuinely anomalous phenomenon. Project Blue Book could find no conventional explanation for Zamora's experience, and the case became the only occupant case listed as "unidentified" in their files.

There were several puzzling inconsistencies, however. A man named Felix Phillips and his wife lived only 1,000 feet from the UFO landing site, and yet they had not heard the rocket blast of the arriving object. Hynek suggested that this was because their house was upwind of the site, and a strong wind had been blowing at the time. The landing prints were in a kite-shaped pattern, which suggested that the object's undercarriage would have been nonsymmetrical and of unequal lengths, meaning that the UFO should have fallen over on landing. Although UFO debunker Philip **Klass** suggested first that Zamora had seen an unusual atmospheric phenomenon, and then that he had hoaxed the whole affair, no convincing evidence for either has ever been found.

SPACE BROTHERS

Term denoting the wise, benevolent alien beings encountered by the **contactees** of the 1950s and 1960s. The Space Brothers were (and perhaps are!) deeply concerned with the spiritual development of humanity, and were troubled by our irresponsible use of nuclear energy. They frequently told the people they contacted that they were prompted to come to Earth by the testing of atomic weapons from the mid-1940s onward, which, they claimed, endangered not only life on Earth, but civilizations on other planets also. It seems that in exploding atomic bombs, humanity was disturbing the balance and harmony of the cosmos.

Entirely human in appearance, the Space Brothers (and Sisters) claimed to have come from a variety of planets both within our Solar System and in other star systems. They were uniformly described as being incredibly handsome (or beautiful), with tall, well-toned bodies and golden hair. Perhaps significantly, the more human scientists learned about conditions on planets such as Venus, Mars and Saturn (conditions that would have killed an unprotected humanoid life-form instantly), the fewer Space Brothers claimed to have come from there.

Sadly, the Space Brothers are seen more and more seldom, having given way to the somewhat less attractive **Grays**, who possess none of their manners or sex appeal.

(See also **Adamski, George; Angelucci, Orfeo; Bethurum, Truman**)

SPECIES (FILM)

Made in 1995, directed by Roger Donaldson and starring Natasha Henstridge, Ben Kingsley and Michael Madsen. A genetic blueprint is transmitted to Earth, which scientists combine with human DNA to produce a humanoid female. The creature, named "SIL," grows rapidly into an unfeasibly attractive woman who is capable of transforming herself at will into a horrific and deadly creature. In this enjoyably mindless science-fiction shocker, the implication is that the hybrid's nastier side is the result of the alien DNA (she was designed by the Swiss surrealist H. R. Giger), until the viewer realizes that it may well be the human component that makes her so unpleasant. (See also *A for Andromeda*)

SPRINGHEEL JACK

Bizarre, apparently nonhuman entity that terrorized London, England, in the 19th century. The mystery began in September 1837, when four people in different parts of London encountered a strange being, which they all described as having large claws, pointed ears and huge glowing eyes. The creature spat gouts of flame from its mouth and made its escape by leaping away across the rooftops. This last ability gave rise to the creature's nickname, for it could leap far higher than any human being, and often jumped clear over houses.

Two more people encountered Springheel Jack on the evening of February 18, 1838. Margaret and Lucy Scales were walking home through the Limehouse area of London, and were passing the entrance to Green Dragon Alley, when a tall figure jumped from the alley's shadows and confronted the terrified girls. The figure opened its mouth, belched a huge blue flame into their faces, and leaped away into the night. The two girls were hysterical with fear for several hours afterward.

On the evening of February 20, Jack struck again at the home of the Alsop family in East London.

When the front doorbell rang, 18-year-old Jane opened the door to see a tall, thin figure, which was partially obscured by shadows. The figure was wearing a helmet, and thus appeared to Jane to be a policeman. Indeed, the figure called out to her to fetch a light, because his colleagues had succeeded in apprehending Springheel Jack. Jane ran into the house, found a candle and returned to the front door to be confronted by Jack himself.

According to the London *Times* of February 22, 1838:

He threw off his outer garment [a large cloak], and applying the lighted candle to his breast, presented a most hideous and frightful appearance, and vomited forth a quantity of blue and white flame from his mouth, and his eyes resembled red balls of fire . . . He wore a large helmet, and his dress, which appeared to fit him very tight, seemed to [Jane Alsop] to resemble white oilskin.

Immediately, the weird creature leaped upon the girl, his sharp, talonlike fingers ripping at her dress and tearing the skin on her neck and arms. Her terrified screams quickly alerted her two sisters, who came running to the front door and managed to wrestle Jane away from her attacker. The three women slammed the door and fled upstairs, but Springheel Jack remained outside the door, trying to get into the house. The three sisters opened an upstairs window and began to scream into the night for help, a ploy which, fortunately, alerted some nearby policemen, who came running to the house. However, Jack was much too fast for them, and made his escape with ease, leaping away across a nearby field.

For the next seven years, Springheel Jack continued to terrorize London with his antics until, in 1845, those antics came to include murder. His victim was a 13-year-old prostitute named Maria Davis, who was walking across the bridge over Folly Ditch, a vile and stinking marsh on Jacob's Island in Bermondsey. Springheel Jack suddenly appeared, performed his by-now-familiar trick of breathing blue fire into his victim's face, and then picked up the hapless girl and threw her from the bridge into the marsh, which quickly swallowed her up. Those nearby, who had watched the murder in horror, could do nothing either to save the girl or to apprehend Jack, who immediately leaped away out of sight.

Springheel Jack's identity has never been discovered, although suspicion did fall for a time upon Henry, marquis of Waterford, who had an extremely cruel sense of humor. Like Jack, he was tall, and had very prominent eyes (although not pointed ears!). Waterford could not have been to blame, however, since Springheel Jack continued his nefarious activities after Waterford's death in 1859. Indeed, he began to widen his sphere of operations to include East Anglia and Liverpool (his last known appearance was in Everton in September 1904).

The most fundamental (and still unanswered) question about Springheel Jack is this: what *was* he? After all, it seems fairly certain that no human being could have performed the feats with which he is accredited. The glowing eyes, the incredible agility, the ability to breathe fire, all argue heavily for a nonhuman nature. (It might be argued that his fire-breathing was a variation on the familiar circus trick; but we are forced to ask how he could actually *generate* the fire inside his mouth, as testified by his numerous victims.)

Some researchers have speculated that he was actually a stranded alien, or a denizen of some bizarre dimension of reality coterminous with our own. Only one thing can be stated for certain: Springheel Jack contained elements of numerous paranormal entities. He was as elusive as a ghost, as destructive as a poltergeist, as evil as a demon, as bizarre as an alien.

STRANGENESS RATING

In his book *The UFO Experience* (1972), Dr. J. Allen **Hynek** proposed a study in which the strangeness of a UFO report is connected with the reliability of the witness, the reason being to establish whether the strangest reports always come from the least reliable people. Hynek states:

The Strangeness Rating is, to express it loosely, a measure of how "oddball" a report is within its particular broad classification. More precisely, it can be taken as a measure of the number of information bits the report contains, each of which is difficult to explain in common-sense terms. A light seen in the night sky the trajectory of which cannot be ascribed to a balloon, aircraft, etc., would nonetheless have a low Strangeness Rating because there is only one strange thing about the report to explain: its motion. A report of a weird craft that descended to within 100 feet of a car on a lonely road, caused the car's engine to die, its radio to stop, and its lights to go out, left marks on the nearby ground, and appeared to be under intelligent control receives a high Strangeness Rating because it contains a number of separate very strange items, each of which outrages common sense. (p. 42)

Hynek goes on to stress that the investigator must depend to a great extent on the credibility of the reporter(s). Balance of mind and reputation are of great importance, as opposed to a propensity for lying. Nevertheless, he discovered in his own researches that there were many cases in which people with a high reliability rating reported incidents containing numerous elements of extreme strangeness.

STRIEBER, WHITLEY

American abductee. Born in San Antonio, Texas, in 1945, Whitley Strieber became a highly successful horror novelist, publishing such books as *The Wolfen* (1978) and *The Hunger* (1981), both of which were filmed. In 1985, Strieber suffered an apparent alien abduction while with his family at their cabin in rural upstate New York. As a result of this event, he began to uncover a number of strange incidents involving what he calls the "Visitors" from earlier years, going back to his childhood.

Strieber wrote of his experiences in the book *Communion: A True Story* (1987), which became a huge best-seller, and was filmed in 1989. This was followed by *Transformation: The Breakthrough* (1988), *Majestic* (a novel about the **Roswell** UFO crash, 1990), *Breakthrough: The Next Step* (1995), *The Secret School: Preparation for Contact* (1996) and *Confirmation: The Hard Evidence of Aliens Among Us* (1998). His UFO- and abduction-related books have made him the single most famous writer in the history of the field, an ironic state of affairs, since Strieber actually prefers to keep the UFO community at arm's length and pursue his own highly sophisticated lines of philosophical inquiry into the mystery of **abductions**.

Indeed, Strieber is rare among UFO commentators in that he openly admits to having no idea what is really going on, whether the Visitors come from another planet, this planet, or another dimension entirely. This has resulted in adverse criticism from some of those ufologists who subscribe to the **extraterrestrial hypothesis**, and Strieber has responded with the cutting (yet amusing) remark that it will take better minds than the average ufologist's to get to the bottom of the UFO enigma.

(See also **children's circles, psychosocial hypothesis**)

TEESDALE INHERITANCE

In his book *Revelations: Alien Contact and Human Deception*, Jacques **Vallée** relates a curious tale from the twilight fringes of ufology. In the chic pages of the *Nouvel Observateur* (March 11–17 1988 issue), a "large-format weekly for elegant leftists," tucked away between the articles on Third World injustices and the advertisements for expensive cars, there appeared a small classified advertisement, which read, in part:

The trustees charged with the estate of
A. P. Teesdale, Esq. of Durham County in England are attempting to enter into contact with those responsible for organizations that may be able to meet the requirements of his will.
... Those concerned may bring their existence to the attention of the trustees by sending a brief summary of their organization and its activities to the paper, reference 1001, before March 31, 1988. (pp. 21–16)

The groups with whom the trustees wished to make contact were "serious organizations that have as their goal the establishment or the maintenance of relationships with extraterrestrial beings."

The advertisement was seen by a French UFO investigator and friend of Vallée's, who responded with some information about himself and his work. On March 31, 1988, he received a telegram informing him that he would soon be contacted.

On January 26, 1989, he received a call from an Englishman calling himself Mr. Wensley, who suggested a meeting in Paris on February 28. The investigator subsequently received a letter typed on the stationery of Theard, Theard, Smith & Theard, 31 Sussex Mansions, London SW7, confirming the meeting at the Intercontinental Hotel in Paris at

7:00 P.M. The investigator was to ask for Mr. Grapinet.

The investigator arrived at the Intercontinental with a friend he had intended as a witness. They were met by two well-dressed men, one of whom introduced himself as Mr. Grapinet. The meeting, it seemed, had been moved to a private room in a Paris restaurant, on the rue du Cloître Notre-Dame; the investigator's friend, unfortunately, was not invited.

At the restaurant, the investigator met the other candidates, two of whom were François Raulin, a respected chemist from Paris University, whose work involved research into the origin of life, and Claude **Vorilhon**, a well-known and highly controversial UFO cult leader who had claimed numerous meetings with alien visitors.

Vallée lists the entire group gathered around the dining table:

Mr. M. Bates from Theard & Co.
Mr. X1, an associate of Mr. Bates
Miss X2, an associate of Mr. Bates
Miss X3, secretary with Theard & Co.
Mr. Grapinet, a Frenchman
Mr. X4, another Frenchman, who had driven over with Mr. Grapinet from the Hotel Intercontinental
Mr. Lalande, who was introduced as a French specialist in computer science and artificial intelligence
Mr. X5, a French lawyer
Mr. X6, a French lawyer
Mr. X7, a French physicist
Mr. X8, a French engineer
Mr. Cellier, a priest (Ibid., pp. 217–18)

None of the guests had any connection with each other, with Theard & Co., or with the mysterious A. P. Teesdale. Mr. Bates then read the "Teesdale Confession," which was the reason for this meeting.

Teesdale, it seems, was born in 1899, enlisted in the British armed forces in 1916 and fought in the trenches of northern France, where, one day in November, he was caught in an explosion which catapulted him into a **near-death experience**. He found himself in a realm of white and gold, with a dark region ahead of him. Teesdale felt that this dark region was intelligent, a suspicion that was confirmed when the region spoke to him, identifying itself as "a sentinel for those who set life on the planet."

The voice said that it had been "trying for eons to get hold of somebody," and that its energy reserves had been exhausted after thousands of years of waiting. It could only manifest when a burst of energy occurred near its target. "It has been decided that the human race shall be given a clue. All that is required is that you place this in the hands of your best scientists." Teesdale then awoke in the battlefield with a strange object in his hand.

Teesdale tried to do as the voice had bid him, and gave the object first to a friend who was a doctor, then to a chemist, and then to a biochemist. All three returned the object without evincing any interest or curiosity whatsoever, so Teesdale decided to keep the object as a kind of personal talisman or charm.

Teesdale also fought in the Second World War, and was injured in the thigh during the retreat from Dunkirk. He and eight other men barely made it to one of the boats, which was then attacked by a German bomber. At that point, Teesdale suddenly found himself once again in the realm of white and gold, where the voice chastised him for not following its instructions. He protested that he had, but could find no one to take any interest in the object. The voice replied that he would be given a second object, and that together the objects would provide scientific proof (presumably of alien reality).

For the remainder of his life, Teesdale made sporadic attempts to have the objects analyzed, but, as before, he could find no one in the scientific community to take any interest. He suffered considerable guilt as a result of this, and ensured that his will would allow "some person or persons to ensure that the meaning, if any, of my experiences in France shall be clarified."

After the reading of the "Teesdale Confession," the candidates each described their backgrounds and the qualifications that would perhaps allow them to fulfil Teesdale's last wish. The Teesdale commission then deliberated in private, before announcing that the recipient of the Teesdale inheritance would be Claude Vorilhon, "because he presents the profile that is closest to the spirit of the Testament."

Vorilhon was then presented with a cryogenic cylinder 12 inches in diameter and 15 inches high, supposedly containing the objects. Vorilhon's sect would also receive the Teesdale fortune. Vorilhon himself assured Vallée's investigator friend and François Raulin that he would allow them to analyze the objects. However, nothing was heard from his sect until March 16, when a member named Dominique Renaudin called to say that the Teesdale fortune had not materialized, and there had been no further word from Theard & Co.

Understandably perplexed, the investigator decided to do some digging in England, where he discovered that Theard, Theard, Smith & Theard had no telephone number; in addition, the address, given as 31 Sussex Mansions in Kensington, does not exist: the numbers only go up to 29.

Vallée writes:

There is a Teesdale River in Durham County, but did a gentleman by the name of A. P. Teesdale ever exist? Quite a few people would very much like to know the answer to this question. They would also like to know why the attorneys for the alleged estate went all the way to Paris to find suitable candidates, while London is filled with groups doing similar research. Why did they hand over the container to Vorilhon, who was clearly preselected, when the other candidates were in a better position to analyze the talisman and to bring the results to the attention of qualified scientists? Why the elaborate charade of a dinner party for 15 people in a Paris restaurant, and why go through the motions of several formal presentations when it was plain that [Vorilhon] would receive the prize? (Ibid., p. 221)

To this we could also add the question: why, if the two objects together would provide obvious and undeniable proof of alien reality, did Teesdale meet with such monumental indifference when he approached representatives of the orthodox sciences? Vallée goes on to describe the Teesdale inheritance as "pure theatre." Although the players in this drama were certainly real, Theard & Co. certainly was not. Why, asks Vallée, did not Teesdale (assuming he existed) simply take the talisman to a forensic analysis firm, pay them to do the necessary work on it, and then publish the results, at his own expense if necessary? "Your answer," says Vallée, "is as good as mine." However, he does make the intriguing suggestion that the Teesdale inheritance may have been the work of a secret group of "social engineers" who are conducting experiments in the creation and manipulation of belief systems.
(See also **UMMO**)

TELEPATHY

The transference of thoughts from one person to another through scientifically unknown or inexplicable means. This technique is frequently used by alien beings when communicating with humans, which in itself is puzzling, since many **contactees** have claimed that the aliens use a mixture of telepathy and verbal speech. Other percipients maintain that telepathy was exclusively used during their encounters, while still others claim that the aliens spoke quite normally.

The entities who speak verbally usually claim to have learned our languages by monitoring radio and television transmissions from Earth, which would seem to make the use of telepathy redundant. Although these races simply may not be capable of telepathy, this does not quite ring true, since a large number of them do seem to have this skill (a skill which is even shared by humans). In cases where telepathy is used, it may be that the percipient has entered an altered state of consciousness resulting in elaborate hallucinations, and the apparent telepathic communications may therefore exist solely in their own minds.

TEROS

A benign race of subterranean humanoid aliens, descended from space travelers who colonized the surface of the Earth millennia ago, but were forced to retreat into vast underground cavern systems when the radiation output of the Sun increased. They are related to the **Dero**, but are their sworn enemies, and try to counteract the Deros' malign power and influences whenever they can. They are entirely human-looking, unlike their twisted, dwarflike cousins, and possess machines capable of transmitting beneficial "telaug rays" to the surface, which have the effect of neutralizing the deleterious rays used by the Deros, which have been responsible for most of the violence and war that has troubled humanity since the dawn of history. Unfortunately, the Teros are fewer in number, hold less territory underground than the Deros, and it seems that they are fighting a losing battle.

TESLA, NIKOLA

Nikola Tesla was born in July 1856 in the village of Smiljan, in Lika, Austria-Hungary. His family originally came from western Serbia. Tesla attended the Technical University of Graz, Austria, and the University of Prague (1879–80). In 1882 he went to Paris to work for the Continental Edison Company, and sailed to America two years later, finding work with Thomas Edison in New Jersey.

In 1885, George Westinghouse of the Westinghouse Electric Company in Pittsburgh, Pennsylvania, bought the patent rights to Tesla's polyphase system of alternating-current transformers and motors. This resulted in a protracted battle between the alternating-current system and Edison's direct-current. Eventually, Tesla's system displayed distinct advantages in long-distance power transmission, and won the battle.

A solitary and brilliant man, Tesla is considered by many to have been born "ahead of his time"; while at the peak of his powers in the 1890s, he invented the induction motor, fluorescent lights and new types of generators and transformers. He was also a highly controversial figure. While in his laboratory in Colorado in 1899, he became convinced that he had received radio signals from another planet, an event which inspired a new interest in life elsewhere in the universe. He also claimed to have invented a death ray capable of destroying 10,000 airplanes from a distance of 250 miles. Such claims have resulted in Tesla becoming something of a posthumous celebrity in the world of fringe ufology, where speculation is rife that he discovered the secret of antigravity propulsion. Some even contend that he was an extraterrestrial.

Tesla died in New York City in January 1943, the holder of more than 700 patents.

TIME TRAVEL HYPOTHESIS

One of the principal objections to the **extraterrestrial hypothesis**, which holds that UFOs are the spacecraft of an alien expeditionary force, is that so many "aliens" are humanoid in form, and have no difficulty whatsoever in communicating with humans. Many scientists contend that any life-form evolving on another planet would not look remotely like us; in addition, their mental development would also be utterly different, resulting in little common ground on which to communicate.

One elegant solution to these problems is presented by the time travel hypothesis, which suggests that UFOs are actually time machines, sent back from some point in the future by our own descendants. This, of course, would explain the similarities between human and ufonaut morphology, not to mention the constant complaints we receive from them about the dismal job we are doing in our management of Earth. It would also rather neatly explain our genetic compatibility with beings such as the **Grays**, who are apparently attempting to revitalize their poor genetic stock with fresh material. It is possible that the ufonauts are perfectly content to allow us to believe that they come from other planets (a belief they themselves have reinforced through numerous contacts), in order to protect their true identity.

It has been speculated by some that UFO occupants are historians conducting research in the "past," which would certainly account for their apparent ubiquity throughout history. However, this is unlikely, since the UFO has become one of the most powerful cultural icons of the 20th century. It is extremely unlikely that our remote descendants would set out to conduct historical research, and then inadvertently contaminate that history with their own presence!

Although time travel has long been considered impossible by orthodox science, recent research in theoretical physics suggests that it may indeed become feasible one day. While such research lies well beyond the mental capabilities of this writer, others have illustrated in layperson's terms how time travel might be achieved. One such illustration involves the warping of space-time. Space-time consists of four dimensions: three of space (up/down, left/right, forward/backward), and one of time. The three spatial axes extend at right angles to each other,

with the time axis extending at right angles to the spatial axes (an arrangement that is expressed far more easily with mathematics than visualized in the mind). If a sufficient gravitational force could be applied to a certain region of space-time, the time axis might become warped so severely that it actually becomes a spatial axis, displacing the spatial axis into the position vacated by the time axis. Once this had been achieved, movement through time would be a simple matter of moving in a certain direction.

"TIN CANS" (ALIENS)

At 7:40 P.M. on the evening of October 23, 1965, a 19-year-old radio announcer trainee named Jerry Townsend was driving home to Long Prairie, Minnesota. About four miles from Long Prairie, Townsend rounded a curve and came upon a large, rocket-shaped object standing in the middle of the road. At that moment, his car engine, lights and radio went dead and he brought the car to a halt. The object was between 30 and 40 feet high and 10 feet in diameter, and was resting on three tail fins.

As Townsend climbed from his car, he saw three tiny objects approach him from beneath the craft. They were six inches high, the size and shape of tin cans, and waddled along on two fin-shaped "legs." When they stopped, a third fin extended to the ground, apparently to stabilize them. Although he could make out no eyes or other sensory organs, Townsend had the distinct impression that the entities were watching him.

Presently, the three "tin cans" returned to the underside of the rocket and disappeared into it. It then took off, casting a "colorless" light onto the road. According to Townsend, the object's ascent looked like someone lifting a flashlight from a table.

During the investigation of this case, Townsend's teachers and friends were asked what sort of fellow he was. They unanimously vouched for his honesty and integrity, and the local sheriff confirmed that

Townsend had appeared genuinely frightened when he had reported the encounter. Sheriff Bain and Long Prairie Police Officer Lavern Lubitz went to the landing site, and found three parallel strips of a curious oily substance about a yard long and four inches apart on the road. According to Bain, two hunters who had been in the vicinity reported a lighted object ascending into the air above the position of Townsend's car.

TOMEY, DEBBIE
(See **Hopkins, Budd**)

TRANS-EN-PROVENCE, FRANCE
Location of a UFO encounter, which yielded an impressive amount of physical evidence. At about 5:00 P.M. on January 8, 1981, Renato Nicolai, 55, was working in his garden. The garden was on a steep slope, and so consisted of four terraces. As Nicolai continued with his gardening, he heard a curious whistling sound behind him, and turned to see a small, disk-shaped object approaching the ground. By the time Nicolai had reached the uppermost terrace, for a better view of the strange sight, the UFO was on the ground, and almost immediately took off again. Nicolai could see four openings in the object's underside as it headed off toward the forest of Trans-en-Provence.

The police examined the landing site the following day. According to their report:

We observed the presence of two concentric circles, one 2.20 meters in diameter and the other 2.40 meters in diameter. The two circles form a sort of corona ten centimeters thick . . . There are two parts clearly visible, and they also show black striations. Nicolai thought he saw two kinds of round pieces, which could have been landing gear or feet as the UFO took off. He felt no heat, no vibration, no illness, neither during the observation nor after. He

was simply very impressed by the inexplicable spectacle.

The encounter was investigated by Groupement d'Etudes des Phénomènes Aerospatiaux Non-identifiés (GEPAN), a unique UFO investigation group, in that it was part of the French space agency, the Centre National d'Etudes Spatiales, and thus had access to the country's best laboratory facilities. GEPAN arranged for the samples of soil and vegetation that had been collected by the police to be biochemically analyzed. They also checked with civil and military aviation authorities that the UFO had not been a terrestrial vehicle.

According to the GEPAN report, based on the results of the analyzes conducted at the Universities of Metz and Rangueill:

The methods of analysis and microscopic observation brought out elements that indicate that the terrain or soil where Nicolai claims to have observed the phenomenon underwent certain specific modifications.

There was a strong mechanical pressure forced on the surface, probably the result of a heavy weight.

The appearance of a superficial structural modification of the soil, with both striations and erosion.

A thermatic heating of the soil, perhaps consecutive to or immediately following the shock, the value of which did not exceed 600 degrees Centigrade.

An eventual residue of material in the form of detectable traces on the samples analyzed, such as a weak quantity of oxidous iron on grains of calcium and minute quantities of phosphate and zinc.

The plant specimens were analyzed at the National Institute of Agronomy Research in Avignon.

It was found that the specimens (as compared with others of the same strain, used as a control) exhibited alterations that were possibly consistent with an "electromagnetic source of stress." However, there was an insufficient amount of information to allow a "precise and unique interpretation to this remarkable combination of results." Most interestingly, the analysis revealed that the plants possessed the physiological characteristics of their age, but had the biochemical characteristics of old age!

It is virtually certain that something extremely unusual landed in Trans-en-Provence. This is one of the very rare UFO landing cases backed up by concrete scientific evidence.

TULPAS

Also known as "thought-forms," tulpas are artificial, nonphysical entities created through the power of thought. According to occult tradition, tulpas are created through manipulation of the psychic aura that is generated by every living creature. Once created, they can develop intelligence and independence from their creator and travel great distances. Tulpas can also be used to attack one's enemies, as long as their energy vibrations match those of the target's aura. If they do not match, the tulpa will immediately return to attack its creator. However, they can also be used to protect and to heal.

The creation process requires intense concentration and visualization. While in Tibet, the French explorer and author Alexandra David-Neel experimented with the creation of a tulpa, which she visualized as a short, fat, jolly monk, in order to make the thought-form as benign as possible. After several months of concentration, the monk appeared, but gradually grew thinner and more malevolent, and it took David-Neel six months to disperse him.

Some researchers have suggested that UFOs and nonhuman entities may be a form of tulpa, since they frequently exhibit capabilities more in keeping with spirit beings than with solid, flesh-and-blood creatures. However, the question of who creates them, and whether this creation is intentional or inadvertent, remains unanswered.
(See also **collective unconscious**)

TURIS, VALENCIA, SPAIN

Location of an encounter with a UFO and nonhuman beings in 1979. At 11:30 A.M. on July 25, 1979, a 54-year-old farmer named Federico Ibáñez was on his way to inspect his vineyards, when he noticed something which he took to be a car ahead. As he approached, he saw that it was actually an object resting on four legs in the middle of the road. The object was shaped like a truncated egg, and was three feet in diameter and nine feet high.

At that point, Ibáñez saw two small beings rushing toward the object. They were three feet tall, and were dressed in white overcoat-like clothing, which completely covered them, including their heads and hands, which seemed to have no fingers. Their heads appeared to be spherical, and were featureless except for narrow, protruding instruments where their eyes should have been. The beings entered the object, which then took off. At a loss for anything else to do, Ibáñez continued with his inspection of the vines. When the landing site was later examined by the authorities, four circular marks were found on the road.

TUYUL

Many researchers have commented on the similarity between modern UFO and alien encounters and the tales of supernatural beings found in folklore (see **psychosocial hypothesis**). However, there are still profound differences in the physical appearance of such creatures, which the psychosociologists put down to some mechanism by which the intelligence responsible for such encounters alters their surface details in order to make them more comprehensible within the contemporary world view. Nevertheless, there are some creatures of folklore that bear a striking resemblance to the diminutive "aliens" said to be visiting Earth. One such creature is the *tuyul*.

The *tuyul* is a creature of Javanese legend, which resembles a bald, naked child with enormous eyes and bright red skin. The color of its skin notwithstanding, this entity bears a striking similarity to the **Grays**, with its lack of hair, prominent eyes and infantlike appearance. In addition, the *tuyul* moves without touching the ground, a trait often reported in modern alien encounters in the West.

The *tuyul* is still seen today from time to time. According to the anomalist Mike Dash:

In 1985 a Javanese *tuyul*-hunting expedition visited the Indonesian island and interviewed a clothing designer in Jakarta. "I saw a *tuyul* about three years ago," the man told his interviewer. "It was real; it looked like a little naked boy and tried to steal my money." (Dash [1997], pp. 39–40)

TWINKLE (PROJECT)

In response to the appearance in the late 1940s of a number of UFOs nicknamed the "green fireballs," a study project was established to identify their origin and nature. The green fireballs were sighted predominantly over the southern United States; it was the intention of Project Twinkle to study them with theodolites, telescopes and cameras, in an effort to ascertain their size, height and speed, and thus come to some conclusions as to what they actually were. One of the key Twinkle investigators was Dr. Lincoln La Paz, an expert in meteor studies.

One of the strangest encounters took place on the night of April 27, 1949, when four U.S. Army personnel stationed near Los Alamos, New Mexico, saw a tiny object flying to the northeast, which gave no indication of being an ordinary meteorite. The soldiers described a four-inch-diameter light, with a two- to four-inch metallic cone attached to the rear. The UFO flew toward the soldiers at a speed of about 70 mph, and at a height of about seven feet, before disappearing suddenly in the southwest.

Unfortunately, Project Twinkle was not successful in finding any answers to the mystery of the green fireballs. The project received neither as much equipment nor as much finance as it needed to conduct proper research into the green fireballs. The military finally stated it had no conclusive opinion concerning the nature of the fireballs, but suggested they may have been the result of Earth passing through a region of space "of high meteoric population." Project Twinkle was closed down in December 1950.

UBATUBA, BRAZIL

Location of an alleged UFO explosion. This case is one of the more intriguing, in that samples of wreckage were retrieved by civilian witnesses and submitted for analysis. On September 14, 1957, a reporter named Ibrahim Sued at the Brazilian newspaper *O Globo* received the following letter, accompanied by several samples of an unusual material:

Dear Mr. Ibrahim Sued:
As a faithful reader of your column and your admirer, I wish to give you something of the highest interest to a newspaper man, about the flying disks. If you believe that they are real, of course. I didn't believe anything said or published about them. But just a few days ago I was forced to change my mind. I was fishing together with some friends, at a place close to the town of Ubatuba, São Paulo, when I sighted a flying disk. It approached the beach at unbelievable speed and an accident, i.e., a crash into the sea seemed imminent. At the last moment, however, when it was almost striking the waters, it made a sharp turn upward and climbed rapidly on a fantastic impulse. We followed the spectacle with our eyes, startled, when we saw the disk explode in flames. It disintegrated into thousands of fiery fragments, which fell sparkling with magnificent brightness. They looked like fireworks, despite the time of the accident, at noon, i.e., midday. Most of these fragments, almost all, fell into the sea. But a number of small pieces fell close to the beach and we picked up a large amount of this material—which was as light as paper. I am enclosing a small sample of it. I don't know anyone that could be trusted to whom I might send it for analysis. I never read about a flying disk being found, or about fragments or parts

of a saucer that had been picked up. Unless the finding was made by military authorities and the whole thing kept as a top-secret subject. I am certain the matter will be of great interest to the brilliant columnist and I am sending two copies of this letter—to the newspaper and to your home address. (Quoted in Randle [1995], pp. 69–70)

Unfortunately, the signature on the letter was unreadable, so Sued had no way of ascertaining the writer's identity. Nevertheless, he published the letter in the pages of *O Globo,* which was read by the Brazilian ufologist and member of APRO, Dr. Olavo Fontes. Although he believed the letter to be a hoax, Fontes requested a meeting with Sued, and together they examined the fragments of material sent by the mysterious correspondent.

The material was three small pieces of dull gray metal, with rough, apparently oxidized surfaces. The pieces were shot through with numerous tiny fissures, and there was a fine white powder adhering strongly to them. Sued, a UFO skeptic, was not particularly interested in following up the story, and allowed Fontes to take the fragments away with him. He took them to the Mineral Production Laboratory, a division of the Brazilian Agriculture Ministry, for analysis.

Dr. Luisa Maria Barbosa submitted one piece of metal to various tests, and concluded that it was in fact magnesium of a particularly high purity. The Brazilian army then ran some tests, which destroyed the sample. They did not publish the results of the test.

Fontes then sent the other two samples to APRO, who in turn sent one of them to the U.S. Air Force for analysis. However, the air force destroyed the sample without managing to obtain any results. When they asked for another piece, APRO understandably refused, instead submitting the last remaining sample to the Atomic Energy Commission. The AEC concluded that the magnesium had come from a much larger object that had been suddenly shattered by an explosion of some kind.

According to chemist Dr. Walter Walker, who reviewed the analyzes conducted on the remaining Ubatuba fragments, magnesium does not occur naturally on Earth, and thus is unlikely to occur naturally anywhere else in the Solar System. It was therefore extremely unlikely, he said, that the fragments were from a meteorite (a suggestion put forward by the University of Colorado UFO Investigation). Neither was unalloyed magnesium used in aircraft, missile or satellite construction. The conclusion, therefore, seemed to be that the Ubatuba material was neither natural in origin, nor part of any man-made machine. However, since the person who wrote the letter to Ibrahim Sued was never traced, a hoax cannot be ruled out, and the Ubatuba "UFO" incident remains a mystery.

UFOCAT

A catalogue of UFO reports compiled by David Saunders for the **Center for UFO Studies (CUFOS)**. While extremely comprehensive, UFOCAT does not distinguish between unexplained UFO sightings and those that have been explained in mundane terms. For this reason it is of little use in research involving the use of statistics.

UFO INCIDENT, THE (FILM)

Made for television in 1975, and starring James Earl Jones and Estelle Parsons, this film is a dramatization of the abduction of Barney and Betty **Hill** in 1961. One of the very few films to draw its inspiration directly from an actual UFO event (see *Fire in the Sky*), *The UFO Incident* is a more or less faithful telling of the Hills' experience, with particularly fine performances from Jones and Parsons.

ULTRATERRESTRIALS

Term coined by the American researcher John A. **Keel** to denote a group of entities residing in one or more parallel dimensions, coterminous with Earth. Keel suggested an interdimensional (as opposed to interstellar) origin for nonhuman entities as a result of his extensive researches and investigations, notably of the **Mothman** visitations in Virginia in the late 1960s. He also examined numerous cases in which UFOs seemed to materialize and dematerialize, rather than simply flying away, and concluded that the frequencies of their matter were being manipulated and altered, shifting them into higher dimensions of reality. In his explanation of this theory, Keel pointed out that UFOs tend to shift their color toward the edge of the visible light spectrum immediately after appearing and immediately prior to vanishing.

Keel compares the ultraterrestrials to the demons of medieval occult lore, since their primary motivation seems to be to play malicious tricks on humanity. Even the apparently benign **Space Brothers** fall into this category, due to their propensity to lie about their origins (they frequently claimed to have come from Venus, Mars and Saturn, even though no humanoid life can exist on those planets), and to utter prophecies that invariably prove to be inaccurate. According to Keel, the ultraterrestrials consider us their playthings, as did the ancient gods of Greece and Rome. They "scramble our brains, destroy our memories and use us in any way they see fit."

In commenting on Keel's ultraterrestrial theory, anomalist Jerome Clark states:

In Keel's revisionist history ultraterrestrials "posing as gods and superkings" once ruled the earth, but when democracy became a force in human affairs, these "gods" and their descendants (royal families whose ancestors had mated with ultraterrestrials in human guise) lost their power and authority. Ever since then the ultraterrestrials have waged war on *Homo sapiens.* They have generated religions, cults, and secret societies, intervened in the lives of influential historical figures at crucial moments, and otherwise directed human life to serve their ends. God himself is an ultraterrestrial dwelling in the superspectrum [Keel's term for their transdimensional habitat]. (Clark [1998], p. 434)

UMMO

An alleged planet, the central element in an extremely elaborate hoax that began in Spain in the mid-1960s. On February 6, 1966 in Aluche, a suburb of Madrid, a number of witnesses reported the landing of a large, disk-shaped spacecraft bearing the unusual symbol)+(on its underside. The following year, another object bearing this insignia was sighted in another Madrid suburb, San José de Valderas, before landing in the neighboring area of Santa Monica. Several photographs were taken, which were sent to the newspaper *Informaciones.* The photographs were sent for analysis to a space research facility in Toulouse, France. They were revealed to be of an eight-inch-diameter model, suspended from a piece of string.

The respected Spanish researcher Antonio Ribera maintained that according to the testimony of numerous people unconnected with each other, some kind of flying object had been seen. However, there is strong evidence to suggest that a complex scheme of human origin was in the process of unfolding.

Soon after the UFO encounters occurred, a number of metallic cylinders were discovered in the areas concerned. When opened, the cylinders were found to contain pieces of flexible material bearing the UMMO symbol)+(. The material was discovered to be made of Tedlar, a weather-resistant plastic used by NASA as a protective covering for rockets. The cylinders were 99 percent nickel.

A large number of documents were then sent out to UFO researchers from an unknown source who mailed them from all over the world. The documents contained scientific, political and sociological information about the planet UMMO, in the IUMMA star system 14.6 light-years from Earth. UMMO was apparently located near the Galactic North Pole, in a highly transparent, hydrogen-free region of the sky. IUMMA should therefore be visible from Earth as a fifth-magnitude star . . . but it isn't. In addition, the documents claim that IUMMA is designated on Earth as the star Wolf 424, which is untrue: there is a Wolf 359, but no Wolf 424.

The information contained in the UMMO documents was impressive in its internal consistency; the sections on science, in particular, seemed to have been written by someone who knew what he was talking about. According to Dr. Teyssandier, a French physicist who examined the documents, the mathematical system used by the "Ummites" was base 12 (a "base" is the number that is raised to various powers to generate the principal counting units of a number system). On Earth, the mathematical system is base 10. The information on Ummite technology, however, was less impressive, reading more like decent **science fiction** than genuine extraterrestrial technology.

The UMMO affair then entered the field of international espionage, with a letter allegedly sent by the "UMMO source" to the **CIA** office in Madrid. The letter stated that two Ummites had stayed at the Albacete house of a society lady, named Doña Margarita Ruiz de Lihory y Resino, marquise of Villasante, baroness of Alcatrali, between 1952 and 1954. Posing as Danish doctors, the Ummites had conducted "psychophysiological experiments" on various domestic animals.

In 1971 the CIA received another document containing instructions on how to detect Ummites living clandestinely on Earth. It seems that in 1953, Margot Shelly, daughter of the marquise of Villasante, who lived on the estate, became seriously ill and was examined by the Danish doctors, who disagreed with each other on the prognosis. Shelly was then treated by physicians in Madrid, but later died. While her body was awaiting burial on the estate, it was mutilated by an unknown person, who removed the eyes, tongue and one of the hands. These body parts were subsequently discovered in the marquise's mansion, along with the mummified bodies of numerous dogs and cats, some of which had been decapitated, others eviscerated.

A criminal suit was instigated against the marquise and her husband. They were sent to a Madrid psychiatric hospital for evaluation, but were found to be "of perfect mental state." The butler, Andres Gomes, was also questioned by police, and later claimed to journalists that the mansion contained a vast network of underground tunnels, a "horrible place," which the marquise would enter through a metal trapdoor in her bathroom. Gomes stated: "I don't know what she did there exactly, but she came up as pale as a corpse."

In 1969 an UMMO document was distributed, which claimed a connection between this macabre, 15-year-old scandal and the Ummites' mission on Earth. However, ufologist Jacques **Vallée** suggests that it is more likely that the UMMO source simply incorporated the scandal into its elaborate tapestry of deceit.

The UMMO controversy is one of the most bizarre in the history of ufology, and has all the elements of science fiction and occultism one might find in a story by H. P. Lovecraft or Colin Wilson. Accepting the extreme unlikelihood that the Ummites really exist, some ufologists have suggested that the whole affair may have been some kind of psychosocial experiment, based on the notion of a verifiable alien presence on Earth. This experiment may then have got out of control when other parties decided to develop it for their own ends. According to Vallée, there is a possible link with an intelligence agency in the former Eastern bloc, which was (and perhaps is) conducting a scientific espionage operation. Since a number of physicists in Europe and America have become deeply involved with UMMO, this would offer the source an insight into current scientific research in the West.

(See also **Teesdale inheritance**)

UNIDENTIFIED FLYING OBJECTS (UFOs)

The most straightforward definition of a UFO is: an aerial object that the observer is unable to identify. However, when we consider the associated term "ufology," we leave simplicity and straight-forwardness far behind, and enter a realm in which virtually all aspects of the paranormal merge and interact with each other, so that, while "UFO" is quite easy to define satisfactorily, "ufology" is virtually impossible to define to the same degree.

It must also be noted that "UFO" is *not* synonymous with "alien spacecraft," although this is almost invariably the first inference drawn when the term "UFO" is mentioned. "UFO" means just that: *unidentified* flying object. In approximately 90 percent of those cases reported and investigated, the UFO turns out to be an *identified* flying object (IFO): a meteorite, a star or planet (ironically, in view of the claims of the **contactees,** Venus is frequently mistaken for an anomalous object), an aircraft seen from an unusual angle, a man-made satellite moving through space, and so on.

In about 10 percent of cases, something truly unusual is seen, such as a large, metallic, disk-shaped object at close proximity to the witness. In these cases, what the witness sees can be called a genuine UFO (which means genuinely unidentified, *not* a genuine extraterrestrial space vessel). There have been many reports of strange flying objects in the vicinity of **Area 51** in Nevada. The nature of many of these reports suggests that something unusual is being seen; however, we must also remember that associated claims of alien activity notwithstanding, the facility is home to some highly advanced terrestrial aircraft, such as the B-2 Stealth Bomber and various highly sophisticated remotely piloted vehicles (RPVs), which are unmanned and thus capable of some astonishing aerial maneuvers. Indeed, as the **psychosocial hypothesis** suggests, even when large metallic disks containing strange, nonhuman entities are seen, it is not *logically necessary* that they be spacecraft and aliens from other worlds.

(See also **collective unconscious, hallucinations**)

UNIVERSAL ARTICULATE INTERDIMENSIONAL UNDERSTANDING OF SCIENCE (UNARIUS)

A flying saucer cult established in California in the 1950s by Ruth and Ernest Norman. Although Unarius bears some similarities to the **Aetherius Society**, the information presented by the Normans was received through the process of **channeling**. According to Unarius, the year 2001 will see the arrival *en masse* of the **Space Brothers** of the Intergalactic Federation, just outside San Diego, California. In an echo of Christianity's promise of a New Jerusalem, there will follow a blissful future of peace, harmony and enlightenment. Ruth Norman herself (she died in 1993) will return to lead the people of Earth.

Like the Aetherius Society, Unarius, which is still going strong today, is seen as something of an embarrassment by serious ufologists, who balk at their pronouncements concerning Lemurian technology and reincarnation, not to mention Norman's pseudonym Uriel (which stands for

Universal Radiant Infinite Eternal Light). Of equal embarrassment (and a source of hilarity to Norman's neighbors) is the Space Cadillac in which she drove around, and which sported a large model of a flying saucer, complete with flashing lights, on its roof. The Space Cadillac, or Cosmic Car, will become her chariot once again, when she returns to Earth in an Intergalactic Federation starship in 2001.

VALENSOLE, FRANCE

Location of an encounter with a UFO and associated entities, which occurred in 1965. At 5:45 A.M. on July 1, farmer Maurice Masse was working in his lavender field, when he heard a whistling sound and saw an elliptical object resting on the ground nearby. The object was resting on six legs, which were joined together at the center of the underside. There was a transparent cockpit on the upper surface. Through an open hatch in the object's side, Masse could see two small seats, back to back.

The farmer then noticed what appeared to be two young boys stealing some lavender plants (he had recently lost some plants to thieves), and began to give chase, when one of the "boys" pointed a tubelike device at him, and he instantly found himself paralyzed. In an interview with ufologist Jacques **Vallée,** Masse said that he did not feel afraid, sensing friendly curiosity from the beings, rather than any

hostility. The beings were about four feet tall, and dressed in dark green single-piece suits. Their heads were large and hairless, with huge eyes and small mouths. They communicated with each other in low gurgling sounds.

The entities then returned to their craft, entered through the open hatch, which then slid shut, and became visible inside the cockpit. The landing gear withdrew, and the craft glided away over the fields.

Masse was unable to move for the next 20 minutes, and by the time he was able to make his way home he had become badly frightened. When he later returned to the landing site, he discovered that it was soaked with moisture, even though it had not been raining. In addition, nothing would grow there for the next 10 years.

In the days following the encounter, Masse's sleep cycle became totally disrupted, and he found that he now needed about 12 hours' sleep a night, instead of his usual five or six. (Disruptions to sleep cycles are commonly reported by witnesses to close-range UFO activity.) This disruption lasted for several months.

The case was investigated by a number of UFO researchers, and also by Lieutenant Colonel Valnet of the Gendarmerie, Maître Chautard, and the mayor and parish priest of Valensole. All concluded that Masse was telling the truth, especially those who knew him personally. As a former Resistance fighter, he was considered to be of unimpeachable moral character.

VALENTICH, FREDERICK

Apparent victim of a UFO abduction who never returned. On October 21, 1978, Valentich took off from Moorabbin airport in Victoria, Australia, in his single-engine Cessna 182 aircraft. His destination was King Island, a one-hour trip that would take him over Bass Strait. At about 7:00 P.M., Valentich watched the approach of another aircraft, which hovered over his own, causing some engine trouble. He radioed controller Steve Robey at Melbourne Air Flight Service, informing him of the situation. Here is the (abridged) conversation:

VALENTICH: Is there any known traffic below five thousand [feet]?
MELBOURNE FLIGHT SERVICE: No known traffic.
V: . . . Seems to be a large aircraft below five thousand.
MFS: What type of aircraft is it?
V: I cannot affirm it is four bright . . . it seems to me like landing lights . . . the aircraft has just passed over me at least a thousand feet above.
MFS: Roger and it is a large aircraft confirm.
V: Er unknown due to the speed it's traveling. Is there any air force aircraft in the vicinity?
MFS: No known aircraft in the vicinity.
V: It's approaching now from due east toward me . . . It seems to me that he's playing some sort of

game, he's flying over me two to three times at a time at speeds I could not identify.
MFS: What is your actual level?
V: My level is four and a half thousand, four five zero zero.
MFS: Confirm that you cannot identify the aircraft.
V: Affirmative.
MFS: Roger standby.
V: It's not an aircraft, it is . . .
MFS: Can you describe the, er, aircraft?
V: As it's flying past, it's a long shape . . . cannot identify more than . . . before me right now, Melbourne.
MFS: Roger, and how large would the, er, object be?
V: It seems like it's stationary. What I'm doing right now is orbiting and the thing is orbiting right now on top of me also. It's got a green light and sort of metallic like it's all shiny on the outside . . . It's just vanished . . . Would you know what kind of aircraft I've got, is it a military aircraft?
MFS: Confirm the, er, aircraft just vanished.
V: Say again.
MFS: Is the aircraft still with you?
V: . . . Approaching from the southwest . . . The engine is rough idling . . .
MFS: Roger. What are your intentions?
V: My intentions are, ah, to go to King Island, ah, Melbourne, that strange craft is hovering on top of me again . . . it's hovering and it's not an aircraft . . .

That was the last anyone ever heard of Frederick Valentich. No trace of him or his aircraft was found. According to **NASA** scientist Dr. Richard Haines, who analyzed the tape of the above conversation, there was a 17-second burst of metallic noise following Valentich's last transmission.

The conclusion of the Aircraft Accident Investigation Summary Report listed the following information:

Location of occurrence:	Not known.
Time:	Not known.
Degree of injury:	Presumed fatal.
Opinion as to cause:	The reason for the disappearance of the aircraft has not been determined.

In 1982 an independent film producer named Ron Cameron was approached by two divers who claimed to have located the wreckage of Valentich's Cessna on the seabed off Cape Otway. They showed him some photographs of a plane with the Cessna's registration marks, and offered to sell them to him, with the plane's exact location, for the sum of $10,000. They also claimed that Valentich's body was not in the plane. Cameron replied that he would need further verification before he handed over that much money. The divers were not heard from again, and their claims are regarded by most researchers to have been a hoax.

The Valentich disappearance remains unsolved, and there is no evidence that he faked his own death. It has been suggested that his plane got into trouble, ditched into the sea and sank immediately. However, the Cessna 182 is designed to float on impact with water. In addition, as ufologist Timothy Good states, "VHF radio would not be able to transmit below 1,000 feet from the aircraft's position of 90 miles from Melbourne, and Valentich's communications with the Flight Service Unit were loud and clear to the last word, as was the 17-second burst of 'metallic' noise which followed."

VALLÉE, DR. JACQUES FRANCIS

French-born computer scientist and highly respected—if controversial—UFO researcher. In 1962, Vallée moved to the United States, where he assisted Dr. J. Allen **Hynek** at Northwestern University. He received his Ph.D. in computer science from that university in 1967. During this period, Vallée and his wife, Janine, compiled the first ever computer database of UFO sightings. He and Hynek offered to improve the U.S. Air Force's antiquated UFO report filing system but were rebuffed.

Vallée first became interested in UFOs while working at the Paris Observatory, tracking satellites (his first job). When he and his colleagues noticed other objects that were obviously not satellites (they traveled in the opposite direction to the rotation of Earth, which no satellite did at that time), they tracked them. However, the project leader confiscated the tracking tape and erased the data, apparently through fear of ridicule from other astronomers.

After writing two highly regarded books on ufology, *Anatomy of a Phenomenon* (1965) and *Challenge to Science: The UFO Enigma* (1966), the latter with Janine Vallée, both of which advocated the **extra-terrestrial hypothesis**, Vallée grew disillusioned with the idea that UFOs are alien spacecraft (he has famously said he will be disappointed if UFOs turn out to be spaceships), and turned his attention to the apparent parallels between modern encounters with nonhuman beings, and historical encounters with supernatural beings, as preserved in the folkloric traditions of many countries. The result of this new line of research was *Passport to Magonia: On UFOs, Folklore and Parallel Worlds* (1969), a classic study that has heavily influenced ufology, particularly in Europe (see **psychosocial hypothesis**). His later books include *The Invisible College* (1975), *Dimensions: A Casebook of Alien Contact* (1988) and *UFO Chronicles of the Soviet Union: A Cosmic Samizdat* (1992).

In 1977, Vallée served as the real-life model for the ufologist Claude Lacombe in Steven Spielberg's epic ***Close Encounters of the Third Kind***.

VAN TASSEL, GEORGE
(See **Integratron**)

VARGINHA, BRAZIL
City in southern Brazilian state of Minas Gerais, situated 180 miles northwest of Rio de Janeiro, which was host to a great deal of UFO and alien-related activity in mid-1996. According to the many reports that came out of the region, a UFO had crashed and its crew had been captured and killed by the authorities.

In January 1996 there had been many UFO sightings in a region already having the reputation as perhaps the world's premier UFO hotspot. At 8:00 A.M. on January 13, the Varginha City Fire Department received an anonymous phone call asking them to come to collect an odd creature that had been seen in a park in the Jardim Andere district of the city. When the firemen arrived, they found the creature crouching at the edge of some woodland. The creature was humanoid, about three and a half feet tall, with brown skin and huge, red eyes. On its head were three large vertical ridges.

While the officer in charge contacted the local military base at Coracoes, 15 miles away, the rest of the firemen captured the creature and put it in a wooden box, which they handed over to the soldiers upon their arrival. It was then taken to the Sergeants' School at Tres Coracoes.

At 3:30 P.M. on the same day, another creature was discovered by three young women on their way home from work in the Jardim Andere district. The creature's appearance reminded them of the Devil, and they ran away screaming. As the young women fled, other witnesses gathered around the creature. The fire department was called, and arrived with more military personnel, who threw a net over it and took it away. Apparently, the creature had been injured by some children, who had been throwing stones at it!

All in all, some 60 witnesses came forward claiming to have encountered the strange beings. The second being was taken to the Varginha Regional Hospital, and then transferred to the nearby Humanitus Hospital, where it died from its injuries at 6:00 P.M. on January 22. According to the doctors who examined the cadaver, there was a powerful, ammonia-like stench. The creature was naked, with no sexual organs, nipples or navel. One of the doctors pried open the mouth and pulled out the black tongue with a pair of forceps. As soon as he let go, the tongue snapped back into the mouth, like a piece of elastic. After the examination, the being was taken away by the military.

According to Brazilian ufologist Rodrigues e Pacaccini, a young policeman had been injured by the first creature during its capture on January 20. He died in hospital two days later, apparently of pneumonia. Pacaccini also claimed that the Brazilian Air Force had been alerted to the approach of a UFO by the United States.

In the months following the events in Varginha, Pacaccini received many threatening phone calls, prompting him to wear a bulletproof vest. In addition, the military forbade all personnel from communicating with UFO investigators. Hospital administrators subsequently denied that any strange creatures had been treated or examined.

Three months after the capture of the alleged aliens in Varginha, Mrs. Terezinha Gallo Clepf was dining in a local restaurant, when she went onto the porch for a cigarette. She found herself facing another creature exactly like the ones apprehended in January.

Three weeks later, a motorist encountered another being (or perhaps the same one) as he was rounding a bend. The being threw up its arms to its face, apparently startled by the car's headlights, before running away.

VILVOORDE, BELGIUM

Location of an encounter with a humanoid entity. On December 19, 1973, the witness, whose name was never revealed, got up early in the morning to use the toilet, which was outside his house, next to the kitchen. As he entered the kitchen, he heard an odd noise and looked into the garden to see a diminutive figure, wearing a single-piece suit that was glowing green. The little man was sweeping an instrument similar to a metal detector over the ground.

The witness found his flashlight and directed it at the being, who turned to face him, swinging its entire body rather than just its head. The entity then raised its hand and made a V-sign with its fingers (it is not clear which way its hand was held, so it could either have meant "peace," or something else!). The being was about three feet tall, and was wearing a goldfish-bowl-type helmet, which revealed its large, oval, yellow eyes and pointed ears. No nose or mouth was visible. On its stomach was a large red box that produced sparkling lights.

The being then walked toward the back of the garden, which was bounded by a wall. It then walked up the wall, remaining *perpendicular* to it as it did so. It then disappeared over the wall, apparently walking down the other side in the same manner. A few moments later, the witness saw a small, disk-shaped object rise from behind the wall and fly away.

VORILHON, CLAUDE

French contactee, founder and leader of the Raelian Movement, a flying saucer sect that awaits the arrival of the "Elohim," a race of benign extraterrestrial beings. Vorilhon, who calls himself "Rael," first met these beings when he encountered a UFO on December 13, 1973, near Clermont Ferrand, France. The white-robed being who emerged from the landed UFO told Vorilhon that he, as a Frenchman, had been chosen to receive the message of the Elohim because France is the "country where democracy was born."

Vorilhon was told that, in order to survive the last days of the present age, humanity had to eliminate politics and disband all military organizations. The Elohim gave him his new name, and also a curious symbol, a swastika set within the star of David. Among the adventures related in his book *Space Aliens Took Me to Their Planet,* Vorilhon tells of a rather pleasant bath he took with five beautiful alien robots.

Over the years since his initial encounter, Vorilhon has appealed for—and received—funds to build a mansion in which the Elohim will live when they eventually arrive on Earth.

VORONEZH, RUSSIA

Location of a series of UFO landings and nonhuman encounters, which the London *Times* called the "story of the century." Some time between September 21, and October 2, 1989, a UFO landed in front of numerous witnesses in Voronezh, 300 miles south of Moscow. According to the news agency TASS, the first witnesses to the UFO landing were children, but many adults quickly came forward to corroborate the reports. Prior to the landing in the Western Park area of the city, a number of disk-shaped and spherical objects were sighted.

At 6:30 P.M. on September 27, commuters watched a "pink haze" moving through the sky over the park. A metallic sphere then emerged from the haze and descended into one of the trees. It then changed shape to that of a bulging cylinder, a hatch opened in the side and a humanoid entity looked out, then withdrew into the object.

The object moved farther toward the ground, before disgorging several huge three-eyed beings, between 12 and 14 feet in height. One of the beings reportedly fired some kind of pistol at a male passerby, who instantly vanished, to reappear, still in mid-stride, after the UFO had departed. According to some witnesses, one of the beings tried to climb an electricity pylon, which caused it to catch fire and vaporize.

The landing site was later examined by scientists, including Professor Genrikh Silanov, director of the Geophysical Laboratory in Voronezh, who concluded that an object weighing 11 tons had landed. Soil samples were also taken, and revealed two to three times the normal background gamma radiation. Although it was later stated that these increased levels were the result of the Chernobyl disaster of 1986, it was still odd that they were concentrated precisely in the depressions made by the UFO's undercarriage.

Jacques **Vallée**, who interviewed Dr. Vladimir Azhazha, professor of mathematics and director of the (then) Soviet Commission for the Study of Paranormal Phenomena, reports that several people vanished during the Voronezh visitations, and reappeared afterward. Azhazha also claimed that the entities' movements were tracked by means of "biolocation," which is "the detection of the bioenergetic field and its application to the analysis of terrain, including the geology." The implication here is that UFOs are investigated in Russia with the aid of parapsychology.

According to skeptics, the Voronezh encounters never took place. The Russians had, in fact, imagined the whole affair, in an attempt to escape the repressive Communist system. One wonders if they also imagined the ground traces, with their increased radiation. Sadly, many American ufologists also dismissed the Voronezh sightings, because the entities reported did not resemble the **Grays**, which are now seen as the standard alien life-form. Vallée was rightly disgusted at this "mockery of the scientific method."

Interestingly, some witnesses described the huge entities as wearing belts, with a certain symbol on the buckles. The symbol was)+(. This insignia is very well known in the field of ufology as being that of the planet UMMO. The **UMMO** affair is widely regarded to be an elaborate hoax, and it therefore seems likely that the testimony of some Voronezh residents had been somehow contaminated by the earlier case.

WALTERS, ED

(See **Gulf Breeze, Florida**)

WALTON, TRAVIS

American abductee who encountered a UFO on November 5, 1975, in Sitgreaves National Park near Snowflake, Arizona. Walton was part of a seven-man woodcutting gang, who had finished work for the day and were on their way home, when they saw a disk-shaped object hovering above the forest to the side of the road. The UFO was approximately 20 feet wide and 8 feet high. There were dark silver vertical lines around the hull, and the central section was encircled by a Saturn-like ring.

As foreman Mike Rodgers stopped the truck, Travis Walton's curiosity overcame his apprehension, and he left the truck and walked into a clearing beneath the object. Ignoring the pleas from his workmates to get back into the truck, Walton continued toward the UFO, which began to emit low bleeping sounds. When the object started to dip in his direction, the bleeping sounds turning into a rumbling roar, Walton decided it was time to leave. He was about to start back, when a beam of intense blue light shot from the UFO and hit him, lifting him about a foot into the air. As his workmates watched in horror, Walton was flung back about 10 feet, his arms and legs outstretched.

Thinking that Walton had been killed (and perhaps that they might be next), the other men fled the scene, Rodgers throwing the truck wildly through the curves in the road. After about a quarter of a mile, the foreman brought the truck to a skidding halt. He told the others that he wanted to go back and get Walton. This was met with incredulity from the others, who had no intention of going anywhere near the clearing again. However, when they had calmed down a little, the agreed that they could not leave their workmate out there, and so Rodgers turned the truck around and headed back.

When they got to the clearing, there was no trace either of Travis Walton or the UFO. The crew then decided that there was nothing to do but to head into Snowflake and inform the police of what had happened.

Travis Walton would not return for five days, during which time the woodcutting gang found themselves under suspicion of murdering their workmate. The witnesses took a polygraph (lie-detector) test; they all passed, with the exception of one, Allen Dalis, whose results were inconclusive. The conclusions of the polygraph examiner, Cy Gilson, who worked for the Arizona Department of Public Safety, read, in part:

These polygraph examinations prove that these five men did see some object that they believe to be a UFO, and that Travis Walton was not injured or murdered by any of these men on [the day of the incident]. If an actual UFO did not exist and the UFO is a man-made hoax, five of these men had no prior knowledge of a hoax. No such determination can be made of the sixth man [Dalis], whose test results were inconclusive. (Clark [1998], p. 633)

Five days after Walton's disappearance, his brother-in-law, Grant Neff, answered the phone and heard a voice mutter: "This is Travis. I'm in a phone booth at the Heber gas station, and I need help. Come and get me."

Under **hypnotic regression**, Walton recalled returning to consciousness onboard the UFO. He was lying in a hospital-like room, his entire body aching. He was shocked and terrified to see three figures, dressed in loose-fitting, orange single-piece suits, approaching him. The beings had large, hairless heads and huge eyes, thus corresponding to the aliens known as the **Grays** (although these beings' eyes

were brown, rather than the jet-black so frequently reported in encounters with the Grays).

Walton immediately jumped off the table, struck one of the beings and pushed another away (it is interesting to note that he was in no way prevented from moving, as is the case with most other abductees—see **abductions**). The beings rapidly retreated from the room. Walton then ran from that room into another, containing an empty chair. When he approached the chair, the walls faded, and were replaced by stars, as if the room were a glass bubble floating in space.

Intrigued in spite of himself, Walton sat in the chair and began to manipulate the controls on the armrests. The stars immediately moved around, while maintaining their relative positions. At that point, he became aware of another being in the room; however, this one was entirely human-looking (a source of much relief to Walton), and was wearing a transparent helmet. The man was blond, tanned, tall and muscular, and was dressed in a blue coverall. Only his eyes were somewhat different from a human's: they were bright gold in color.

Ignoring his questions, the man took Walton into a large hangar containing three UFOs. Walton was led through the hangar to yet another room, where two men and a woman were sitting. They were all extremely attractive, and bore something of a resemblance to each other. Walton asked them who they were, where they came from, and where this place was, but they did not answer him. Instead, they took him to a table, forced him to lie down and placed a device resembling an oxygen mask over his face. At that point, he lost consciousness again, and woke up on the highway just outside Heber, about 10 miles from where he had seen the UFO.

The Walton abduction split the UFO community. Some suggested that the entire affair had been a hoax perpetrated by the woodcutting crew to get out of their logging contract (they were seriously behind schedule at the time of the encounter). However, this is merely a suggestion, and it must be said that the only piece of evidence that might point to a hoax is the inconclusive polygraph test on Allen Dalis. In other words, the skeptical case is rather thin at this time.

WEEKI-WACHI SPRINGS, FLORIDA

Location of an encounter with a UFO and occupant in 1965. At about 2:00 P.M. on March 3, 65-year-old John Reeves was out walking, when he came upon a disk-shaped object 30 feet in diameter, and about eight feet thick. Around the rim of the object were a number of "slats," similar to a Venetian blind, which opened and closed. The object was resting on four struts, and a fifth extended from its underside, holding several disk-shaped "steps."

At that point, a humanoid figure approached Reeves, and regarded him with obvious curiosity. The entity was dressed in a silver gray, tight-fitting suit, with a transparent, spherical helmet. Its head was similar to a human's, except for the very wide-set eyes. When the creature drew a small, boxlike instrument from its side and pointed it at Reeves, the latter decided to leave; however, the instrument was apparently harmless. As he looked over his shoulder, Reeves saw that the box was flashing.

Footprints were later found at the landing site, and Reeves later claimed that the entity had come so close to him that his helmet banged against Reeves's head. It has been suggested, however, that this later claim was merely an exaggeration.

Reeves also discovered two pieces of tissuelike paper at the scene of the encounter, which bore strange symbols, and which he turned over to the U.S. air force, which managed partly to decode the message. It read: "Planet Mars—are you coming home soon—we miss you very much—why did you stay away too long." According to the American researcher Coral Lorenzen of APRO, it has been suggested that this rather silly message was an attempt to mislead humans, for some reason—assuming, of course, that the encounter itself was genuine.

WHISTLE-BLOWERS

(See **Aviary**)

WINDOW AREA

A geographical area in which a high level of UFO activity is reported. It is unclear why such activity should seem to be targeted on specific areas, which is unsurprising in view of the fact that so little is known about the true nature of UFOs and associated phenomena. For instance, the so-called Washington Invasion of 1952, in which large numbers of UFOs were sighted over the U.S. capital, is an example of high activity in a window area. Ufologists who subscribe to the **extraterrestrial hypothesis** contend that this was actually a demonstration of strength by the aliens, a none-too-subtle implication that they can operate anywhere on Earth they choose. This, of course, presupposes that the extraterrestrial hypothesis is correct.
(See also **liminal zones**)

WISE BABIES

A rather bizarre and subtly disturbing element in memories of alien **abductions**. Frequently, female abductees will report encounters with babies that give the impression of possessing great intelligence—much more than is evident in human infants. This feeling is primarily conveyed through eye contact.

It has been suggested that these "wise babies" are actually alien/human **hybrids**, which have been produced through the manipulation of genetic material from humans and **Grays**, as part of their breeding program. Although apparently possessing great intelligence, the babies are almost invariably described as being exceptionally weak and sickly, and it has been speculated that human women are encouraged by the Grays to hold them, in an effort to increase their chances of survival through close contact with their mothers.

WODEWOSE

In medieval Europe, there were numerous legends of man-beasts living in the vast forest tracts that then covered much of the continent. These creatures were known as *wodewose*, or "wild man of the woods." Frequently hostile toward the occasional human who met them, they were also credited with being able to control, to a certain extent, the behavior of the other forest animals.

While there are certain parallels with the **Bigfoot** legends of North America, it is most unlikely that the *wodewose* were relict hominids, as has been suggested of Bigfoot. As anomalist Mike Dash states: ". . . there is some reason to suppose that a few men really did live wild in the forests at this time, many of whom were lunatics or mentally handicapped people who were liable to be violent or unpredictable." Dash goes on to remind us that the legends of the wild men of the woods survived until the 16th century, and may well have been taken to America by early colonists. While a few wild men may well have existed in Europe, they became part of the folklore of the forest, the inhabitants of wild places, and objects of fear due to their disinclination, or inability, to observe the conventions of society.

It may not be overstating the case to suggest a parallel with modern reports of alien encounters and abductions. Just as in the Middle Ages, the small communities of Europe were surrounded by the dark unknown of the forest, with its fearful denizens (whether real or legendary), so 20th-century humanity finds itself surrounded by the infinite darkness of deep space, which may well also harbor dreadful things. Throughout the 20th century in the industrialized First and Second Worlds, the idea that the glory and beneficence of God pervaded all of space was constantly under attack (much more so in the Second World, for obvious reasons), so that contemporary society is now not nearly as reassured about what deep space contains as was medieval society.

If our ancestors' relationship with the primeval forest of the Middle Ages can be likened to our own relationship with infinite space, the very essence of the deep unknown, then modern encounters with "alien" beings might well fulfill a function similar to the wild men stories of medieval times, as personifications of our deep-seated apprehensions regarding our place in the universe.

WOLSKI, JAN

Polish farmer who encountered an extremely unusual UFO and occupants in 1978. At about 8:00 A.M., 71-year-old Wolski was traveling through a forest in his horse-drawn cart, when he came upon two small men who were bounding along the road in the same direction, their movements reminding Wolski of deep-sea divers. As Wolski drew level with them, the men jumped up onto his cart, sat down next to him and gestured for him to keep going. The men spoke in an incomprehensible language. When the cart neared a clearing in the forest, Wolski saw a curious white object hovering in the air.

British ufologist Timothy Good comments on the apparent uniqueness of the UFO, which was shaped like a house, with "a roof like a barn." On each corner of the object was mounted a barrel-shaped device, from which extended vertically two black rods with rapidly rotating corkscrewlike spirals. Beneath the craft extended four cables, supporting a box-shaped elevator, which descended as the cart approached.

Wolski then became aware of an intense humming, which he likened to the sound of bumblebees in flight, as his two companions jumped down from the cart and entered the elevator. One of them turned and invited Wolski to join them on their craft. Since he could detect no hostility from the beings (rather, he had the impression of friendliness and joviality), the farmer accepted the invitation.

The interior of the craft was unlit, the only illumination coming from outside, and was uniformly grayish black in color, with seats against each of the four walls. There were no controls as such, only two black tubes extending from one gable wall to the other, and two holes into which the entities placed small, black rods. More bizarrely, Wolski noticed about ten black birds, perhaps crows or rooks, that seemed to have been paralyzed, and were lying on the floor.

The beings themselves were slim, about four feet tall, and were dressed in tight-fitting one-piece suits of a dark gray material, which covered the whole of their bodies, with the exception of the face and hands. Their heads were quite large, their eyes almond-shaped, their noses small, and their mouths lipless.

Wolski was then given a physical examination. One of the beings gestured that he should remove his clothes, and then another passed a pair of hand-held, disk-shaped instruments over his body. When the examination had been completed, Wolski was given his clothes, and when he had dressed, the beings showed him the way out.

All in all, it had been quite a civilized meeting, and Wolski doffed his hat and bowed politely to the beings when he stepped out of the elevator. The beings smiled and returned the bow, before disappearing inside their craft, which then departed.

When Wolski told his family about his encounter, they went to the landing site with some neighbors, and discovered several rectangular footprints, broken ears of corn and tree branches, and some black feathers. It later emerged that a woman was preparing breakfast for her children between 8:00 and 9:00 A.M. that day, when one of the children rushed in and told her that a "little house" had just flown overhead. The woman's house was about 800 yards from the scene of Wolski's encounter.

WRIGHT-PATTERSON AIR FORCE BASE

Formerly known as Wright Field, Wright-Patterson Air Force Base in Dayton, Ohio, has entered the folklore of ufology as the place where the ultimate proof of the alien presence on Earth is guarded. In a kind of modern reworking of the legends of the Holy Grail, the so-called **Blue Room** (sometimes known as "Hangar 18," or "Building 18-F, 3rd Floor") is claimed by many UFO devotees to house recovered artifacts from alien spacecraft, many of which are said to have crashed, for various reasons.

Whether or not this is true, it is easy to see how such legends could have arisen. Indeed, if the U.S. government does possess pieces of captured alien technology, Wright-Patterson AFB would be the natural choice for their storage, since it houses the U.S. Air Force's Foreign Technology Division (FTD).

In recent years, however, it has been suggested that Wright-Patterson's role as the central repository of alien devices has been superseded by the infamous **Area 51**, where new aircraft designs based on cutting-edge technology are routinely tested. Some of these designs, it is claimed, are based on the **reverse engineering** of alien spacecraft.

(See also **Interplanetary Phenomenon Unit (IPU)**)

X, COMMANDER

A prolific writer on UFO conspiracy and hollow earth theories and self-styled "ex-military intelligence operative," Commander X is a rather mysterious figure in fringe ufology. His books invariably read like the nightmarish ravings of an utter madman, his writing style a stream-of-consciousness rant covering everything from **abductions** to UFO **crash-retrievals**, from secret alien-human treaties to underground **bases** and the worldwide subterranean tunnel system allegedly built by the Atlanteans and Lemurians.

Commander X's books include *The Ultimate Deception* (1990), *Underground Alien Bases* (1990), *Nikola **Tesla**: Free Energy and the White Dove* (1992) and *The Controllers: The Hidden Rulers of Earth Identified* (1994), on the back cover of which is a warning: "This book is meant for serious researchers only!" It has been suggested by some researchers that Commander X is actually the American ufologist Timothy Green Beckley.

X, DR.

French biologist who had a number of UFO experiences in the late 1960s, and who has always maintained absolute anonymity, hence his pseudonym, Dr. X. At 4:00 on the morning of November 2, 1968, the 38-year-old doctor, who was living with his wife and 14-month-old son in the countryside in southern France, was awakened by the cries of the infant. He got out of bed and limped to his son's room. Three days earlier, Dr. X had badly cut his leg while chopping wood. An artery had been severed, resulting in a hematoma, a pocket of accumulated blood under the skin. The wound was not healing well, and was causing considerable pain.

On reaching his son's room, Dr. X found the child standing up in his crib and pointing toward the window. Through the closed shutters, Dr. X could see flashes of lightning, and assumed that the thunderstorm must have woken the boy. He then realized that there *was* no thunder, although it was raining very hard.

Dr. X refilled his son's water bottle, and was on his way back to bed, when he heard the sound of a shutter banging in an upstairs room. After struggling up the stairs and opening the window where the shutter was banging, Dr. X was astonished to see two silvery, disk-shaped objects hovering in the distance. Each object had a deep red light on its base, a vertical antenna on top and a horizontal antenna extending from the side. The objects moved together slowly across the rolling landscape, projecting cylindrical beams of light onto the ground. The light beams pulsed in one-second intervals as electrical discharges flashed between the objects, via their antennae.

As they approached the house, they merged into a single object, which then flipped up on end and turned on its horizontal axis, until it appeared as a shining circle. The cylindrical beam was aimed directly at the window at which Dr. X was standing, bathing him in light. This was followed by a sudden loud bang; the object vanished, leaving behind a white glow that gradually dissipated. A single shaft of light then shot up to the sky, and there was a final explosion high in the air.

Although utterly astonished at what he had just witnessed, Dr. X nevertheless had the presence of mind to sit down and make detailed notes of his experience, accompanied by sketches of the objects. When he had finished, he went to his wife, woke her and told her about the strange visitation. As might be expected, she was unsure whether her husband had simply dreamed the whole encounter . . . until she noticed that the swelling on his leg had completely disappeared. When she pointed this out to him, Dr. X realized that the pain, too, had vanished.

After discussing the matter at some length, Dr. X and his wife returned to bed. While she had difficulty sleeping, he immediately entered a profound slumber, during which he began to speak. Having similar presence of mind to her husband, she began to take notes of what he was saying (he had never talked in his sleep before). At one point, he muttered: "Contact will be reestablished by falling down the stairs on November 2."

Dr. X slept until 2:00 P.M. the following afternoon, and when he awoke he had no memory of what had occurred the previous night. When his wife showed him the sketches and notes he had made, he was deeply alarmed. Later that afternoon, he tripped and fell down the stairs in the living room, bumping his head. At that moment, his memories of the objects returned.

Ten years earlier, in the Algerian war, Dr. X had been badly injured in a mine explosion; the left hemisphere of his brain had been damaged, resulting in severe weakness down the right side of his body. After his encounter with the objects, this weakness also disappeared.

On November 8, Dr. X was visited by his friend, the respected French ufologist Aimé Michel, who was concerned to find him tired and depressed. Dr. X complained of abdominal cramps, weight loss and a curious red rash in the shape of a triangle on his stomach. A dermatologist was called in to examine the rash, which he found so intriguing that he asked Dr. X if he might present the case to the French Academy of Medicine. Dr. X, however, was afraid that his UFO encounter might inadvertently become publicly known, and so demurred.

The rash would return again and again in the following years. Dr. X and his wife also experienced a profound alteration in their attitudes to the world; they became much more spiritually orientated and able to appreciate the sublime harmony of the Universe. In addition, their home seemed to become the focus for poltergeist activity, and Dr. X experienced levitation on one occasion. It seemed to him and his wife that there were unseen, nonhuman entities moving around the house, and various electrical devices malfunctioned frequently.

X-DEVICES

Term denoting the small minority of UFOs and other objects that give the appearance of being intelligently guided machines of nonhuman origin. Although now obsolete, the term is actually semantically more useful than the term "UFOs" (**Unidentified Flying Objects**), when referring to machines that appear not to have been designed and built by humans. UFOs can refer to objects that, in many cases, are unidentified for mere seconds, before the percipient realizes what they actually are (an aircraft seen at an odd angle can seem very strange, until its position alters and it is recognized for what it is), and thus the term "UFO" is far too general to describe a genuinely anomalous and possibly extraterrestrial phenomenon under intelligent control. The term "X-device" is more satisfactory, since it marks the phenomenon as a piece of equpment of a genuinely anomalous nature.

X-DRONES

Alien devices postulated by researcher George Leonard to account for the presence of cross- or X-shaped features photographed on the surface of the Moon. These features are extremely puzzling, as are many other objects on the Moon (see **artifacts (alien)**), and have been seen by astronomers on a number of occasions. Leonard himself has seen the X-shaped features in various lunar locations, including the Alpine Valley, the Sea of Crises and the crater Tycho.

Leonard has speculated that these objects are actually pieces of alien-built machinery, which he has called X-drones. Since the huge X-drones have often been seen in or near craters, Leonard suggests that they may be mining devices, able to scoop up lunar rocks, process the raw materials contained in them and then discard what is left. Since X-drones seem to have the capacity to appear and disappear, Leonard believes that they are also self-propelled and capable of moving over large distances. This, he says, would also account for the unusual sprays of material, which are sometimes seen issuing from craters. These may be waste material ejected by X-drones, or they may be evidence of underground facilities.

X-drones have also been seen apparently "stitching up" or repairing lunar chasms. Some researchers speculate that the Moon is actually a colossal alien spacecraft, and that the strange objects seen moving about on its surface are actually devices designed to maintain the vessel's outer hull.

X-FILES, THE (TV SHOW)

Created by Chris Carter in 1993, and starring David Duchovny and Gillian Anderson, *The X-Files* has gained phenomenal popularity throughout the world, and is responsible to a considerable degree for the renaissance of public interest in the paranormal in general, and UFOs in particular, in the last six years or so.

The X-Files of the title are reports held by the **FBI**, detailing paranormal events throughout the United States and, occasionally, other countries. Special Agent Fox Mulder (Duchovny) has been given the responsibility of investigating these reports, along with his partner, Special Agent Dana Scully (Anderson), a medical doctor instructed to evaluate Mulder's work. (Scully's initial skepticism of the paranormal was maintained for far too long, in the face of weekly encounters with UFOs, ghosts, demons, monsters, and genetic freaks.)

The basic premise of *The X-Files* is that a political and military elite (the "secret government" of UFO and conspiracy legend) is aware of the alien presence on Earth, and has covered up all evidence for the last 50 years. The FBI itself seems to be involved with this huge conspiracy (the precise nature of which is never made absolutely clear), and much of the dramatic tension is maintained by Mulder's uncertainty as to whom he can trust (two phrases crop up frequently: "trust no one" and "the truth is out there").

The series also features several supporting characters, such as the immensely sinister "Cigarette-smoking Man" (played by William B. Davis), who belongs to a shadowy group that may or may not be **Majestic 12**, and Mulder and Scully's immediate boss and ally, Walter Skinner (Mitch Pileggi).

While *The X-Files* is clearly inspired by the supernatural thriller series *The Night Stalker* from the 1970s (although it is far more intelligent and sophisticated), its true inspiration is the "damned data" accumulated by the American anomalist Charles Fort. By *damned*, Fort meant all those data derided or ignored by orthodox science as being incompatible with current paradigms. Contrary to the opinion of many skeptics, Fort did not confine his attention to spurious and unsubstantiated superstitions; in fact, the majority of the copious notes he made on strange phenomena were taken from respected scientific journals and newspapers. His work has been continued since the early 1970s by the British journal *Fortean Times,* the pages of which are routinely scoured by the writers of *The X-Files* for ideas!

Paradoxically, the reason for the appeal of the series is also the reason why it frequently becomes irritating: in utilizing the full range of Fortean phenomena, *The X-Files* has little choice but to be frequently contradictory in its treatment of the possible explanations for the events it dramatizes. The one thing any in-depth study of the paranormal teaches us, is that there are no clear-cut answers to any of the genuine mysteries of which it is composed—mysteries that frequently shade into one another, leaving us with little to do but ponder Professor C. E. M. Joad's famous maxim that the universe is not only stranger than we imagine, but stranger than we *can* imagine.

(See also **conspiracy theories**)

YEREN

A mysterious semi-human beast said to inhabit remote regions of Asia, in particular the Shennongjia Mountains of central China. The yeren is said to be between five and six feet in height, with shaggy red hair and large feet. Some cryptozoologists have suggested that the yeren may be a relict *Gigantopithecus*. According to Dr. Karl Shuker:

In recent years, yeren hair samples found on trees and bushes have been analyzed by proton-induced X-ray emission (PIXE) spectrometry, to discover the relative concentrations of the elements contained in them. The resulting profile proved to be totally different from that of any known species in China, with an exceptionally (but consistently) high iron/zinc ratio.

(See also **Bigfoot,** *wodewose*)

YETI

Also known as the Abominable Snowman, the Yeti is an apparently nonhuman biped whose natural habitat is the Himalayas. This creature was first mentioned in 1832 in the *Journal of the Asiatic Society of Bengal*. B. H. Hodgson described how a group of Nepalese hunters were collecting specimens in a province in northern Nepal, when they came upon a large, humanoid creature with long, dark red hair covering its body.

According to the anomalist Jerome Clark:

The first Westerner actually to see what may have been such creatures (though there are other, unsubstantiated claims for that distinction) was Lt. Col. C. K. Howard-Bury, who led a reconnaissance expedition up Mount Everest in September 1921. At 20,000 feet on the side of the mountain that faces northern Tibet, the group found a large number of footprints three times the size human beings would make. The Sherpas attributed them to what Howard-Bury, apparently incorrectly, transcribed as *metoh-kangmi*. A *Calcutta Statesman* columnist who was shown the colonial officer's official report mistranslated the word as "abominable snowman." Apparently Howard-Bury had misunderstood the Sherpa term *meh-teh*, which means, approximately, "manlike thing that is not a man." (Clark [1993], p. 430)

A number of respected mountaineers have sighted the yeti over the years, including the British climber Don Whillans, who reported that while on Mount Annapurna in 1970, he and his Sherpa heard the cries of a yeti. The following day, Whillans discovered large, humanlike tracks in the snow. That night, he had the feeling that a yeti was near, so he looked out of his tent and saw one picking food from some nearby tree branches. Whillans was able to watch the creature for approximately 20 minutes.

Aside from footprints, other physical evidence of the yeti's existence has been discovered from time to time, including droppings found during a 1959 expe-dition which, when examined, were found to contain eggs from a previously unknown parasitic worm.

Possible candidates for the yeti include relict hominids such as *Gigantopithecus* (see **yeren**), *Australopithecus* and the orangutan.
(See also **Bigfoot**)

YTTRIUM

A silvery metallic element, not a rare earth but occurring in nearly all rare-earth minerals, yttrium is used in various metallurgical applications, such as the strengthening of magnesium and aluminium alloys. The element is of interest to ufologists because of a reference made to it after a UFO abduction in Gustavslund, Sweden, in March 1974. The abductee, who was given the pseudonym "Anders," had a dream in which he was told to "search in yttrium."

UFO investigator Arne Groth subsequently replaced the rock crystals he had been experimenting with, in an attempt to construct a telepathic communication instrument (with which he hoped to contact the aliens), with yttrium. Apparently, this had the effect of causing waves of energy to extend from Groth's apparatus, waves that could be physically felt when standing close to it.

ZETA RETICULI STAR SYSTEM

A close pair of stars approximately 37 light-years from Earth. The two stars, Zeta 1 and Zeta 2, are located in the southern constellation of Reticulum (the Net), are between 6 and 8 billion years old and are relatively close to a loose cluster of stars first defined in 1958, and known as the Zeta Hercules group. Although Zeta Reticuli is often described as a binary system, this is not so: Zeta 1 and 2 are actually close companion stars, which are moving together in the same direction at the same speed, rather than orbiting about a common center, as with binary systems. The stars are very similar to our own sun, Sol, with luminosities of 0.7 (Zeta 1) and 0.9 (Zeta 2), as compared with Sol's luminosity of 1.0.

Zeta Reticuli has often been cited as the home system of the **Grays**, an assertion based principally on the "star map" reconstructed by Marjorie Fish, from information supplied by Betty **Hill** after the abduction of her and her husband, Barney. Although there is no direct evidence of a planetary system associated with Zeta Reticuli, the Sun-like characteristics of these stars certainly do not rule it out.

In a 1997 article posted on the Internet, Robert M. Collins lists four important points that support the idea that Zeta Reticuli might well possess life-bearing planets. First, that they are Sun-like stars; second, since it has now been established that they are not binary stars, it becomes possible for planets to exist in stable orbits within the so-called habitable zone (the region in which life can begin), which is not the case in binary systems; third, that the stars are between 6 and 8 billion years old—1 to 3 billion years older than Sol, suggesting that any life on their planets would also be far older than Earth life, and thus may well be much more scientifically advanced than humanity; and fourth, that the Grays have been described as having an extremely tough skin and several eyelids, which would be expected of creatures living near a star with a high ultraviolet output.

ZIGEL, DR. FELIX YUREVICH

Doctor of science and assistant professor of cosmology at the Moscow Aviation Institute, who published an article in the Russian magazine *Smena* (Change) in 1967, stating that UFOs were worthy of serious scientific attention. This was an extremely unusual (not to mention courageous) stance to take in the Soviet Union, where official statements regarding UFOs had been uniformly dismissive. Zigel also stated that numerous Soviet scientists had also witnessed UFO activity, and that the government was deeply concerned about the phenomenon.

In his book *Beyond Top Secret: The Worldwide UFO Security*, Timothy Good quotes a startling statement made by Dr. Zigel in a 1981 interview with the American journalist Henry Gris:

We have seen these UFOs over the USSR; craft of every possible shape: small, big, flattened, spherical. They are able to remain stationary in the atmosphere or to shoot along at 100,000 kilometers per hour. They move without producing the slightest sound, by creating around themselves a pneumatic vacuum that protects them from the hazard of burning up in our stratosphere. Their craft also have the mysterious capacity to vanish and reappear at will. They are also able to affect our power resources, halting our electricity-generating plants, our radio stations, and our engines, without, however, leaving any permanent damage. So refined a technology can only be the fruit of an intelligence that is indeed far superior to man. (Good [1996], pp. 245–6)

Zigel ultimately collected more than 50,000 UFO reports, which he stored in the computer at the Moscow Aviation Institute. He only published one volume based on his own researches, although he stated that he had material for seven more. Zigel was reluctant to publish any more, he said, because he feared the shocking information would create mass unrest in the Soviet Union.

There were, according to Zigel, three basic categories of alien visiting Earth: Spacemen, who were very tall (about nine feet); Humanoids, who were entirely human-looking; and Aliens, diminutive beings corresponding to the **Grays**.

ZOMDIC

A planet in an unknown star system, which was visited by a British engineer named James Cooke in September 1957. Cooke, from Runcorn in Cheshire, witnessed the arrival of a 120-foot-diameter disk-shaped spacecraft, from which a ladder extended, accompanied by a voice which said to him: "The ground is damp. Jump. Don't have one foot on the ground or you will be hurt."

Cooke did as he was instructed, jumped onto the ladder and entered the craft, which turned out to be unmanned. Presently, the voice told him to exit the vessel, and he found himself in the hangar of a larger craft. There he was met by tall, beautiful humanoid beings with exceptionally fine complexions. Cooke later discovered that each being was a mixture of male and female.

The large spacecraft then arrived on the planet Zomdic, where Cooke was shown around by his hermaphroditic hosts. He saw a ground transportation system that was apparently operated through the manipulation of musical vibrations. Cooke was told that the civilization on Zomdic was not based on any monetary system, since they had long ago discovered how to convert energy to whatever form was needed.

A rather trite and pointless exchange then occurred between Cooke and one of the masters of

Zomdic. The master said to him: "The inhabitants of your planet will upset the balance if they persist in using force instead of harmony. Warn them of the danger."

"But they won't listen to me," replied Cooke.

"Or anybody else either," lamented the master.

And that, it seems, was that.

ZRET

A humanoid alien being belonging to a race known as the Norcans who befriended a very early contactee named Albert Coe in June 1920. Coe, then 16 years old, was on a canoeing vacation in Ontario, Canada, with his friend Rod. While out by himself one day, Coe heard a voice crying for help from below the rocks over which he was climbing. Coe eventually located the source of the voice, a young man who had become trapped in a cleft in the rocks. With some difficulty, Coe managed to rescue the trapped man, who thanked him profusely and said that he had been fishing when he accidentally stumbled into the cleft.

The handsome, blond-haired young man, who was dressed in a strange silver gray suit, told Coe that he had a small aircraft in a nearby clearing, and when Coe helped him return to it, he realized that it was unlike anything he had ever seen. It was a 20-foot-diameter disk, resting on three landing struts in a tripod arrangement. Having made Coe promise not to mention their encounter, the young man opened a hatch in the underside of the craft and climbed in. The disk then took off with a high-pitched whine.

Six months later, Coe received a short note requesting a lunchtime meeting at the McAlpine Hotel in Ottawa. It was signed "Xretsim" (Mister X spelled backward). Coe went to the hotel, and there met the young man he had rescued, although this time he was dressed in an ordinary suit. The young man introduced himself as Zret, and over lunch he explained that he was part of a survey team charged with monitoring Earth's scientific progress. His race,

he said, had originated on the planet Norca in the Tau Ceti star system. Fourteen thousand years ago, Norca had begun to dehydrate, forcing the inhabitants to migrate to another system. Our own Solar System was explored, and chosen as the Norcans' new home.

According to Zret, 243,000 Norcans embarked on the journey of colonization in 62 colossal spacecraft. However, due to some tragic navigational error, all but one of these ships plunged into the Sun. The remaining ship then crash-landed on Mars, killing 1,300 of its 5,000 passengers. The survivors then set about colonising Mars, then moved on to Venus and Earth, where they founded Atlantis and Lemuria. Zret went on to state that the Norcans now live mainly on Venus, although they maintain several research bases on Mars.

Coe maintained contact with Zret and other Norcans for the next 60 years, meeting them on average once a month. In 1969 he privately published a book entitled *The Shocking Truth,* which detailed these encounters.

(See also **contactees**)

ZUCCALÀ, MARIO

Italian tailor who encountered a UFO and occupants in 1962. At about 9:30 P.M. on April 10, Zuccalà was walking from a bus stop to his home in San Casciano, Val di Pesa, near Florence, central Italy, when he felt a sudden gust of wind. The 26-year-old tailor turned to see a disk-shaped object, about 25 feet in diameter, hovering nearby. A cylinder descended from the underside of the craft, and then withdrew, revealing a second cylinder inside it. This cylinder contained a doorway, from which a bright light shone. Two humanoid beings, each about four feet tall and dressed in what looked like suits of shining metal, then came out of the craft and approached Zuccalà. They took hold of him and gently ushered him into the craft, which was filled with a bright light with no obvious source. Zuccalà asked the beings where the light came from, but did not receive a reply.

At that point, a voice (which apparently did not come from either of the two beings) echoed through the craft. It said, in Italian: "At the fourth moon we shall come at one o'clock in the morning to bring you a message for humanity. We shall give notice of this to another person in order to confirm that that which you have seen is true." (Good [1998], p. 231) It is unclear whether the "fourth moon" was from the beginning of the year, or from the day of the encounter.

Zuccalà was then taken from the craft, and the next thing he knew, he was standing outside his home; the time was 9:45 P.M. He told his wife about what had happened, and she was alarmed at his obvious state of confusion and distress. The next morning, one of Zuccalà's colleagues at work, to whom he had told his story, informed a newspaper, and the encounter was subsequently widely reported. Although no physical evidence could be found at the landing site, all those who knew Zuccalà testified to his honesty and trustworthiness.

Ufologist Timothy Good remarks on how silly the message given to Zuccalà was, and also how inaccurate, for there were no further visitations from the strange beings. If Zuccalà was telling the truth about his experience, then we are left, once again, to ponder in frustration the odd and apparently senseless tricks so often played upon humanity by the mysterious and elusive occupants of the UFOs.

BIBLIOGRAPHY AND SUGGESTED FURTHER READING

A NOTE TO THE READER

While the following list refers exclusively to books, with a few periodicals at the end, a certain amount of useful material (consisting mainly of snippets of information) for *The Encyclopedia of Alien Encounters* was found scattered on a wide variety of Internet sites. I have not included these in the Bibliography, since it will be more convenient for the computer-equipped reader simply to search the Net by keyword.

★ Andrews, George C. *Extra-Terrestrials Among Us* St. Paul, Minn.: Llewellyn Publications, 1993.
Extra-Terrestrial Friends and Foes, Lilburn, Ga: IllumiNet Press, 1993.

★ Ashpole, Edward. *The UFO Phenomena: A Scientific Look at the Evidence for Extraterrestrial Contacts*, London: Headline Books, 1996.

★ Baker, Alan. *UFO Sightings* London: Orion Media, 1997.
Destination Earth. A History of Alleged Alien Presence, London: Blandford Books, 1998.

★ Barker, Gray. *They Knew Too Much About Flying Saucers*. Lilburn, Ga: IllumiNet Press, 1997.

★ Bernard, Raymond: *The Hollow Earth*. New York: Carol Publishing, 1991.

★ Blum, Howard. *Out There*. New York: Simon & Schuster, 1990.

★ Blum, Ralph, and Judy Blum. *Beyond Earth, Man's Contact with UFOs*. New York: Bantam Books, 1974.

★ Bord, Janet, and Colin. *Alien Animals: A Worldwide Investigation*. London: Book Club Associates, 1980.

Life Beyond Planet Earth? Man's Contact with Space People. London: Grafton, 1992.

★ Bowen, Charles, ed. *The Humanoids*. London: Futura Publications, 1977.

★ Brookesmith, Peter. *UFO: The Complete Sightings Catalogue*. London: Blandford Press, 1995.

★ Brookesmith, Peter, ed. *The Age of the UFO*. London: Orbis Publishing, 1984.

★ Bryan, C.D.B. *Close Encounters of the Fourth Kind: Alien Abduction and UFOs—Witnesses and Scientists Report*, London: Orion Books, 1996.

★ Bulwer-Lytton, E.G.E. *The Coming Race*. Stroud: Alan Sutton Publishing, 1995.

★ Childress, David Hatcher. *Extraterrestrial Archaeology*. Stelle, Ill.: Adventures Unlimited Press, 1994.

★ Clark, Jerome. *Unexplained!* Detroit: Visible Ink Press, 1993.
The UFO Book: Encyclopedia of the Extraterrestria. Detroit: Visible Ink Press, 1998.

★ Commander X: *Underground Alien Bases*. Wilmington, Del.: Abelard Productions, 1990.

★ Corso, Philip J. *The Day After Roswell*. London: Pocket Books, 1997.

★ Craft, Michael. *Alien Impact*. New York: St. Martin's Paperbacks, 1996.

★ Dash, Mike. *Borderlands*. London: Heinemann, 1997.

★ Devereux, Paul, and Peter Brookesmith. *UFOs and Ufology: The First 50 Years*. London: Blandford Books, 1997.

★ Drake, Frank, and Dava Sobel. *Is Anyone Out There?*. London: Pocket Books, 1994.

★ Drury, Nevill. *The Elements of Shamanism*. Shaftesbury, Dorset: Element Books, 1992.

★ Emenegger, Robert. *UFOs Past, Present and Future*, New York: Ballantine Books, 1978.

★ Evans, Hilary, and Dennis Stacy, eds. *UFO 1947–1997: Fifty Years of Flying Saucers*. London: John Brown Publishing, 1997.

★ Fawcett, Lawrence, and Barry J. Greenwood. *The UFO Cover-Up* (originally published as *Clear Intent*). New York: Simon & Schuster, 1992.

★ Fort, Charles. *Book of the Damned*. London: John Brown Publishing, 1995.

★ Fowler, Raymond E. *The Watchers: The Secret Design Behind UFO Abduction*. New York: Bantam Books, 1991.

★ Friedman, Stanton. *TOP SECRET/MAJIC*. New York: Marlowe & Company, 1996.

★ Fuller, John G. *The Interrupted Journey*. New York: MJF Books, 1996.

★ Godwin, Joscelyn. *Arktos: The Polar Myth in Science, Symbolism and Nazi Survival*. London: Thames and Hudson, 1993.

★ Good, Timothy. *Alien Liaison: The Ultimate Secret*, London: Arrow Books, 1992.

Beyond Top Secret: The Worldwide UFO Security Threat. London: Sidgwick & Jackson, 1996.

Alien Base: Earth's Encounters with Extraterrestrials, London: Century, 1998.

★ Gribbin, John. *In Search of Schrödinger's Cat*, London: Black Swan, 1993.

★ Guiley, Rosemary Ellen. *Harper's Encyclopedia of Mystical & Paranormal Experience*. Edison, N.J.: Castle Books, 1991.

★ Harbinson, W. A. *Projekt UFO: The Case for Man-Made Flying Saucers*. London: Boxtree, 1996.

★ Harpur, Patrick. *Daimonic Reality: A Field Guide to the Otherworld*. London: Arkana, 1995.

★ Herbert, Nick. *Faster Than Light: Superluminal Loopholes in Physics*. New York: Plume Books, 1989.

★ Hoagland, Richard C. *The Monuments of Mars: A City on the Edge of Forever*. Berkeley: North Atlantic Books, 1996.

★ Hopkins, Budd. *Missing Time: A Documented Study of UFO Abductions*. New York: Richard Marek Publishers, 1981.

Intruders: The Incredible Visitations at Copley Woods, New York: Ballantine Books, 1992.

Witnessed: The True Story of the Brooklyn Bridge Abduction. London: Bloomsbury, 1997.

★ Hough, Peter, and Moyshe Kalman. *The Truth About Alien Abductions*. London: Blandford Press, 1997.

★ Hough, Peter, and Jenny Randles. *Looking For the Aliens: A Psychological, Scientific and Imaginative Investigation*. London: Blandford Press, 1991.

The Complete Book of UFOs. London: Piatkus, 1994.

★ Huyghe, Patrick. *The Field Guide to Extraterrestrials*. London: New English Library, 1997.

★ Hynek, J. Allen. *The UFO Experience*. London: Corgi Books, 1975.

★ Jacobs, David M. *Alien Encounters: First-hand Accounts of UFO Abductions* (originally published as *Secret Life*). London: Virgin Books, 1994.

★ Jessup, Morris K. *The Case for the UFO*. London: Arco, 1955.

★ Jung, C. G. *Flying Saucers: A Modern Myth of Things Seen in the Sky*. London: Ark, 1987.

Man and His Symbols. London: Aldus Books, 1979.

★ Keel, John A.: *UFOs: Operation Trojan Horse*, London: Abacus, 1973.

The Mothman Prophecies, Avondale Estates, Ga: IllumiNet Press, 1991.

★ Keith, Jim. *Casebook on Alternative 3*. Lilburn, Ga: IllumiNet Press, 1994.

Casebook on the Men in Black. Lilburn, Ga: IllumiNet Press, 1997.

★ Keyhoe, Donald E. *Flying Saucers from Outer Space*. London: Tandem Books, 1974.

Aliens from Space. London: Panther Books, 1976.

★ Klass, Philip J. *UFOs Explained*. New York: Random House, 1974.

The Real Roswell Crashed-Saucer Coverup. Amherst: Prometheus Books, 1997.

★ Kraspedon, Dino. *My Contact with UFOs.* London: Sphere Books, 1977.

★ LePage, Victoria. *Shambhala,* Wheaton, Ill: Quest Books, 1996.

★ Mack John E. *Abduction: Human Encounters with Aliens.* London: Pocket Books, 1995.

★ Maclellan, Alec. *The Lost World of Agharti: The Mystery of Vril Power.* London: Souvenir Press, 1996.

★ Monroe, Robert A. *Journeys Out of the Body,* London: Souvenir Press, 1986.

★ Nichols, Preston, and Peter Moon. *The Montauk Project: Experiments in Time.* New York: Sky Books, 1992.

★ Peebles, Curtis. *Watch the Skies!: A Chronicle of the Flying Saucer Myth.* New York: Berkeley Books, 1995.

★ Pringle, David, ed. *The Ultimate Encyclopedia of Science Fiction.* London: Carlton Books, 1996.

★ Randle, Kevin D. *A History of UFO Crashes.* New York: Avon Books, 1995.

★ Randle, Kevin D., and Russ Estes. *Faces of the Visitors: An Illustrated Reference to Alien Contact.* New York: Simon & Schuster, 1997.

★ Randle, Kevin D., and Donald R. Schmitt. *UFO Crash at Roswell.* New York: Avon Books, 1991.

The Truth About the UFO Crash at Roswell. New York: Avon Books, 1994.

★ Randles, Jenny. *Alien Contacts and Abductions.* New York: Sterling Publishing, 1994.

UFO Retrievals: The Recovery of Alien Spacecraft. London: Blandford Books, 1995.

MIB: Investigating the Men in Black Phenomenon. London: Piatkus, 1997.

UFO Crash Landing? Friend or Foe?. London: Blandford Press, 1998.

★ Ring, Kenneth. *The Omega Project: Near-Death Experiences, UFO Encounters, and Mind at Large.* New York: William Morrow, 1992.

★ Sagan, Carl, and Thornton Page eds.: *UFOs: A Scientific Debate.* New York: Barnes & Noble Books, 1996.

★ Schnabel, Jim. *Dark White: Aliens, Abductions and the UFO Obsession.* London: Penguin Books, 1995.

★ Shuker, Karl P. N. *The Unexplained.* London: Carlton Books, 1996.

★ Siegel, Ronald K. *Fire in the Brain: Clinical Tales of Hallucination.* New York: Dutton, 1992.

★ Spencer, John. *The UFO Encyclopedia.* London: Headline, 1991.

★ Strieber, Whitley. *Communion: A True Story.* New York: William Morrow & Company, 1987.

Transformation: The Breakthrough. New York: Avon Books, 1989.

Breakthrough: The Next Step. New York: HarperPaperbacks, 1996.

The Secret School: Preparation for Contact London: Simon & Schuster, 1997.

★ Talbot, Michael. *The Holographic Universe,* London: HarperCollins, 1996.

★ Temple, Robert. *The Sirius Mystery.* London: Century, 1998.

★ Thompson, Keith. *Angels and Aliens: UFOs and the Mythic Imagination.* New York: Fawcett Columbine, 1993.

★ Thompson, Richard L. *Alien Identities: Ancient Insights into Modern UFO Phenomena.* San Diego: Govardhan Hill Publishing, 1993.

★ Vallée, Jacques. *Anatomy of a Phenomenon.* London: Tandem Books, 1974.

UFOs: The Psychic Solution (originally published as *The Invisible College*). London: Panther Books, 1975.

Dimensions: A Casebook of Alien Contact, London: Sphere Books, 1990.

UFO Chronicles of the Soviet Union: A Cosmic Samizdat. New York: Ballantine Books, 1992.

Revelations: Alien Contact and Human Deception. New York: Ballantine Books, 1993.

Passport to Magonia: On UFOs, Folklore, and Parallel Worlds. Chicago: Contemporary Books, 1993.

★ Vesco, Renato, and David Hatcher Childress. *Man-Made UFOs 1944–1994: 50 Years of Suppression*. Stelle, Ill: Adventures Unlimited Press, 1994.

★ Warren, Larry, and Peter Robbins. *Left at East Gate*. London: Michael O'Mara Books, 1997.

★ Wilkins, Harold T. *Flying Saucers on the Attack*. New York: Ace Books, 1954.

JOURNALS

Flying Saucer Review
FSR Publications Ltd.
P.O. Box 162,
High Wycombe,
Bucks HP13 5DZ,
UK

Fortean Times
Box 2409,
London NW5 4NP,
UK

International UFO Reporter
J. Allen Hynek Center for UFO Studies
2457 West Peterson Avenue
Chicago, Il 60659

Mutual UFO Network *MUFON UFO Journal*
Mutual UFO Network
103 Oldtowne Road
Seguin, Texas 78155-4099

UFO Magazine
Quest Publications International Ltd,
Wharfebank House,
Wharfebank Business Center,
Ilkley Road,
Otley, nr Leeds LS21 3JP,
UK

INDEX

A

ABCs. *See* alien big cats
abduction(s) 9–10, 16, 20,
  32–33, 46, 47, 48, 54, 57, 63,
  87, 90, 108, 110, 116, 120, 124,
  125, 143, 149, 156, 162, 164,
  185, 196, 203, 204, 208, 217,
  219, 220, 221, 223, 226, 231,
  254, 255, 259
*Abduction: Human Encounters
  with Aliens* 79, 149
Aboard a Flying Saucer 35
*Account of a Meeting with
  Denizens of Another World, An*
  10–11
Adams, Thomas 93
Adamski, George 11–12, 13, 19,
  51, 55, 62, 173, 180, 188
Aerial Phenomena Enquiry
  Network 12–13
Aetherius 13
Aetherius Society 13–14, 60,
  135, 136, 245
AFIP. *See* Armed Forces Institute
  of Pathology
A for Andromeda (TV show) 14
AFOSI. *See* Air Force Office of
  Special Investigations
Air Force Office of Special
  Investigations 35
Akon 136
Alien (film), 14–15
alien(s) 15–17
  contact 51

DNA, harvesting 14, 47, 87
encounters 6, 10–11, 49, 53,
  54, 173, 189
alien big cats 15
Aliens from Space 135, 146
Allagash abductions 17–19
Allagash Abductions, The 19
Allan, Christopher 19
Allingham, Cedric 19–20
Almas 20
Amazing Stories 184, 223
amnesia 20
ancient astronauts 21–22, 62,
  196
Andreasson, Betty 22–23, 51,
  196–197
Andreasson Affair, The 22
*Andreasson Affair—Phase Two,
  The* 22
Andreasson Legacy, The 22
Andrews, George C. 204–205
Angelucci, Orfeo 23, 51, 55
APEN. *See* Aerial Phenomena
  Enquiry Network
Appleton, Cynthia 23–24
Applewhite, Marshall 60
Apollo Program 26
Area 51 24, 28, 141, 191, 245,
  257
*Arktos: The Polar Myth in Science,
  Symbolism and Nazi Survival*
  106
Armed Forces Institute of
  Pathology 18

Arnold, Kenneth 5, 6, 51
artifacts (alien) 24–26, 75, 166,
  261
Ashtar (aka Ashtar Command)
  26
Asket 26 157, 222
Atlanteans 31
Atlantis 65, 135, 163, 267
Aurora 31
Ausso 200–201
Aveley, Essex, U.K. 27
aviary 27–28, 74, 142, 166
Avis, Elaine 27
Avis, John 27
Aztec, New Mexico 28, 104

B

Babalon Working 166
Babylonian History 66
Badajoz, Spain 29–30
Baden-Württemberg, Germany
  30
Bahía Blanca, Argentina 30–31
Bailey, Harrison 179–180
Barker, Gray 34, 161
Barnett, Paul 11
bases (alien) 31, 34, 50, 53, 179,
  187, 259
Beast of Bodmin 15
Beast of Inkberrow 15
Bebedouro, Brazil, 31–32
Beckley, Timothy Green. *See* X,
  Commander

bedroom visitors 18, 32–33, 99, 144

Begay, Wil 205–206

Behind the Flying Saucers 28, 58–59

Belgrave, Australia 33

Bender, Albert K. 33–34, 161

Bennewitz, Dr. Paul 34–35, 47, 167, 187

Bergier, Jacques 21

Berliner, Don 153

Berlitz, Charles 166

Berossus 66

Bethurum, Truman 35, 55

Beyond Top Secret: The Worldwide UFO Security Threat 170

Bigfoot 35, 82, 132, 145, 256

black helicopters 35–36, 43

Blackmore, Dr. Susan 72

Blob, The (film) 36

blobs, aliens 36, 37, 123

Blue Book (project) 28, 37–38, 92, 111, 207, 228

Blue Room 38, 99, 257. *See also* Hangar 18

Boas, Antonio Villas 38–39, 220

Bohm, David 107

Bord, Colin 120

Bord, Janet 120

Bosak, William 82

Bottomley, Peter 12–13

Bower, Doug 59

Brady, Dr. Brian 71

British UFO Research Association 13, 39

Bronk, Dr. Detlev 74

Brookesmith, Peter 94, 136, 208

Brookings Institute 25, 26

Brown, T. Townsend 170–171

Brunvand, Jan Harold 73–74

BUFORA. *See* British UFO Research Association

Bukit Mertajam, Malaysia 39–40

Bullard, Thomas 16

Bulwer-Lytton, Edward 49–50

Butler, Rich 57–58

Byrd, Richard E. 106

C

Cabo Rojo 46

Cahill, Kelly 33

Campbell, Steuart 19

Canovanas 46, 47

Caracas, Venezuela 41–42

Carr, Frank 42

Carr, Robert Spencer 146

Cascade Mountains 5

Case for the UFO, The 186–187

Caspar mummy 42

cattle mutilations 36, 42–44, 47, 93, 105, 109, 127,167

Celtic legend 6. *See also* Gentry

Center for UFO Studies 44, 111, 242

Centers for Disease Control 18

Central Intelligence Agency 44–45, 57, 153. *See also* CIA

Centurus 163

channeling 26, 45–46, 52, 58, 132, 154, 245

Chapman, Robert 19

Chariots of the Gods? 62

Cheney, Dick 58

children's circles 46

Chomsky, Noam 54

Chorley, David 59

Christian era 63

Christianity 5

Chupacabras 46–47, 164

CIA 34, 36, 63, 159, 171, 181, 204, 206, 226, 244. *See also* Central Intelligence Agency

Cimarron, New Mexico 47–48, 144

Clarion 35

Clark, Jerome 20, 103, 139, 140, 150, 151, 161–162, 171, 192. 243, 263

close encounters 48, 49, 75, 111, 128, 136, 182

Close Encounters of the Third Kind (film), 49, 73, 90, 111, 210, 220, 249

Coe, Albert 267

Cold, Indrid 64

Coleman, Loren 68, 73, 192

collective unconscious 46, 49, 191

Collins, Robert M. 28

Coming Race, The (novel) 49–50

Commander X. *See* X, Commander

Committee for the Scientific Investigation of Claims of the Paranormal 50–51, 137

communications with aliens 51–52

Communion: A True Story 52, 231

communion (concept) 52

Communion (film) 53

Computer UFO Network 121–123

Condon, Dr. Edward U. 111, 218

Condon Committee 62

conspiracy theories 43, 50, 53–54, 55, 59, 74, 94, 110, 123, 126, 142, 150, 166, 196, 204

Constable, Trevor James 227

Constantino, Anthony (Tony) 18
contactee(s) 11, 14, 22, 23, 26, 35, 48, 51, 54–55, 62, 66, 75, 84, 100, 104, 117, 120, 135, 136, 137, 146, 157, 158, 162, 163, 173, 188, 190, 193, 203, 204, 222, 228, 235, 245, 251
Cooke, James 266–267
Cooper, Milton William ("Bill") 55, 115, 126, 127, 137–138, 150
Corso, Philip J. 51, 55–56
Cortile, Linda 56–57, 108
Council of Nine 46, 58. *See also* Nine, The
crash-retrievals 58–59, 104, 121, 204, 259
Creighton, Gordon 82
crop circles 59–60, 86, 209
CSICOP. *See* Committee for the Scientific Investigation of Claims of the Paranormal
CUFON. *See* Computer UFO Network
CUFOS. *See* Center for UFO Studies
cult(s) 13, 60
cyclops (alien) 60
Cydonia Plain 25

D

Dakelia Barracks, Cyprus 30, 61–62
DAL 26, 222
Däniken, Erich von 21, 62
da Silva, José Antônio 32
Davies, Peter 19–20
Davis, Christopher 218

Day After Roswell, The 55, 56
Day the Earth Stood Still, The (film) 62, 220
DEA. *See* Drug Enforcement Agency
debunker(s) 44, 62–63, 137, 144, 203
Dedeu, Eduardo Fernando 30–31
Defense Intelligence Agency 63
Delphos Republican 140
Delphos ring 140
demon(s) 5, 63, 243
Derenberger, Woodrow 63–65, 167
DERN universe 26, 222
Deros 31, 65, 223, 224, 236
Desvergers, D. S. 65–66
Devereux, Paul 71, 136, 208
Dewilde, M. Marius 195, 196
DIA. *See* Defense Intelligence Agency
Dieterlen, Germaine 66
Dimensions: A Casebook of Alien Contact 152
Di Pietro, Vincent 25
DiPietro-Molenaar Pyramid 166
disinformation 11, 34, 47, 56, 66, 94, 167, 187
Dogon 66–67
dolphinoids (aliens) 67
Doty, Richard C. 27–28, 34, 167
Douglas family 206
Dover demon 67–68
"Dr. Gee" 28
DRACO 31
Drake, Frank 68
Drake equation 68
dreams 68–69, 99, 124
Druffel, Ann 185

Drug Enforcement Agency 36
Dulce 31, 34
Duncan, James 19
Dyke, Nick 15
Dyke, Sally 15

E

Earthlights 71–72
East Midlands UFO group 13
EBEs. *See* extraterrestrial biological entities
Edwards, Ernest 34
Element 115 24, 72, 141
elementals 72
Elliston, Jon 45
Emery 199 200
encounter-prone personalities 72, 173
English, William S. 93, 94
"Estimate of the Situation" 73, 92, 153, 225
Eszterhas, Joe 186
ET: The Extraterrestrial (film) 73, 210
ETH. *See* extraterrestrial hypothesis
Etherians 146
"Etherian World" 145
evil clowns 73–74, 101
extraterrestrial beings 48, 60, 62, 72, 150
extraterrestrial biological entities 28, 74, 90
extraterrestrial hypothesis 5, 6, 16, 31, 49, 63, 74–75, 82, 83, 97, 100, 109, 110, 119, 125–126, 132, 134, 137, 172, 182, 192, 193, 217, 231, 236, 249, 255

extraterrestrial travel agents 75
Ezekiel 76

F

fairies (aliens) 77–78
False Memory Syndrome
78–79
fantasy-prone personalities 55,
79
Fate 184
Fatima, Portugal 79–80, 127
FBI 12, 45, 261. *See also* Federal
Bureau of Investigation
Federal Bureau of Investigation
80. *See also* FBI
Federal Emergency
Management Agency 36
FEMA. *See* Federal Emergency
Management Agency
*Fire in the Brain: Clinical Tales of
Hallucination* 97
Fire in the Sky (film), 80, 242
Fish, Marjorie 102, 103
Flatwoods, West Virginia 80–81
flying humanoids 81–82, 87
flying saucers 5, 19, 62, 107
activity 11
crashed 59
*Flying Saucers: A Modern Myth of
Things Seen in the Sky* 49, 191,
192
Flying Saucers and the Three Men
34
Flying Saucers Are Real, The 135
Flying Saucers from Mars 19–20
Flying Saucers Have Landed 12
Flying Saucers on the Attack 131,
145
Flying Saucer Review 39, 82, 136

FMS. *See* False Memory
Syndrome
FOIA. *See* Freedom of
Information Act
folklore 31, 48, 77
Foltz, Charlie 17
Fontaine, Luce 162
Fontes, Olavo 39
Forbidden Planet (film) 200
Fort, Charles 106
Fortean Times 15, 94, 154, 156
Fowler, Raymond E. 18, 22–23
Frederick, Wisconsin 82–83
Freedom of Information Act 80,
83, 121, 122, 123, 203
Freixedo, Salvador 164
Friedman, Stanton T. 55, 56,
83–84, 141, 153, 209
From Outer Space to You 158
Fry, Daniel 84
Fuller, John G. 102, 125

G

Gaetano, Paolo 85–86
Gaia Hypothesis 59, 86
Gardea, Larry 43
Garuda 87
Geller, Uri 58
Gentry 6. *See also* Celtic legend
giant birds 87–88
Gill, George 42
Gill, Father William Booth
88–89
Gina Foiro 89
Godwin, Joscelyn 106
Goldwater, Barry 38
Gonzales, Gustavo 41–42
Good, Timothy 170, 191, 202,
216, 256, 266,268

Gould, Dr. Laurence M. 106
Gray(s) 9, 14, 17, 22, 23, 27, 31,
33, 46, 47, 49, 53, 56, 63, 67,
74. 80, 87, 89–90, 102, 108,
118, 120, 124, 140, 150, 162,
167, 174, 179, 182, 190, 197,
203, 204, 205, 216, 217, 228,
237, 240, 254 255, 265, 266.
See also large grays
Gray, Glen 174–175
great airships 90–91, 104
green children of Woolpit 91–92
Griaule, Marcel 66
Groom Lake 24
Groth, Arne 264
Grudge (project) 37, 92–93, 225
Grudge Report 13 93–94
Guiley, Rosemary Ellen 48
Gulf Breeze, Florida 94–95
Gulf Breeze Sentinel 94–95
Gustafsson, Hans 36, 37

H

Haines, Gerald 45
Hall, Mark 88
hallucinations 97–99, 124
Halt, Charles 201–202
Hamilton, William F. III 31
Hangar 18 189, 257. *See also*
Blue Room
Hangar 18 (film) 38, 99–100
Hanssen, Myrna 47–48
Harbison, W. A. 172
Harpur, Patrick 144, 145
Hanssen, Myrna 34
Harder, James 186
Harris, Paul 92
Hastings, Robert 28
healings by aliens 100

Heaven's Gate sect 60

Heinonen, Aarno 116, 117

Helge (pseudonym) 180–181

Hickson, Charlie 185–186

Higdon, Carl 200–201

high strangeness 23, 53, 68, 82, 100–101, 143, 162, 167, 175, 179

Hill, Barney 90, 101–103, 125, 160, 220, 242, 265

Hill, Betty 90, 101–103, 125, 220, 242, 265

Hingley, Jean 77–78

Hitler, Adolf 50

Hitt, Jack 44

Hoagland, Richard 25, 26

hoaxes 11, 28, 56, 103–105, 220

Holloman Air Force Base, New Mexico 105–106, 137

Hollow Earth Theory 50, 106–107, 133, 207

holographic theory 107–108

Holographic Universe, The 107

Hopkins, Elliott Budd 56, 108–109, 110, 119, 123, 125, 149, 208

Hopkins, Dr. Herbert 159–160

Hough, Peter 19, 75, 114, 115

Howe, Linda Moulton 27–28, 44, 105, 109

Hoyle, Fred 109

Hubbard, L. Ron 166

humanoid(s) 11, 12, 16, 17, 30, 38, 58, 60, 61, 67, 100, 102, 109, 128, 178, 181, 184, 185, 188, 200, 218, 251, 255, 267

Huyghe, Patrick 16, 17

hybrids 10, 87, 110, 121, 126, 179, 256

Hynek, J(oseph) Allen 38, 44, 48, 49, 73, 89, 92, 105, 110–111, 124, 134, 185, 189, 226, 228, 230, 249

hypnagogic and hypnopompic states 79

hypnotic regression 18, 56, 79, 102, 111–112, 114, 116, 123, 126, 143, 144, 157, 159, 164, 177, 179, 185, 197, 219, 221, 227, 254

Hyslop, James 155

I

Ibáñez, Federico 239

IFSB. *See* International Flying Saucer Bureau

Ilkley Moor, Yorkshire, England 113–115

Illuminati 115–116

Illuminatus! 115

Imjärvi, Finland 116–117

implant(s) 10, 22, 117–118, 185, 223, 226

insectoids (aliens) 118–119, 196, 216

Institute of Terrestrial Ecology 15

Integratron 26, 119–120

interiors of UFOs 120–121

International Flying Saucer Bureau 33, 34

International UFO Reporter (IUR) 44

Interplanetary Parliament 13

Interplanetary Phenomenon Unit 121–123

Interrupted Journey, The 102, 125

Intruders (TV miniseries) 123

Intruders: The Incredible Visitations at Copley Woods 56, 123

Intruders Foundation 108–109

Invaders from Mars (film) 123–124

IPU. *See* Interplanetary Phenomenon Unit

Isle of Wight 15

Invaders, The (TV show) 123

Invaders from Mars (film) 123–124, 220

invisible college 124

J

J. Allen Hynek Center for UFO Studies 44, 95, 168, 171

Jacobs, David M. 9, 10, 100, 110, 120, 123, 125–126, 208

Jacolliot, Louis 106

JANAP (Joint Army/Navy/Air Force Publication) 146 126

Janos people 126

Jason Society 126–127

Jersey Devil 127–128

Jessup, Morris K. 186–187

Joan Rivers Show, The 18

Johannis, Professor Rapuzzi 128–129

Johnson family 140

Journal of UFO Studies 44

Journey to the Center of the Earth 50

Jung, C. G. 46, 49, 154, 191–192. *See also* collective unconscious

Jupiter 12, 26

K

Kalman, Moyshe 115
Kareeta 131–132, 145
Kearney, Betty 150
Keel, John Alva 51, 52, 63, 64–65, 132–133, 146, 167, 217, 218
Keith, Jim 36, 43, 64–65
Kelly, Kentucky 133–134
Kennedy, Robert 52
Keyhoe, Donald Edward 126, 134–135, 146, 170–171
King, George 13, 14, 135–136
Klarer, Elizabeth 136
Klass, Philip Julian 137, 154, 186
Klotz, Jim 121, 123
Kofman, Dr. Marie-Jeanne 20
Korff, Kal 158
Kraspedon, Dino 137
Krll, O. H. 137–138
Kruuk, Dr. Hans 15

L

Lafrenière, Ghislaine 71
landing traces 139–140
Langford, David 10–11
Langford, Hazel 11
Lanulos 64
large grays 140–141. See also Grays
La Rubia, Antonio 183–184
Lauritzen, Hans 100
Lawson, Alvin 116
Lazar, Robert Scott 24, 55, 72, 74, 90, 141–142, 191–192
Lear, John 126, 141, 142, 150, 167
Leir, Roger 118

LeMay, Curtis 38
Lemuria 65, 135, 163, 267
Lemurians 31, 65, 259
León, Dr. Padrón 142–143
Leonard, George 261
Leslie, Desmond 12
Ley, Willy 50
leys 143, 181
Liberty, Kentucky 143–144
lie-detector tests 143, 144, 185
liminal zones 144–145
"lizard man" 145
Llandrillo 12
Loka 132, 145–146
London UFO Research Association 39
Loosley, William Robert 11
Lovelock, Dr. James 86
Lure, Operation 146–147
Lyra 23

M

Mack, John E. 79, 117, 118, 123, 149–150, 208
Mad Gasser of Mattoon 150–152
Magonia 152, 192
Main, Cecil 42
Majestic 12 28, 74, 104, 152–154, 166, 262. See also Majority 12, MJ-12
Majority 12 28. See also Majestic 12, MJ-12
Manzano Nuclear Weapons Storage Area 34
Margulis, Dr. Lynn 86
Mars 13, 14, 19, 25, 55, 75, 86, 154, 155, 156, 188, 217
Martian mediums 46, 154–156
Martians 13, 124, 196

Martian Sphinx 25
Martins, Joao 39
Marzano, Genoa, Italy 156–157
Masse, Maurice 247–248
Mawnan Church 181–182
Meier, Eduard Albert "Billy" 26–27, 157–158, 163, 193, 197, 210, 222
Menger, Howard 104, 158–159, 188
Men in Black 33, 34, 46, 64, 73, 101, 132, 133, 159–162, 167
Men in Black (film) 159
Mercury 135
metalogic 101, 162
MIBs 180. See also Men in Black
"Michelin man" (alien) 162
Miller, Richard 162–163
"mines" (aliens) 163–164
missing time 18, 20, 114, 119, 123, 126, 143, 157, 164, 177, 179, 184, 219, 226, 227
Missing Time 108, 125
MJ-12 28, 187. See also Majestic 12, Majority 12
Moca vampire 164–165
Molenaar, Gregory 25
Montauk Project 54, 74, 165–166, 186
Montauk Project: Experiments in Time, 189 166
Montauk Revisited: Adventures in Synchronicity 166
Monteleone, Thomas 64
Moon 17, 25, 26, 75, 169, 170, 217, 261, 267
Moon, Peter 166
Moore, Patrick 19, 20
Moore, William Leonard 27, 34, 35, 47, 55, 152, 161, 166–167

Mormon Mesa 35
Morrison, Earl 82
Moseley, James W. 217
Mothman 167
Mothman Prophecies, The 51, 63, 132, 167
Mothman visitations 63, 64, 81, 88, 101, 243
Mount Palomar Observatory 11
MUFON 167. *See also* Mutual UFO Network
Muller, Frederick 19
Mutual UFO Network 18, 22, 35, 57, 95, 100, 135, 143, 168
My Contact with Flying Saucers 137

N
NASA 26, 86, 191, 216, 225, 248. *See also* National Aeronautics and Space Administration
National Aeronautics and Space Administration 25, 169–170
National Enquirer 22, 143
National Investigations Committee on Aerial Phenomena 102, 135, 146, 170–171, 188
National Reconnaissance Office 45
National Security Agency 153, 171–172
Natural History of Stafford-Shire, The 59
Nazcan Lines 21
Nazi flying saucers 172
NDEs. *See* near-death experiences
near-death experiences 72, 172–173, 234

Neptune 23, 26
Newton, Silas M. 28
Niagara Falls, New York 173
NICAP. *See* National Investigations Committee on Aerial Phenomena
Nichols, Preston 165–166
Nickell, Joe 79
Nicolai, Renato 238
Nine, The 58. *See also* Council of Nine
Nommos 22, 66
Nordics 173–174, 205
Norway, Maine 159, 174–175
NSA. *See* National Security Agency

O
Oakensen, Elsie 177–178
O'Barski, George 178
Office of Scientific Intelligence 45
Official UFO 104
O Globo 241, 242
Old Saybrook, Connecticut 178
Omega Project: Near-Death Experiences, The 173
Only Planet of Choice, The 58
orang bati 178–179
Oranges (aliens) 179
Ordo Templi Orientis 115
Orion, 23
Orland Park, Illinois 179–180
Orocovis, 46
OSI. See Office of Scientific Intelligence
Overlords 180–181
owlman 181–182
owls 182, 221

Oz Factor 68, 72, 108, 128, 159, 173, 182

P
Pacal 21
Paciencia, Rio de Janeiro, Brazil 183–184
Palmer, Raymond A. 50, 107, 184, 223
Palos Verdes, California 184–185
Parker, Calvin 185–186
Parris, Lee 227
Pascagoula, Mississippi 185–186, 188
Pereira, Jader U. 16
Pérez de Cuéllar, Javier 57, 58
Persinger, Michael 71, 72
Philadelphia Experiment 165, 186–187
photographs of aliens 187–189
Plaja 157
Pleiadians/Plejarans 26, 27, 157, 158, 189, 193, 222
Plott, Robert 59
Ponce, José 41
pop music and ufology 189–190
Porshnev, Dr. Boris 20
prayer battery 13
Presley, Elvis 189–190, 208
Pribram, Karl 107, 108
Probert, Mark 132
Project Stigma 93
Proposed Studies on the Implications of Peaceful Space Activities for Human Affairs 25
propulsion of UFOs 170, 190–191
psychosocial hypothesis 15, 49, 72, 110, 126, 150. 152, 182,

191–193, 220, 222, 239, 245, 249

Ptaah 157, 193, 222

Puddy, Maureen 86, 182, 193–194

Q

Quarouble, France 140, 195–196

Quatermass and the Pit (film) 196

Quazgaa 22, 196–197

Quetzal 157, 197

Quezet, Meagan 197

R

Rainbow City 199–200

Rak, Chuck 17, 18, 19

Randles, Jenny 12, 13, 19, 59, 61, 75, 105, 108, 114, 128–129, 160, 161, 177–178, 203

Raulin, François 234

Rawlins, Wyoming 200–201

Reeves, John 255

Reiche, Maria 21

Reid, Ernest C. 19

Rendlesham Forest, Suffolk, England 201–203

repeater witnesses 203

Report on Unidentified Flying Objects, The 37–38

reproductive procedures 10

Reptoids (aliens) 67, 179, 203–204

Revelations: Alien Contact and Human Deception 94, 233

reverse engineering 24, 56, 141, 204, 257

Rhanes, Aura 35

Rhodes, Rosemary 15

Rigelians 204, 205

Rigel-Procyon War 204–205

Ring, Dr. Kenneth 72, 173

Ririe, Idaho 205–206

Riverside, California 206

Robertson, Dr. H. P. 206

Robertson Panel 45, 206–207, 225

de Rochas, Colonel 154, 156

Roerich, Nicholas 207–208

Rommel, Ken 44

Roper Organization 109, 208

Roper Poll 109, 208

Rossi, Carlo 160

Roswell, New Mexico 12, 51, 56, 59, 74, 83, 105, 132, 153, 166, 189, 209, 211–213, 225, 231

Roswell: The UFO Cover-up (film) 213

Roswell autopsy footage 208–211

Roswell Incident, The 166

Ruppelt, Edward J. 37

Rydberg, Stig 36, 37

S

Sagan, Carl 87, 215–216

Salinas corpse 216

Salzburg, Austria 216–217

Sandia National Laboratories 28, 34

Santilli, Ray 208–209, 210

Saturn 12

Saucer Smear (publication) 217

Saunders, David 242

scape ore monster 218

Schaefler, Lothar 30

Schirmer, Herbert 218–219

Schlemmer, Phyllis 58

Schwa 219–220

science fiction 121, 124, 196, 220–221, 244

Scott, Brian 31

screen memories 86, 182. 221

Scully, Frank 28, 58–59

Search for Extraterrestrial Intelligence 52, 79, 221

Secret Life: Firsthand Accounts of UFO Abductions 125

Secret of the Saucers 23

Secret School, The 46

Semjase 157, 193, 197, 222

SETI 215. *See also* Search for Extraterrestrial Intelligence

Sfath 222

shamanic hypothesis 222–223

shamanic peoples 45

Shard 26

Shaver, Richard S. 31, 50, 65, 107, 184, 223–224

Shaw, H. G. 90–91

Shea, Mike 118–119

Shea, Robert 115

Shuker, Dr. Karl 20, 35, 42, 68, 92, 178, 226, 263

Siegel, Ronald K. 97, 98, 99

Sign (project) 37, 92, 224–225

Simon, Dr. Benjamin 102, 103

Simonton, Joe 225–226

Sims, Derrel 25, 226

Sinus Medii 26

Sirius 66, 67

Sirius Mystery 22

sky-beast hypothesis 226–227

"slabs" (aliens) 227

sleep paralysis 32–33

Smith, Helene 154, 155

Smith, Louise 143–144

Smith, Thaddia 140

Socorro, New Mexico 227–228

Solar System 12, 26, 35, 55, 127, 158, 159, 242, 267

Solganda 119

Soltec 163

Space Brothers 12, 22, 23, 55, 66, 72, 119, 120, 135, 136, 146, 150, 203, 228, 243, 245

Space Review 33, 34

Species (film) 14, 229

Spencer, John 39, 73, 116, 220, 221

Spencer, Philip (pseudonymn) 113–115

Spooner, Dr. Edward 114

Springheel Jack 152, 229–230

Sprinkle, Dr. Leo 47, 143, 218

Stafford, Mona 143–144

Starr, Mary 178

Stefula, Joe 57–58

Stephens, David 174–175

Story, Ronald D. 106

Strange Harvest, A 44

strangeness rating 230

Strieber, Whitley 10, 22, 25, 46, 52, 53, 63, 231–232

Stringer, Chris 20

Stringfield, Leonard H. 58, 144

Sued, Ibrahim 241–242

Sun 17, 25, 31, 65, 75, 267

Superstition Mountain 31

Sutton family 133, 134

T

Talavera la Real 29

Talbot, Michael 107

Taylor, Bill 133, 134

Taylor, Bob 163–164

Teesdale inheritance 233–235

telepathy 235–236

Telos 31

Temple, Robert K. G. 22, 66

Teros 223, 236

Tesla, Nikola 236, 259

They Knew Too Much About Flying Saucers 34, 161

Thomas, Elaine 143–144

Threat, The 126

Timars 26, 27

time travel hypothesis 236–237

"tin cans" (aliens) 237–238

Tomlinson, Arthur 114

Tossie, Guy 205–206

Townsend, Jerry 237–238

Trans-en-Provence 140, 238–239

Trench, Brinsley Le Poer 107

True 134

Truman, Harry 28, 153, 154, 171, 209

tulpas 161, 239

Turis, Valencia, Spain 239

Turner, Victor 144

tuyul 239–240

Twentieth Century Times, The 23

Twinkle (project) 37, 240

U

Ubatuba, Brazil 241–242

UFO(s) 9, 10, 12, 14, 17, 18, 22, 24, 27, 30, 31, 33, 34, 35, 36, 37, 38, 43, 46, 48, 49, 51, 54, 60, 62, 63, 64, 65, 66, 67, 72, 73, 74, 82, 82, 83, 84, 85, 86, 87, 88, 89, 90, 93, 95, 97, 98, 99, 104, 105, 108, 109, 111, 113, 114, 116, 117, 119, 123, 126, 132, 133, 139, 142, 143, 144, 145, 149, 152, 153, 162, 165, 169, 170, 171, 179, 180, 185, 186, 187, 188, 189, 190, 191, 192, 193, 194, 195, 197, 202, 203, 204, 205, 206, 207, 217, 219, 220, 223, 224, 225, 226, 227, 228, 236, 237, 240, 243, 249, 251, 253, 254, 255, 256, 261, 266, 267, 268

age of 5

alien phenomenon 74

community 47

crashes 59, 121, 153, 188, 189, 209, 210, 225, 250

cults, 60

encounters 6, 23, 44, 49, 53, 54, 72, 75, 80, 94, 100, 118, 162, 174–175, 182, 183–184, 186, 238, 239, 243, 247

entities 75

events 12, 111

explosion 241

film of 27

hoax 28, 103

incident 201–203

investigators 12, 33, 110

landings 75, 105–106, 146, 251

mythology 184

percipient, 52

phenomenon 45, 49, 116, 124, 134, 137, 168, 220, 222

photographs 95, 210

reports 28, 45, 74, 225, 230

research 39, 124

researchers 5, 6, 11, 12, 13, 31, 38, 42, 55, 65, 161, 248

retrieval 56

secret government study
group 13
sightings 5, 6, 44, 59, 68,
72, 73, 79, 84, 88, 92, 97,
102, 111, 166, 167, 172,
177, 178, 192, 203, 250
See also interiors of;
propulsion of; uniden-
tified flying objects
UFO Brigantia 11
UFOCAT 44, 242
UFO Controversy in America, The
125
UFO Experience, The 111, 230
UFO Incident, The (film) 242
ufologists 12, 13, 50, 54, 56, 63,
66, 75, 104, 123, 136, 187, 190,
192, 215, 264
ufology 44, 53, 58, 59, 60, 111,
125, 154, 171, 184, 223, 233,
244. *See also* pop music and
ufology
UFO Magazine 89
*UFOs and Ufology: The First Fifty
Years* 136, 208
UFOs Identified 137
ultraterrestrials 51, 132, 146,
167, 243
UMMO 55, 181, 243–245, 252
UNARIUS. *See* Universal
Articulate Interdimensional
Understanding of Science
Underground Alien Bases 199
Unexplained! 150
Unexplained, The 92, 178
unidentified flying objects 245.
See also UFO(s)
Unidentified, The 192
Universal Articulate
Interdimensional

Understanding of Science
245–246
UN Security Investigation Unit,
58
Unsolved Mysteries 19
Uriel 245–246
U.S. Air Force 34, 37, 62, 110,
122, 167, 201, 207, 212, 242
Air Force Special Activities
Center 161
Air Technical Intelligence
Center (ATIC) 73
UFO investigation project
37–38, 92
U.S. government 24, 28, 36, 43,
74, 84, 105, 126, 138, 167, 204,
224
U.S. intelligence community 27

V

Valensole, France 247–248
Valentich, Frederick 248–249
Vallée, Jacques 5, 49, 52, 55,
72, 75, 79, 86, 94, 101, 103,
110, 111, 138, 152, 162, 187,
192, 220, 233, 244, 247, 249,
252
Vandenberg, Hoyt S. 73, 153,
225
van Tassel, George 26, 119, 120
Varginha, Brazil 250
Venus 12, 14, 26, 55, 136, 158,
159, 245
Venusian 12, 13, 19, 62, 158,
200
Verne, Jules 50
Vesco, Renato 172
Vidal, Dr. Gerardo 104
Viljo, Esko 116, 117

Vilvoorde, Belgium 251
Visitors 46, 52
Vorilhon, Claude 234, 251
Voronezh, Russia 251–252
Vril Society 50

W

Walters, Edward 94–95
Walton, Travis 80, 164, 253–255
Walton Experience, The 80
Warren, Lawrence 202
Watchers 22, 51, 196, 197
Watchers, The 22
Watchers II 22
Watkins, Alfred 143
Watson, Paula 145
Watson, Ron 145
Webb, David 18
Weeki-Wachi Springs, Florida
255
Weiner, Jack 17–19
Weiner, Jim 17–18
Weishaupt, Adam 115
White Sands Incident, The 84
Wilkins, Harold T. 131–132,
145–146
Williams, Gordon 202
Williams, Mark 44
Wilson, Jack 97–99
Wilson, Peter 97
Wilson, Robert Anton 115
window area 255
wise babies 255–256
*Witnessed: The True Story of the
Brooklyn Bridge Abduction* 56,
108
woodwose 256
Wolf, Fred Alan 72
Wolski, Jan 256–257

Wonder Stories 184
Wright, Dan 100
Wright-Patterson Air Force Base
28, 37, 38, 73, 99, 153, 189,
212, 225, 257

X
X, Commander 31, 115–116, 199,
200, 204, 259
X, Dr. 259–261
x-devices 261
x-drones 261

X-Files, The (TV show) 7,
261–262

Y
yeren 263, 264
yeti 263–264
You Are Responsible 13
yttrium 264

Z
Zamora, Lonnie 227–228

Zanfretta, Fortunato 156–157
Zeta Reticuli 74, 90, 103, 167,
204, 265–266
Zhamtsarano, Tsyben 20
Zigel, Dr. Felix Yurevich 189,
266
Zomdic 266–267
Zret 267
Zuccalà, Mario 267–268